The "OFF-LAWN" MOWER

> "We're so positive that these patterns and designs will open up a new world of woodworking for you that we'll send you a free gift just for trying them."

"312 WOODWORKING SCROLL SAW PATTERNS"

DESIGNS THAT OPEN UP THE WORLD OF WOODWORKING

(By Gene Keith)

FC&A, a Peachtree City, Georgia, publisher, announced today that it has released for sale the eagerly awaited book, *"Encyclopedia of 312 Scroll Saw Woodworking Patterns"*.

LOOK AT WHAT YOU WILL FIND IN THIS NEW BOOK

▶ Diagrams and sizing instructions.

▶ How to enlarge and reduce scroll saw patterns.

▶ Many popular designs.

▶ Decorate your refrigerator with these magnets.

▶ Dress up your Christmas tree with these patterns.

▶ Alphabets and numerals.

▶ Hang one of these blackboards beside the phone.

▶ Sconces to decorate a wall.

▶ Make this towel holder.

▶ Key and jewelry holders.

▶ Fun to make patterns like Heart Candle Holder.

▶ Make a nice street scene.

▶ Handy Oven Rack Tool.

▶ Goose Towel Holder.

▶ Great children's games.

▶ Make your own shelves.

▶ Give someone special these Hanging Hearts.

▶ Many original designs for popular subjects like pigs, ducks, bears, chickens, hearts, tulips, stars, sheep, apples, butterflies, melons, musical instruments, pineapples, cows, and doves.

▶ Make a great educational puzzle map of the U.S.

▶ Plus hundreds of great ideas and helpful hints for wood enthusiasts.

▶ Easy patterns for beginners and more difficult patterns for experts.

THE

OLD FARMER'S ALMANAC

CALCULATED ON A NEW AND IMPROVED PLAN
FOR THE YEAR OF OUR LORD

1989

Being 1st after LEAP YEAR and (until July 4)
213th year of American Independence

FITTED FOR BOSTON, AND THE NEW ENGLAND STATES, WITH SPECIAL COR-
RECTIONS AND CALCULATIONS TO ANSWER FOR ALL THE UNITED STATES.

Containing, besides the large number of Astronomical Calculations
and the Farmer's Calendar for every month
in the year, a variety of

NEW, USEFUL, AND ENTERTAINING MATTER.
ESTABLISHED IN 1792

BY ROBERT B. THOMAS

I stepped from Plank to Plank
A slow and cautious way
The Stars about my Head I felt
About my Feet the Sea.

I knew not but the next
Would be my final inch —
This gave me that precarious Gait
Some call experience.
— Emily Dickinson

COVER T.M. REGISTERED
IN U.S. PATENT OFFICE

ISSN 0078-4516

LIBRARY OF CONGRESS
CARD NO. 56-29681

Address All Correspondence to
Publisher
Rob Trowbridge
THE OLD FARMER'S ALMANAC
DUBLIN, NH 03444
Editor
Jud Hale

TO PATRONS

About nine million people read this publication every year. Their median age is 59.5, 55 percent of them live on more than one acre of land, and 81 percent own their own home. (Eight percent live on more than 50 acres.) Thirteen percent live in the Deep South, 19 percent in the mid-Atlantic states, almost 25 percent in the Midwest, and 12 percent live where the almanac has always been published, New England. We've learned this sort of data during the past year by means of a professional reader survey. Some of our advertisers asked us to do it, and so, well, we did it.

To be candid, however, we have never felt the necessity for statistical information about our readers. We've always felt that we knew them well. After all, we — and the eleven editors before us — have been corresponding with them daily for 197 years!

"I wish the man who'd changed the Moon signs in this year's almanac had died before he done it," wrote a Texas reader when we changed printers. Almanac readers, as we know, are not fond of sudden change. Or breaking with tradition.

Three readers have written in the last year to say they've acquired a complete set of *The Old Farmer's Almanac*. "It took me five years and cost me $580 all told," wrote one, a Troy, New York, man. He went on to say an antiquarian book shop in Portsmouth, New Hampshire, offered him 200 "old almanacs" for only $500. "But," he wrote, "they weren't the Thomas almanac, and besides, the price didn't include the fun of the hunt." Spoken like a bona fide almanac reader!

Many letters good-naturedly (?) scold us for our weather predictions. "Don't print unpleasant forecasts," wrote a Kentucky lady last winter. "People in this valley would rather have mild winters. No snow, please. We get tired of it."

Questions, of course, abound from every direction, and we attempt to answer them all. "Will you tell me when a conjunction of Mars, Jupiter, and Saturn took place during spring between 1,992 and 1,995 years ago?" from Wyandotte, Michigan. "Years ago you ran an ad for a recording of rodents screaming in pain. Worked better than any mousetrap. Can you send me the address?" That from Massachusetts.

We're regularly informed that Jesus Christ was born in the spring and that Rome fouled up his birthday in subsequent calendar reforms. In fact, calendar reform is a favorite topic. For instance, this from Englewood, New Jersey, recently: ". . . our actual year is 365.2422 days long, but our present calendar is based on 365.2425 days. This can be remedied by leaving out one leap year every 80,000 years."

Only almanac readers — and almanac makers — would correspond about "leaving out one leap year every 80,000 years." That's why we'll leave the cold facts about our readership to magazine statisticians. Frankly, we'd rather ponder a picture postcard of Stoystown, Pennsylvania, which arrived yesterday from "a long-time almanac reader," as it was signed, and was addressed to "America's Best Friend, Dublin, NH 03444." "Seas can be stormy, but they're full of fish," was the first of its two sentences, shakily written in red ink. Then, "What R U full of?"

"Like the ocean," we replied. As a longtime almanac reader, she'll understand.

J.D.H.

* * *

We're indebted to: Dr. Richard Head for all the weather data; Susan Peery, assisted by Martha W. Temple, Lida Stinchfield, Jody Saville, Mary Sheldon, Anna Larson, and Andrew Rothovius, for the editorial work; John Pierce as managing editor; Jill Shaffer as designer; Mary Lewis and Fran Frasca for production work; Steve Klett and staff for graphic services; Dottie Guy and staff for ad production; George Greenstein, astronomer; Fred Schaaf, astronomical consultant; and Castle Freeman, Jr., for the Farmer's Calendar work.

However, it is by our works and not our words that we would be judged. These, we hope, will sustain us in the humble though proud station we have so long held in the name of

Your ob'd servant,

June 1988

90

FEATURES

116

164

INDEX OF CHARTS, TABLES, FORECASTS, AND DEPARTMENTS

REWARD $3,000.00
FOR THIS PENNY!

OUR COIN
CATALOGUE TELLS
YOU HOW TO
SHIP COINS
TO US AND
QUICKLY
GET THE MOST
MONEY WE PAY
FOR COINS! SEND
FOR IT TODAY!

**We'll Pay You $3,000.00
For A 1943 Copper Penny
Like this One;**

Stop spending valuable coins worth hundreds of dollars. New 1989 catalogue with NEW HIGHER PRICES, lists hundreds of coins we want to buy and gives the price range we will pay for these United States Coins. Certain half-cent coins are worth up to $3,500.00 for Canadian Coins. Our valuable Coin Book may reward you many thousands of dollars. Coins do not have to be old to be valuable. Thousands of dollars have been paid for coins dated as recently as 1940 or 1956. Now you, too, can learn the rare dates and how to identify rare coins in your possession with our new 1989 catalogue. A fortune may be waiting for you. Millions of Dollars have been paid for rare coins. Send your order for this valuable coin catalogue now. Hold onto your coins until you obtain our catalogue. Send $5.00 plus $1.50 postage and handling for 1989 Coin Catalogue to:

Best Values Co., Dept. D575
P.O. Box 802, E. Orange, N.J. 07019

$500,000 SEARCH
FOR RARE COINS!
OLD and NEW!
MAIL MONEY-SAVING NO-RISK
FREE TRIAL COUPON NOW!

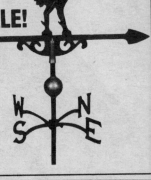

My Feet Were Killing Me...Until I Discovered the Miracle in Germany!

It was the European trip we had always dreamed about. We had the time and money to go where we wanted—see what we wanted. But I soon learned that money and time don't mean much when your feet hurt too much to walk. After a few days of sightseeing my feet were killing me.

Oh, my wife tried to keep me going. In Paris I limped through Notre Dame and along the Champs-Elysées. And I went up in the Eiffel Tower although I can't honestly say I remember the view. My feet were so tired and sore my whole body ached. While everybody else was having a great time, I was in my hotel room. I didn't even feel like sitting in a sidewalk cafe.

The whole trip was like that until we got to Hamburg, Germany. There, by accident, I happened to hear about an *exciting break-through for anyone who suffers from sore, aching feet and legs.*

This wonderful invention was a custom formed foot support called Flexible Featherspring.® When I got a pair and slipped them into my shoes *my pain disappeared almost instantly.* The flexible shock absorbing support they gave my feet was like cradling them on a cushion of air. I could walk, stand, even run. The relief was truly a miracle.

And just one pair was all I needed. I learned that my wife also can wear them—even with sandals and open backed shoes. They're completely invisible.

Imagine how dumbfounded I was to discover these miraculous devices were sold only in Europe. Right then I determined that we would share the miracle we discovered in Germany with our own countrymen.

Since 1948, over 3,000,000 people of all ages — many with foot problems far more severe than mine— have experienced this blessed relief for themselves.

MADE FOR YOUR FEET ALONE

Here's why Feathersprings work for them and *why they can work for you.* These supports are like nothing you've ever seen before. They are custom formed and made for *your feet alone!* Unlike conventional devices, they actually imitate the youthful elastic support that Nature originally intended your feet to have.

NO RISK OFFER

Whatever your problem—corns, calluses, pain in the balls of your feet, burning nerve ends, painful ankles, old injuries, backaches or just generally sore, aching feet, Flexible Feathersprings will bring you relief with every step you take or your money back.

Don't suffer pain and discomfort needlessly. If your feet hurt, the miracle of Germany can help you. Write for more detailed information. There is no obligation whatsoever. No salesman will call. Just fill out the coupon below and mail it today.

WHAT PEOPLE SAY ABOUT THE MIRACLE:

"... *I have thoroughly enjoyed the comfort Feathersprings have provided me. You would not believe the difference they have made my feet feel—before I had such pain when walking because I have severe callus' on both of my feet.*"   M.W.R./Richmond, VA

"*I want to thank you for refunding to me the full amount of what I ordered. I admire your company for this with no strings or red tape.*"
G.K.M./Warwick, Rhode Island

© 1988 Featherspring International, Inc.
712 N. 34th Street, Seattle, Washington 98103

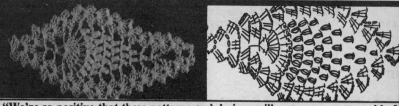

"300 CROCHET PATTERNS STITCHES AND DESIGNS"

DESIGNS THAT OPEN UP THE WORLD OF CROCHET

(By Brenda Keith)

I'm no dummy. But, I've always had trouble following written instructions. So, I laughed when I picked up a new book and saw these funny looking crochet symbols. They looked like chicken scratches. But then, an amazing thing happened . . .

AN EASY MAP TO FOLLOW

I opened the book, *"Encyclopedia of 300 Crochet Patterns, Stitches and Designs"*, and quickly made one of the patterns. It was so easy. Each of these new International Crochet Symbols looks like its stitch. When I lost my place in the instructions, I just looked at the drawing to see where I was. Instead of starting over, I had an easy map to follow. Then . . .

When I finished each segment, I compared it to the photograph in the book to make sure it was right.

Soon, I connected the segments to make a beautiful afghan. Later, I looked through the whole 250-page book and had a pleasant surprise . . .

LOOK AT WHAT YOU WILL FIND IN THIS NEW BOOK

▶ Photos, written instructions and diagrams showing each of 300 patterns and designs.
▶ Hand-drawn diagrams using the new International Crochet Symbols.
▶ Many original designs.
▶ All the great classic crochet patterns.
▶ Designs using all types of crochet stitches.
▶ Use designs such as Granny-Square or Shamrock to create bedspreads, tablecloths, scarves, and afghans.
▶ Give your handwork a neatly finished, decorative edge with laces and trims.
▶ Piece together doilies using patterns.
▶ Start now — trim your Christmas tree with beautiful crocheted snowflakes.
▶ Fashion collars using charts in this book.

IT'S EASY TO ORDER

Just return this notice with your name and address and a check for **$5.99** plus $2.00 shipping and handling to our address: **FC&A, Dept. COF-89**, 103 Clover Green, Peachtree City, GA 30269. We will send you *"Encyclopedia of 300 Crochet Patterns, Stitches and Designs"* right away.

Save! Return this notice with **$11.98** + $2.00 for two books. (No extra shipping.) Satisfaction guaranteed or your money back.

Cut out and return this notice with your order. Copies will not be accepted.

IMPORTANT — FREE GIFT OFFER EXPIRES IN 30 DAYS

All orders mailed within 30 days will receive a free gift. Order right away!

VITA-MIX®
"THE PENNY STRETCHER"

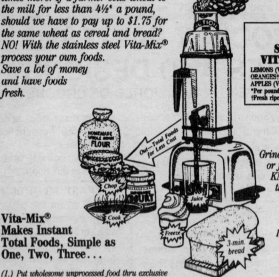

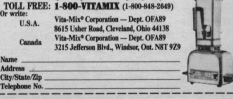

Going Bald?
Try This, At No Risk

HOUSTON, Texas—if you are gradually going bald, obviously, something is causing your hair loss to be <u>greater</u> than the growth. It stands to reason that if you can reduce your hair loss to where it is <u>less</u> than the growth...you can stop the balding process ...and gradually thicken your hair.

It is a known fact that "sebum" which is discharged through the sebaceous glands in the scalp, can cause excessive hair loss. (Seborrhea) The symptoms of a sebum problem are: greasy forehead; dandruff; dry or oily; itchy scalp; and if your hair pulls out easily on top of your head. If you have one or more of these symptoms, sebum could be the cause of your problem.

A firm of laboratory consultants has developed a scientifically advanced formula and regimen to remove and control the continuous discharge of toxic sebum, so the scalp can function normally and effectively. This, in turn, greatly reduces excessive hair loss...and, helps promote natural hair cell production.

A study of these formulas and regimen recently completed by a California medical school shows the average subject reduced hair loss by 87%. Forty percent of the subjects also showed an increase in hair density in just 90 days, <u>reversing the balding process</u>.

This scientific regimen has proven so successful the firm invites you to try it for 32 days, at their risk, and see for yourself.

Everyone has a full head of hair until some time after puberty. In the case of hair loss caused by "sebum", the problem starts when the male hormone production reaches its peak. This causes an excessive discharge of toxic sebum, which if not properly controlled, will gradually destroy the hair-producing cells on top of the head.

Hair loss caused by sebum can also run in your family, and, if you wait until you are slick bald and your hair-producing cells are destroyed, you are beyond help.

So, if you have sebum symptoms and still have any hair on top of your head...now is the time to do something about it before it's too late.

Experts believe that the majority of cases of excessive hair fall and baldness are the beginning and more fully developed stages of male pattern baldness and cannot be helped.

But, if your hair loss is caused or effected by sebum, here is help.

Loesch Laboratory Consultants, Inc., will supply you with treatment for 32 days ...at their risk...if you have the sebum symptoms and are not already slick bald. Just send them the information below. Or, call them toll-free at 1-800-231-7157 (in Texas 1-800-833-8387) 8:00 a.m. to 4:00 p.m., Monday thru Thursday, and they will send complete information. Your reply places you under no obligation whatsoever. ADV. ©

NO OBLIGATION COUPON

TO: Loesch Laboratory Consultants, Inc.
    Dept F-40, 3311 West Main Street
    P.O. Box 66001   Houston, Texas 77266

I am submitting the following information with the understanding that it will be kept strictly confidential and that I am under no obligation whatsoever.

Does your forehead become oily or greasy? _____

How soon after washing? _____

Do you have dandruff? _____ Dry or oily? _____

Does hair pull out easily on top of head? _____

Any thin areas? _____ Where? _____

Any slick bald areas? _____ Where? _____

NAME _____ Sex _____ Age _____

ADDRESS _____

CITY _____ STATE _____ ZIP _____

Plenty of water, no water bills.

Drink. Bathe. Splash. Water the garden. Wash the car. Do the laundry. Scrub the dog. Give the lawn a drink. Fill the pool. There's no limit to the wonderful things you can do when you have your own private water system and no water bills.

Join the thousands of homeowners who have drilled their own water well to supplement their expensive city water.

With a **Hydra-Drill**, you can drill your own water well 50-100-200 feet deep. It's as simple to operate as a power lawn mower. Don't wait for the next drought or big increase in your water bills.

Get the facts. You owe it to yourself to find out about this practical, economical way to provide good, year 'round water for your home and garden.

For a FREE BROCHURE, call today TOLL-FREE 1-800-DEEPROCK (Ext. 7063) or mail coupon below. Learn how over 100,000 home water wells have been drilled this easy, low-cost way since 1962.

"What a thrill to strike pure water at just 59 feet. Just think--that sparkling water has been so close all these years. Now I can make good use of it!"
— P.H., Minnesota

"My lawn and garden benefit greatly from my 750 gallon per hour well I drilled."
— G.W.F., New Jersey

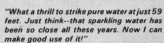

FREE BOOKLET

The Energy Efficient LOG HOME

Traditional full log or insulated log kits with up to R-40 roof system. Handcrafted Northern White CEDAR or PINE logs. Complete kits priced from $9,900. Nationwide FREE DELIVERY. Dealership's available at no charge.

Send for the Free Log Home Lovers Design Booklet or order our new color Plan Book of 100 beautiful models.

MasterCard or Visa accepted.
Call TOLL FREE 1-800-558-5812 In Wisconsin Call 1-800-242-1021

Hand crafted

Log Homes
Greatwood®

©1986

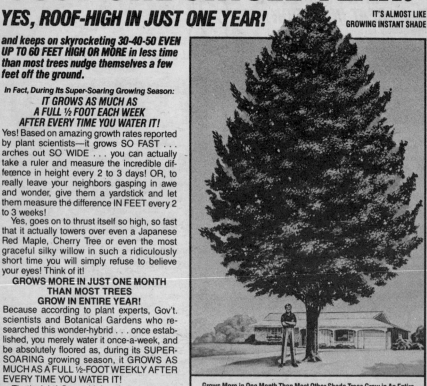

AMAZING SUPER-GROWING SPECIES SOARS INTO A MAGNIFICENT TREE IN JUST ONE SINGLE YEAR!

Best of all, unlike most trees that demand constant care, constant pampering . . . about the only thing you do after you plant this super-growing wonder-hybrid is water it and enjoy it! That's why leading botanical gardens . . . landscape artists . . . garden editors . . . can't stop raving about its indescribable beauty . . . its trouble-free care . . . its surging, towering growth.

Small wonder that leading experts hail it in the most glowing terms . . . recommended it again and again for homeowners who want a stunning display of beauty . . . both a wind and privacy screen and deep, cool shade . . . and with practically no more work than a thorough watering each week!

VITAL STATISTICS FROM LEADING EXPERTS

MATURE GROWTH SIZE: as much as 40 to 65 feet

MATURE SPREAD: as much as 30 to 35 feet

ZONE OF HARDINESS: Hardy from the deepest South to as far North as Vermont, Minn., Quebec, British Columbia, Winter Hardy in areas where temp. drops as low as 30 degrees below zero.

LIGHT NEEDS: Grows beautifully in Sunny location.

DECORATIVE MERITS: Highly recommended by landscape architects as beautiful decorative specimens for homes, parks, highways, etc., where exceptional fast growth and beauty are required. Perfect for fast screening and privacy.

RAPID RATE OF GROWTH: Experts report growth rates on specimen trees that measure up to 8 FEET THE VERY FIRST YEAR ALONE. That's more than most shade trees grow in 3 . . . 4 . . . 5 . . . even 7 years. Yes, once established will grow ranch-house-roof high IN JUST ONE SINGLE YEAR, that's right—

The very next year after planting! Experts also report it soars an amazing 5 to 8 feet each year for YEARS thereafter. Naturally results are based on optimum growing conditions. Takes but 10 minutes to plant and normal care rewards you with a lifetime of beauty starting this very year.

CARE: Nothing special—just normal garden care. Water fully once weekly. Naturally resistant to most diseases, pests or insects.

**WE HAVE AT THIS MOMENT
ONLY A LIMITED SUPPLY AVAILABLE
FOR RELEASE TO THE PUBLIC—
FULL SUPPLY WON'T BE READY
UNTIL 1989 SO *ACT NOW!***

Now the price of this super growing shade tree is not $20 or $30 as you might expect, but a mere $3.95!

That's right, only $3.95 for this magnificent Beauty that rewards you with such a glorious display of growth IN JUST ONE SINGLE YEAR. However, our supply is limited! Full supplies from the growing fields will not be ready until late 1988 or early 1989. Therefore, all orders must be shipped on a first-come, first-shipped basis. To make sure you don't miss out . . . ACT NOW!

SATISFACTION GUARANTEED OR MONEY BACK!

Remember: Satisfaction is fully guaranteed. You must be thrilled in every way with this spectacular f-a-s-t growing shade tree or RETURN AT ANYTIME within 90 days for a full refund of purchase price . . . ANYTIME within 1 year for free replacement. Could anything be fairer? Now is the time to order and replant—so send no-risk coupon today!

JUST MINUTES TO PLANT— REWARDS YOU WITH A LIFETIME OF BEAUTY!

Here's a luxurious sight you don't have to wait half a lifetime growing—a matched pair of these towering show-pieces.

Picture your patio bathed in the cool beauty of this show-stopping miracle tree from early spring to the first snows of winter.

Just a few minutes planting time—a few seasons' growing time, rewards you with twin towers of beauty.

© 1988 Spring River™ Nurseries, Inc., Spring River Road, Hartford, MI 49057

– – – – – MAIL NO-RISK COUPON TODAY – – – – –

**Spring River Nurseries, Inc., Dept. SB50MN
Spring River Road, Hartford, Michigan 49057**

Yes, please send me for proper planting time in my area the SUPER GROWING HYBRID(S) indicated below:

☐ (#001) 1 for only $3.95 plus 75¢ postage and handling.

☐ (#002) 2 for only $6.95 **(SAVE OVER $1.00)** plus $1.00 postage and handling.

☐ (#004) 4 for only $10.00 **(SAVE OVER $7.00)** plus $1.50 postage and handling.

☐ (#010) 10 for only $20.00 **(SAVE OVER $20.00)** plus $3.00 postage and handling.

☐ (#020) 20 for only $30.00 **(SAVE OVER $55.00)** plus $5.00 postage and handling.

If after receiving my order I am not fully delighted, I may return anytime within 90 days and you will refund my purchase price in full (less postage and handling, of course).

Total amount enclosed $ _____ IL, IN, MI, MN, OH & WI Residents please add appr. Sales Tax. No C.O.D.'s please.

Name _____

Address _____

City _____ State _____ Zip _____

USE NUMEROLOGY TO WIN THE LOTTERY

State sponsored lotteries and daily numbers games are helping to make Numerology and Numerologists more popular than ever. The gifted Numerologist, Gela, from upstate New York, has been helping people from all over the world discover their own LUCKY NUMBERS and put the awesome power of Numerology to work for themselves. Some of these Lucky people are winning thousands and thousands of dollars.

Take Laverne Wedow for example. The LUCKY NUMBERS Gela predicted for Laverne came out in the Canadian Lottery and Laverne won $25,000.00. She writes:

Dear Gela,

I used the Lucky Numbers that I received from you and I've been a big winner in the Wintario Lottery for $25,000.00 dollars. And a few weeks later I was at the Horse Races and played a trifecta and won $575.00 on a $2.00 bet. I owe all the thanks to you Gela. It sure was a dream come true. Thanks again.
Laverne Wedow
Hanover, Ontario

You could also be a Big Winner in the Lottery if you put Gela's LUCKY NUMBERS to work for yourself. These LUCKY NUMBERS can also be used in Daily Numbers Games, Horse and Dog Racing, Keno, Jai Alai, and many other forms of gambling. In fact, June Aldinger used her LUCKY NUMBERS to win $10,000.00 in the Pick Four Numbers Game. Her letter reads:

Dear Gela:

On March 17, I received my LUCKY NUMBERS in the mail and on April 4, I played my Lucky 4 digit number for $2.00 and won $10,000.00. Thank you so much for sending my LUCKY NUMBERS.
June Aldinger
Norristown, PA

And of course, Laverne and June aren't the only ones winning a lot of money using LUCKY NUMBERS that Gela predicted for them. Here is a small sampling of the thousands of testimonials that Gela has received:

Lucena Kilburn wins $3050.00 at Bingo.

Albert Senner hits 5 out of 6 lottery numbers for $4019.10

Anna Joray hits 4 digit number for $7604.00.

Evelyn Bocek Wins $1936.00 at the races.

Now it's your turn to put the ancient science of Numerology to work for yourself and join the growing list of BIG MONEY WINNERS. For a small recording fee of $10.00, Gela will send you your own set of LUCKY NUMBERS. Gela is so sure that they will work for you and help you win lots of money that she is able to make this incredible guarantee:

If you play your LUCKY NUMBERS the way that Gela tells you to, YOU MUST WIN AT LEAST $500.00 WITHIN 30 DAYS OF RECEIVING YOUR LUCKY NUMBERS or you are entitled to a full refund of your $10.00 recording fee **PLUS** a $10.00 bonus ($20.00 total) for a **double your money back guarantee!** How can you possibly lose with those odds? Send for your LUCKY NUMBERS today and be a Big Winner tomorrow.

! DOUBLE YOUR MONEY !
BACK GUARANTEE

————- Mail No Risk Coupon Today ————

GELA Numerology
Dept. FA-3, Box 265, Delanson, NY 12053

Enclosed is $10.00. Please send me my own set of LUCKY NUMBERS. I understand that if I play my LUCKY NUMBERS the way Gela tells me to, I must win at least $500.00 within thirty days of receiving my LUCKY NUMBERS or I am entitled to a full refund of my $10.00 recording fee plus a $10.00 BONUS for a DOUBLE MY MONEY BACK GUARANTEE.

Name ....

Address ....

City.................... State.......... Zip ....

Date of Birth .... Time of Birth ....

If Unknown, check here ☐

TRIMMER USERS!
MOWER USERS!

YOU'LL LOVE our totally new **DR™ TRIMMER/MOWER** compared to the hassle of using any *hand-held trimmer* or any *small-wheels rotary mower* !

Trimmer Hassle!

Mower Hassle!

The Revolutionary **DR**™ rolls "light as a feather" on two BIG WHEELS! Trims precisely under/along fences, buildings, borders, low branches, lawn furniture, etc. Plus, has the POWER TO MOW everything from whole lawns to tough waist-high growth with incredible ease!

Rocks, roots, stumps, etc. do it no harm because the DR has no steel blades to bend, break or dull. Perfect for use with your hand-held trimmer AND small-wheels rotary mower for finish-up trimming and mowing. Wonderfully useful SPRING, SUMMER & FALL. The ONLY machine you may need if you have a fairly small lawn! For **FREE DETAILS**, prices, specifications of Manual &Electric Starting Models, "Off-Season" Savings and our 30-Day Risk-Free Trial, please mail coupon at right. Or, call (802)425-2196. Either way, we'll look forward to hearing from you!

COUNTRY HOME PRODUCTS
Box 89, Cedar Beach Road, Charlotte, VT 05445

The
EASY
WAY!

INTRODUCTION
Including How to Use This Almanac Anywhere in the U.S.A.
THE LEFT-HAND CALENDAR PAGES
(Pages 48-74)

THESE PAGES will provide you with the phases of the Moon; the hour and minute of the Sun's rising and setting for each day of the year and month; the length of each day; the times of high tides in Boston in the morning and evening ("11¼" under "Full Sea Boston, A.M." means that the high tide that morning will be at 11:15 A.M. — with the number of feet of high tide shown for some of the dates on the right-hand calendar pages); the hour and minute of the Moon's rising and setting; the declination of the Sun in degrees and minutes (angular distance from the celestial equator); the Moon's place in the heavens; and finally, in the far right column, the Moon's age. The Moon's place and age apply, without correction, throughout the United States.

The Moon's place given on the left-hand pages is its *astronomical* place in the heavens. (*All* calculations in this Almanac, except for the astrological information on pages 181 and 202-205, are based on astronomy, not astrology.) As well as the 12 constellations of the Zodiac, five other abbreviations appear in this column: Ophiuchus (OPH) is a constellation primarily north of the Zodiac, but with a small corner between Scorpio and Sagittarius. Orion (ORI) is a constellation whose northern limit just reaches the Zodiac between Taurus and Gemini. Auriga (AUR) lies just northeast of Taurus. Sextans (SEX) lies south of the Zodiac except for a corner that just touches it near Leo. Cetus (CET) lies south of the Zodiac, just south of Pisces and Aries.

Eastern Standard Time is used throughout this Almanac. (Be sure to add one hour for Daylight Saving Time between April 2 and October 29.) **All of the times on the left-hand calendar pages are calculated for Boston.** Key letters accompany much of the data; they are provided for the correction of Boston times to other localities. Here's how . . .

SUNRISE, SUNSET

Note the Key Letter to the right of each time for sunrise and sunset in the column entitled "Key." To find the time of sunrise or sunset for your area, consult the Time Correction Tables (pages 80-84). Find your city or the city nearest you and locate the figure, expressed in minutes, in the appropriate Key Letter column. Add, or subtract, that figure to the time given for Boston. The result will be accurate to within 5 minutes for latitudes north of 35°, 10 minutes for latitudes 30°-35°, and 15 minutes for latitudes 25°-30°.

Example: March 26 (Easter) sunrise in Boston is 5:38 A.M., EST, with Key Letter C (p. 56). To find the time of sunrise in Seattle, Washington, look on page 83. Key Letter C for Seattle is +24 minutes, so sunrise in Seattle is 6:02 A.M., PST. Use the same process for sunset. (For dates between April 2 and October 29, add one hour for Daylight Saving Time.)

MOONRISE, MOONSET

Moonrise and moonset are figured the same way except that an additional correction factor (see table below) based on longitude should be used. For the longitude of your city, consult pages 80-84.

Longitude of city	Correction minutes
58°- 76°	0
77°- 89°	+1
90°-102°	+2
103°-115°	+3
116°-127°	+4
128°-141°	+5
142°-155°	+6

Example: To determine moonrise in Eastport, Maine, for October 19, 1989, see page

70. Moonrise in Boston is 8:39 P.M., EST, with Key Letter A. For Eastport, Key Letter A (page 81) is -26 minutes, moving moonrise to 8:13 P.M. The longitude of Eastport is 67° 0′, so the additional correction is 0 minutes. Moonrise in Eastport is therefore 8:13 P.M., EST. (Add one hour for Daylight Saving Time.) Follow the same procedure to determine moonset.

SUNDIALS

Also in the left-hand calendar pages is a column headed "Sun Fast." This is for changing sundial time into local clock time. A sundial reads natural, or Sun, time which is neither Standard nor Daylight time except by coincidence. Simply *subtract* Sun Fast time to get local clock time and use Key Letter C (pages 80-84) to correct the time for your city. (Add one hour for Daylight Saving Time April 2-October 29.)

Example:	Boston
Sundial reading, April 1	12:00
Subtract Sun Fast	−12
Clock Time	11:48 EST

Example:	El Paso
Sundial reading, April 1	12:00
Subtract Sun Fast	−12
Add Key C (for El Paso)	+22
Clock Time	12:10 MST

RISING AND SETTING OF THE PLANETS

The times of rising and setting of visible planets, with the exception of Mercury, are given for Boston on pages 36-37. To convert these times to those of other localities (pages 80-84), follow the same procedure as that given for finding the times of sunrise and sunset.

LENGTH OF DAY

The "Length of Day" column for Boston (pages 48-74) tells how long the Sun will be above the horizon. Use the Time Correction Tables (pages 80-84) to determine sunrise and sunset times for your city. Add 12 hours to the time of sunset, subtract the time of sunrise, and you will have the length of day.

LENGTH OF TWILIGHT

Subtract from time of sunrise for dawn. Add to time of sunset for dark.

Latitude	25°N to 30°N	31°N to 36°N	37°N to 42°N
	h m	h m	h m
Jan. 1 to Apr. 10	1 20	1 26	1 33
Apr. 11 to May 2	1 23	1 28	1 39
May 3 to May 14	1 26	1 34	1 47
May 15 to May 25	1 29	1 38	1 52
May 26 to July 22	1 32	1 43	1 59
July 23 to Aug. 3	1 29	1 38	1 52
Aug. 4 to Aug. 14	1 26	1 34	1 47
Aug. 15 to Sept. 5	1 23	1 28	1 39
Sept. 6 to Dec. 31	1 20	1 26	1 33

Latitude	43°N to 47°N	48°N to 49°N
	h m	h m
Jan. 1 to Apr. 10	1 42	1 50
Apr. 11 to May 2	1 51	2 04
May 3 to May 14	2 02	2 22
May 15 to May 25	2 13	2 42
May 26 to July 22	2 27	—
July 23 to Aug. 3	2 13	2 42
Aug. 4 to Aug. 14	2 02	2 22
Aug. 15 to Sept. 5	1 51	2 04
Sept. 6 to Dec. 31	1 42	1 50

DAWN AND DARK

The approximate times dawn will break and dark descend are found by applying the length of twilight taken from the table above to the times of sunrise and sunset at any specific place. The latitude of the place (see pages 80-84) determines the column from which the length of twilight is to be selected.

Boston (latitude 42° 22′)
Sunrise March 1	6:20 A.M.
Length of twilight	−1:33
Dawn breaks	4:47 A.M.
Sunset March 1	5:34 P.M.
Length of twilight	+1:33
Dark descends	7:07 P.M.

Tampa (latitude 27° 57′)
Sunrise March 1	6:45 A.M.
Length of twilight	−1:20
Dawn breaks	5:25 A.M.
Sunset March 1	6:38 P.M.
Length of twilight	+1:20
Dark descends	7:58 P.M.

THE RIGHT-HAND CALENDAR PAGES
(Pages 49-75)

THESE PAGES are a combination of astronomical data; specific dates in mainly the Anglican church calendar, inclusion of which has always been traditional in American and English almanacs (though we also include some other religious dates); tide heights at Boston (the left-hand calendar pages include the daily times of high tides; the corrections for your locality are on pages 86-87); quotations; anniversary dates; appropriate seasonal activities; and a rhyming version of the weather forecasts for New England. (Detailed forecasts for the entire country are presented on pages 134-159.)

The following is a summary of the highlights from this year's right-hand calendar pages, the signs used, and a sample (the first part of December 1988) of a calendar page explained. . . .

MOVABLE FEASTS AND FASTS FOR 1989

Septuagesima Sunday	Jan. 22
Shrove Tuesday	Feb. 7
Ash Wednesday	Feb. 8
Palm Sunday	Mar. 19
Good Friday	Mar. 24
Easter Day	Mar. 26
Low Sunday	Apr. 2
Rogation Sunday	Apr. 30
Ascension Day	May 4
Whit Sunday-Pentecost	May 14
Trinity Sunday	May 21
Corpus Christi	May 25
1st Sunday in Advent	Dec. 3

THE SEASONS OF 1989

Winter 1988	Dec. 21	10:28 A.M., EST
		(Sun enters Capricorn)
Spring	Mar. 20	10:28 A.M., EST
		(Sun enters Aries)
Summer	June 21	4:53 A.M., EST
		(Sun enters Cancer)
Fall	Sept. 22	8:20 P.M., EST
		(Sun enters Libra)
Winter 1989	Dec. 21	4:22 P.M., EST
		(Sun enters Capricorn)

CHRONOLOGICAL CYCLES FOR 1989

Golden Number (Lunar Cycle)	14
Epact	22
Solar Cycle	10
Dominical Letter	A
Roman Indiction	12
Year of Julian Period	6702

ERA	Year	Begins
Byzantine	7498	Sept. 14
Jewish (A.M.)*	5750	Sept. 29
Roman (A.U.C.)	2742	Jan. 14
Nabonassar	2738	Apr. 26
Japanese	2649	Jan. 1
Grecian	2301	Sept. 14
(Seleucidae)		(or Oct. 14)
Indian (Saka)	1911	Mar. 22
Diocletian	1706	Sept. 11
Islamic (Hegira)*	1410	Aug. 3
Chinese (Lunar)	4626	Feb. 6
(Snake)		

*Year begins at sunset

DETERMINATION OF EARTHQUAKES

Note, on right-hand pages 49-75, the dates when the Moon (☽) "runs high" or "runs low." The date of the high begins the most likely five-day period of earthquakes in the northern hemisphere; the date of the low indicates a similar five-day period in the southern hemisphere. You will also find on these pages a notation for Moon on the Equa-

tor (☾ on Eq.) twice each month. At this time, in both hemispheres, is a two-day earthquake period.

NAMES AND CHARACTERS OF THE PRINCIPAL PLANETS AND ASPECTS

Every now and again on these right-hand calendar pages, you will see symbols conjoined in groups to tell you what is happening in the heavens. For example, ☌ ♂ ☾ opposite December 17, 1988, on page 51 means that Mars ♂ and the Moon ☾ are on that date in conjunction ☌ or apparently near each other.

Here are the symbols used . . .

☉ The Sun
○ ● ☾ The Moon
☿ Mercury
♄ Saturn
♀ Venus
⊕ The Earth
♂ Mars
♃ Jupiter
♅ Uranus
♆ Neptune
♇ Pluto

☌ Conjunction, or in the same degree
☍ Opposition, or 180 degrees
☊ Ascending Node
☋ Descending Node

EARTH AT APHELION AND PERIHELION 1989

The Earth will be at Perihelion on January 1, 1989, when it will be 91,400,005 miles from the Sun. The Earth will be at Aphelion on July 4, 1989, when it will be 94,512,258 miles from the Sun.

SAMPLE PAGE

(from December 1988—page 51)

Day of the month. Day of the week. For detailed regional forecasts, see pages 134-159.

Conjunction — closest approach — of Venus and the Moon.

Second Sunday in Advent. (Events in the church calendar generally appear in this typeface.)

The Dominical Letter for 1988 was C during January and February because the first Sunday of the year fell on the third day of January; after Leap Year Day it became B. The letter for 1989 is A.

Feast Day of the Conception of Virgin Mary, instituted by St. Anselm about 1070, to commemorate the escape of the fleet of William the Conqueror from a storm. (Certain religious feasts and civil holidays appear in this typeface.)

Morning tide at Boston, shown to be at 1:00 A.M. on the left-hand page, will be 8.8 feet. Evening tide, at 1:00 P.M., will be 10.4 feet.

The Moon is at perigee, the closest point to the Earth in its orbit.

D.M.	D.W.	Dates, Feasts, Fasts, Aspects, Tide Heights	Weather ↓
1	Th.	☾ at ☋ • ☿ in sup. ☌ • Tides {8.2 8.4 •	*Batten*
2	Fr.	☾ on Eq. • ☾ at apo. • Monroe Doctrine proclaimed, 1823 {8.3 8.2	*hatches —*
3	Sa.	*The school of life is a compulsory education.* • {8.5 8.1 •	*Northeaster*
4	B	**2nd S. Advent • Chanukah** • {8.8 8.2	*brings*
5	M.	Mozart died, 1791 • Ty Cobb died, 1951 • Tides {9.1 8.2	*batches!*
6	Tu.	**St. Nicholas** • ☌♀☾ • {9.4 8.3 •	*Attitude*
7	W.	Mary Stuart, Queen of Scots, born, 1542 • {9.7 8.5 •	*depends*
8	Th.	**Conception of Virgin Mary** • Tides {10.0 8.6 •	*on*
9	Fr.	New ● • 61° F., Boston, at 1 A.M., 1980 • {10.2 8.7 •	*latitude:*
10	Sa.	*Strange that a man who has wit enough to write a satire should have folly enough to publish it.*	*rain*
11	B	**3rd S. Advent** • ☾ runs low • ☌♆☾	*or snow?*
12	M.	Dr. Joel R. Poinsett, who introduced poinsettia plant to U.S., died, 1851 • {8.8 10.4	*Sunny*
13	Tu.	**St. Lucy** • 30° F., Los Angeles, 1938 • {8.9 10.3 •	*reprieve,*
14	W.	☾ at ☊ • Ember Day • Alabama joined U.S., 1819 • {9.1 10.0 •	*then*
15	Th.	☾ at peri. • *Nine-tenths of wisdom consists in being wise in time.* •	*colder*

NOTE: The values of Key Letters are given in the Time Correction Tables. (See pages 80-84.)

Holidays, 1989

(*) Are recommended as holidays with pay for all employees.
(**) State observances only.

Jan. 1 (*) New Year's Day
Jan. 16 (*) Martin Luther King Jr.'s Birthday (observed)
Jan. 19 (**) Robert E. Lee's Birthday (Ala., Ark., Miss., S.C., Tenn.)
Feb. 2 Groundhog Day
Feb. 7 Mardi Gras (Ala., La.)
Feb. 8 Ash Wednesday
Feb. 12 (**) Abraham Lincoln's Birthday
Feb. 14 Valentine's Day
Feb. 20 (*) George Washington's Birthday observed (Presidents' Day)
Mar. 2 (**) Texas Independence Day
Mar. 15 (**) Andrew Jackson Day (Tenn.)
Mar. 17 (**) St. Patrick's Day; Evacuation Day (Boston and Suffolk Co., Mass.)
Mar. 24 Good Friday
Mar. 26 Easter
Mar. 27 (**) Seward's Day (Alaska)
Apr. 13 (**) Thomas Jefferson's Birthday (Ala., Okla.)
Apr. 17 (**) Patriots Day (Maine, Mass.)
Apr. 20 Passover
Apr. 24 (**) Fast Day (N.H.)
Apr. 28 Arbor Day (except Alaska, Neb., Wyo.)
Apr. 30 Greek Orthodox Easter
May 1 May Day
May 14 (**) Mother's Day
May 20 Armed Forces Day
May 29 (*) Memorial Day (observed)
June 1 (**) Statehood Day (Tenn.)
June 5 World Environment Day
June 14 Flag Day
June 11 (**) King Kamehameha Day (Hawaii)
June 17 (**) Bunker Hill Day (Boston and Suffolk Co., Mass.)
June 18 Father's Day
July 1 Canada Day
July 4 (*) Independence Day
Aug. 13 (**) Herbert Hoover Day (Iowa)
Aug. 14 (**) Victory Day (R.I.)
Aug. 16 (**) Bennington Battle Day (Vt.)
Aug. 26 Women's Equality Day
Aug. 27 (**) Lyndon B. Johnson's Birthday (Tex.)
Sept. 4 (*) Labor Day
Sept. 10 Grandparents' Day

Sept. 12 (**) Defenders' Day (Md.)
Sept. 22 Native American Day
Sept. 28 (**) Frances Willard Day (Minn., Wis.)
Sept. 30 Rosh Hashanah
Oct. 9 (*) Columbus Day; (**) Pioneer Day (S. Dak.); Yom Kippur; Thanksgiving (Canada)
Oct. 18 (**) Alaska Day
Oct. 24 United Nations Day
Oct. 31 Halloween
Nov. 7 Election Day
Nov. 11 (*) Veterans Day (Armistice Day)
Nov. 23 (*) Thanksgiving Day
Dec. 10 (**) Wyoming Day
Dec. 15 Bill of Rights Day
Dec. 23 Chanukah
Dec. 25 (*) Christmas Day
Dec. 26 Boxing Day (Canada)

How the Almanac Weather Forecasts Are Made

Our weather forecasts are determined both by the use of a secret weather-forecasting formula devised by the founder of this almanac in 1792 and by the most modern scientific calculations based on solar activity. We believe nothing in the universe occurs haphazardly; there is a cause-and-effect pattern to all phenomena, including weather. It follows, therefore, that we believe weather is predictable. It is obvious, however, that neither we nor anyone else has as yet gained sufficient insight into the mysteries of the universe to predict weather with anything resembling total accuracy.

Price Breakthrough

AT LAST! A Small, LOW-PRICED rear-tine tiller for backyard gardens!

The All-New TROY-BILT® TUFFY

☐ So easy to operate, you guide it with JUST ONE HAND!

☐ Has its tines in the REAR, and POWER-DRIVEN wheels!

☐ Legendary TROY-BILT performance, at about the same price of a hard-to-handle front-tine tiller!

Which gardening machine would YOU rather use?

This One?...

This ordinary tiller has its tines in the front and no power to its tiny wheels. (The tines propel the machine... and you... forward, while you try to hold it back!) It's an exhausting strain on your arms and back.

Or This One!...

TROY-BILT Tillers are different. Their tines are in the rear (so they leave no wheel-marks or footprints), and forward speed is controlled by separately powered wheels. As a result, the TROY-BILT is so easy to control, you simply guide it with just one hand!

 For NEWS about the low-priced TROY-BILT Tuffy Model please see over...then mail the card below TODAY!

The TROY-BILT® Tiller is so easy to use... you can guide it with Just One Hand!

1989   OLD FARMER'S ALMANAC   33

Aph. — Aphelion: Planet reaches point in its orbit farthest from the Sun.

Apo.— Apogee: Moon reaches point in its orbit farthest from the Earth.

Conj. — Conjunction: Time of apparent closest approach to each other of any two heavenly bodies.

Declination: Measure of angular distance any celestial object lies perpendicularly north or south of celestial equator; analogous to terrestrial latitude. The Almanac gives the Sun's declination at noon E.S.T.

Dominical Letter: Used for the ecclesiastical calendar and determined by the date on which the first Sunday of the year falls. If Jan. 1 is a Sunday, the Letter is A; if Jan. 2 is a Sunday, the Letter is B.; and so to G when the first Sunday is Jan. 7. In leap year the Letter applies through February and then takes the Letter before.

Eclipse, Annular: An eclipse in which sunlight shows around the Moon.

Eclipse, Lunar: Opposition of the Sun and Moon with the Moon at or near node.

Eclipse, Solar: Conjunction of Sun and Moon with the Moon at or near node.

El. — Elongation: Apparent angular distance of a member of the solar system from the Sun as seen from the Earth.

Epact: A number from 1 to 30 to harmonize the lunar year with the solar year, used for the ecclesiastical calendar. Indicates the Moon's age at the instant Jan. 1 begins at the meridian of Greenwich, England.

Eq. — Equator: A great circle of the Earth equidistant from the two poles.

Equinox, Fall: Sun passes from northern to southern hemisphere.

Equinox, Spring: Sun passes from southern to northern hemisphere.

Evening Star: A planet that is above the horizon at sunset and less than 180° east of the Sun.

Golden Number: Denoting the year in the 19-year cycle of the Moon. The Moon phases occur on the same dates every 19 years.

Gr. El. — Greatest Elongation: See El.

Inf. — Inferior: Conjunction in which the planet is between the Sun and the Earth.

Julian Period: A period of 7,980 Julian years, being a period of agreement of solar and lunar cycles. Add 4,713 to year to find Julian year.

Moon's Age: The number of days since the previous new Moon. First Quarter: Right half of Moon illuminated. Full Moon: Moon reaches opposition. Last Quarter: Left half of Moon illuminated. New Moon: Sun and Moon in conjunction.

Moon Runs High or Low: Day of month Moon is highest or lowest exactly above the south point of the observer's horizon.

Morning Star: A planet that is above the horizon at sunrise and less than 180° west of the Sun in right ascension.

Node: Either of the two points where the Moon's orbit intersects the ecliptic.

Occultations: Eclipses of stars by the Moon.

Opposition: Time when the Sun and Moon or planet appear on opposite sides of the sky (El. 180°).

Perig. — Perigee: Moon reaches point in its orbit closest to the Earth.

Perih. — Perihelion: Planet reaches point in its orbit closest to the Sun.

R.A. — Right Ascension: The coordinate on the celestial sphere analogous to longitude on the Earth.

Roman Indiction: A cycle of 15 years established Jan. 1, A.D. 313 as a fiscal term. Add 3 to the number of years in the Christian era and divide by 15. The remainder of the year is Roman Indiction — no remainder is 15.

Solar Cycle: A period of 28 years, at the end of which the days of the month return to the same days of the week.

Solstice, Summer: Point at which the Sun is farthest north of the celestial equator: Sun enters Cancer. **Winter:** Point at which the Sun is farthest south of the celestial equator: Sun enters Capricorn.

Stat. — Stationary: Halt in the apparent movement of a planet against the background of the stars just before the planet comes to opposition.

Sun Fast: Subtract times given in this column from your sundial to arrive at the correct Standard Time.

Sunrise & Sunset: Visible rising and setting of the Sun's upper limb across the unobstructed horizon of an observer whose eyes are 15' above ground level.

Sup. — Superior: Superior Conjunction; indicates that the Sun is between the planet and the Earth.

Twilight: Begins or ends when stars of the sixth magnitude disappear or appear at the zenith; or when the Sun is about 18 degrees below the horizon.

A PILLAR OF FLAMING TRUMPETS
HARDY HUMMINGBIRD VINE
(Campsis radicans)

PRICES SLASHED

AS LOW AS **$2.24** EACH IN QTY.

AVAILABLE ALL YEAR

ZOOMS ROOF HIGH THE FIRST YEAR!

No other flowering plant you can grow will attract hummingbirds faster than the fabulous trumpet vine. The very first year of planting the beautiful, hardy vines will climb skyward, grasping any kind of support . . . man-high within a few weeks . . . roof-high by mid-summer . . . a pillar of flaming red trumpet flowers, each loaded with nectar that hummingbirds find so irresistible, they return year after year to thrill you and your family. These plants are foolproof to grow, thrive even in poor soils, sun or shade. Climbs on its own, covering walls, arbors and fences in no time at all.

© 1988 Spring River™ General Offices: P.O. Box 25, Hartford, MI 49057

THE VISIBLE PLANETS, 1989

The times of rising or setting of the planets Venus, Mars, Jupiter, and Saturn on the 1st, 11th, and 21st of each month are given below. The approximate time of rising or setting of these planets on other days may be found with sufficient accuracy by interpolation. For an explanation of Key Letters (used in adjusting the times given here for Boston to the time in your town), see page 28 and pages 80-84. Key Letters appear as capital letters beside the time of rising or setting. (For definitions of morning and evening stars, see page 34.)

VENUS is brilliant in the morning sky from January until late February when it becomes too close to the Sun for observation, and in the evening sky from mid-May until the end of the year. Venus is in conjunction with Saturn on January 16 and November 15, with Mercury on February 1, with Jupiter on May 23, and with Mars on July 12.

Boldface — P.M.   Lightface — A.M.

Jan. 1	.... rise	5:33	E	May 1	....set	7:17	D	Sept. 1	......set	7:42	B
Jan. 11	.... "	5:52	E	May 11	.... "	7:42	E	Sept. 11	..... "	7:28	B
Jan. 21	.... "	6:06	E	May 21	.... "	8:06	E	Sept. 21	..... "	7:15	B
Feb. 1	.... rise	6:14	E	June 1	......set	8:28	E	Oct. 1	......set	7:04	A
Feb. 11	.... "	6:16	D	June 11	.... "	8:43	E	Oct. 11	..... "	6:57	A
Feb. 21	.... "	6:12	D	June 21	.... "	8:51	E	Oct. 21	..... "	6:55	A
Mar. 1	.... rise	6:07	D	July 1	......set	8:53	E	Nov. 1	......set	6:57	A
Mar. 11	.... "	5:57	D	July 11	.... "	8:49	D	Nov. 11	..... "	7:03	A
Mar. 21	.... "	5:46	C	July 21	.... "	8:41	D	Nov. 21	..... "	7:10	A
Apr. 1	.... rise	5:32	B	Aug. 1	......set	8:28	D	Dec. 1	......set	7:15	A
Apr. 11	....set	6:27	D	Aug. 11	.... "	8:14	C	Dec. 11	..... "	7:14	A
Apr. 21	.... "	6:52	D	Aug. 21	.... "	7:59	C	Dec. 21	...., "	7:02	A
								Dec. 31	.....set	6:34	A

MARS can been seen more than half the night in Pisces for the first two weeks of the year, after which it can be seen in the evening sky as it passes through Aries, Taurus, Gemini, Cancer, and Leo until mid-August, when it becomes too close to the Sun for observation. It reappears in the morning sky around mid-November, moving from Virgo into Libra. A few days after mid-December it moves into Scorpius, and in late December into Ophiuchus. Mars is in conjunction with Jupiter on March 12, with Venus on July 12, and with Mercury on August 5. Mars passes 7° N. of Aldebaran on March 28, 5° S. of Pollux on June 7, 0.7° N. of Regulus on August 2, and 5° N. of Antares on December 30.

Jan. 1	..... set	12:49	D	May 1	.... set	10:55	E	Sept. 1	......set	6:42	C
Jan. 11	..... "	12:37	D	May 11	.... "	10:42	E	Sept. 11	..... "	6:17	C
Jan. 21	..... "	12:27	D	May 21	..... "	10:27	E	Sept. 21	..... "	5:51	C
Feb. 1	.... set	12:16	D	June 1	..... set	10:09	E	Oct. 1	.....set	5:26	C
Feb. 11	..... "	12:08	D	June 11	..... "	9:50	E	Oct. 11	.... rise	5:32	C
Feb. 21	..... "	12:00	E	June 21	..... "	9:31	E	Oct. 21	..... "	5:27	D
Mar. 1	.... set	11:53	E	July 1	.... set	9:10	E	Nov. 1	.... rise	5:21	D
Mar. 11	..... "	11:45	E	July 11	..... "	8:48	D	Nov. 11	..... "	5:17	D
Mar. 21	..... "	11:37	E	July 21	..... "	8:25	D	Nov. 21	..... "	5:13	D
Apr. 1	.... set	11:27	E	Aug. 1	.... set	7:59	D	Dec. 1	.... rise	5:09	D
Apr. 11	..... "	11:18	E	Aug. 11	.... "	7:35	D	Dec. 11	..... "	5:05	D
Apr. 21	..... "	11:07	E	Aug. 21	..... "	7:10	D	Dec. 21	..... "	5:01	E
								Dec. 31	.... rise	4:57	E

JUPITER is visible in Taurus until mid-February, after which it can be seen only in the evening sky until late May, when it becomes too close to the Sun for observation. It reappears in late June in the morning sky, still in Taurus, and in late July moves into Gemini, where it remains for the rest of the year. It is at opposition on December 27, when it can be seen throughout the night. Jupiter is in conjunction with Mars on March 12, with Venus on May 23, and with Mercury on July 2.

IVPITER

Jan. 1	set 3:53	E	May 1	set 9:04	E	Sept. 1	rise 11:55	A
Jan. 11	" 3:12	D	May 11	" 8:36	E	Sept. 11	" 11:22	A
Jan. 21	" 2:32	D	May 21	" 8:08	E	Sept. 21	" 10:48	A
Feb. 1	set 1:50	E	June 1	set 7:37	E	Oct. 1	rise 10:09	A
Feb. 11	" 1:14	E	June 11	rise 4:05	A	Oct. 11	" 9:33	A
Feb. 21	" 12:39	E	June 21	" 3:34	A	Oct. 21	" 8:55	A
Mar. 1	set 12:12	E	July 1	rise 3:04	A	Nov. 1	rise 8:12	A
Mar. 11	" 11:36	E	July 11	" 2:34	A	Nov. 11	" 7:32	A
Mar. 21	" 11:05	E	July 21	" 2:04	A	Nov. 21	" 6:49	A
Apr. 1	set 10:32	E	Aug. 1	rise 1:31	A	Dec. 1	rise 6:06	A
Apr. 11	" 10:02	E	Aug. 11	" 1:00	A	Dec. 11	" 5:21	A
Apr. 21	" 9:33	E	Aug. 21	" 12:29	A	Dec. 21	" 4:36	A
						Dec. 31	set 7:03	E

SATURN may be observed starting in mid-January in the morning sky, rising before sunrise in Sagittarius, in which constellation it remains throughout the year. Its westward elongation gradually increases, and in early April it becomes visible for more than half the night. It is at opposition on July 2 when it can be seen throughout the night, after which its eastward elongation gradually decreases. From the end of September until mid-December it can only be seen in the evening sky. Saturn is in conjunction with Venus on January 16 and November 15 and with Mercury on December 16.

SATVRN9

Jan. 1	rise 6:50	E	May 1	rise 11:27	E	Sept. 1	set 12:08	A
Jan. 11	" 6:15	E	May 11	" 10:47	E	Sept. 11	set 11:25	A
Jan. 21	" 5:40	E	May 21	" 10:06	E	Sept. 21	" 10:46	A
Feb. 1	rise 5:02	E	June 1	rise 9:20	E	Oct. 1	set 10:07	A
Feb. 11	" 4:27	E	June 11	" 8:39	E	Oct. 11	" 9:30	A
Feb. 21	" 3:51	E	June 21	" 7:57	E	Oct. 21	" 8:53	A
Mar. 1	rise 3:22	E	July 1	rise 7:15	E	Nov. 1	set 8:13	A
Mar. 11	" 2:46	E	July 11	set 3:45	A	Nov. 11	" 7:38	A
Mar. 21	" 2:09	E	July 21	" 3:03	A	Nov. 21	" 7:03	A
Apr. 1	rise 1:27	E	Aug. 1	set 2:16	A	Dec. 1	set 6:28	A
Apr. 11	" 12:49	E	Aug. 11	" 1:34	A	Dec. 11	" 5:54	A
Apr. 21	" 12:10	E	Aug. 21	" 12:53	A	Dec. 21	" 5:20	A
						Dec. 31	set 4:46	A

MERCURY can only be seen low in the east before sunrise or low in the west after sunset. It is visible mornings between these approximate dates: January 31-March 26, June 2-July 11, October 2-28. The planet is brighter at the end of each period (best viewing conditions in northern latitudes occur the second week of October). It is visible evenings between these approximate dates: January 1-19, April 13-May 14, July 27-September 18, November 28-December 31. The planet is brighter at the beginning of each period (best viewing conditions in northern latitudes occur in late April and early May).

DO NOT CONFUSE 1) Venus with Saturn at mid-January or mid-November, with Mercury in early February and mid-May, with Jupiter in late May, and with Mars at mid-July; on all occasions Venus is the brighter object. 2) Mars with Jupiter in March and with Mercury in early August (Mars is the dimmer). 3) Mercury with Jupiter in late June (Jupiter is the brighter) and with Saturn at mid-December (Mercury is the brighter).

The Planetary Odd Couple

Pluto, the smallest planet in our solar system, is also the most enigmatic. Is it a double planet — or maybe even more?

by Andrew E. Rothovius

☐ THERE CAN BE NO SORT OF GUARANTEE that what follows concerning Pluto, the presently known outermost planet of the solar system, will not have been radically revised or even superseded by new discoveries before this appears in print. For of all the members of the Sun's planetary family, none has proved as difficult to pin down as this misfit, named for the classical god of the underworld. And since 1978 the problem of defining it has been vastly complicated by the discovery of its traveling companion, Charon, bearing the name of the ferryman of Hades.

Less than 60 years ago, the very existence of Pluto was totally unknown, although not wholly unsuspected. Observations made over a quarter of a century, beginning in 1905, convinced astronomers Percival Lowell and W. H. Pickering (otherwise noted for their wrongheaded insistence on the habitability of Mars) that perturbations in the orbit of Neptune indicated the presence of another planet.

Lowell and Pickering worked out the likely position of the mysterious planet, and it was very close to their predicted location that Clyde Tombaugh of the Lowell Observatory at Flagstaff, Arizona, first spotted a new dot of light on a photographic plate exposed on January 21, 1930. A second exposure a few weeks later confirmed this sighting, and after further double checking, Tombaugh announced on March 12 the discovery of the ninth planet. Suggestions for naming the new sibling came from around the world; "Pluto" was proposed by 11-year-old Venetia Burney of Oxford, England.

The new planet turned out to be a mere 1,400 miles in diameter — less by a third than the Earth's Moon — and far too small to account for the irregularities in the Neptunian orbit. Pluto also proved to have other odd and puzzling features. Its orbit is the most eccentric of any in the solar system, ranging from 2.8 billion to 4 billion miles away from the Sun, with an orbital period of 248 years. At the innermost point of the orbit, which it is now entering, Pluto cuts 13 million miles inside the orbit of Neptune, which is thus temporarily restored to the position of outermost planet.

The new planet also departed wildly from the progression of planetary sizes that had hitherto held good, with the single exception of Mars. From Mercury out to Jupiter, the planets increase progressively in size (except for Mars); beyond Jupiter, they decrease in the same ratio. But Pluto is far smaller than the formula would predict.

Being so far from the Sun, it is understandable that Pluto appears to be very cold — about 370° below zero, F. But oddly for so small an object, and hence with tiny gravity, it seems to have a sizable atmosphere of methane gas, though mostly in the form of ice. To retain that, it must have a core of rock.

All of these anomalies have continued to puzzle astronomers

through six decades. One, Maurice Wemyss, predicted as early as 1935 that part of Neptune's orbital wobbles were caused by another planet, even smaller than Pluto, between Uranus and Saturn, and proposed that it be named Jason, for the legendary leader of the treasure-hunting Argonauts.

Forty years later, on November 1, 1977, Wemyss's conjectured planet was discovered by Charles Kowal of the California Institute of Technology. And a strange object it is, with dimensions only vaguely estimated at 100 to 400 miles in diameter, orbiting between Saturn and Uranus at a mean distance of 2.5 billion miles from the Sun. This planetoid, finally named Chiron for the half-man, half-horse of ancient myth, originally may have been one of a trio (with Pluto and Charon) of closely grouped asteroids or minor planets before it was deflected by the huge gravitational pull of Saturn or Jupiter. There is still no agreement on how to classify Kowal's find. Chiron is too small to be a full-fledged planet, yet there are no other known asteroids in that part of the solar system. It is doubtful if it has more than the smallest effect on Neptune's orbit.

In July of 1978, while scientists were puzzling over Chiron, James W. Christy of the U.S. Naval Observatory discovered Charon when he noticed an odd bulge on one side of a photographic image of Pluto. In fact, the bulge had been noted before but had always been dismissed as an imperfection in the film. This time the 158-inch Interamerican telescope at Cerro Tololo in Chile was trained on Pluto, and the bulge was determined to be a satellite half the size of Pluto, orbiting at so close a distance — a mere 12,000 miles — as to make the system virtually a double planet, the only one in our solar system.

In the 10 years since, the mysteries of Pluto and its companions have deepened. Early in 1988, taking advantage of the closest approach of Pluto to the Earth in 124 years, a concerted effort began to explain some of the enigmas. Among the early findings was that Charon appears to be of the same composition as Pluto — i.e., a frozen methane coating over a rocky core — but some of the methane on both bodies is somehow sublimated into gas, forming a halo atmosphere that enfolds both bodies in a single gaseous envelope, the only such formation known in the solar system. (We do not yet know if Chiron is similarly covered with methane.) Yet Pluto and Charon do not appear to be the same color, Pluto having a reddish cast and Charon appearing as a dull gray. Astronomers hope that the launch of the Hubble Space Telescope, scheduled for 1989, will fill in the picture of conditions on Pluto and Charon.

And though the combined gravitational effect of Charon and Pluto orbiting in tandem is greater than we had thought, it still is insufficient to fully explain neighbor Neptune's orbital inequalities. New electronic sensors capable of seeing an object as small as 30 miles in diameter are searching the region of Pluto for signs of other moons. Perhaps there is yet an even more remote outlier of the solar system, waiting to be discovered. □ □

ECLIPSES FOR 1989

There will be four eclipses in 1989, two of the Moon and two of the Sun. Lunar eclipses technically are visible from the entire night side of the Earth; solar eclipses are visible only in certain local areas. Both of the lunar eclipses and one of the solar eclipses will be visible in certain locations in the United States and Canada, as specified below.

1. Total eclipse of the Moon, February 20. Only the umbral phases will be visible from North America, and this only in the western half. Totality begins at 9:56 A.M. EST and ends at 11:15 A.M. EST. Magnitude of the eclipse is 1.279.

2. Partial eclipse of the Sun, March 7. The eclipse will be visible through central, western, and northern North America, but not from the eastern or south-central regions. The eclipse begins at about 1:30 P.M. EST in central regions and at about noon EST in western regions. It will last between one and two hours, depending on the viewer's location. The magnitude of greatest eclipse is 0.827.

3. Total eclipse of the Moon, August 16. The eclipse will be visible throughout most of North America. The beginning of the umbral phase will be visible from the eastern half of North America; the end will be visible throughout all of North America except Alaska. Totality begins at 9:20 P.M. EST and ends at 10:56 P.M. EST. Magnitude of the eclipse is 1.604.

4. Partial eclipse of the Sun, August 30-31. This eclipse will be visible only from southern Africa and parts of Antarctica. The magnitude of greatest eclipse is 0.635.

FULL MOON DAYS

	1989	1990	1991	1992	1993
Jan.	21	10	30	19	8
Feb.	20	9	28	18	6
Mar.	22	11	30	18	8
Apr.	20	9	28	16	6
May	20	9	28	16	5
June	19	8	26	14	4
July	18	7	26	14	3
Aug.	16	6	25	13	2/31
Sept.	15	4	23	11	30
Oct.	14	4	23	11	30
Nov.	13	2	21	10	29
Dec.	12	2/31	21	9	28

PRINCIPAL METEOR SHOWERS

Shower	Best Hour (EST)	Radiant Direction*	Date of Maximum**	Approx. Peak Rate (/hr.)	Associated Comet
Quadrantid	5 A.M.	N.	Jan. 4	40-150	—
Lyrid	4 A.M.	S.	Apr. 21	10-15	1861 I
Eta Aquarid	4 A.M.	S.E.	May 4	10-40	Halley
Delta Aquarid	2 A.M.	S.	July 30	10-35	—
Perseid	4 A.M.	N.	Aug. 11-13	50-100	1862 III
Draconid	9 P.M.	N.W.	Oct. 9	10	Giacobini-Zinner
Orionid	4 A.M.	S.	Oct. 20	10-70	Halley
Taurid	midnight	S.	Nov. 9	5-15	Encke
Andromedid	10 P.M.	S.	Nov. 25-27	10	Biela
Leonid	5 A.M.	S.	Nov. 16	5-20	1866 I
Geminid	2 A.M.	S.	Dec.13	50-80	—
Ursid	5 A.M.	N.	Dec. 22	10-15	—

* Direction from which the meteors appear to come.

** Date of actual maximum occurrence may vary by one or two days in either direction.

BRIGHT STARS, 1989

The upper table shows the Eastern Standard Time when each star transits the meridian of Boston (i.e., lies directly above the horizon's south point there) and its altitude above that point at transit on the dates shown. The time of transit on any other date differs from that on the nearest date listed by approximately four minutes of time for each day. For a place outside Boston the local time of the star's transit is found by correcting the time at Boston by the value of Key Letter "C" for the place. (See footnote.)

Star	Constellation	Magni-tude	Jan. 1	Mar. 1	May 1	July 1	Sept. 1	Nov. 1	Alt.
			Boldface—P.M.			Lightface—A.M.			
Altair	Aquila	0.8	**12 49**	8 57	4 57	12 57	**8 49**	4 50	56.3
Deneb	Cygnus	1.3	**1 40**	9 48	5 48	1 48	**9 40**	5 40	87.5
Fomalhaut	Psc. Austr.	1.2	**3 54**	**12 02**	8 02	4 03	**11 55**	7 55	17.8
Algol	Perseus	2.2	**8 05**	**4 13**	**12 13**	8 13	4 10	12 10	88.5
Aldebaran	Taurus	0.9	**9 32**	**5 40**	**1 41**	9 41	5 37	1 37	64.1
Rigel	Orion	0.1	**10 11**	**6 19**	**2 19**	10 19	6 15	2 15	39.4
Capella	Auriga	0.1	**10 12**	**6 20**	**2 21**	10 21	6 17	2 17	85.4
Bellatrix	Orion	1.6	**10 21**	**6 29**	**2 30**	10 30	6 26	2 26	54.0
Betelgeuse	Orion	0.7	**10 51**	**6 59**	**3 00**	11 00	6 56	2 56	55.0
Sirius	Can. Maj.	-1.4	**11 41**	**7 49**	**3 49**	11 49	7 46	3 46	31.0
Procyon	Can. Min.	0.4	12 39	**8 43**	**4 43**	**12 43**	8 39	4 40	52.9
Pollux	Gemini	1.2	12 45	**8 49**	**4 49**	**12 49**	8 45	4 46	75.7
Regulus	Leo	1.4	3 08	**11 12**	**7 12**	**3 12**	11 08	7 09	59.7
Spica	Virgo	1.0	6 24	2 32	**10 28**	**6 28**	**2 25**	10 25	36.6
Arcturus	Bootes	-0.1	7 15	3 23	**11 19**	**7 19**	**3 16**	11 16	66.9
Antares	Scorpius	var. 0.9	9 28	5 36	1 36	**9 32**	**5 28**	1 29	21.3
Vega	Lyra	0.0	11 35	7 43	3 43	**11 40**	**7 36**	3 36	86.4

Time of Transit (E.S.T.)

RISINGS AND SETTINGS

The times of the star's rising and setting at Boston on any date are found by applying the interval shown to the time of the star's transit on that date. Subtract the interval for the star's rising; add it for its setting. The times for a place outside Boston are found by correcting the times found for Boston by the values of the Key Letters shown. (See footnote.) The directions in which the star rises and sets shown for Boston are generally useful throughout the United States. Deneb, Algol, Capella, and Vega are circumpolar stars — this means that they do not appear to rise or set but are above the horizon.

Star	Int. hr.m.	Rising Key	Dir.	Setting Key	Dir.
Altair	6 36	B	EbN	D	WbN
Fomalhaut	3 59	E	SE	A	SW
Aldebaran	7 06	B	ENE	D	WNW
Rigel	5 33	D	EbS	B	WbS
Bellatrix	6 27	B	EbN	D	WbN
Betelgeuse	6 31	B	EbN	D	WbN
Sirius	5 00	D	ESE	B	WSW
Procyon	6 23	B	EbN	D	WbN
Pollux	8 01	A	NE	E	NW
Regulus	6 49	B	EbN	D	WbN
Spica	5 23	D	EbS	B	WbS
Arcturus	7 19	A	ENE	E	WNW
Antares	4 17	E	SEbE	A	SWbW

NOTE: The values of Key Letters are given in the Time Correction Tables (see pages 80-84).

THE OLD FARMER'S GENERAL STORE

As the World *Really* Turns

*It seems that all of us are whirling in at least
seven different directions at once — and at speeds of more than
a million miles an hour!*   by Dennis L. Mammana

☐ YOU MIGHT THINK YOU'RE SITTING still. But we on planet Earth are rotating, revolving, and whirling through the universe in at least seven different directions and at speeds of more than a million miles an hour! If that's not too dizzying, read on. . . .

Today we know with confidence that our world rotates from west to east around an axis that joins its north and south poles. Its rotation was proved little more than a century ago by French physicist J. B. L. Foucault, who suspended a freely swinging pendulum beneath the dome of the Pantheon in Paris. Onlookers became astounded during the course of the day, for the plane of the pendulum's swing turned slowly clockwise.

The Earth's rotation affects the trajectory of rockets and projectiles, air traffic, and weather systems. We are being carried along around our globe's circumference once every 24 hours; those at midnorthern latitudes are moving at some 820 miles per hour. Yet as remarkable as this motion seems, it is relatively insignificant compared to an-

other — the annual orbit of our planet around the Sun.

As we circle our star each year, nighttime observers can watch the stars change through the seasons. The springtime Leo replaces Orion, Scorpius replaces Leo, and so on, all because we are moving. Astronomers now know that we are zipping along our orbit at the blinding speed of 66,527 miles per hour, or 18½ miles per second. At that rate, we travel over a million and a half miles each day. Before a baby celebrates its first birthday, it will have traveled some 583 million miles. And during the course of a human lifetime, we all will have journeyed 45 billion miles — five times the size of our solar system!

Although we traverse millions of miles around the Sun, our view of the heavens doesn't change much from year to year. The stars and constellations we see on any clear night are the same as those seen thousands of years ago. But in 1718 the famous astronomer Edmund Halley found something peculiar. The positions of several stars did not coincide with those cataloged by Ptolemy centuries earlier. In fact, some had changed by the width of the full Moon. Astronomers found a pattern in the movements. Many stars seemed to be radiating from a point southwest of the bright summertime star Vega, while many on the opposite side of the sky seemed to be converging toward a point south of Orion.

Other astronomers studied these stellar motions with a phenomenon known as the Doppler effect. Much as the ear discerns direction and speed of an automobile from the changing pitch of its horn, the Doppler effect allows scientists to study fine details within the spectrum of stars to learn how fast they are approaching or receding from us. What they found was that stars in the direction of Vega were approaching us at some 12 miles per second, while those on the opposite side of the sky were receding just as fast.

Our Sun, it seemed, was tearing along through our stellar neighborhood in the direction of the bright star Vega at some 12 miles per second, and pulling us and the other planets with it. At this speed, we cross a distance equal to the width of our solar system in just 20 years. In one human lifetime we come nearly 40 billion miles closer to Vega, yet even at that speed it would take more than 5,300 human lifetimes to get there. That is, of course, if Vega itself stood still!

Each day we travel nearly 12 million miles; each year, the distance of Pluto from the Sun.

Until the beginning of the 20th century, these were the only motions known for our Sun and Earth. But with larger and larger telescopes being trained on the heavens, the situation changed rapidly.

Doppler studies soon showed that the swarm of stars in which we reside seemed to be moving systematically toward the constellation Cygnus, and away from Canis Major, both within the band of the Milky Way. Astronomer B. Linblad of Stockholm explained why in 1926. Our Milky Way galaxy, the highly flattened pinwheel of stars, clusters, and interstellar clouds stretching some 600 billion miles across space, was itself rotating on its own axis.

And with it, our Sun and its retinue of planets are wheeling around at 490,000 miles per hour — 136 miles every second. Each day we travel nearly 12 million miles; each year, the distance of Pluto from the Sun. And a human lifetime takes us on a galactic journey of nearly 322 billion miles. Yet on the scale of our galaxy, these vast distances are an invisible dot, for an incredible 240 million years are required to complete the two-billion-billion-mile trek around the galactic center.

Only two dozen times in the five-billion-year history of the Earth have we passed this way. The last time, the first small dinosaurs were beginning to appear on Earth. The next . . . who knows?

Our Milky Way, we discovered early in this century, is not the only galaxy in this universe. In fact, ours is part of a gravitationally bound family of some 30 galaxies known as the Local Group. Some of these galaxies are visible through a small backyard telescope as faint smudges of light in our nighttime sky. One, perhaps the most famous of all, is even visible to the naked eye.

Stand under a clear, dark autumn sky and look off to the northeastern corner of the Great Square of Pegasus. You should be able to see a hazy patch of light smaller in size than the full Moon. This is the Andromeda galaxy, similar in many respects to our own Milky Way, but located 12 billion billion miles away from us — so far that its light has taken two million years to reach our eyes. (We say that its distance is two million light years.)

Within the last decade astronomers trying to measure the rotational speed of our Milky Way relative to external galaxies noticed that it seemed to be turning 50 miles per second faster than anyone had thought. They soon realized that this extra velocity was not caused by our galaxy's rotation, but by its motion through the Local Group. Today we know that our Milky Way galaxy is careening in the direction of the Andromeda galaxy at some 50 miles per second. But there is no immediate danger of a collision, for it will take at least 75 million centuries to get there!

The Local Group, vast and imposing as it may seem, is actually classified as a "dwarf irregular cluster." It lies on the outskirts of a larger grouping known as the Local Supercluster, which in turn contains some 50 galactic families like our own. Near its center some 70 million light years away lies the Virgo Cluster, home to at least a thousand individual galaxies. Doppler studies have shown that our Local Group is falling toward the Virgo Cluster at the speed of 150 miles per second.

As far beyond as the largest telescopes can see, astronomers see more clusters of galaxies and clusters of clusters. It was in the 1920s that Edwin Hubble and Milton Humason of the Mount Wilson Observatory found that most of these were rushing away from each other as if hurled from a huge cosmic fireball 15 or 20 billion years ago — the Big Bang. In the 1960s astronomers used radio telescopes to find the background radiation from this explosion. And today we know that our Milky Way galaxy, the Local Group, and the Local Supercluster participate in this universal expansion. In fact, our galaxy is moving at more than a million miles per hour — 322 miles every second — relative to this cosmic background radiation.

Within only a century or so, astronomers have proven that we on Earth are:

• rotating on our axis — at about 820 mph in midnorthern latitudes

• revolving about the Sun — at 66,527 mph

• speeding through the nearby stars — at 12 miles per second

• orbiting our Milky Way galaxy — at 490,000 mph

• rushing toward Andromeda — at 50 miles per second

• falling into the Local Supercluster — at 150 miles per second

• and flying outward from the Big Bang — at 322 miles per second

Is there more to come? Is our universe moving in some unknown direction at some incredible speed? Is it rotating upon its own axis as we on Earth and the Milky Way are rotating? The answers may be forthcoming as larger and larger telescopes are aimed toward the heavens.

In the meantime, when you feel that things just aren't going anywhere at all, gaze toward a starry night sky and think again!   □ □

LETTERS TO THE ASTRONOMER

Dr. George Greenstein, astronomer
for *The Old Farmer's Almanac,* answers readers' questions.

Why does the Sun continue to rise later each day for a couple of weeks after the winter solstice, even though the days are getting longer?

If you were to use your wristwatch to check on this, you would indeed find the Sun rising later each day. But using a *sundial* you would not. Which is right? The sundial is. Why, then, do we use watches that run wrong? Because we want our watches to run at the same rate every day. Sundials do not run at such a steady rate; this is because the Earth is orbiting the Sun at an irregular pace. For instance, on the first of January this year we are closest to the Sun and moving fastest; on the Fourth of July we are farthest away from the Sun and moving slowest.

Why is twilight short in the tropics and long at higher latitudes?

Watch the Sun as it sets. If you live in the tropics, you will see it moving straight down. But if you live at higher latitudes, you will see it moving down and to the right. The farther north you live, the more slanting the Sun's path — and the longer it takes the Sun to move far below the horizon and give us total darkness.

What will be the most exciting day of 1989, astronomically speaking?

August 24th, for on this day *Voyager II* is scheduled to encounter the planet Neptune. This one-ton space probe was launched in August of 1977. It passed by Jupiter in 1979, Saturn in 1981, and Uranus in 1986, each time returning spectacular photographs and other scientific data. Neptune is so distant that we know very little about it. *Voyager II* will be giving us our first close look.

What causes the Earth to tilt on its axis?

No one knows. We do know that different planets have different tilts: Mercury's axis does not tilt at all, while Uranus's points right at the Sun. The tilt of a planet's axis, of course, is responsible for its seasons. It is enjoyable to speculate what seasons on other planets must be like.

What accounts for the morning and evening brightness of Venus?

Venus is ideally situated to be the brightest of all the planets. It is close to the Sun and so receives a lot of sunlight; it is covered with brilliant white clouds and so reflects a lot of this light back into space; and it is relatively nearby so we can pick up a lot of the light.

Why don't eclipses occur each month?

If the Moon always moved on exactly the same path, and if that path crossed in front of the Sun, there would indeed be an eclipse each month — two of them, in fact, one of the Sun and one of the Moon. But the Moon's path is more complicated, and it actually passes above or below the Sun most months.

We see so many sights in the night sky. Are there any sounds?

None. Sound cannot pass through the vacuum of space.

I have been reading a lot about "dark matter" in the universe. What is it?

If I knew that, I would be famous. We know there is a lot of matter up there because we can measure its gravitational pull. On the other hand, when we look for it we don't find it: all the planets, comets, stars, and so forth that we know of are not enough to yield such a big gravitational force. It's a slightly ominous situation, a bit like hearing an invisible person muttering in the dark. □□

1988 NOVEMBER, THE ELEVENTH MONTH

The chain of stars called Andromeda extends up and to the right from the Great Square, for evening viewers near 40° north latitude. Country observers can see the elongated glow of the Great Andromeda Galaxy. A few Leonid meteors zoom from the south before dawn on the 18th. Mighty Jupiter lies between the beautiful Pleiades and Hyades star clusters of Taurus. On the 22nd it reaches opposition, rises at sunset, and is biggest and brightest. At mid evening it now greatly outshines Mars, which is in the south, lower left from the Great Square of Pegasus. K-shaped Perseus is high in the northeast, near the Pleiades, and Andromeda's mother, Cassiopeia the Queen, forms a bright letter M. The bright star Regulus is occulted by the Moon at 6 A.M. EST on the 30th, visible throughout North America except the southwest.

ASTRONOMICAL CALCULATIONS

☾	Last Quarter	1st day	5th hour	12th min.
●	New Moon	9th day	9th hour	21st min.
☽	First Quarter	16th day	16th hour	36th min.
○	Full Moon	23rd day	10th hour	54th min.

FOR POINTS OUTSIDE BOSTON SEE KEY LETTER CORRECTIONS — PAGES 80-84

Day of Year	Day of Month	Day of Week	☉ Rises h. m.	Key	☉ Sets h. m.	Key	Length of Days h. m.	Sun Fast m.	Full Sea Boston A.M.	Full Sea Boston P.M.	☽ Rises h. m.	Key	☽ Sets h. m.	Key	Declination of sun ° ′	☽ Place	☽ Age
306	1	Tu.	6 17	D	4 38	B	10 21	32	4½	4¾	$11^{P}_{M}17$	B	$1^{P}_{M}18$	E	14s.39	CAN	22
307	2	W.	6 19	D	4 37	B	10 18	32	5½	5¾	— —	–	1 42	D	14 58	CAN	23
308	3	Th.	6 20	D	4 35	B	10 15	32	6½	6¾	$12^{A}_{M}21$	C	2 02	D	15 16	LEO	24
309	4	Fr.	6 21	D	4 34	B	10 13	32	7½	7¾	1 22	C	2 20	C	15 35	LEO	25
310	5	Sa.	6 22	D	4 33	B	10 11	32	8	8½	2 23	D	2 38	C	15 53	VIR	26
311	6	**B**	6 24	D	4 32	A	10 08	32	8¾	9¼	3 25	D	2 56	B	16 11	VIR	27
312	7	M.	6 25	D	4 31	A	10 06	32	9½	10	4 28	E	3 16	B	16 29	VIR	28
313	8	Tu.	6 26	D	4 30	A	10 04	32	10	10½	5 33	E	3 39	B	16 46	VIR	29
314	9	W.	6 27	D	4 28	A	10 01	32	10¾	11¼	6 40	E	4 07	A	17 04	LIB	0
315	10	Th.	6 29	D	4 27	A	9 58	32	11¼	11¾	7 49	E	4 42	A	17 20	LIB	1
316	11	Fr.	6 30	D	4 26	A	9 56	32	—	12	8 56	E	5 27	A	17 37	SCO	2
317	12	Sa.	6 31	D	4 25	A	9 54	32	12½	12½	9 58	E	6 23	A	17 53	OPH	3
318	13	**B**	6 32	D	4 24	A	9 52	32	1¼	1¼	10 52	E	7 29	A	18 09	SAG	4
319	14	M.	6 34	D	4 23	A	9 49	32	2	2¼	$11^{A}_{M}36$	E	8 42	B	18 24	SAG	5
320	15	Tu.	6 35	D	4 23	A	9 48	31	3	3	$12^{P}_{M}12$	E	9 58	B	18 39	CAP	6
321	16	W.	6 36	D	4 22	A	9 46	31	4	4	12 41	E	$11^{P}_{M}14$	C	18 54	CAP	7
322	17	Th.	6 37	D	4 21	A	9 44	31	5	5¼	1 06	D	— —	–	19 09	AQU	8
323	18	Fr.	6 38	D	4 20	A	9 42	31	6	6¼	1 29	C	$12^{A}_{M}30$	C	19 23	AQU	9
324	19	Sa.	6 40	D	4 19	A	9 39	31	6¾	7¼	1 52	C	1 44	D	19 37	PSC	10
325	20	**B**	6 41	D	4 19	A	9 38	30	7¾	8¼	2 15	B	3 01	E	19 51	PSC	11
326	21	M.	6 42	D	4 18	A	9 36	30	8½	9¼	2 43	B	4 19	E	20 04	PSC	12
327	22	Tu.	6 43	D	4 17	A	9 34	30	9½	10	3 15	B	5 37	E	20 17	ARI	13
328	23	W.	6 45	D	4 17	A	9 32	30	10¼	11	3 54	A	6 56	E	20 29	TAU	14
329	24	Th.	6 46	D	4 16	A	9 30	29	11	11¾	4 44	A	8 09	E	20 41	TAU	15
330	25	Fr.	6 47	E	4 15	A	9 28	29	11¾	—	5 43	A	9 13	E	20 53	TAU	16
331	26	Sa.	6 48	E	4 15	A	9 27	29	12½	12¾	6 48	A	10 05	E	21 04	GEM	17
332	27	**B**	6 49	E	4 14	A	9 25	28	1½	1½	7 56	B	10 46	E	21 15	GEM	18
333	28	M.	6 50	E	4 14	A	9 24	28	2¼	2¼	9 03	B	11 18	E	21 25	CAN	19
334	29	Tu.	6 51	E	4 14	A	9 23	28	3	3¼	10 08	C	$11^{A}_{M}44$	E	21 36	CAN	20
335	30	W.	6 52	E	4 13	A	9 21	27	4	4	$11^{P}_{M}11$	C	$12^{P}_{M}05$	D	21s.45	LEO	21

These are the days when
birds come back,
A very few, a bird or two,
To take a backward look.

These are the days when skies put on
The old, old sophistries of June, —
A blue and gold mistake.
— *Emily Dickinson*

Farmer's Calendar

November 26. This afternoon, walked through the woods, across the brook, and up the hill to hit the powerline, then followed the powerline to a spot where it looked like you'd be able to see the village. It's hard to get a look out from these wooded hills. The trees close in, and when you come to the top of a rise, expecting to see out over the country, you find another hill, another woods, like the first.

The powerline clearing is probably 100 feet broad. It looks like easy going, but it isn't. The ground is covered with dead fern, wild grasses, and tough low brush, and it's broken ground, full of ledges, holes, and drops. In the woods you'd be able to spot them, but here the brush hides them.

It's mild today, without the damp and chill of a November day. The clouds are November clouds, though: high, gray, and passing. The powerline crosses a hidden brook with steep banks. On the south-facing slope above it are places where deer have lain to get the sun. The grass is flattened down, and the dead ferns are broken and scattered. Yesterday hunting season ended. The deer have this remote little corner to themselves again. It must be strange to be a hunter and leave your job and everyday life behind to come out here and wait all day where nobody ever goes.

Up ahead a hawk passes across the clearing on steady, tilting wings, low above the trees. At the top of the hill where it disappeared the woods part a little, and you can see the highway down in the valley, and a house. Farther off is the top of the steeple of the church in the village. What are they, a mile away, two miles? But up here are only the wind and the gray sky. From the hills it seems that the village is distant by more than miles. Tiny, noiseless, it might be in another world, another time.

D.M.	D.W.	Dates, Feasts, Fasts, Aspects, Tide Heights	Weather ↓
1	Tu.	**All Saints** National Weather Service founded, 1870 • {8.1 8.9	Three-
2	W.	**All Souls** • ♂ Regulus • 7″ snow, N.Y., 1810 • {8.0 8.6	day
3	Th.	*A man of courage never needs weapons, but he may need bail.* • {8.2 8.6	pass,
4	Fr.	☾ at ☊ • ☿ at apo. • ◖ P ☉ • Tides {8.5 8.6	then
5	Sa.	**St. Elisabeth** • ☾ on Eq. • Wind 78 m.p.h., Block Is., 1894	more
6	**B**	**24ᵗʰ S. af. P.** • **St. Leonard** • ♂ ♂ ☾ • {9.2 8.8	
7	M.	"Galloping Gertie" bridge collapsed, Tacoma, Wash., 1940 • {9.5 8.9	rain,
8	Tu.	**Election Day** • Halley's Comet spotted, 1985 • Tides {9.8 8.9	alas!
9	W.	New ● Dylan Thomas died, 1953 • {9.9 8.9	Frost
10	Th.	Henry Stanley found missionary David Livingstone, Africa, 1871 • {10.0 8.8	bite,
11	Fr.	**St. Martin** Veterans Day • ♂ Antares ☾ • Remembrance Day, Canada	
12	Sa.	☾ runs low • ♂ ♂ ☾ • ♂ ♄ ☾ • Tides {8.7 10.1	warm
13	**B**	**25ᵗʰ S. af. P.** • ♂ ♅ ☾ • {8.6 10.0	and
14	M.	Lech Walesa freed, Poland, 1982 • Tides {8.5 9.9	bright!
15	Tu.	*A pun is the lowest form of humor— when you don't think of it first.* • {8.4 9.7	Did I
16	W.	♂ ♀ Spica • Clark Gable died, 1960 • Tides {8.5 9.6	mention
17	Th.	**St. Hugh of Lincoln** • ☾ at ☊ • {8.8 9.5	a
18	Fr.	☾ on Eq. • Ub Iwerks first drew Mickey Mouse, 1928 • {9.3 9.5	drenchin'?
19	Sa.	♂ ♂ ☾ • Lincoln spoke at Gettysburg, 1863 • {9.8 9.6	Hope
20	**B**	**26ᵗʰ S. af. P.** • **St. Edmund** • ☾ at peri.	your
21	M.	*We are not punished for our sins, but by them.* • {10.9 9.8	turkey
22	Tu.	♃ at ☊ • JFK assassinated, 12:30 P.M., CST, 1963 • Tides {11.3 9.8	has
23	W.	**St. Clement** • Full Beaver ○ • ♂ ♃ ☾	water-
24	Th.	**Thanksgiving Day** • *A full belly makes a dull brain.* • {11.4 9.5	wings!
25	Fr.	**St. Catherine** • ☾ runs high • Tides {11.1	Fall
26	Sa.	Hurricane, Cape Cod to Nova Scotia, 1888 • {9.3 10.7	slips
27	**B**	**1ˢᵗ S. in Advent** Portland gale, Cape Cod, 1898 • {8.9 10.2	away,
28	M.	Stalin, FDR, and Churchill met in Teheran, 1943 • Tides {8.6 9.7	dank
29	Tu.	L. Hammond patented electric bridge table, 1932 • {8.4 9.2	and
30	W.	**St. Andrew** • Occult. Regulus by ☾	gray.

Where ignorance is bliss it's foolish to borrow your neighbor's newspaper.

1988 DECEMBER, THE TWELFTH MONTH

Mars, still outshining all but the brightest star, is visible in midevening in the southwest. Far more brilliant Jupiter dominates the south, however, there drawing attention to the little dipper-shaped Pleiades star cluster and the big V-shaped Hyades star cluster. Seemingly part of the latter is the orange eye of Taurus the Bull, Aldebaran. Yellow Capella shines high above Taurus in Auriga the Charioteer. Through the middle of the night on December 13, the Geminid meteors spray at rates of up to one per minute from Gemini, above Orion. Winter begins at 10:28 A.M. EST on December 21. On the 23rd is just about the lowest full Moon possible. Saturn is passing the Sun on the 26th. Before dawn on the 20th, Venus is low but still visible.

ASTRONOMICAL CALCULATIONS

☾	Last Quarter	1st day	1st hour	50th min.
●	New Moon	9th day	0 hour	37th min.
☽	First Quarter	16th day	0 hour	41st min.
○	Full Moon	23rd day	0 hour	29th min.
☾	Last Quarter	30th day	23rd hour	58th min.

FOR POINTS OUTSIDE BOSTON SEE KEY LETTER CORRECTIONS — PAGES 80-84

Day of Year	Day of Month	Day of Week	☉ Rises h. m.	Key	☉ Sets h. m.	Key	Length of Days h. m.	Sun Fast m.	Full Sea Boston A.M.	Full Sea Boston P.M.	☽ Rises h. m.	Key	☽ Sets h. m.	Key	Declination of sun ° ′	☽ Place	☽ Age
336	1	Th.	6 54	E	4 13	A	9 19	27	4¾	5	— —	–	12$^{P}_{M}$24	C	21s.54	LEO	22
337	2	Fr.	6 55	E	4 13	A	9 18	26	5¾	6	12$^{A}_{M}$31	D	12 42	C	22 03	VIR	23
338	3	Sa.	6 56	E	4 12	A	9 16	26	6½	7	2 31	E	12 60	B	22 11	VIR	24
339	4	**B**	6 57	E	4 12	A	9 15	26	7¼	7¾	2 14	E	1 19	B	22 19	VIR	25
340	5	M.	6 58	E	4 12	A	9 14	25	8	8½	3 18	E	1 41	B	22 27	VIR	26
341	6	Tu.	6 59	E	4 12	A	9 13	25	8¾	9¼	4 25	E	2 07	A	22 34	LIB	27
342	7	W.	7 00	E	4 12	A	9 12	24	9½	10	5 33	E	2 40	A	22 41	LIB	28
343	8	Th.	7 01	E	4 12	A	9 11	24	10	10¾	6 42	E	3 22	A	22 47	SCO	29
344	9	Fr.	7 01	E	4 12	A	9 11	24	10¾	11½	7 48	E	4 15	A	22 53	OPH	0
345	10	Sa.	7 02	E	4 12	A	9 10	23	11½	—	8 46	E	5 19	A	22 58	SAG	1
346	11	**B**	7 03	E	4 12	A	9 09	23	12¼	12¼	9 34	E	6 31	B	23 03	SAG	2
347	12	M.	7 04	E	4 12	A	9 08	22	1	1	10 13	E	7 48	B	23 07	CAP	3
348	13	Tu.	7 05	E	4 12	A	9 07	22	1¾	2	10 45	E	9 05	C	23 11	CAP	4
349	14	W.	7 06	E	4 12	A	9 06	21	2¾	2¾	11 11	D	10 21	C	23 15	CAP	5
350	15	Th.	7 06	E	4 12	A	9 06	21	3½	3¾	11 34	D	11$^{P}_{M}$35	D	23 18	AQU	6
351	16	Fr.	7 07	E	4 13	A	9 06	20	4½	4¾	11$^{A}_{M}$56	C	— —	–	23 20	PSC	7
352	17	Sa.	7 08	E	4 13	A	9 05	20	5½	6	12$^{P}_{M}$18	B	12$^{A}_{M}$48	D	23 22	PSC	8
353	18	**B**	7 08	E	4 13	A	9 05	19	6½	7	12 43	B	2 03	E	23 24	PSC	9
354	19	M.	7 08	E	4 13	A	9 05	19	7¼	8	1 12	B	3 19	E	23 25	ARI	10
355	20	Tu.	7 09	E	4 14	A	9 05	18	8¼	9	1 48	A	4 36	E	23 26	TAU	11
356	21	W.	7 10	E	4 15	A	9 05	18	9¼	10	2 33	A	5 50	E	23 26	TAU	12
357	22	Th.	7 11	E	4 15	A	9 04	17	10	10¾	3 27	A	6 57	E	23 26	TAU	13
358	23	Fr.	7 11	E	4 16	A	9 05	17	10¾	11½	4 30	A	7 54	E	23 25	GEM	14
359	24	Sa.	7 11	E	4 16	A	9 05	16	11½	—	5 37	B	8 39	E	23 24	GEM	15
360	25	**B**	7 12	E	4 17	A	9 05	16	12¼	12¼	6 46	B	9 16	E	23 22	GEM	16
361	26	M.	7 12	E	4 17	A	9 05	15	1	1	7 52	B	9 44	E	23 20	CAN	17
362	27	Tu.	7 13	E	4 18	A	9 05	15	1¾	1¾	8 57	C	10 07	D	23 17	LEO	18
363	28	W.	7 13	E	4 19	A	9 06	14	2½	2½	9 59	C	10 27	D	23 14	LEO	19
364	29	Th.	7 13	E	4 20	A	9 07	14	3¼	3½	11$^{P}_{M}$00	D	10 45	C	23 11	VIR	20
365	30	Fr.	7 13	E	4 20	A	9 07	13	4	4¼	— —	–	11 03	C	23 07	VIR	21
366	31	Sa.	7 13	E	4 21	A	9 08	13	4¾	5¼	12$^{A}_{M}$01	D	11$^{A}_{M}$21	B	23s.02	VIR	22

Nature is never spent;
There lives the dearest freshness deep down things;
And though the lost lights off the black West went,
Oh, morning, at the brown brink eastward, springs—
— *Gerard Manley Hopkins*

Farmer's Calendar

When it is snowing hard at bedtime, sleep is sound and waking is full of anticipation, like the anticipation felt by a child on Christmas morning when he wakes and keeps his bed a minute before getting up, knowing he will find the world excitingly changed by the lights, the tree, the decorations, the gifts. Here, it is the gift of snow people wake to discover, and if the storm has been a big one, it's an exciting moment when you first look out the window to see what the snow has done.

Even if the snow is bad news for you because you must make your way through it to go about your business, there is a quick pleasure in first looking upon its work the morning after a storm. Every dwelling has its own set of impromptu snow gauges that tell you immediately, and more eloquently than a bare account of inches of depth ever could, what size storm has passed. Can you see the stone walls? How deeply is the car snowed in? To the wheel tops? To the door handles? How much of the rhododendron still shows? Where is the woodpile?

At my house the best snow gauge last year was a large metal lawn chair that got left outside. Nobody ever got around to putting it away in the shed with the rest of the summer things. The winter was the snowiest in some years. One morning the chair was standing to its seat in snow; another morning the snow was up to its arms. Then there came a hard storm that blew all through the night, and the next day, under clearing, shifting cloud and sun, the chair was gone. I looked for it and saw only the featureless plain of white. For just a second I asked myself what uncharacteristically order-obsessed member of my family had gone out into that blizzard the night before and moved the chair, at last, into the shed where it belonged.

D.M.	D.W.	Dates, Feasts, Fasts, Aspects, Tide Heights	Weather ↓
1	Th.	☾ at �rž • ☿ in sup. ♂ • Tides {8.2 {8.4	*Batten*
2	Fr.	☾ on Eq. • ☾ at apo. • Monroe Doctrine proclaimed, 1823 {8.3 {8.2	*hatches —*
3	Sa.	*The school of life is a compulsory education.* • {8.5 {8.1	*Northeaster*
4	B	**2ⁿᵈ S. Advent • Chanukah •** {8.8 {8.2	*brings*
5	M.	Mozart died, 1791 • Ty Cobb died, 1951 • Tides {9.1 {8.2	*batches!*
6	Tu.	**St. Nicholas •** ♂☾☾ • {9.4 {8.3	*Attitude*
7	W.	Mary Stuart, Queen of Scots, born, 1542 • {9.7 {8.5	*depends*
8	Th.	**Conception of Virgin Mary •** Tides {10.0 {8.6	*on*
9	Fr.	New ● 61° F., Boston, at 1 A.M., 1980 • {10.2 {8.7	*latitude:*
10	Sa.	*Strange that a man who has wit enough to write a satire should have folly enough to publish it.*	*rain*
11	B	**3ᵈ S. Advent • ☾ runs low • ♂♇☾**	*or snow?*
12	M.	Dr. Joel R. Poinsett, who introduced poinsettia plant to U.S., died, 1851 • {8.8 {10.4	*Sunny*
13	Tu.	**St. Lucy •** 30° F., Los Angeles, 1938 • {8.9 {10.3	*reprieve,*
14	W.	☾ at �×ᵍ • Ember Alabama joined Day • U.S., 1819 • {9.1 {10.0	*then*
15	Th.	☾ at peri. • *Nine-tenths of wisdom consists in being wise in time.*	*colder*
16	Fr.	☾ on Eq. • Ember Jane Austen Day • born, 1775 • {9.5 {9.4	*than*
17	Sa.	♂♂☾ • Ember Wright brothers' Day • first flight, 1903 • {9.8 {9.1	*you*
18	B	**4ᵗʰ S. Advent •** 36″ snow, Muskegon, Mich., 1963 • {10.1 {9.0	*can*
19	M.	*Scepticism is a barren coast, without a harbor or a lighthouse.* {10.4 {9.0	*believe!*
20	Tu.	♂☿♇ • ♂♃☾ • Mayor Daley died, 1976 • {10.6 {9.0	*Still*
21	W.	**St. Thomas •** Solstice, 10:28 A.M., EST • Tides {10.8 {9.0	*frightful:*
22	Th.	**Sts. Cyril and Methodius •** ♂�⊙ •	
23	Fr.	☾ runs high • Full ○ • Cold ○ • Tides {10.8 {9.0	*Christmas*
24	Sa.	**Christmas Eve •** ♂♀ Antares • Kit Carson born, 1809 •	*is*
25	B	**𝕮𝖍𝖗𝖎𝖘𝖙𝖒𝖆𝖘 𝕯𝖆𝖞 •** {8.9 {10.4	*whiteful!*
26	M.	**St. Stephen •** ♂♄⊙ • Boxing Day, Canada •	*Snow*
27	Tu.	**St. John •** ♂ Regulus ☾ • Tides {8.7 {9.7	*stopping*
28	W.	**Holy Innocents •** ☾ at �×ᵍ • {8.6 {9.2	*in*
29	Th.	**St. Thomas à Becket •** ☾ at apo. •	*time*
30	Fr.	*Fatigue is the best pillow.* • Tides {8.4 {8.3 •	*for cork-*
31	Sa.	**St. Sylvester •** ♂♇⊙ • Hail and farewell!	*popping!*

1989

JANUARY, THE FIRST MONTH

On New Year's Day, the Earth reaches perihelion (closest to the Sun) at 5 P.M. EST, the earliest in the year for the rest of the century. Rural observers see the Quadrantid meteor shower, the largest of them all, just before dawn on the 4th. Mercury is visible just after sunset in the west on the 8th, when it reaches its greatest elongation. From southwest to southeast, the evening's brightest points of light are now reddish planet Mars, brighter planet Jupiter, and blue-white star Sirius. The Moon makes beautiful patterns with Mars and Jupiter around midmonth. The Milky Way arches overhead, and Orion dominates the southern sky. Venus passes near Uranus (use binoculars) on the 12th, near Saturn on the 16th, and near Neptune (use a telescope) on the 18th. On the 23rd is an occultation of Regulus by the Moon, 11 P.M. EST.

ASTRONOMICAL CALCULATIONS

● New Moon	7th day	14th hour	23rd min.
☽ First Quarter	14th day	9th hour	0 min.
○ Full Moon	21st day	16th hour	34th min.
☾ Last Quarter	29th day	21st hour	4th min.

FOR POINTS OUTSIDE BOSTON SEE KEY LETTER CORRECTIONS — PAGES 80-84

Day of Year	Day of Month	Day of Week	☉ Rises h. m.	Key	☉ Sets h. m.	Key	Length of Days h. m.	Sun Fast m.	Full Sea Boston A.M.	Full Sea Boston P.M.	☽ Rises h. m.	Key	☽ Sets h. m.	Key	Declination of sun ° ′	☽ Place	☽ Age
1	1	A	7 14	E	4 22	A	9 08	12	5½	6	1 A.M. 03	E	11 A.M. 41	B	22s.57	VIR	23
2	2	M.	7 14	E	4 23	A	9 09	12	6½	7	2 08	E	12 P.M. 05	B	22 52	VIR	24
3	3	Tu.	7 14	E	4 24	A	9 10	11	7¼	8	3 15	E	12 34	A	22 46	LIB	25
4	4	W.	7 14	E	4 25	A	9 11	11	8	8¾	4 23	E	1 12	A	22 40	SCO	26
5	5	Th.	7 14	E	4 26	A	9 12	11	9	9½	5 31	E	2 00	A	22 33	SCO	27
6	6	Fr.	7 14	E	4 27	A	9 13	10	9¾	10¼	6 33	E	3 01	A	22 26	SAG	28
7	7	Sa.	7 13	E	4 28	A	9 15	10	10½	11	7 26	E	4 12	A	22 18	SAG	0
8	8	A	7 13	E	4 29	A	9 16	9	11¼	—	8 10	E	5 30	B	22 10	SAG	1
9	9	M.	7 13	E	4 30	A	9 17	9	12	12	8 44	E	6 49	B	22 02	CAP	2
10	10	Tu.	7 13	E	4 31	A	9 18	8	12¾	12¾	9 13	D	8 07	C	21 52	CAP	3
11	11	W.	7 13	E	4 32	A	9 19	8	1½	1¾	9 38	D	9 24	D	21 43	AQU	4
12	12	Th.	7 12	E	4 33	A	9 21	8	2¼	2½	10 01	C	10 39	D	21 33	PSC	5
13	13	Fr.	7 12	E	4 34	A	9 22	7	3	3½	10 23	C	11 P.M. 54	E	21 23	PSC	6
14	14	Sa.	7 12	E	4 36	A	9 24	7	4	4½	10 47	B	— —	–	21 13	PSC	7
15	15	A	7 11	E	4 37	A	9 26	7	5	5½	11 14	B	1 A.M. 09	E	21 02	ARI	8
16	16	M.	7 11	E	4 38	A	9 27	6	6	6¾	11 A.M. 47	A	2 25	E	20 50	ARI	9
17	17	Tu.	7 10	E	4 39	A	9 29	6	7	7¾	12 P.M. 28	A	3 39	E	20 38	TAU	10
18	18	W.	7 10	E	4 40	A	9 30	6	8	8¾	1 18	A	4 46	E	20 26	TAU	11
19	19	Th.	7 09	E	4 42	A	9 33	5	9	9¾	2 17	A	5 46	E	20 13	TAU	12
20	20	Fr.	7 08	E	4 43	A	9 35	5	9¾	10½	3 22	A	6 35	E	20 00	GEM	13
21	21	Sa.	7 08	E	4 44	A	9 36	5	10½	11¼	4 30	B	7 14	E	19 47	GEM	14
22	22	A	7 07	D	4 45	A	9 38	4	11¼	—	5 38	B	7 45	E	19 34	CAN	15
23	23	M.	7 06	D	4 47	A	9 41	4	12	12	6 43	C	8 10	E	19 20	LEO	16
24	24	Tu.	7 05	D	4 48	A	9 43	4	12½	12¾	7 46	C	8 31	D	19 05	LEO	17
25	25	W.	7 05	D	4 49	A	9 44	4	1¼	1½	8 48	D	8 49	D	18 50	LEO	18
26	26	Th.	7 04	D	4 50	A	9 46	3	1¾	2	9 49	D	9 07	C	18 35	VIR	19
27	27	Fr.	7 03	D	4 52	A	9 49	3	2½	2¾	10 50	E	9 25	C	18 20	VIR	20
28	28	Sa.	7 02	D	4 53	A	9 51	3	3¼	3½	11 P.M. 53	E	9 44	B	18 04	VIR	21
29	29	A	7 01	D	4 54	A	9 53	3	4	4½	— —	–	10 06	B	17 47	VIR	22
30	30	M.	7 00	D	4 56	A	9 56	3	4¾	5¼	12 A.M. 58	E	10 32	A	17 31	LIB	23
31	31	Tu.	6 59	D	4 57	A	9 58	3	5½	6¼	2 A.M. 05	E	11 A.M. 05	A	17s.14	LIB	24

The poetry of earth is ceasing never:
On a lone winter evening, when the frost
Has wrought a silence, from the stove there shrills
The Cricket's song, in warmth increasing ever...
— John Keats

Farmer's Calendar

The snowshoer in the winter woods is a locomotor contradiction: an elephant in flight. He flounders along strapped onto a pair of platforms whose design and construction have evolved perversely through centuries to make effective walking clumsy, labored, and difficult. If the outdoorsman owns the popular round "bearpaw" snowshoe, he is obliged to hold his legs as though he were on the back of a fat old horse and to walk like a ruptured gander. If he has chosen a longer, slimmer shoe with a tail, he will trip over his heels and kick himself in the bottom, and his turning radius will be comparable to that of the S.S. *France*. In either case the snowshoer will hang up on the brush, sideslip hopelessly if he descends a hill obliquely, and fall on his face if he goes straight at it, plunging awkwardly on at the head of a trail that might have been left by an army tank.

But consider now the snowshoer's advantage: snowshoes make difficult what without them is impossible. In much of the hilly woodland around my house the snow can lie as deep as a man's chest. Skis aren't practical in the thick woods. Even a snowmobile can't get you where snowshoes — however clumsily — can. They're the only game in town. And when you accept that, you see the best fun of snowshoeing, the flight. You are up on top of all that snow, walking through the air over the white surface like a spirit over the water. The little fir beside your trail, waist high, is the top of a ten-foot tree. The branches of the maples you must duck are where the birds will nest in the spring. You have traded grace and ease for access to a new world; and which of us who watched our brothers in the Apollo program 20 years ago would refuse that trade? The Apollo astronauts walked heavily, clumsily, like snowshoers. But they were walking on the Moon.

D.M.	D.W.	Dates, Feasts, Fasts, Aspects, Tide Heights	Weather ↓
1	A	**New Year's Day • Circumcision** ⊕ at perihelion	
2	M.	*History is something that never happened,* {9.0 *written by a man who wasn't there.* {7.9	Egg-
3	Tu.	Alaska admitted Bobby Hull {9.2 to United States, 1959 • born, 1939 • {8.2	nogged,
4	W.	Washington's Army hit by Tides {9.5 snowstorm, Morristown, N.J., 1780 {8.2	snow-
5	Th.	♂♂☽ • Twelfth Diane Keaton {9.9 Night • born, 1946 • {8.5	bogged.
6	Fr.	**Epiphany • ☽** runs low Tides {10.4 {8.9	Frozen
7	Sa.	New ● Marian Anderson sang with Metropolitan Opera, N.Y.C., 1955	nose 'n'
8	A	**1ˢᵗ S. af. Epiph.** ☿ Gr. Elong. East (19°) • ♂♂☽	
9	M.	Plough *The course of true anything* {9.6 Monday *never does run smooth.* {11.3	then
10	Tu,	☽at☊ ☽ at peri. • Sal Mineo {9.9 born, 1939 • {11.3	a
11	W.	5" snow. St. -23°F., Kingston, {10.2 Mary's River, Fla., 1800 • R.I., 1942 {11.1	thaw.
12	Th.	☽ on Eq. • ♂♀♇ • Sunshine today foretells much wind.	Pshaw!
13	Fr.	**St. Hilary** • Coldest day of the year. {10.5 {10.2	Warmish
14	Sa.	♂♂☽ • Propitious day for birth of women. Tides {10.5 {9.6	but
15	A	**2ⁿᵈ S. af. Epiph.** ☿ stat.	stormish;
16	M.	Martin Luther King Jr.'s birthday • ♂♀♇ • ♂♃☽ •	the
17	Tu.	Coldest day of the century in Tides {10.3 many eastern cities, 1982 • {8.6	sleet's
18	W.	♂♀♆ • Start of 60" snowfall, {10.3 Giant Forest, Cal., 1933 • {8.6	in!
19	Th.	☽ runs high • 42" snow, Depew, Snowflakes, N.Y., 1978 • Miami, Fla., 1977 •	Cold
20	Fr.	♃ stat. • 24" snow, George Burns Boston, 1978 • born, 1896 •	enough?
21	Sa.	**St. Agnes** • Full Wolf ○ • Tides {10.5 {9.0	Tough.
22	A	**Septuagesima • St. Vincent**	More
23	M.	Occult. Reg. by ☽ • 91° F., McAllen, {9.1 Texas, 1982 • {10.3	white
24	Tu.	☽at☊ • Temp. fell from +44°F. to -56°F., Browning, Mont., 1916 •	stuff!
25	W.	**Conv. of Paul** • Clear betides {9.2 a happy year. {9.8	Everything's
26	Th.	☽ on Eq. • ☽ at apo. • Rotten wood cannot be carved.	jake
27	Fr.	Mozart Jerome Kern Tides {9.2 born, 1756 • born, 1885 • {9.0	out;
28	Sa.	First rope ski tow in Tides {9.1 operation, Woodstock, Vt., 1934 • {8.5	time
29	A	**Sexagesima** • U.C.L.A. won 88th straight basketball game, 1974	to
30	M.	Charles I *The greatest prayer* {8.9 beheaded, 1649 • *is patience.* {7.8	flake
31	Tu.	♂♀♀ • -59° C., Smith Tides {8.9 River, B.C., 1947 • {7.7	out!

FEBRUARY, THE SECOND MONTH

Mercury and Venus are in conjunction low in the southeast before dawn on the first. There will be three conjunctions on the 3rd: the Moon with Saturn, Uranus, and Neptune. The next night, the Moon is in conjunction with Mercury. Just after sunset on the 6th is a nearly world-record-thin Moon, possibly glimpsed very low in the west. Sirius and its constellation Canis Major, the Big Dog, are prominent in the southern sky around 9 P.M. EST. Sirius is the brightest of all stars, but the planet Jupiter, near the Pleiades and Hyades clusters in the southwest, outshines it. Far less bright Mars draws closer to Jupiter all month. Between Sirius and Jupiter, Orion the Hunter slants westward with his "blue giant" star Rigel and "red giant" star Betelgeuse. Mercury reaches its greatest elongation on the 18th. At 6 A.M. EST on the 20th, is another occultation of Regulus by the Moon, followed about 4½ hours later by a total eclipse of the full Moon, visible for 78 minutes by Alaska and Hawaii.

ASTRONOMICAL CALCULATIONS

●	New Moon	6th day	2nd hour	38th min.
☽	First Quarter	12th day	18th hour	15th min.
○	Full Moon	20th day	10th hour	33rd min.
☾	Last Quarter	28th day	15th hour	8th min.

FOR POINTS OUTSIDE BOSTON SEE KEY LETTER CORRECTIONS — PAGES 80-84

Day of Year	Day of Month	Day of Week	☉ Rises h. m.	Key	☉ Sets h. m.	Key	Length of Days h. m.	Sun Fast m.	Full Sea Boston A.M.	Full Sea Boston P.M.	☽ Rises h. m.	Key	☽ Sets h. m.	Key	Declination of sun ° ′	☽ Place	☽ Age
32	1	W.	6 58	D	4 58	A	10 00	2	6½	7¼	3 A.M. 12	E	11 A.M. 47	A	16s.57	SCO	25
33	2	Th.	6 57	D	4 59	A	10 02	2	7½	8¼	4 16	E	12 P.M. 40	A	16 40	OPH	26
34	3	Fr.	6 56	D	5 01	A	10 05	2	8¼	9	5 13	E	1 46	A	16 22	SAG	27
35	4	Sa.	6 55	D	5 02	A	10 07	2	9¼	10	6 01	E	3 01	B	16 05	SAG	28
36	5	**A**	6 54	D	5 03	A	10 09	2	10	10¾	6 40	E	4 21	B	15 46	CAP	29
37	6	M.	6 53	D	5 05	A	10 12	2	10¾	11½	7 12	E	5 43	C	15 28	CAP	0
38	7	Tu.	6 52	D	5 06	B	10 14	2	11¾	—	7 39	D	7 03	D	15 09	AQU	1
39	8	W.	6 50	D	5 07	B	10 17	2	12¼	12½	8 03	C	8 22	D	14 50	AQU	2
40	9	Th.	6 49	D	5 09	B	10 20	2	1	1¼	8 26	C	9 39	E	14 31	PSC	3
41	10	Fr.	6 48	D	5 10	B	10 22	2	1¾	2¼	8 50	B	10 P.M. 57	E	14 11	PSC	4
42	11	Sa.	6 47	D	5 11	B	10 24	2	2¾	3¼	9 17	B	— —	–	13 51	ARI	5
43	12	**A**	6 45	D	5 12	B	10 27	2	3½	4¼	9 48	A	12 A.M. 15	E	13 31	ARI	6
44	13	M.	6 44	D	5 14	B	10 30	2	4½	5¼	10 27	A	1 30	E	13 11	TAU	7
45	14	Tu.	6 43	D	5 15	B	10 32	2	5½	6¼	11 A.M. 14	A	2 40	E	12 51	TAU	8
46	15	W.	6 41	D	5 16	B	10 35	2	6¾	7½	12 P.M. 10	A	3 42	E	12 30	TAU	9
47	16	Th.	6 40	D	5 18	B	10 38	2	7¾	8½	1 12	A	4 33	E	12 10	AUR	10
48	17	Fr.	6 38	D	5 19	B	10 41	2	8¾	9½	2 19	B	5 15	E	11 49	GEM	11
49	18	Sa.	6 37	D	5 20	B	10 43	2	9¾	10¼	3 26	B	5 47	E	11 28	CAN	12
50	19	**A**	6 36	D	5 21	B	10 45	2	10½	11	4 32	B	6 14	E	11 06	CAN	13
51	20	M.	6 34	D	5 23	B	10 49	2	11	11½	5 36	C	6 36	D	10 45	LEO	14
52	21	Tu.	6 33	D	5 24	B	10 51	2	11¾	—	6 38	D	6 54	D	10 23	LEO	15
53	22	W.	6 31	D	5 25	B	10 54	2	12¼	12¼	7 39	D	7 13	C	10 01	LEO	16
54	23	Th.	6 30	D	5 26	B	10 56	3	12¾	1	8 40	E	7 31	C	9 39	VIR	17
55	24	Fr.	6 28	D	5 28	B	11 00	3	1¼	1½	9 42	E	7 49	B	9 17	VIR	18
56	25	Sa.	6 26	D	5 29	B	11 03	3	2	2¼	10 45	E	8 09	B	8 54	VIR	19
57	26	**A**	6 25	D	5 30	B	11 05	3	2½	3	11 P.M. 51	E	8 33	B	8 32	VIR	20
58	27	M.	6 23	D	5 31	B	11 08	3	3¼	3¾	— —	–	9 03	A	8 09	LIB	21
59	28	Tu.	6 22	D	5 33	B	11 11	3	4	4¾	12 A.M. 57	E	9 A.M. 40	A	7s.47	SCO	22

Come when the rains
Have glazed the snow and clothed the trees with ice,
While the slant sun of February pours
Into the bowers a flood of light.
— *William Cullen Bryant*

Farmer's Calendar

Those people who believe themselves superior to talking about the weather, and who despise country folk because they are supposed to have no other conversation, miss a whole realm of language and its particular delights. Do not imagine that when we exchange remarks on the weather we are stupidly, irrelevantly reciting information that we already have. Weather talk is not reporting or description. It's more like poetry or song, and its end is not conveying fact, but the pleasure taken in using our language in a dramatic, even poetic way.

We personify the weather, as a poet would. We give it purpose, feelings, mind. On a day of changing snow, cloud, and sun we say, "It can't make up its mind what it wants to do." To describe the weather we use poetic figures right out of the rhetoric texts, as when we call a heavy rain a "cow-drowner" or a "lamb-killer" or refer to the winter wind of this time of year as the "Montreal Express." All weather talk is essentially metaphorical: its meaning is not in its words but in their images and associations: "It's raining cats and dogs."

The best weather talk often proceeds like a play. There are parts: the one who wonders, the one who knows. We ask: "Is it going to stop snowing?" He answers: "It always has." The same dialogue took place last winter, will take place again next. Repetition is of the essence of talk about the weather. We aren't telling each other something new; we're telling each other something old. That's why we engage in weather talk. We could use numbers or any other empty code merely to report on the weather. To enjoy the old, familiar conceits and similes of real weather talk, you need language. Animals and birds, perhaps, and city people too wised-up for weather talk, undoubtedly, can pass on information about the weather as well as we can, but they can't have so much fun doing it.

D.M.	D.W.	Dates, Feasts, Fasts, Aspects, Tide Heights	Weather ↓
1	W.	*You have not converted a man because you have silenced him.* • {9.1 / 7.7	*Groundhog*
2	Th.	**Purif. of Mary** • ☾ runs low • Candlemas	*frightened,*
3	Fr.	☌♂☾ • ☌♄☾ • ☌♅☾ • Tides {9.9 / 8.5	*ground*
4	Sa.	☌☿☾ • Auspicious for marriage and repair of ships. • {10.4 / 9.0	*is*
5	A	**Quinquagesima** • **St. Agatha** • ☿ stat. • {11.0 / 9.7	
6	M.	New ● • Most snow of year. • Tides {11.4 / 10.3	*whitened.*
7	Tu.	**Shrove Tues.** • ☾ at ☍ • ☾ at peri. •	*Ten*
8	W.	**Ash Wed.** ☾ on Eq. • Tea picking begins, China • {10.8 / 11.6	*below,*
9	Th.	Congress prohibited importation of opium, 1909 • Gypsy Rose Lee born, 1914	*then*
10	Fr.	-54° F., Seneca, Oregon, 1933 • Leontyne Price born, 1927 • {11.2 / 10.8	*a*
11	Sa.	Blizzard from Va. to Conn., 1983; 22" snow, Baltimore • Tides {11.1 / 10.1	*blow.*
12	A	**1st Sun. in Lent** • Lincoln's Birthday • ☌♂☾ • {10.8 / 9.4	
13	M.	☌♃☾ • 1.9" snow, Jacksonville, Florida, 1899 • {10.4 / 8.7	*Sugar's*
14	Tu.	**St. Valentine** • *He who falls in love with himself will have no rivals.* • {10.0 / 8.3	*sweet*
15	W.	☾ runs high • Ember Day • Winter's back breaks. • Tides {9.8 / 8.2	*but*
16	Th.	*Love grants in a moment What toil can hardly achieve in an age.* • {9.7 / 8.3	*sap is*
17	Fr.	Ember Day • Redwing blackbird seen, Block Island, R.I., 1942 • Tides {9.8 / 8.6	*sappier;*
18	Sa.	☿ Gr. Elong. West (26°) • Ember Day • Kim Novak born, 1933 • {10.0 / 8.8	*cold*
19	A	**2nd S. Lent** • Tides {10.1 / 9.1	*nights make*
20	M.	Presidents' Day • ☾ at ☍ • Eclipse ○ • Full Snow ○	
21	Tu.	Fog in February means frost in May. • W. H. Auden born, 1907	*the farmers*
22	W.	☾ on Eq. • Wind blew 96 m.p.h. for 5 min., New York City, 1912 • {9.5 / 9.9	*happier!*
23	Th.	☾ at apo. • Siege of Alamo began, 1836 • {9.6 / 9.7	*A*
24	Fr.	**St. Matthias** • *A barking dog is more useful than a sleeping lion.* • {9.6 / 9.4	*snowy*
25	Sa.	Thunder now means poor sugaring. • 18" snow, Society Hill, S.C., 1914 •	*reminder,*
26	A	**3rd S. Lent** • Buffalo Bill Cody born, 1845 • Fats Domino born, 1928	*then*
27	M.	First day above zero in 47days, Amenia, N.D., 1936 • Tides {9.2 / 8.1	*it's*
28	Tu.	Sunny day means an excellent year. • Linus Pauling born, 1901 • {9.1 / 7.8	*kinder.*

Sing, for faith and hope are high —
None so true as you and I —
Sing the Lovers' Litany:
"Love like ours can never die!"
— Rudyard Kipling

1989 MARCH, THE THIRD MONTH

Telescopes show the close Saturn-Neptune conjunction before dawn on the 3rd, their first meeting in 26 years, but the first of three for these planets in 1989. On March 7th, Hawaii and Alaska get their second eclipse in two weeks, a partial solar eclipse best observed around 8 A.M. Hawaii time. The new Moon causing that eclipse occurs with the Moon close to Earth, leading to a higher tide that day. Look for a spectacular, ruddy Mars just 2° north of brilliant Jupiter in the west early on March 12th. The constellations of winter, the Milky Way, Orion, the Pleiades, Taurus, and Gemini the Twins are moving westward as the seasons advance, and set in the early evening this month. Spring begins at 10:28 A.M. EST on March 20th. Easter has not fallen earlier than it does this year since March 25, 1951 nor will it again until March 23, 2008.

ASTRONOMICAL CALCULATIONS

●	New Moon	7th day	13th hour	20th min.
☽	First Quarter	14th day	5th hour	11th min.
○	Full Moon	22nd day	4th hour	59th min.
☾	Last Quarter	30th day	5th hour	23rd min.

FOR POINTS OUTSIDE BOSTON SEE KEY LETTER CORRECTIONS — PAGES 80-84

Day of Year	Day of Month	Day of Week	☉ Rises h. m.	Key	☉ Sets h. m.	Key	Length of Days h. m.	Sun Fast m.	Full Sea Boston A.M.	Full Sea Boston P.M.	☽ Rises h. m.	Key	☽ Sets h. m.	Key	Declination of sun ° ′	☽ Place	☽ Age
60	1	W.	6 20	D	5 34	B	11 14	4	5	$5\frac{1}{2}$	2 A.M. 00	E	10 A.M. 27	A	7S. 24	OPH	23
61	2	Th.	6 19	D	5 35	B	11 16	4	$5\frac{3}{4}$	$6\frac{3}{4}$	2 59	E	11 A.M. 25	A	7 01	SAG	24
62	3	Fr.	6 17	D	5 36	B	11 19	4	$6\frac{3}{4}$	$7\frac{3}{4}$	3 51	E	12 P.M. 34	A	6 38	SAG	25
63	4	Sa.	6 15	D	5 38	B	11 23	4	$7\frac{3}{4}$	$8\frac{1}{2}$	4 33	E	1 51	B	6 15	SAG	26
64	5	**A**	6 14	D	5 39	B	11 25	4	$8\frac{3}{4}$	$9\frac{1}{2}$	5 07	E	3 11	C	5 51	CAP	27
65	6	M.	6 12	D	5 40	B	11 28	5	$9\frac{3}{4}$	$10\frac{1}{4}$	5 36	D	4 32	C	5 28	CAP	28
66	7	Tu.	6 10	D	5 41	B	11 31	5	$10\frac{1}{2}$	11	6 02	D	5 52	D	5 05	AQU	0
67	8	W.	6 09	D	5 42	B	11 33	5	$11\frac{1}{4}$	$11\frac{3}{4}$	6 26	C	7 13	E	4 41	PSC	1
68	9	Th.	6 07	D	5 43	B	11 36	5	—	$12\frac{1}{4}$	6 50	B	8 34	E	4 18	PSC	2
69	10	Fr.	6 05	D	5 45	B	11 40	6	$12\frac{1}{2}$	1	7 17	B	9 54	E	3 54	PSC	3
70	11	Sa.	6 04	C	5 46	B	11 42	6	$1\frac{1}{2}$	2	7 47	A	11 P.M. 14	E	3 31	ARI	4
71	12	**A**	6 02	C	5 47	B	11 45	6	$2\frac{1}{4}$	$2\frac{3}{4}$	8 24	A	— —	-	3 08	ARI	5
72	13	M.	6 00	C	5 48	B	11 48	7	$3\frac{1}{4}$	$3\frac{3}{4}$	9 09	A	12 A.M. 29	E	2 44	TAU	6
73	14	Tu.	5 58	C	5 49	B	11 51	7	4	5	10 03	A	1 35	E	2 21	TAU	7
74	15	W.	5 57	C	5 50	B	11 53	7	$5\frac{1}{4}$	6	11 A.M. 05	A	2 31	E	1 57	AUR	8
75	16	Th.	5 55	C	5 52	B	11 57	7	$6\frac{1}{4}$	$7\frac{1}{4}$	12 P.M. 11	A	3 15	E	1 32	GEM	9
76	17	Fr.	5 53	C	5 53	B	12 00	8	$7\frac{1}{2}$	$8\frac{1}{4}$	1 18	B	3 50	E	1 09	CAN	10
77	18	Sa.	5 52	C	5 54	B	12 02	8	$8\frac{1}{2}$	$9\frac{1}{4}$	2 24	B	4 18	E	0 46	CAN	11
78	19	**A**	5 50	C	5 55	C	12 05	8	$9\frac{1}{4}$	10	3 27	C	4 41	D	0S. 21	LEO	12
79	20	M.	5 48	C	5 56	C	12 08	9	10	$10\frac{1}{2}$	4 30	C	5 01	D	0N.01	LEO	13
80	21	Tu.	5 46	C	5 57	C	12 11	9	$10\frac{3}{4}$	11	5 30	D	5 19	C	0 25	LEO	14
81	22	W.	5 45	C	5 59	C	12 14	9	$11\frac{1}{4}$	$11\frac{1}{2}$	6 32	D	5 37	C	0 49	VIR	15
82	23	Th.	5 43	C	6 00	C	12 17	9	—	12	7 33	E	5 55	B	1 12	VIR	16
83	24	Fr.	5 41	C	6 01	C	12 20	10	$12\frac{1}{4}$	$12\frac{1}{2}$	8 36	E	6 15	B	1 36	VIR	17
84	25	Sa.	5 39	C	6 02	C	12 23	10	$12\frac{3}{4}$	$1\frac{1}{4}$	9 41	E	6 38	B	1 59	VIR	18
85	26	**A**	5 38	C	6 03	C	12 25	10	$1\frac{1}{4}$	$1\frac{3}{4}$	10 46	E	7 05	A	2 23	LIB	19
86	27	M.	5 36	C	6 04	C	12 28	11	2	$2\frac{1}{2}$	11 P.M. 50	E	7 39	A	2 47	SCO	20
87	28	Tu.	5 34	C	6 05	C	12 31	11	$2\frac{1}{2}$	$3\frac{1}{4}$	— —	-	8 22	A	3 10	SCO	21
88	29	W.	5 32	C	6 06	C	12 34	11	$3\frac{1}{2}$	$4\frac{1}{4}$	12 A.M. 50	E	9 14	A	3 33	OPH	22
89	30	Th.	5 31	C	6 08	C	12 37	12	$4\frac{1}{4}$	5	1 42	E	10 17	A	3 57	SAG	23
90	31	Fr.	5 29	B	6 09	C	12 40	12	$5\frac{1}{4}$	6	2 A.M. 27	E	11 A.M. 28	B	4N.20	SAG	24

Yet still on every side we trace the hand
Of Winter in the land,
Save where the maple reddens on the lawn,
Flushed by the season's dawn.
— *Henry Timrod*

D.M.	D.W.	Dates, Feasts, Fasts, Aspects, Tide Heights	Weather ↓
1	W.	**St. David** • Blackthorn winds • Avalanche, Wellington, Wash., 1910 • {9.0 7.7	*In*
2	Th.	☾ runs low • ☌♂☾ • ☌♄♆ • Tides {9.1 7.8 •	*like*
3	Fr.	☌♆☾ • ☌♄☾ • 10″ snow, Savannah, Ga., 1837 • {9.4 8.2	*a*
4	Sa.	James Garfield first President to use a telephone, 1881 • Tides {9.9 8.8	*mastodon,*
5	A	**4th S. Lent** • Patsy Cline killed, 1963 • {10.5 9.6	*bearded*
6	M.	☾ at ☊ • Great gale along mid-Atlantic coast, 1962 • Tides {11.0 10.4	*with*
7	Tu.	**St. Perpetua** • New ● • Eclipse ☉ • {11.5 11.1	*icicles!*
8	W.	☾ on Eq. • ☾ at peri. • *Happiness* is *virtue, not its reward.* • {11.7 11.6	*Out*
9	Th.	**Sts. Cyril and Methodius** • Mail box patented, 1858 •	*come*
10	Fr.	Skunks mate. • Home for Aged Pioneers estab., Prescott, Ariz., 1909 • {11.8 11.2	*bicycles!*
11	Sa.	*Three may keep a secret if two of them are dead.* • Tides {11.8 10.6 •	*Drizzly*
12	A	**5th S. L. • Passion** • ☌♂♃ • ☌♃☾	
13	M.	Blizzard Vermont-Maine dumped 3 feet of snow, 1984 • {10.9 9.2 •	*misery.*
14	Tu.	☾ runs high • Albert Einstein born, 1879 • Tides {10.3 8.6 •	*Winter*
15	W.	*Stick to your winter flannels 'til your flannels stick to you.* • {9.8 8.2 •	*redux*
16	Th.	Germany occupied Czechoslovakia, 1939 • Tides {9.4 8.2 •	*then*
17	Fr.	**St. Patrick** • Evacuation Day, Boston • Rubber band patented, 1845	*it's*
18	Sa.	Tornado hit Midwest, 692 killed, 1925 • {9.4 8.7 •	*deluxe!*
19	A	**Palm Sun.** • ☾ at ☋ • Swallows return to Capistrano. •	*This*
20	M.	Vernal Equinox • U.S. Marines landed in Nicaragua, 1896 • {9.7 9.3	*weather's*
21	Tu.	**St. Benedict** • ☾ on Eq. • J.S. Bach born, 1685 • {9.8 9.6	*just*
22	W.	Full Sap ○ • ☾ at apo. • Stamp Act imposed, 1765 • {9.8 9.8	*made*
23	Th.	*Some are weather-wise, some are otherwise.* • P. Henry's "Liberty or death" speech, 1775	*for*
24	Fr.	**Good Friday** • 25″ snow, Kansas City, 1912 • {9.9 9.5	*an*
25	Sa.	**Annunciation** • Clear today means a fertile year. • {9.9 9.2	*Easter*
26	A	**Easter Sunday** • Tides {9.8 8.9 •	*parade!*
27	M.	*Having a good wife and rich cabbage soup, seek not other things.* • {9.7 8.6	*Sun's*
28	Tu.	36 tornadoes in Carolinas, 1984 • Tides {9.5 8.3 •	*dimmer;*
29	W.	☾ runs low • ☌♂☾ • Coca-Cola intro., 1886 • {9.3 8.0 •	*grayer*
30	Th.	☌♆☾ • ☌♄☾ • U.S. bought Alaska for $7.2 million, 1867 {9.3 8.0	*and*
31	Fr.	Listen for the peepers. • Rene Descartes born, 1596 • Tides {9.3 8.2	*grimmer.*

Farmer's Calendar

Every winter the glacier, which 20,000 years ago covered this country with a mile-thick mantel of moving ice that scooped out the valleys and scoured the mountains, is reborn in miniature. Yes, it's only a little glacier, but if it's on your roof, you pay attention to it because the thing to remember about glaciers is: they're *heavy.*

Just as ancient snowfields on the Laurentian highlands gave rise to the great glacier of the last Ice Age, so the successive snows of the winter, if they have accumulated on your roof, will have compacted into a mass of solid ice. The weight of the snow above, bearing on the snow beneath, turns the bottom of the pile to ice.

The little roof glacier isn't big enough to move of its own weight, as the great glacier did, sliding down to the sea like a river of ice. The roof glacier slides when warmer days melt it enough to loosen its hold on the house. Nor does the roof glacier move with the geologic stateliness of its grand original. It comes down with a rush and a bang. Around my house the moment of the roof glacier's descent is awaited with some anxiety. Over my kitchen window, in a good snow year, hangs a shelf of ice not much smaller, or much lighter, than a billiard table. When it comes down, it can, it does, rebound off the snow on the ground and destroy windows and storm doors. To prevent that I erect an elaborate system of two-by-four studs each year under the eaves below the ice. Carefully placed and sturdily propped and braced, they will, I hope, deflect the ice when it slides, shooting it harmlessly out into the yard. Of all the structures I build and unbuild year after year to accommodate the seasons, my wall-stud ice catcher seems the silliest — perhaps because of the association of the ice it is designed to counteract with the inexorable continent-shaper of the Pleistocene.

APRIL, THE FOURTH MONTH

Reset your clocks this month. Both Mercury and Venus are in superior conjunction on the 4th; by rare coincidence, they both reached inferior conjunction last June 4th. The new Moon on the 5th is only about seven hours after perigee (Moon's closest approach to the Earth), so tides will be considerably raised. Jupiter, Taurus, Orion, and Sirius start setting before twilight ends. Fading Mars evades twilight, pulling rapidly away from Jupiter. The south displays noble Leo the Lion with bright star Regulus, almost overhead, marking both his heart and the handle of the pattern called "the Sickle." Dominating the north sky is the upside-down Big Dipper, part of Ursa Major, the Great Bear. The Lyrid meteors are spoiled by the full Moon on the night of April 20-21. On the 26th, the Moon is in conjunction with Saturn, Uranus, and Neptune.

ASTRONOMICAL CALCULATIONS

●	New Moon	5th day	22nd hour	34th min.
☽	First Quarter	12th day	18th hour	14th min.
○	Full Moon	20th day	22nd hour	14th min.
☾	Last Quarter	28th day	15th hour	46th min.

ADD 1 hour for Daylight Saving Time at 2 A.M. April 2nd.

FOR POINTS OUTSIDE BOSTON SEE KEY LETTER CORRECTIONS — PAGES 80-84

Day of Year	Day of Month	Day of Week	☉ Rises h. m.	Key	☉ Sets h. m.	Key	Length of Days h. m.	Sun Fast m.	Full Sea Boston A.M.	Full Sea Boston P.M.	☽ Rises h. m.	Key	☽ Sets h. m.	Key	Declination of sun ° ′	☽ Place	☽ Age
91	1	Sa.	5 27	B	6 10	C	12 43	12	6¼	7	3 A.M. 04	E	12 P.M. 44	B	4N.43	CAP	25
92	2	A	5 26	B	6 11	C	12 45	12	7½	8	3 34	E	2 02	C	5 06	CAP	26
93	3	M.	5 24	B	6 12	C	12 48	13	8¼	9	4 01	D	3 22	C	5 29	AQU	27
94	4	Tu.	5 22	B	6 13	D	12 51	13	9¼	9¾	4 25	D	4 41	D	5 52	PSC	28
95	5	W.	5 20	B	6 14	D	12 54	13	10¼	10½	4 49	C	6 02	E	6 15	PSC	0
96	6	Th.	5 19	B	6 15	D	12 56	14	11	11¼	5 14	B	7 24	E	6 37	PSC	1
97	7	Fr.	5 17	B	6 17	D	13 00	14	—	12	5 43	B	8 47	E	7 00	ARI	2
98	8	Sa.	5 15	B	6 18	D	13 03	14	12¼	12¾	6 18	A	10 07	E	7 22	ARI	3
99	9	A	5 14	B	6 19	D	13 05	14	1	1¾	7 01	A	11 P.M. 20	E	7 45	TAU	4
100	10	M.	5 12	B	6 20	D	13 08	15	1¾	2½	7 54	A	— —	–	8 07	TAU	5
101	11	Tu.	5 10	B	6 21	D	13 11	15	2¾	3½	8 55	A	12 A.M. 22	E	8 29	AUR	6
102	12	W.	5 09	B	6 22	D	13 13	15	3¾	4½	10 00	B	1 12	E	8 51	GEM	7
103	13	Th.	5 07	B	6 23	D	13 16	15	4¾	5¾	11 A.M. 08	B	1 51	E	9 12	CAN	8
104	14	Fr.	5 05	B	6 24	D	13 19	16	6	6¾	12 P.M. 15	B	2 22	E	9 34	CAN	9
105	15	Sa.	5 04	B	6 26	D	13 22	16	7	7¾	1 20	C	2 46	D	9 55	LEO	10
106	16	A	5 02	B	6 27	D	13 25	16	8	8½	2 22	C	3 07	D	10 17	LEO	11
107	17	M.	5 01	B	6 28	D	13 27	16	8¾	9¼	3 23	D	3 26	C	10 38	LEO	12
108	18	Tu.	4 59	B	6 29	D	13 30	17	9½	9¾	4 24	D	3 44	C	10 59	VIR	13
109	19	W.	4 57	B	6 30	D	13 33	17	10¼	10½	5 25	E	4 02	B	11 19	VIR	14
110	20	Th.	4 56	B	6 31	D	13 35	17	11	11	6 28	E	4 21	B	11 40	VIR	15
111	21	Fr.	4 54	B	6 32	D	13 38	17	11½	11½	7 32	E	4 43	B	12 01	VIR	16
112	22	Sa.	4 53	B	6 33	D	13 40	18	—	12¼	8 38	E	5 09	A	12 21	LIB	17
113	23	A	4 51	B	6 35	D	13 44	18	12¼	12¾	9 42	E	5 41	A	12 41	LIB	18
114	24	M.	4 50	B	6 36	D	13 46	18	12¾	1½	10 43	E	6 21	A	13 01	SCO	19
115	25	Tu.	4 48	B	6 37	D	13 49	18	1½	2	11 P.M. 38	E	7 10	A	13 20	OPH	20
116	26	W.	4 47	B	6 38	D	13 51	18	2¼	3	— —	–	8 10	A	13 39	SAG	21
117	27	Th.	4 45	B	6 39	D	13 54	18	3	3¾	12 A.M. 24	E	9 17	A	13 59	SAG	22
118	28	Fr.	4 44	B	6 40	D	13 56	19	4	4¾	1 02	E	10 29	B	14 17	CAP	23
119	29	Sa.	4 43	B	6 41	D	13 58	19	5	5¾	1 34	E	11 A.M. 43	C	14 36	CAP	24
120	30	A	4 41	B	6 42	D	14 01	19	6	6½	2 A.M. 01	D	12 P.M. 59	C	14N.54	AQU	25

APRIL hath 30 days. 1989

Sparrows far off, and nearer, April's bird,
Blue-coated, — flying before from tree to tree,
Courageous sing a delicate overture
To lead the tardy concert of the year.
— Ralph Waldo Emerson

D.M.	D.W.	Dates, Feasts, Fasts, Aspects, Tide Heights	Weather ↓
1	Sa.	*Voice of the turtle is heard in the land.* • Great Plague hit London, 1665 • {9.6 8.7	*Sunny,*
2	A	**Low Sun.** • Daylight Saving Time begins. • {10.0 9.4	*toastier.*
3	M.	☾ at ☊ • Fog now means flood in June. • Doris Day born, 1924 {10.5 10.3	*Roller*
4	Tu.	**St. Ambrose** • ☾ on Eq. • ☿ in sup. ☌ • ♀ in sup. ☌ •	
5	W.	☾ at peri. • New ● • Tornado, Tupelo, Miss., 1936 {11.2 11.7	*coastier!*
6	Th.	Blue herons return to Vinalhaven, Maine • Andre Previn born, 1929 • Tides {11.3 12.1	*It's*
7	Fr.	16.5″ snow, El Paso, Tex., 1983 • Italy invaded Albania, 1939 • {— 11.2	*drearier*
8	Sa.	*Care more for the patient than for the disease.* • Tides {12.2 10.9 •	*in*
9	A	**2nd S. af. Easter** • ♅ stat. • ☌♃☾ •	*the*
10	M.	☌♅☾ • Atomic sub *Thresher* lost in N. Atlantic, 1963 • {11.5 9.7	*interior.*
11	Tu.	☾ runs high • U.S. troops liberated Buchenwald, 1945 • Tides {10.9 9.1 •	*The*
12	W.	World's top wind speed, 231 m.p.h., Mt. Washington, N.H., 1934 • {10.2 8.6	*Whites*
13	Th.	♆ stat. • Thomas Jefferson born, 1743 • Tides {9.6 8.4 •	*are*
14	Fr.	*The best qualification of a prophet is to have a good memory.* • {9.2 8.4	*whiter,*
15	Sa.	Occult. Reg. by ☾ • Leonardo da Vinci born, 1542 • Tides {9.1 8.6	*but*
16	A	**3rd S. af. E.** • ☾ at ☋ • Lily Pons born, 1904 • {9.1 8.9	*now*
17	M.	☾ on Eq. • *Tyranny is always better organized than freedom.* • {9.2 9.2 •	*it's*
18	Tu.	☾ at apo. • First laundromat in U.S. opened, Fort Worth, Tex., 1934	*brighter.*
19	W.	Battles of Lexington and Concord, 1775 • {9.3 9.8 •	*Rainbows*
20	Th.	**Passover** • Full Pink ○ • Lionel Hampton born, 1914 {9.4 10.0	*arc*
21	Fr.	*Anger is never without a reason, but seldom with a good one.* • {9.3 10.1 •	*as*
22	Sa.	♄ stat. • First Oklahoma land rush began, 1889 •	*you*
23	A	**4th S. af. E.** • **St. George** • Tides {10.1 9.0	*walk*
24	M.	Joshua Slocum left Boston on solo circumnavigation sail, 1895 • {10.0 8.9 •	*in*
25	Tu.	**St. Mark** • ☾ runs low • John James Audubon born, 1785 {10.0 8.7	*the*
26	W.	☌♅☾ • ☌♆☾ • ☌♄☾ • {9.8 8.5 •	*park.*
27	Th.	73″ snow, Red Lake, Mont., 1984 • Coretta Scott King born, 1927 • {9.7 8.5	*Hark!*
28	Fr.	Fletcher Christian led mutiny on *Bounty,* 1789 • Tides {9.7 8.6 •	*Build*
29	Sa.	2″ rain in 10 minutes, Taylor, Texas, 1905 • Hirohito born, 1901 • {9.7 8.9 •	*an*
30	A	**Rogation S.** • ☾ at ☊ • ☿ Gr. Elong. East (21°) •	*ark!*

Take care of the minutes, for the hours will take care of themselves.

Farmer's Calendar

Before the hardwood trees have gotten their leaves, the soft spring wind from the south blows through the woods with a hundred voices. Wait for a sunny day with a gentle spring breeze, then find yourself a seat in the woods and listen. The wind in the trees at this time is not a single sound but a complex, orchestral multitude.

Near here is a little wooded hill that drops off toward the south. At the top of the knoll the ground is rocky. Slim oaks and hop hornbeams grow in an open, parklike woods. To the west are dense hemlock thickets, and to the east, brushy logged-over hardwoods. Going downhill to the south the woods are bigger: old oaks, beeches, and maples and here and there an enormous, towering pine.

The spring wind, arriving at the hilltop from the south or backing around to come out of the west, plays among the different woodlands with a rich variety of sound. Every section of the woods has its own pitch, its own key. The wind in the hemlocks has a low, bass tone. As it blows through the scrubby second growth, its pitch is still low, but it's a cello now rather than a bass fiddle. The wind among the bare branches of the open woods has a far higher pitch, a soprano that can be hard to hear at all. In the bigger but still bare trees of the mature woods the wind is a strong tenor line, and where it blows among last year's dry leaves in a grove of beeches, it sounds almost like distant voices.

Once the leaves are on the trees, the sound of the wind in the woods is less various. The leaves muffle the different pitches, reducing them to a single constant rushing, like the sound of surf on a beach. At this time of year, however, before the leaves, each tree is a string, each grove a section of the orchestra, each hollow and brook a hall, each hillside a great harp for the winds.

1989	MAY, THE FIFTH MONTH

Pluto reaches opposition on May 1, but a 6" telescope just barely shows it; nonetheless, it is at its best in 248 years. (See September.) Also on May Day, the second smallest planet, Mercury, has dashed out of the Sun's glow to reach greatest elongation (21°). It is easily visible to the naked eye, though low in the west in late twilight. Watch for Eta Aquarid meteors from the southeast in the predawn hours during May's first week. The bright Venus and Jupiter pair are very close together in twilight on the 22nd. Between Pollux and Regulus in the west, after nightfall, is faint Cancer the Crab and its naked-eye star cluster, the Beehive. On the 23rd, an embarrassment of riches: conjunction of the Moon with Saturn, Uranus, and Neptune; and Mercury in inferior conjunction.

ASTRONOMICAL CALCULATIONS

● New Moon	5th day	6th hour	48th min.
☽ First Quarter	12th day	9th hour	21st min.
○ Full Moon	20th day	13th hour	17th min.
☾ Last Quarter	27th day	23rd hour	1st min.

ADD 1 hour for Daylight Saving Time.

FOR POINTS OUTSIDE BOSTON SEE KEY LETTER CORRECTIONS — PAGES 80-84

Day of Year	Day of Month	Day of Week	☉ Rises h. m.	Key	☉ Sets h. m.	Key	Length of Days h. m.	Sun Fast m.	Full Sea Boston A.M.	Full Sea Boston P.M.	☽ Rises h. m.	Key	☽ Sets h. m.	Key	Declination of sun ° ′	☽ Place	☽ Age
121	1	M.	4 40	B	6 44	D	14 04	19	7	7½	2 A.M. 25	D	2 P.M. 15	D	15N.12	AQU	26
122	2	Tu.	4 39	B	6 45	D	14 06	19	8	8½	2 48	C	3 33	D	14 48	PSC	27
123	3	W.	4 37	A	6 46	D	14 09	19	9	9¼	3 12	C	4 53	E	15 31	PSC	28
124	4	Th.	4 36	A	6 47	D	14 11	19	9¾	10	3 40	B	6 15	E	16 06	PSC	29
125	5	Fr.	4 35	A	6 48	D	14 13	19	10¾	11	4 12	B	7 37	E	16 23	ARI	0
126	6	Sa.	4 33	A	6 49	D	14 16	19	11½	11¾	4 50	A	8 55	E	16 40	TAU	1
127	7	**A**	4 32	A	6 50	D	14 18	19	—	12½	5 39	A	10 05	E	16 56	TAU	2
128	8	M.	4 31	A	6 51	D	14 20	20	12½	1¼	6 38	A	11 02	E	17 13	TAU	3
129	9	Tu.	4 30	A	6 52	D	14 22	20	1½	2¼	7 44	A	11 P.M. 47	E	17 29	AUR	4
130	10	W.	4 29	A	6 53	D	14 24	20	2¼	3¼	8 54	B	— —	–	17 44	GEM	5
131	11	Th.	4 27	A	6 54	D	14 27	20	3¼	4¼	10 03	B	12 A.M. 21	E	18 00	CAN	6
132	12	Fr.	4 26	A	6 55	D	14 29	20	4¼	5	11 A.M. 09	C	12 49	E	18 15	LEO	7
133	13	Sa.	4 25	A	6 57	D	14 32	20	5¼	6	12 P.M. 13	C	1 11	D	18 29	LEO	8
134	14	**A**	4 24	A	6 58	E	14 34	20	6¼	7	1 15	C	1 30	D	18 44	LEO	9
135	15	M.	4 23	A	6 59	E	14 36	20	7¼	7¾	2 15	D	1 49	C	18 58	LEO	10
136	16	Tu.	4 22	A	7 00	E	14 38	20	8¼	8½	3 17	D	2 07	C	19 12	VIR	11
137	17	W.	4 21	A	7 01	E	14 40	20	9	9¼	4 19	E	2 26	B	19 26	VIR	12
138	18	Th.	4 20	A	7 02	E	14 42	20	9¾	9¾	5 22	E	2 47	B	19 39	VIR	13
139	19	Fr.	4 19	A	7 03	E	14 44	20	10½	10½	6 28	E	3 12	A	19 52	LIB	14
140	20	Sa.	4 18	A	7 04	E	14 46	20	11	11	7 34	E	3 42	A	20 04	LIB	15
141	21	**A**	4 17	A	7 05	E	14 48	19	11¾	11¾	8 37	E	4 20	A	20 16	SCO	16
142	22	M.	4 17	A	7 06	E	14 49	19	—	12½	9 33	E	5 07	A	20 28	OPH	17
143	23	Tu.	4 16	A	7 07	E	14 51	19	12½	1	10 22	E	6 03	A	20 39	SAG	18
144	24	W.	4 15	A	7 07	E	14 52	19	1	1¾	11 03	E	7 09	B	20 50	SAG	19
145	25	Th.	4 14	A	7 08	E	14 54	19	1¾	2½	11 P.M. 36	E	8 20	B	21 01	SAG	20
146	26	Fr.	4 14	A	7 09	E	14 55	19	2¾	3½	— —	–	9 34	B	21 12	CAP	21
147	27	Sa.	4 13	A	7 10	E	14 57	19	3½	4¼	12 A.M. 04	D	10 A.M. 47	C	21 22	CAP	22
148	28	**A**	4 12	A	7 11	E	14 59	19	4½	5¼	12 28	D	12 P.M. 01	D	21 32	AQU	23
149	29	M.	4 12	A	7 12	E	15 00	19	5½	6¼	12 51	C	1 15	D	21 41	PSC	24
150	30	Tu.	4 11	A	7 13	E	15 02	19	6½	7	1 14	C	2 31	E	21 50	PSC	25
151	31	W.	4 11	A	7 14	E	15 03	18	7½	8	1 A.M. 38	B	3 P.M. 50	E	21N.58	PSC	26

When breezes are soft and skies are fair,
I steal an hour from study and care,
And hie me away to the woodland scene,
Where wanders the stream with waters of green.
— *William Cullen Bryant*

Farmer's Calendar

The Book of Genesis tells how God created the birds on the Fifth Day, the same day He did the great whales and other sea life. The Fifth Day was a busy day, coming right before the weekend, and the Creator took a short-cut when He furnished birds for the mixed-hardwood uplands of northern New England. Rather than create three different woodpeckers to populate our trees, He created the same woodpecker three different times.

The downy, hairy, and pileated woodpeckers are the same tune played in different keys. Soberly black and white, but with an antic, bright-red topknot for the males, they look like a firm of small-town undertakers at a birthday party. All three have big heads, strong, thick tails, and a vigorous, dipping flight over short courses from tree to tree. Alike as they are, they differ in size. The downy is the size of a sparrow, the hairy, of a robin. The pileated, with a wing span exceeding a foot and a half, is as big as a crow or a medium-sized hawk.

The three woodpeckers have the same range. They forage over the same trees for the same grubs and bugs. All three are active by day, and all three are present year-round in my neighborhood. They remind me of the three brothers in a fairy tale. Each has his fortune to make, and each must make it by the same tasks. In a fairy tale the two larger brothers, perhaps representing strength and force, generally fail and must be bailed out by the littlest brother, who succeeds by guile. If numbers are a measure of success, then the three woodpeckers' fortunes work out pretty much as folklore would predict. The littlest of them, the downy, is a much commoner bird than the others, and he has an easier time of it, at least in one way, for the downy comes willingly to bird feeders, while, as far as I can see, the hairy seldom does and the pileated never.

D.M.	D.W.	Dates, Feasts, Fasts, Aspects, Tide Heights	Weather ↓	
1	M.	**Sts. Philip and James** • ☾ on Eq.	Tides {10.0 {10.2	*Rain*
2	Tu.	Yankee first-baseman Lou Gehrig missed 1st game after 2,130 consecutive starts, 1939		*diminishes,*
3	W.	**Invention of Cross** • ☾ at peri.	{10.5 {11.5 •	*then*
4	Th.	**Ascension** • ♈☍	{10.7 {12.0 •	*finally*
5	Fr.	New ● • 12″ snow, Denver, Col., 1917 • Year's highest P.M. tide: 12.2′		*finishes.*
6	Sa.	♂☾ • Willie Mays born, 1931 • Tides {10.6 {12.1		*Steamy*
7	A	**1st S. af. Ascen.** • ♂♃☾ •		*breath;*
8	M.	☾ runs high • ♂♌☾ • Men's Dacron suits introduced, 1951	{11.8 {10.0	*you*
9	Tu.	Plant corn now, or lose a bushel a day past the middle of May. •	{11.3 {9.5 •	*might*
10	W.	*Be at war with your vices, at peace with your neighbors.* • Tides {10.7 {9.1		*catch*
11	Th.	**Three** to Thailand, 1949 • Tornado hit Waco, Tex., 1953	{9.5 {8.7	*your*
12	Fr.	**Chilly** • ☿ stat. • Berlin blockade lifted, 1949	{9.5 {8.7 •	*death!*
13	Sa.	**Saints** • ☾ at ♉ • Enormous sandstorm, New Jersey, 1866	{9.1 {8.7	*How*
14	A	**Whit Sun.** • **Pentecost** •	{8.9 {8.9 •	*do*
15	M.	☾ on Eq. • *An eel held by the tail is not yet caught.*	{8.8 {9.1	*you*
16	Tu.	♂♀☾ • ☾ at apo. • First "Oscars" awarded, 1929 • Tides {8.8 {9.4		*spell*
17	W.	Ember Day • Racial segregation ruled unconstitutional, 1954 •	{8.8 {9.6 •	*relief?*
18	Th.	Gamaliel Wayte planted garden on Milne St., Boston, 1642 • Tides {8.9 {9.9		*B-*
19	Fr.	**St. Dunstan** • Ember Day • Hang up horseshoes for good luck.		*R-*
20	Sa.	Full Flower ○ • Ember Day • Cranberries in bud.	{8.9 {10.2	*I-*
21	A	**Trinity Sun.** • "Fats" Waller born, 1904 • Albrecht Dürer born, 1471		*E-*
22	M.	♂♂♃ • *Common sense in an uncommon degree is what the world calls wisdom.* •		*F!*
23	Tu.	☾ runs low • ♂♂☾ • ☿ inf. ♂ • ♂♇☾ • ♂♄☾ •		
24	W.	18% of all tornadoes occur this month. • Tides {10.3 {8.9		*Floods*
25	Th.	**Corpus Christi** • 9″ snow in mtns. of New England, 1967 •		*ebbing,*
26	Fr.	**St. Augustine of Canterbury** • Tides {10.2 {9.1		*feet*
27	Sa.	**St. Bede** • ☾ at ♌ • 113° F., Greenville, Georgia, 1978		*webbing.*
28	A	**2nd Sun. af. Pent.** • Tides {9.9 {9.7 •		*Glorious!*
29	M.	**Memorial Day** • ☾ on Eq. • John F. Kennedy born, 1917	{9.8 {10.2	
30	Tu.	Lincoln Memorial dedicated, 1922 • Benny Goodman born, 1909	{9.8 {10.7	*Down-*
31	W.	☾ at peri. • Johnstown, Pa., flood, 1889	{9.8 {11.2	*pourious!*

The summer Milky Way is rising as a dreamy background to Saturn and to the bright stars Vega, Deneb, and Altair, comprising the Summer Triangle. The semicircle of Corona Borealis, the Northern Crown, is to the upper left of bright Arcturus, high in the south. Saturn and Neptune have the second of their rare (and telescopic) conjunctions of the year, the former shining bright in the southeast, after nightfall on the 24th, even to the unaided eye. Uranus is dimly visible to the naked eye when it obtains opposition that same day. Anything north of the arctic circle receives 24 hours of daylight from the solstice on, beginning at 4:53 A.M. EST on June 21st. Antares is in the southeast; its name ("not Mars") indicates that it is red like Mars and should not be confused with it. Spica is high overhead, the brightest star of long Virgo the Virgin.

ASTRONOMICAL CALCULATIONS

● New Moon	3rd day	14th hour	54th min.
☽ First Quarter	11th day	2nd hour	0 min.
○ Full Moon	19th day	1st hour	58th min.
☾ Last Quarter	26th day	4th hour	10th min.

ADD 1 hour for Daylight Saving Time.

FOR POINTS OUTSIDE BOSTON SEE KEY LETTER CORRECTIONS — PAGES 80-84

Day of Year	Day of Month	Day of Week	☼ Rises h. m.	Key	☼ Sets h. m.	Key	Length of Days h. m.	Sun Fast m.	Full Sea Boston A.M.	Full Sea Boston P.M.	☽ Rises h. m.	Key	☽ Sets h. m.	Key	Declination of sun ° ′	☽ Place	☽ Age
152	1	Th.	4 10	A	7 14	E	15 04	18	8½	9	2$^{A}_{M}$07	B	5$^{P}_{M}$10	E	22N.06	ARI	27
153	2	Fr.	4 10	A	7 15	E	15 05	18	9½	9¾	2 42	A	6 30	E	22 14	ARI	28
154	3	Sa.	4 09	A	7 16	E	15 07	18	10½	10½	3 26	A	7 43	E	22 21	TAU	0
155	4	**A**	4 09	A	7 17	E	15 08	18	11¼	11½	4 20	A	8 47	E	22 28	TAU	1
156	5	M.	4 08	A	7 17	E	15 09	18	—	12¼	5 24	A	9 38	E	22 35	AUR	2
157	6	Tu.	4 08	A	7 18	E	15 10	17	12¼	1	6 34	B	10 17	E	22 42	GEM	3
158	7	W.	4 08	A	7 18	E	15 10	17	1¼	2	7 45	B	10 48	E	22 48	CAN	4
159	8	Th.	4 08	A	7 19	E	15 11	17	2	2¾	8 55	B	11 13	D	22 53	CAN	5
160	9	Fr.	4 08	A	7 20	E	15 12	17	2¾	3½	10 00	C	11 34	D	22 58	LEO	6
161	10	Sa.	4 07	A	7 20	E	15 13	17	3¾	4½	11$^{A}_{M}$03	D	11$^{P}_{M}$53	C	23 02	LEO	7
162	11	**A**	4 07	A	7 21	E	15 14	16	4¾	5¼	12$^{P}_{M}$05	D	— —	–	23 06	LEO	8
163	12	M.	4 07	A	7 21	E	15 14	16	5½	6	1 06	D	12$^{A}_{M}$11	C	23 10	VIR	9
164	13	Tu.	4 07	A	7 22	E	15 15	16	6½	7	2 07	E	12 30	B	23 14	VIR	10
165	14	W.	4 07	A	7 22	E	15 15	16	7½	7¾	3 11	E	12 50	B	23 17	VIR	11
166	15	Th.	4 07	A	7 23	E	15 16	16	8¼	8½	4 16	E	1 14	A	23 20	VIR	12
167	16	Fr.	4 07	A	7 23	E	15 16	15	9	9¼	5 22	E	1 42	A	23 22	LIB	13
168	17	Sa.	4 07	A	7 23	E	15 16	15	9¾	10	6 26	E	2 16	A	23 23	SCO	14
169	18	**A**	4 07	A	7 24	E	15 17	15	10½	10½	7 26	E	3 00	A	23 24	OPH	15
170	19	M.	4 07	A	7 24	E	15 17	15	11¼	11¼	8 18	E	3 55	A	23 25	SAG	16
171	20	Tu.	4 07	A	7 24	E	15 17	15	—	12	9 02	E	4 59	A	23 26	SAG	17
172	21	W.	4 07	A	7 24	E	15 17	14	12	12¾	9 38	E	6 10	B	23 26	SAG	18
173	22	Th.	4 08	A	7 25	E	15 17	14	12¾	1½	10 07	E	7 24	B	23 26	CAP	19
174	23	Fr.	4 08	A	7 25	E	15 17	14	1½	2¼	10 33	D	8 38	C	23 25	CAP	20
175	24	Sa.	4 08	A	7 25	E	15 17	14	2½	3	10 56	D	9 52	C	23 24	AQU	21
176	25	**A**	4 08	A	7 25	E	15 17	13	3¼	4	11 18	C	11$^{A}_{M}$06	D	23 22	PSC	22
177	26	M.	4 09	A	7 25	E	15 16	13	4¼	4¾	11$^{P}_{M}$41	B	12$^{P}_{M}$20	E	23 20	PSC	23
178	27	Tu.	4 09	A	7 25	E	15 16	13	5¼	5¾	— —	–	1 35	E	23 18	PSC	24
179	28	W.	4 10	A	7 25	E	15 15	13	6¼	6¾	12$^{A}_{M}$08	B	2 53	E	23 15	ARI	25
180	29	Th.	4 10	A	7 25	E	15 15	13	7¼	7½	12 40	B	4 11	E	23 12	ARI	26
181	30	Fr.	4 10	A	7 25	E	15 15	12	8¼	8½	1 18	A	5$^{P}_{M}$26	E	23N.08	TAU	27

The Sun, as common, went abroad,
The flowers, accustomed, blew,
As if no soul the solstice passed
That maketh all things new.
— Emily Dickinson

Farmer's Calendar

Someone left a light burning in a window last night, and this morning a luna moth is clinging to the screen. It came out of the night woods, drawn by the lighted window, and now it rests motionless in the daylight, hardly stirring its wings when I touch them. With its size and its astonishing color, the moth *(Actias luna)* seems to have come from a different world. No other insect looks so out of place in New England's cold northern setting. The luna's wings, which can span five inches, are the palest blue-green, the color of a Caribbean pool. Its wings have long, slender tails which trail like the feathers of a bright tropical bird. The front edges of its wings are purple or maroon, and its body is the whitest thing in nature.

Despite its exotic look, the luna is about the commonest big moth in northern New England. Its larva, a fat, light-green caterpillar the size of a man's thumb, feeds all summer on the leaves of hickories, oaks, butternuts, and cherry trees. It makes a rough silk cocoon among dry leaves on the ground in late summer and spends the winter under the snow as a pupa. In June the adult moths emerge from their cocoons, fly, mate, lay eggs, and die — all in the space of four or five days. Like the other large silkmoths, the luna has no working mouth parts and so does not feed. Its brief life is devoted to mating and egg laying.

The moth has long been associated with the Moon — hence its name, *luna* — although the origin of the association isn't clear. Henry David Thoreau speculated on the point when on June 27, 1859, he found one of the moths on the edge of a swamp near Concord, Massachusetts. The luna, he wrote, "has more relation to the Moon by its pale, hoary-green color and its sluggishness by day than by the form of its tail," which some old naturalists had thought resembled the crescent Moon.

D.M.	D.W.	Dates, Feasts, Fasts, Aspects, Tide Heights	Weather ↓	
1	Th.	National Dairy Month and Ragweed Control Month begin. ●	{9.9 {11.5	*Something's*
2	Fr.	P.T. Barnum's circus began first U.S. tour, 1835 ●	Tides {10.0 {11.8	*fishy;*
3	Sa.	New ● ● Tornado killed 175, Camanche, Iowa, 1860	{10.0 {11.8	*still squishy.*
4	A	3ʳᵈ S. af. P. ● ☾ runs high ● ♂♀☾ ● ☿ stat.		
5	M.	St. Boniface ● "Know-Nothings" held first national convention, 1855		*We*
6	Tu.	☌♂☾ ● Laurel in blossom, N.H. ● Nathan Hale born, 1755	{11.4 {9.6	*seem*
7	W.	20″ snow, Danville, Vt., 1816 ●	Tides {11.0 {9.4	*fated*
8	Th.	*It is useless to try to reason a man out of a thing he was never reasoned into.* ●	Tides {10.5 {9.2	*to*
9	Fr.	Shavuot ● ☾at☋ ● ☌♃☉ ●	Tides {10.0 {9.5	*be*
10	Sa.	Mich., Ill., and Wis. ratified woman suffrage (19th) amendment, 1919 ●	{9.5 {9.0	*inundated.*
11	A	4ᵗʰ S. af. P. ● St. Barnabas ● ☾ on Eq.	{9.0 {9.0	
12	M.	☾ at apo. ● Baseball Hall of Fame dedicated, Cooperstown, N.Y., 1939	{8.7 {9.0	*Avast!*
13	Tu.	*N.Y. Times* began publishing "The Pentagon Papers," 1971 ●	{8.4 {9.2	*It's*
14	W.	"If St. Vitus Day be rainy weather, It will rain for 30 days together." (1697) ●		*clearing*
15	Th.	1″ snow, Ellentown, Penn., 1918 ● Waylon Jennings born, 1937	{8.3 {9.6	*up*
16	Fr.	*Never let the bottom of your purse or your mind be seen.* ●	Tides {9.4 {9.8	*at*
17	Sa.	St. Alban ● Bunker Hill Day, Boston ●	Tides {8.5 {10.0	*last!*
18	A	5ᵗʰ S. af. P. ● ☿ Gr. Elong. West (23°)		*Brisk*
19	M.	☾ runs low ● Full Strawberry ○ ● ☌♂☾	{8.8 {10.4	*but*
20	Tu.	☌♆☾ ● ☌♄☾ ● Chet Atkins born, 1924		*beamier;*
21	W.	Summer Solstice ● *Don't marry for money; you can borrow it cheaper.* ●		*Midsummer*
22	Th.	Don't brew while beans blossom. ● France surrendered to Germany, 1940	{10.7 {9.4	*night's*
23	Fr.	☾at☋ ● First matador killed in bullfight, Spain, 1771	{10.7 {9.6	*dreamier.*
24	Sa.	Nativ. John Baptist ● ☌♃☾ ● ☍☉		*Sumer*
25	A	6ᵗʰ S. af. P. ● ☾ on Eq. ● Custer's Last Stand, 1876	{10.3 {10.1	*is*
26	M.	Abner Doubleday born, 1819 ●	Tides {10.0 {10.4	*icumen*
27	Tu.	☾ at peri. ● Helen Keller born, 1880	{9.7 {10.6	*in,*
28	W.	*When the cat mourns for the mouse, do not take her seriously.* ●	{9.5 {10.8	*Lhude*
29	Th.	St. Peter ● Lucky day for fishermen. ● Nelson Eddy born, 1901	{9.3 {11.0	*sing*
30	Fr.	St. Paul ● 138 m.p.h. winds, Havre, Mont., 1978 ●	Tides {9.3 {11.2	*cuccu!*

The tyrant dies and his rule is over;
the martyr dies and his rule begins.

1989 JULY, THE SEVENTH MONTH

Saturn is at opposition, biggest and brightest, on July 2nd, just ten hours before Neptune is, and the Moon runs high. Observers with a small telescope should be able to pick out Messier 13, a spectacular cluster of stars in the trapezoid of Hercules, high overhead. Earth is at aphelion (farthest from the Sun in space) on Independence Day at 7 A.M. EST. Exactly 24 hours later is a very close conjunction (1/10th of a degree) of the Moon and Mars. Can you spot Mercury, very near Jupiter, low in the dawn on the 2nd, or Mars, very near Venus, low in the dusk on the 12th? The Venus-Regulus conjunction on July 22nd and 23rd is easier to see. Mars is at aphelion on July 22nd. Look for several dozen Delta Aquarid meteors an hour after midnight around the month's end.

ASTRONOMICAL CALCULATIONS

●	New Moon	3rd day	0 hour	0 min.
☽	First Quarter	10th day	19th hour	20th min.
○	Full Moon	18th day	12th hour	43rd min.
☾	Last Quarter	25th day	8th hour	33rd min.

ADD 1 hour for Daylight Saving Time.

FOR POINTS OUTSIDE BOSTON SEE KEY LETTER CORRECTIONS — PAGES 80-84

Day of Year	Day of Month	Day of Week	☉ Rises h. m.	Key	☉ Sets h. m.	Key	Length of Days h. m.	Sun Fast m.	Full Sea Boston A.M.	Full Sea Boston P.M.	☽ Rises h. m.	Key	☽ Sets h. m.	Key	Declination of sun ° ′	☽ Place	☽ Age
182	1	Sa.	4 11	A	7 25	E	15 14	12	9¼	9½	2 07 A.M.	A	6 32 P.M.	E	23N.05	TAU	28
183	2	**A**	4 12	A	7 25	E	15 13	12	10¼	10¼	3 07	A	7 28	E	23 00	AUR	29
184	3	M.	4 12	A	7 24	E	15 12	12	11¼	11¼	4 14	A	8 12	E	22 55	GEM	0
185	4	Tu.	4 13	A	7 24	E	15 11	12	—	12	5 25	B	8 46	E	22 50	GEM	1
186	5	W.	4 13	A	7 24	E	15 11	11	12	12¾	6 36	B	9 14	E	22 44	CAN	2
187	6	Th.	4 14	A	7 24	E	15 10	11	12¾	1½	7 45	C	9 37	D	22 38	LEO	3
188	7	Fr.	4 14	A	7 23	E	15 09	11	1½	2¼	8 50	C	9 56	D	22 32	LEO	4
189	8	Sa.	4 15	A	7 23	E	15 08	11	2½	3	9 52	D	10 15	C	22 25	LEO	5
190	9	**A**	4 16	A	7 23	E	15 07	11	3¼	3¾	10 54	D	10 33	C	22 18	VIR	6
191	10	M.	4 16	A	7 22	E	15 06	11	4	4½	11 55 A.M.	E	10 53	B	22 10	VIR	7
192	11	Tu.	4 17	A	7 22	E	15 05	11	4¾	5¼	12 58 P.M.	E	11 15	B	22 02	VIR	8
193	12	W.	4 18	A	7 21	E	15 03	10	5¾	6	2 01	E	11 40 P.M.	A	21 54	VIR	9
194	13	Th.	4 19	A	7 21	E	15 02	10	6¾	7	3 07	E	— —	–	21 45	LIB	10
195	14	Fr.	4 20	A	7 20	E	15 00	10	7½	7¾	4 11	E	12 12 A.M.	A	21 36	LIB	11
196	15	Sa.	4 20	A	7 19	E	14 59	10	8½	8½	5 14	E	12 52	A	21 26	SCO	12
197	16	**A**	4 21	A	7 19	E	14 58	10	9¼	9½	6 10	E	1 42	A	21 16	OPH	13
198	17	M.	4 22	A	7 18	E	14 56	10	10	10¼	6 58	E	2 43	A	21 06	SAG	14
199	18	Tu.	4 23	A	7 17	E	14 54	10	10¾	11	7 36	E	3 53	B	20 56	SAG	15
200	19	W.	4 24	A	7 17	E	14 53	10	11½	11¾	8 09	E	5 07	B	20 46	CAP	16
201	20	Th.	4 25	A	7 16	E	14 51	10	—	12¼	8 36	D	6 24	C	20 34	CAP	17
202	21	Fr.	4 26	A	7 15	E	14 49	10	12½	1	9 00	D	7 40	C	20 23	AQU	18
203	22	Sa.	4 27	A	7 14	E	14 47	10	1¼	1¾	9 23	C	8 55	D	20 11	AQU	19
204	23	**A**	4 28	A	7 13	E	14 45	10	2	2¾	9 46	B	10 10	D	19 58	PSC	20
205	24	M.	4 28	A	7 12	E	14 44	10	3	3½	10 11	B	11 26 A.M.	E	19 46	PSC	21
206	25	Tu.	4 29	A	7 11	D	14 42	10	4	4¼	10 41	B	12 43 P.M.	E	19 33	PSC	22
207	26	W.	4 30	A	7 10	D	14 40	10	5	5¼	11 17 P.M.	A	1 59	E	19 20	ARI	23
208	27	Th.	4 31	A	7 09	D	14 38	10	6	6¼	— —	–	3 14	E	19 06	TAU	24
209	28	Fr.	4 32	A	7 08	D	14 36	10	7	7¼	12 01 A.M.	A	4 22	E	18 53	TAU	25
210	29	Sa.	4 33	A	7 07	D	14 34	10	8¼	8¼	12 56	A	5 21	E	18 38	TAU	26
211	30	**A**	4 34	A	7 06	D	14 32	10	9¼	9¼	1 59	A	6 09	E	18 24	AUR	27
212	31	M.	4 35	A	7 05	D	14 30	10	10	10¼	3 09 A.M.	B	6 46 P.M.	E	18N.09	GEM	28

"Mantis weighs just 20 pounds, but it does tons of work!"

– J. Hosinski
South Bend, IN

Our 20-lb. Mantis Tiller handles like a dream, *yet works like a dynamo.*

It starts with a flick of the wrist, turns on a dime, lifts nimbly over hedges, but *never* gets out of control. Just pull it back and forth the way you would a hoe. Couldn't be simpler!

Best of all, our tough little Mantis does *more* gardening jobs than any other tiller!

Mantis prepares perfect seedbeds.   Its 36 *serpentine* "tine teeth" spin at up to 240 RPM, *twice* the speed of other tiller tines! That's why Mantis can till down to 8" *deep* ... and churn tough soils into soft, *fluffy* loam!

Mantis weeds your garden in minutes. And, since it works a sensible 6" to 9" *wide,* it weeds *precisely* between narrow rows, next to walkways, even right along fences — without disturbing your growing plants.

Mantis even does your lawn care and yard work!   See other side for full details!

Test Mantis RISK FREE FOR A FULL MONTH and see for yourself! For free details, call toll free, 1-800/344-4030. (Within PA, call 1-800/342-0052.) Or mail postpaid card below!

Mail this card today!

☐ YES! Rush me complete FREE details on the amazing 20-lb. Mantis. Tell me about your lifetime warranties, your risk-free full-month trial, *and* your early-order bonus!

Name

Address

City

State

Mantis. Changing the way Americans garden.®

Zip

Mantis. Because tilling is just the beginning.

Most tillers do nothing but till. But our 20-lb. Mantis works hard for you *all season long.*

Mantis creates smooth seedbeds *in minutes.* Then, when your garden's up and growing, Mantis "speed-weeds" between narrow rows . . . and right along walks, drives, and fences.

Your Complete Precision Gardening System™

Mantis does your landscaping, too! With its low-cost, *custom* attachments, it cuts crisp

borders for your garden beds . . . digs planting furrows and drainage ditches . . . aerates and de-thatches your lawn . . . even *trims and prunes your hedges!* No other tiller, big *or* small, is so versatile or useful!

Try Mantis RISK FREE FOR A FULL MONTH right in your own backyard! FOR FREE DETAILS, MAIL CARD BELOW, OR CALL TOLL FREE, 1-800-344-4030. (WITHIN PENNSYLVANIA, CALL 1-800-342-0052.) ©1988 MMC

JULY hath 31 days. 1989

But far in the fierce sunshine tower the hills,
With all their growth of woods, silent and stern,
As if the scorching heat and dazzling light
Were but an element they loved.
— William Cullen Bryant

D.M.	D.W.	Dates, Feasts, Fasts, Aspects, Tide Heights	Weather ↓
1	Sa.	☌☿☾ • ☌♃☾ • Canada Day • {9.3 / 11.3	*Rocket's*
2	A	**7th S. af. P.** • Visit. of Mary • ☾ runs high • ☌☿♃ • New ●	
3	M.	Dog Days begin. • "Blondie" first broadcast, 1939 • Tides {9.4 / 11.2 •	*red*
4	Tu.	**Independence Day** • ⊕ at aphelion •	*glare,*
5	W.	☌♅☾ • 120°F., Gannvalley, South Dakota, 1936 • Tides {11.0 / 9.5 •	*then*
6	Th.	☾ at ☋ • *You'll never get ahead trying to get even.* • {10.7 / 9.4 •	*beware!*
7	Fr.	Debut of "Dragnet," with Jack Webb, NBC radio, 1949 • Tides {10.4 / 9.4 •	*A*
8	Sa.	☾ on Eq. • Temperatures 105°-110° F. in East, 1936 • {9.9 / 9.3 •	*peach:*
9	A	**8th S. af. P.** • Invasion of Sicily, 1943 • Tides {9.4 / 9.2 •	*go*
10	M.	☾ at apo. • Wyoming admitted to Union with suffrage for women, 1890 •	*to*
11	Tu.	First Romanov Czar crowned, 1613 • John Quincy Adams born, 1767 •	*the*
12	W.	☌♀♅ • Minimum wage set at 40¢/hour, 1933 • Tides {8.2 / 9.1 •	*beach!*
13	Th.	*No wife can endure a gambling husband, unless he's a steady winner.* • {8.0 / 9.2 •	*Cumulo-*
14	Fr.	Bastille Day • 118° F., Warsaw and Union, Mo., 1954 • Tides {8.0 / 9.4 •	*stratus*
15	Sa.	**St. Swithin** • Apples watered by St. Swithin's tears are the most luscious.	*coming*
16	A	**9th S. af. P.** • ☾ runs low • ☌♅☾ •	*at*
17	M.	☌♄☾ • ☌♆☾ • 44° C., Lytton, B.C., 1941 • {8.6 / 10.4 •	*us.*
18	Tu.	☿ sup. ☌ • Full Buck ○ • Tides {9.0 / 10.7 •	*Drip,*
19	W.	Washington Senators stole 8 bases in first inning, 1915 • {9.4 / 11.0 •	*drip,*
20	Th.	**St. Margaret** • ☾ at ☊ • Armstrong and Aldrin landed on Moon, 1969 •	*this*
21	Fr.	*A proverb is a short sentence based on long experience.* • {11.1 / 10.2 •	*weekend's*
22	Sa.	**St. Mary Magdalene** • ☾ on Eq. • Tides {11.1 / 10.5 •	*a*
23	A	**10th S. af. P.** • ☾ at peri. • Tides {10.8 / 10.7 •	*pip!*
24	M.	Detroit founded, 1701 • Mormons reached Great Salt Lake, 1847 • {10.4 / 10.8 •	*Zeus*
25	Tu.	**St. James** • *Keep company with good men and you'll increase their number.* •	*on*
26	W.	**St. Anne** • Republic of Liberia established, 1847 • {9.5 / 10.7 •	*the*
27	Th.	Beware of cornscateous air. • "Detroit City" hit Top 20 records, 1963 •	*loose.*
28	Fr.	♇ stat. • Jacqueline Kennedy Onassis born, 1929 • {8.8 / 10.6 •	*Shooting*
29	Sa.	☾ runs high • ☌♃☾ • First motorcycle race in U.S., 1899 • {8.8 / 10.6	*stars,*
30	A	**11th S. af. P.** • Kellogg invented corn flakes, 1898 •	*birdies,*
31	M.	**St. Ignatius of Loyola** • Tides {9.1 / 10.8 •	*pars.*

Farmer's Calendar

In a well-stocked fishing shop today the casual buyer is lost. A veritable Louvre of baits is exhibited to his bewildered senses. Time was, you could go to work with a plug that looked like a fishing lure ought to look: a red-headed torpedo with big googly eyes and two sets of huge treble hooks that would have held a plesiosaur.

No more. You need an engineering degree at least to equip yourself for fishing today. The wall of the fishing shop is stacked to the ceiling with lures. The old bass plug was made of pine wood and covered with boat paint. Modern lures are made of every known material except wood. There are lures of steel, tin, brass, aluminum, epoxy, fiberglass, rubber, and 500 kinds of plastic. There are lures in every color and in every combination of colors. There are lures that imitate living things like worms, frogs, mice, bugs, baby muskrats, and fish; and there are lures that imitate nothing — or, not nothing, but *other fishing lures.* What else are we to make of a spoon that's half a foot long and takes two men to cast? There are lures that swim and lures that splash, and there are lures that make little beeping sounds that are supposed to attract fish.

"To attract fish," did you say? That's part of the program, certainly, but it's only part. There is another term in the system that relates the fish to the fishing shop, and that term is the fisherman. Those fancy lures don't catch fish on the shelves. Before they can hook a fish they must hook a fisherman, and *there* is the point of the profusion of styles, materials, colors, and sizes of lure. The fish were just as happy with the old bass plug. They don't care. It's the owners of the fishing shops who have seen the light, just as saints Peter and Andrew did beside the Sea of Galilee in the gospel. "Follow me," the Lord said unto them, "and I will make you fishers of men."

AUGUST, The Eighth Month

The closest planetary conjunction visible from the U.S. in this part of the century can be seen after sunset on August 5th. Binoculars help find Mercury and dimmer Mars (plus Regulus a degree away) low in the bright west twilight. Only binoculars separate the two, less than 1/30th of the Moon's apparent diameter apart. Look for the Perseid meteor showers from the 11th to the 13th. The longest total lunar eclipse since 1982 occurs on the night of August 16-17. Eastern U.S. gets the best view; Alaska and Hawaii get none. Earth's central shadow first touches the Moon at 8:22 P.M. EST; last touches at about 11:56 P.M. EST. Mercury's best viewing of the year is on the 29th, low in the west after sunset, 27° from the Sun. Voyager II is scheduled to encounter Neptune on August 24.

ASTRONOMICAL CALCULATIONS

●	New Moon	1st day	11th hour	6th min.
☽	First Quarter	9th day	12th hour	29th min.
○	Full Moon	16th day	22nd hour	7th min.
☾	Last Quarter	23rd day	13th hour	41st min.
●	New Moon	31st day	0 hour	45th min.

ADD 1 hour for Daylight Saving Time.

FOR POINTS OUTSIDE BOSTON SEE KEY LETTER CORRECTIONS — PAGES 80-84

Day of Year	Day of Month	Day of Week	☉ Rises h. m.	Key	☉ Sets h. m.	Key	Length of Days h. m.	Sun Fast m.	Full Sea Boston A.M.	P.M.	☽ Rises h. m.	Key	☽ Sets h. m.	Key	Declination of sun ° ′	☽ Place	☽ Age
213	1	Tu.	4 36	A	7 04	D	14 28	10	11	11	4ᴹ19	B	7ᴾᴹ15	E	17 N.54	CAN	0
214	2	W.	4 37	A	7 03	D	14 26	10	11¾	11¾	5 29	B	7 39	D	17 38	CAN	1
215	3	Th.	4 38	A	7 02	D	14 24	10	—	12¼	6 35	C	8 00	D	17 22	LEO	2
216	4	Fr.	4 39	A	7 00	D	14 21	10	12½	1	7 39	C	8 19	C	17 06	LEO	3
217	5	Sa.	4 40	A	6 59	D	14 19	10	1¼	1¾	8 42	D	8 38	C	16 50	LEO	4
218	6	A	4 42	A	6 58	D	14 16	10	1¾	2¼	9 43	E	8 56	B	16 33	VIR	5
219	7	M.	4 43	A	6 57	D	14 14	10	2½	3	10 45	E	9 17	B	16 17	VIR	6
220	8	Tu.	4 44	A	6 55	D	14 11	10	3¼	3¾	11ᴾᴹ48	E	9 41	B	16 00	VIR	7
221	9	W.	4 45	A	6 54	D	14 09	11	4¼	4½	12ᴾᴹ52	E	10 10	A	15 42	LIB	8
222	10	Th.	4 46	A	6 53	D	14 07	11	5	5¼	1 56	E	10 45	A	15 25	LIB	9
223	11	Fr.	4 47	A	6 51	D	14 04	11	6	6¼	2 59	E	11ᴾᴹ30	A	15 08	SCO	10
224	12	Sa.	4 48	A	6 50	D	14 02	11	7	7¼	3 57	E	— —	-	14 50	OPH	11
225	13	A	4 49	A	6 49	D	14 00	11	7¾	8	4 49	E	12ᴬᴹ25	A	14 31	SAG	12
226	14	M.	4 50	B	6 47	D	13 57	11	8¾	9	5 31	E	1 31	A	14 13	SAG	13
227	15	Tu.	4 51	B	6 46	D	13 55	12	9½	9¾	6 07	E	2 44	B	13 54	SAG	14
228	16	W.	4 52	B	6 44	D	13 52	12	10½	10½	6 37	E	4 01	C	13 35	CAP	15
229	17	Th.	4 53	B	6 43	D	13 50	12	11	11¼	7 02	D	5 19	C	13 16	AQU	16
230	18	Fr.	4 54	B	6 41	D	13 47	12	11¾	—	7 26	C	6 36	D	12 56	PSC	17
231	19	Sa.	4 55	B	6 40	D	13 45	12	12	12½	7 50	B	7 54	D	12 37	PSC	18
232	20	A	4 56	B	6 38	D	13 42	13	1	1¼	8 14	B	9 11	E	12 17	PSC	19
233	21	M.	4 57	B	6 37	D	13 40	13	1¾	2¼	8 43	B	10 30	E	11 57	PSC	20
234	22	Tu.	4 58	B	6 35	D	13 37	13	2¾	3	9 17	A	11ᴬᴹ49	E	11 37	ARI	21
235	23	W.	4 59	B	6 33	D	13 34	13	3½	4	9 59	A	1ᴾᴹ05	E	11 17	ARI	22
236	24	Th.	5 01	B	6 32	D	13 31	14	4¾	5	10 50	A	2 15	E	10 56	TAU	23
237	25	Fr.	5 02	B	6 30	D	13 28	14	5¾	6	11ᴾᴹ51	A	3 17	E	10 36	TAU	24
238	26	Sa.	5 03	B	6 29	D	13 26	14	7	7¼	— —	-	4 07	E	10 15	AUR	25
239	27	A	5 04	B	6 27	D	13 23	15	8	8¼	12ᴬᴹ58	B	4 46	E	9 54	GEM	26
240	28	M.	5 05	B	6 25	D	13 20	15	9	9¼	2 07	B	5 18	E	9 33	CAN	27
241	29	Tu.	5 06	B	6 24	D	13 18	15	9¾	10	3 16	B	5 43	D	9 11	CAN	28
242	30	W.	5 07	B	6 22	D	13 15	15	10½	10¾	4 23	C	6 05	D	8 50	LEO	29
243	31	Th.	5 08	B	6 20	D	13 12	16	11¼	11½	5ᴬᴹ28	C	6ᴾᴹ24	D	8 N.28	LEO	0

The opal heart of afternoon
Was clouding on to throbs of storm,
Ashen within the ardent west
The lips of thunder muttered harm.
— *William Vaughn Moody*

Farmer's Calendar

Every gardener who plants a sweet corn patch in the spring knows the raccoons are watching from the woods. Now August has come, the corn is ripe, and we are ready to eat it. The raccoons are ready, too.

If you decide to pick corn for your dinner on Tuesday, the raccoons will show up Monday night. They will eat it all, every ear, just when the corn is at its best. Many animals are smart, but the raccoon is both smart and *patient*. They will wait until the corn is ready, just as you do.

You will try all the common tricks for repelling raccoons. None of them works — or none of them works for long. Pie pans that rattle and bang, squash plants with prickly leaves, loud radios playing, rags soaked in kerosene, shaving cream on the fence posts, mothballs on the ground, blood meal, rubber snakes, plastic owls — no raccoon is going to be put off for very long by any of those. He may hold back for a night, but soon he'll understand that the pie pan, the kerosene are no real threat to him, and in he'll come. If you would keep him out, remember: the raccoon thinks the same way you do. He likes what you like (ripe sweet corn). He doesn't like what you don't like. Would a plastic owl repel you? No. Therefore neither will it repel a raccoon. You need a repellent that you know would work for you as well as for him. The Ayatollah Khomeini, say, or a well-armed member of the Right Wing Fundamentalist Muslim Jihad. Effective repellents, those, no doubt, but complicated from the point of view of international restrictions on imports and exports. More practical repellents might be a vicious dog or a friend who likes to talk at length about investments, or television programs, or computers, or cars, or cameras. Either of these, stationed in your corn patch at night, will surely keep the raccoons away.

D.M.	D.W.	Dates, Feasts, Fasts, Aspects, Tide Heights	Weather ↓
1	Tu.	**Lammas Day** • New ● • Tides {9.3 10.7	*Tan*
2	W.	☾at☍ • ♂☿☾ PT-*109* rammed and sunk, 1943 • Tides {9.4 10.6	*your*
3	Th.	♂♂☾ U.S.S. *Nautilus* cruised under North Pole, 1958	*hide.*
4	Fr.	♂♀☾ *A mile walked with a friend has only 100 steps.* • Tides {10.4 9.6	*Stay*
5	Sa.	☾ on Eq. • ♂♀☌ Conrad Aiken born, 1889 • {10.1 9.6	*inside!*
6	**A**	**12ᵗʰ ⅀. af. ℙ.** • **Transfiguration**	*Dog*
7	M.	**Name of Jesus** • ☾at apo. • Bank holiday, Great Britain	*days,*
8	Tu.	Snowstorm on Lake Michigan, 1882, covered ships with 6″ snow and slush • {8.8 9.3	*heat*
9	W.	President Richard Nixon resigned, 1974 • Tides {8.9 9.1	*and*
10	Th.	**St. Laurence** • Sun today means a fine autumn. • Tides {8.0 9.0	*haze.*
11	Fr.	Dog Days end. • Barbados hurricane began, 1780 • Tides {7.8 9.1	*It's*
12	Sa.	**St. Clare** • Perseid meteors after midnight • {7.8 9.3	*wet*
13	**A**	**13ᵗʰ ⅀. af. ℙ.** • ☾ runs low • ♂♂☾ • ♂♄☾ •	
14	M.	*If you tell the truth, you don't have to remember anything.* • Tides {8.4 10.1	*you'll*
15	Tu.	40° C., Bark Lake, Quebec, 1928 • Napoleon Bonaparte born, 1769 •	*get*
16	W.	Full Sturgeon ○ • Eclipse ○ • Tides {9.5 11.0	*in*
17	Th.	☾at☍ • Cat nights commence. • Mae West born, 1892 • {10.1 11.3	*Connect-*
18	Fr.	**St. Helena** • ☾ on Eq. • Hurricane Alicia hit Houston, 1984 •	*icut!*
19	Sa.	☾ at peri. • 37° C., Charlottetown, Prince Edward Island, 1935 • {11.4 11.1	*C'est*
20	**A**	**14ᵗʰ ⅀. af. ℙ.** • Tides {11.3 11.3	*magnifique!*
21	M.	W.S. Burroughs patented adding machine, 1888 • Tides {10.9 11.3	*Up*
22	Tu.	Wallpaper printing press patented, 1822 • Tides {10.4 11.2	*the*
23	W.	*A cynic knows the price of everything and the value of nothing.* • Tides {9.8 10.9	*creek.*
24	Th.	**St. Bartholomew** • *Voyager II* scheduled to encounter Neptune, 1989	*Good-bye*
25	Fr.	☾ runs high • "Father Knows Best" first broadcast on NBC, 1949 • {8.8 10.3	*to*
26	Sa.	♂♃☾ • John Wilkes Booth born, 1838 • {8.6 10.1	*summer —*
27	**A**	**15ᵗʰ ⅀. af. ℙ.** • Tides {8.7 10.2	*flashes,*
28	M.	**St. Augustine of Hippo** • Charles Boyer born, 1899 •	*crashes,*
29	Tu.	**John Bap. beheaded** • ☿ Gr. Elong. East (27°) • {9.2 10.3	*tin*
30	W.	☾at☍ *They who give have all things, they who withhold have nothing.*	*roof*
31	Th.	New ● • Eclipse ☉ • Tides {9.6 10.3	*drummer!*

SEPTEMBER, THE NINTH MONTH

On the 1st, Uranus is farthest south in 84 years. On the 9th, the Moon is in conjunction with stationary Uranus and with Saturn. Pluto reaches perihelion on the 12th, for the only time in almost 500 years. Pluto, closer than Neptune until 1999, is now only 6/10ths as distant as when farthest out, just after the Civil War. Venus dazzles after dusk with the star Beta Virginis right beside it on the 14th and 15th. The autumnal equinox is reached at 8:20 P.M. EST on the 22nd. The Milky Way, our home galaxy with a hundred billion stars seen on its edge, is shifting from its midsummer north-south position to an east-west alignment by November. The Summer Triangle is high overhead with Corona and Hercules to its west and tiny Delphinus the Dolphin to its east. Look for the great square of Pegasus low in the east.

ASTRONOMICAL CALCULATIONS

☽	First Quarter	8th day	4th hour	50th min.
○	Full Moon	15th day	6th hour	51st min.
☾	Last Quarter	21st day	21st hour	11th min.
●	New Moon	29th day	16th hour	48th min.

ADD 1 hour for Daylight Saving Time.

FOR POINTS OUTSIDE BOSTON SEE KEY LETTER CORRECTIONS — PAGES 80-84

Day of Year	Day of Month	Day of Week	☉ Rises h. m.	Key	☉ Sets h. m.	Key	Length of Days h. m.	Sun Fast m.	Full Sea Boston A.M.	Full Sea Boston P.M.	☽ Rises h. m.	Key	☽ Sets h. m.	Key	Declination of sun ° ′	☽ Place	☽ Age
244	1	Fr.	5 09	B	6 19	D	13 10	16	11¾	—	6 A.M. 30	D	6 P.M. 43	C	8N.06	LEO	1
245	2	Sa.	5 10	B	6 17	D	13 07	16	12	12½	7 32	D	7 02	B	7 44	VIR	2
246	3	**A**	5 11	B	6 15	D	13 04	17	12¾	1	8 33	E	7 21	B	7 22	VIR	3
247	4	M.	5 12	B	6 14	D	13 02	17	1¼	1½	9 36	E	7 44	B	7 00	VIR	4
248	5	Tu.	5 13	B	6 12	D	12 59	17	2	2¼	10 39	E	8 10	A	6 38	VIR	5
249	6	W.	5 14	B	6 10	D	12 56	18	2¾	3	11 A.M. 43	E	8 42	A	6 15	LIB	6
250	7	Th.	5 15	B	6 08	D	12 53	18	3½	3¾	12 P.M. 46	E	9 22	A	5 53	SCO	7
251	8	Fr.	5 16	B	6 07	C	12 51	18	4½	4¾	1 45	E	10 12	A	5 30	OPH	8
252	9	Sa.	5 17	B	6 05	C	12 48	19	5¼	5½	2 38	E	11 P.M. 12	A	5 08	SAG	9
253	10	**A**	5 19	B	6 03	C	12 44	19	6¼	6½	3 24	E	— —	–	4 45	SAG	10
254	11	M.	5 20	B	6 01	C	12 41	19	7¼	7½	4 02	E	12 A.M. 20	B	4 22	SAG	11
255	12	Tu.	5 21	B	6 00	C	12 39	20	8¼	8½	4 34	E	1 34	B	3 59	CAP	12
256	13	W.	5 22	B	5 58	C	12 36	20	9	9¼	5 01	D	2 51	C	3 36	CAP	13
257	14	Th.	5 23	B	5 56	C	12 33	20	9¾	10	5 26	D	4 09	C	3 13	AQU	14
258	15	Fr.	5 24	B	5 54	C	12 30	21	10½	11	5 50	C	5 28	D	2 50	PSC	15
259	16	Sa.	5 25	B	5 53	C	12 28	21	11¼	11¾	6 15	B	6 47	E	2 27	PSC	16
260	17	**A**	5 26	B	5 51	C	12 25	22	—	12	6 44	B	8 08	E	2 04	PSC	17
261	18	M.	5 27	B	5 49	C	12 22	22	12½	1	7 16	B	9 29	E	1 41	ARI	18
262	19	Tu.	5 28	C	5 47	C	12 19	22	1½	1¾	7 56	A	10 A.M. 50	E	1 18	ARI	19
263	20	W.	5 29	C	5 46	C	12 17	23	2½	2¾	8 46	A	12 P.M. 05	E	0 54	TAU	20
264	21	Th.	5 30	C	5 44	C	12 14	23	3¼	3¾	9 45	A	1 11	E	0 31	TAU	21
265	22	Fr.	5 31	C	5 42	C	12 11	23	4½	4¾	10 50	A	2 05	E	0N.07	AUR	22
266	23	Sa.	5 32	C	5 40	C	12 08	24	5½	5¾	11 P.M. 59	B	2 48	E	0S. 15	GEM	23
267	24	**A**	5 33	C	5 39	C	12 06	24	6¾	7	— —	–	3 21	E	0 38	CAN	24
268	25	M.	5 34	C	5 37	C	12 03	24	7¾	8	1 A.M. 07	B	3 48	E	1 02	CAN	25
269	26	Tu.	5 36	C	5 35	C	11 59	25	8¾	9	2 15	C	4 11	D	1 25	LEO	26
270	27	W.	5 37	C	5 33	B	11 56	25	9½	9¾	3 19	C	4 30	D	1 49	LEO	27
271	28	Th.	5 38	C	5 31	B	11 53	25	10	10¼	4 21	D	4 49	C	2 12	LEO	28
272	29	Fr.	5 39	C	5 30	B	11 51	26	10¾	11	5 23	D	5 08	C	2 35	VIR	0
273	30	Sa.	5 40	C	5 28	B	11 48	26	11¼	11¾	6 A.M. 24	E	5 P.M. 27	B	2S. 59	VIR	1

SEPTEMBER hath 30 days. 1989

Season of mists and mellow fruitfulness,
Close bosom-friend of the maturing sun;
Conspiring with him how to load and bless
With fruit the vines that round the thatch-eves run . . .
— *John Keats*

D.M.	D.W.	Dates, Feasts, Fasts, Aspects, Tide Heights	Weather ↓
1	Fr.	**St. Giles** • ☾ on Eq. • Hurricane Elena hit Gulf Coast, 1985 •	*Moist*
2	Sa.	☌☿☾ • Ho Chi Minh proclaimed Dem. Rep. of Vietnam, 1945 • {10.1 9.8 •	*at*
3	A	**16th S. af. P.** • ☌♀☾ • Tides {9.8 9.8 •	*foist.*
4	M.	**Labor Day** • ☾ at apo. • Paul Harvey born, 1918 • {9.5 9.7 •	*Ask*
5	Tu.	Cranberry harvest begins, Cape Cod • UFO sighting, Dresser, Wis., 1979 • {9.1 9.5 •	*not*
6	W.	*Science is the slaying of a beautiful hypothesis by an ugly fact.* • {8.7 9.3	*for*
7	Th.	First settlement at Boston, 1630 • Grandma Moses born, 1860 •	*whom*
8	Fr.	**Nativity of Mary** • Tides {8.0 9.0 •	*the*
9	Sa.	☾ runs low • ☌♅☾ • ♅ stat. • ☌♄☾ • {7.8 9.0 •	*school*
10	A	**17th S. af. P.** • ☌♆☾ • ♄ stat. •	*bells*
11	M.	☿ stat. • N.Y. Yankees drew 11 walks, 3rd inning, 1949 • Tides {8.2 9.7 •	*toll.*
12	Tu.	*The "silly" question is the first intimation of some totally new development.* • {8.8 10.2	*Dole-*
13	W.	☾ at ☊ • Rhinoceros first seen in New York City, 1826 •	*ful*
14	Th.	**Holy Cross** • 36″ snow, Red Lodge, Mont., 1982 • Tides {10.2 11.2 •	*skies*
15	Fr.	☾ on Eq. • Full Harvest ○ • Jackie Cooper born, 1922 • {11.0 11.4 •	*and*
16	Sa.	**St. Ninian** • ☾ at peri. • Tides {11.5 11.5 •	*direful*
17	A	**18th S. af. P.** • Tides {— 11.9 •	*deluges;*
18	M.	First issue of *New York Times* published, 1851 • Tides {11.2 11.9 •	*all*
19	Tu.	*What is patriotism but the love of the good things we ate in our childhood?* • {10.8 11.7	*of*
20	W.	♆ stat. • Ember Day • Tides {10.2 11.3 •	*a*
21	Th.	**St. Matthew** • Independence for Malta, 1964 • {9.6 10.8 •	*sudden,*
22	Fr.	☾ runs high • ☌♃☾ • Autumnal Equinox • Ember Day •	*it's*
23	Sa.	Ember Day • Rocky Marciano K-O'ed Jersey Joe Walcott, 1952 • Tides {8.7 9.9 •	*hotter*
24	A	**19th S. af. P.** • ☿ inf. ☌ • {8.6 9.8 •	*than*
25	M.	*Let me smile with the wise, and feed with the rich.* • {8.8 9.8	*helluges!*
26	Tu.	**St. Cyprian** • ☾ at ☋ • Tides {9.1 9.9 •	*Sox*
27	W.	*Visits always give pleasure — if not the arrival, then the departure.* •	*in first,*
28	Th.	☾ on Eq. • 1st World Series color TV broadcast, 1955 • {9.7 9.9	*expect*
29	Fr.	**St. Michael** • ☌♅☉ • New ● • {9.9 9.8 •	*the*
30	Sa.	**Rosh Hashanah** • **St. Jerome** • {10.0 9.7 •	*worst.*

Wisdom is ofttimes nearer when we stoop
Than when we soar.

Farmer's Calendar

There are ghosts in our gardens — pale, unearthly shapes shining under the harvest Moon. Frost is predicted for tonight, and people in the cold lowlands have carried sheets and blankets from their houses to cover tender plants against the cold. By moonlight it looks as though vegetables must celebrate Halloween a month earlier than the rest of us. Spirits in every form walk among the garden rows.

The forms that the spectral garden takes on are peculiarly medieval. We see mounted knights. Staked tomatoes in their former life, now draped and sheeted, they stand lined up in ranks for the tournament. There are creeping ghosts, lowly serfs and villeins, the spirits of squash plants and melons. Thin ghosts of monks and fat ghosts of friars, lords and ladies in every degree, each of them the mysterious, enduring essence of one crop or another. There is even ghost architecture from the Middle Ages: towers that were pole beans, and ghost castles, formerly tomato and cucumber cages. Any learned doctor of Paris of the time who had decided plants don't have souls would have to think again if he passed today through a New England village on the night of the first frost.

And then, the next day, resurrection! The dead are raised. The cerements are flung off, a little damp with the dew, a little muddy at the hem. The tomatoes, melons, beans, and the rest awake, shake themselves, and begin to frolic about in the morning sun, looking a little peaked, perhaps, at first, but soon stepping about as good as new. Eggplants and peppers reborn! Witchcraft! Confronted with creatures whose ghosts walked about each night and who then resumed normal life by day, our medieval doctor would not hesitate. He'd burn them at the stake. Seven centuries later, we do the same thing. The learned doctor called it *auto da fé*. We call it veg-kabob.

OCTOBER, THE TENTH MONTH

Tides will be increased by the closest, biggest-looking Moon of 1989, being only four hours after full Moon (Hunter's Moon) on October 14. The farthest Moon of the year is on the 28th, the day before we set the clocks back. The Orionid meteors are spoiled by the waning Moon. Fomalhaut is a solitary brilliant star low in the south, under the higher four bright stars from the great square of Pegasus. Around dawn on the 10th comes a good chance to see Mercury at greatest elongation of 18°. The Big Dipper is hardly seen, skimming the northern horizon, and the Pleiades and Aldebaran, harbingers of fall, are low in the east. After Venus sets, second-brightest Jupiter rises to dominate the sky. Across the southern sky at mid evening are the faint patterns of Capricornus, Aquarius, and Pisces.

ASTRONOMICAL CALCULATIONS

☽ First Quarter	7th day	19th hour	53rd min.
○ Full Moon	14th day	15th hour	33rd min.
☾ Last Quarter	21st day	8th hour	19th min.
● New Moon	29th day	10th hour	29th min.

ADD 1 hour for Daylight Saving Time until 2 A.M. October 29th.

FOR POINTS OUTSIDE BOSTON SEE KEY LETTER CORRECTIONS — PAGES 80-84

Day of Year	Day of Month	Day of Week	☉ Rises h. m.	Key	☉ Sets h. m.	Key	Length of Days h. m.	Sun Fast m.	Full Sea Boston A.M.	Full Sea Boston P.M.	☽ Rises h. m.	Key	☽ Sets h. m.	Key	Declination of sun ° ′	☽ Place	☽ Age
274	1	**A**	5 41	C	5 26	B	11 45	26	11¾	—	7 A.M. 26	E	5 P.M. 49	B	3s.22	VIR	2
275	2	M.	5 42	C	5 25	B	11 43	27	12¼	12½	8 29	E	6 14	A	3 45	VIR	3
276	3	Tu.	5 43	C	5 23	B	11 40	27	12¾	1	9 33	E	6 44	A	4 08	LIB	4
277	4	W.	5 44	C	5 21	B	11 37	27	1½	1¾	10 36	E	7 21	A	4 31	LIB	5
278	5	Th.	5 45	C	5 19	B	11 34	28	2¼	2¼	11 A.M. 35	E	8 06	A	4 55	SCO	6
279	6	Fr.	5 47	C	5 18	B	11 31	28	3	3¼	12 P.M. 30	E	9 01	A	5 18	OPH	7
280	7	Sa.	5 48	C	5 16	B	11 28	28	4	4	1 17	E	10 04	B	5 41	SAG	8
281	8	**A**	5 49	C	5 14	B	11 25	28	4¾	5	1 57	E	11 P.M. 13	B	6 03	SAG	9
282	9	M.	5 50	C	5 13	B	11 23	29	5¾	6	2 30	E	— —	–	6 26	CAP	10
283	10	Tu.	5 51	C	5 11	B	11 20	29	6¾	7	2 59	D	12 A.M. 26	B	6 49	CAP	11
284	11	W.	5 52	C	5 09	B	11 17	29	7¾	8	3 25	D	1 42	C	7 11	AQU	12
285	12	Th.	5 53	C	5 08	B	11 15	30	8½	8¾	3 49	D	2 58	D	7 34	AQU	13
286	13	Fr.	5 54	D	5 06	B	11 12	30	9¼	9¾	4 13	C	4 16	D	7 56	PSC	14
287	14	Sa.	5 56	D	5 04	B	11 08	30	10	10½	4 41	B	5 37	E	8 19	PSC	15
288	15	**A**	5 57	D	5 03	B	11 06	30	10¾	11½	5 12	B	7 00	E	8 41	PSC	16
289	16	M.	5 58	D	5 01	B	11 03	30	11¾	—	5 50	A	8 23	E	9 03	ARI	17
290	17	Tu.	5 59	D	5 00	B	11 01	31	12¼	12½	6 37	A	9 44	E	9 25	TAU	18
291	18	W.	6 00	D	4 58	B	10 58	31	1¼	1¼	7 34	A	10 56	E	9 47	TAU	19
292	19	Th.	6 01	D	4 56	B	10 55	31	2	2¼	8 39	A	11 A.M. 57	E	10 08	TAU	20
293	20	Fr.	6 03	D	4 55	B	10 52	31	3	3¼	9 49	B	12 P.M. 46	E	10 30	GEM	21
294	21	Sa.	6 04	D	4 53	B	10 49	31	4¼	4¼	10 P.M. 59	B	1 23	E	10 51	GEM	22
295	22	**A**	6 05	D	4 52	B	10 47	32	5¼	5½	— —	–	1 52	E	11 12	CAN	23
296	23	M.	6 06	D	4 50	B	10 44	32	6¼	6½	12 A.M. 07	C	2 15	A	11 33	LEO	24
297	24	Tu.	6 07	D	4 49	B	10 42	32	7¼	7½	1 12	C	2 36	A	11 54	LEO	25
298	25	W.	6 09	D	4 48	B	10 39	32	8¼	8½	2 15	D	2 55	C	12 15	LEO	26
299	26	Th.	6 10	D	4 46	B	10 36	32	9	9¼	3 16	D	3 14	C	12 36	VIR	27
300	27	Fr.	6 11	D	4 45	B	10 34	32	9½	10	4 17	E	3 33	B	12 56	VIR	28
301	28	Sa.	6 12	D	4 43	B	10 31	32	10¼	10½	5 18	E	3 54	B	13 16	VIR	29
302	29	**A**	6 14	D	4 42	B	10 28	32	10¾	11¼	6 21	E	4 18	B	13 36	VIR	0
303	30	M.	6 15	D	4 41	B	10 26	32	11¼	11¾	7 24	E	4 47	A	13 56	LIB	1
304	31	Tu.	6 16	D	4 39	B	10 23	32	—	12	8 A.M. 28	E	5 P.M. 21	A	14s.15	LIB	2

The trees all richly clad, yet void of pride,
Were gilded o'er by his rich golden head;
Their leaves and fruits seemed painted, but were true
Of green, of red, of yellow, mixéd hue.
— *Anne Bradstreet*

D.M.	D.W.	Dates, Feasts, Fasts, Aspects, Tide Heights	*Weather* ↓
1	**A**	**20th S. af. P.** • **St. Remigius** • ☾ at apo. • {10.0 —	
2	M.	"The Cisco Kid" debuted on WOR-Mutual radio, 1942 • Tides {9.5 10.0	*Mountain*
3	Tu.	☿ stat. • ☌♀☾ • Gore Vidal born, 1925 • {9.2 9.9 •	*snow,*
4	W.	**St. Francis d'Assisi** • *Sputnik I* launched, 1957 • Tides {8.9 9.7	*rain*
5	Th.	October always has 19 fine days. • N.Y. Yankees won World Series, 1953 •	*down*
6	Fr.	**St. Faith** • ☾ runs low • ☌♅☾ • Tides {8.2 9.2 •	*below.*
7	Sa.	☌♄☾ • ☌♆☾ • Tides {8.0 9.1 •	*Visit*
8	**A**	**21st S. af. P.** • John Lennon born, 1940 • {8.0 9.2 •	*an*
9	M.	**Columbus Day** • **Yom Kippur** • Tides {8.2 9.4	*orchard*
10	Tu.	☾ at ☊ • ☿ Gr. Elong West (18°) • 9″ snow, Worcester, Mass., 1979 •	*before*
11	W.	*A host is like a general: it takes a mishap to reveal his genius.* • Tides {9.4 10.2 •	*we*
12	Th.	☾ on Eq. • Lambing season, New Zealand • Tides {10.2 10.7 •	*get*
13	Fr.	Molly Pitcher born, 1754 • Boston Red Sox won first World Series, 1903 •	*tortured.*
14	Sa.	**Succoth** • Full Hunter's ○ • ☾ at peri. • Tides {11.7 11.2 •	
15	**A**	**22nd S. af. P.** • Tides {12.2 11.2 •	*Rain-*
16	M.	*Take care to get what you like, or you will be forced to like what you get.* •	*whipped,*
17	Tu.	**St. Ethelred** • Rita Hayworth born, 1918 • Tides {10.9 12.2 •	*leaves*
18	W.	**St. Luke** • St. Luke's "little summer" • Tides {10.5 11.8 •	*stripped.*
19	Th.	☾ runs high • ☌♃☾ • Marlon Brando's stage debut, 1944 • {10.0 11.3 •	*A*
20	Fr.	Saturday Night Massacre, 1973 • Art Buchwald born, 1925 •	*break,*
21	Sa.	Columbus landed at San Salvador Island, 1492 • Tides {9.0 10.0 •	*then*
22	**A**	**23rd S. af. P.** • Annette Funicello born, 1942 •	*a*
23	M.	☾ at ☋ • Hungarian uprising, 1956 • Tides {8.8 9.4 •	*battering.*
24	Tu.	Chipmunks hibernate. • Temperatures in 90s, N.E., 1947 • {9.0 9.4 •	*Rake*
25	W.	**St. Crispin** • ☾ on Eq. • Picasso born, 1881 • {9.3 9.4 •	*those*
26	Th.	*There is no such thing as a pretty good omelet.* • Tides {9.6 9.4 •	*lawns*
27	Fr.	Snowstorm with high winds from New England to Baltimore, 1859 •	*before*
28	Sa.	**Sts. Simon and Jude** • ☾ at apo. • ♃ stat. • Tides {10.0 9.4	
29	**A**	**24th S. af. P.** • New ● • D.S.T. ends •	*the*
30	M.	*Unanimity is almost always an indication of servitude.* • Tides {10.1 9.1 •	*next*
31	Tu.	**All Hallows Eve** • Dale Evans born, 1912 •	*splattering.*

Farmer's Calendar

Everybody builds woodpiles the same way, and everybody is subject to the same frustration and despair when his woodpile inevitably collapses. But until today nobody has elevated both the construction and the collapse to the level of mathematics.

In making a woodpile you produce a freestanding rectangle that gravity wants to turn into a triangle by causing the upper corners to fall down. To counter this, you buttress the ends of the pile, building towers log-cabin-style with pieces of wood placed at right angles to form a square. You build the towers up by the thickness of each piece of wood. Between the end buttresses you stack all the pieces in the same direction. It is this central stack that tends to fall down at the high corners, exerting force against the end buttresses. The higher the buttresses, the more wood they retain, and the greater the forces pulling the whole pile apart. The moment comes when you reach the critical point and an end buttress collapses, dumping the stacked wood inside it.

How can you predict when your woodpile has reached its maximum height, a height at which adding another stick's thickness would bring catastrophe? Up to now you have had to guess blindly, but henceforth you can apply the following formula: $h = y - 1$. Where h is the height at which the pile will collapse, expressed as a number of pieces of wood of whatever thickness; and y is the height you want your woodpile to be, expressed similarly. Therefore, if you want a 20-stick-high pile, collapse will occur when you reach 19 sticks, and so forth. In plain English, our formula states that your woodpile will always fall down just before you quit building it up. And if you needed mathematics to convince yourself of *that*, you are probably a person of tender years and little experience of our common predicament.

1989 NOVEMBER, THE ELEVENTH MONTH

On the 3rd, the Moon is in conjunction with Saturn, Uranus, and Neptune. On the 8th, Venus (not Mars this time) reaches its greatest elongation from the Sun. Look for it after sunset in the west. Saturn and Neptune are one half a degree apart on the 12th, their last conjunction together until 2025. A few hours after sundown, Jupiter rises in the east. Venus is in conjunction with Neptune and Saturn on the 15th. At midmonth and mid evening, the Great Galaxy of Andromeda is a hazy patch of light just about overhead. High in the north is the now-sideways chair of Cassiopeia the Queen. Climbing the northeast, ahead of bright yellow Capella, is constellation Perseus with its star Algol — a "variable star" which you can watch dim dramatically in the course of some nights. Leonid meteors are spoiled by the Moon. Mars, the only visible planet in the morning sky, is very close to double star Alpha Librae on the 26th.

ASTRONOMICAL CALCULATIONS

☽	First Quarter	6th day	9th hour	12th min.
○	Full Moon	13th day	0 hour	52nd min.
☾	Last Quarter	19th day	23rd hour	45th min.
●	New Moon	28th day	4th hour	42nd min.

FOR POINTS OUTSIDE BOSTON SEE KEY LETTER CORRECTIONS — PAGES 80-84

Day of Year	Day of Month	Day of Week	☉ Rises h. m.	Key	☉ Sets h. m.	Key	Length of Days h. m.	Sun Fast m.	Full Sea Boston A.M.	Full Sea Boston P.M.	☽ Rises h. m.	Key	☽ Sets h. m.	Key	Declination of sun ° '	☽ Place	☽ Age
305	1	W.	6 17	D	4 38	B	10 21	32	12½	12½	9 A.M. 28	E	6 P.M. 04	A	14s.34	SCO	3
306	2	Th.	6 19	D	4 37	B	10 18	32	1¼	1¼	10 25	E	6 55	A	14 53	OPH	4
307	3	Fr.	6 20	D	4 35	B	10 15	32	1¾	2	11 13	E	7 56	A	15 12	SAG	5
308	4	Sa.	6 21	D	4 34	B	10 13	32	2½	2¾	11 A.M. 55	E	9 02	B	15 30	SAG	6
309	5	A	6 22	D	4 33	B	10 11	32	3½	3½	12 P.M. 30	E	10 11	B	15 49	SAG	7
310	6	M.	6 24	D	4 32	B	10 08	32	4¼	4½	12 59	E	11 P.M. 23	C	16 07	CAP	8
311	7	Tu.	6 25	D	4 31	A	10 06	32	5¼	5½	1 25	D	— —	–	16 25	CAP	9
312	8	W.	6 26	D	4 30	A	10 04	32	6¼	6½	1 48	D	12 A.M. 36	D	16 42	AQU	10
313	9	Th.	6 27	D	4 28	A	10 01	32	7	7½	2 12	C	1 50	D	17 00	PSC	11
314	10	Fr.	6 29	D	4 27	A	9 58	32	8	8½	2 37	B	3 07	E	17 16	PSC	12
315	11	Sa.	6 30	D	4 26	A	9 56	32	8¾	9¼	3 05	B	4 26	E	17 33	PSC	13
316	12	A	6 31	D	4 25	A	9 54	32	9½	10¼	3 40	B	5 49	E	17 49	ARI	14
317	13	M.	6 32	D	4 24	A	9 52	32	10½	11	4 23	A	7 13	E	18 05	ARI	15
318	14	Tu.	6 34	D	4 23	A	9 49	32	11¼	—	5 16	A	8 31	E	18 20	TAU	16
319	15	W.	6 35	D	4 23	A	9 48	31	12	12¼	6 21	A	9 40	E	18 36	TAU	17
320	16	Th.	6 36	D	4 22	A	9 46	31	1	1	7 31	B	10 36	E	18 51	GEM	18
321	17	Fr.	6 37	D	4 21	A	9 44	31	1¾	2	8 44	B	11 19	E	19 05	GEM	19
322	18	Sa.	6 38	D	4 20	A	9 42	31	2¾	3	9 55	B	11 A.M. 52	E	19 19	CAN	20
323	19	A	6 40	D	4 19	A	9 39	31	3¾	4	11 P.M. 02	C	12 P.M. 19	D	19 33	CAN	21
324	20	M.	6 41	D	4 19	A	9 38	30	4¾	5	— —	–	12 41	D	19 47	LEO	22
325	21	Tu.	6 42	D	4 18	A	9 36	30	5¾	6	12 A.M. 06	C	1 00	D	20 01	LEO	23
326	22	W.	6 43	D	4 17	A	9 34	30	6¾	7	1 08	D	1 19	C	20 14	VIR	24
327	23	Th.	6 45	D	4 17	A	9 32	30	7½	8	2 10	D	1 38	B	20 26	VIR	25
328	24	Fr.	6 46	D	4 16	A	9 30	29	8¼	8¾	3 11	E	1 58	B	20 38	VIR	26
329	25	Sa.	6 47	D	4 15	A	9 28	29	9	9½	4 13	E	2 22	B	20 50	VIR	27
330	26	A	6 48	E	4 15	A	9 27	29	9½	10¼	5 16	E	2 49	A	21 01	LIB	28
331	27	M.	6 49	E	4 14	A	9 25	28	10¼	10¾	6 19	E	3 22	A	21 12	LIB	29
332	28	Tu.	6 50	E	4 14	A	9 24	28	10¾	11½	7 22	E	4 02	A	21 23	SCO	0
333	29	W.	6 51	E	4 14	A	9 23	28	11½	—	8 19	E	4 52	A	21 33	OPH	1
334	30	Th.	6 52	E	4 13	A	9 21	27	12	12	9 A.M. 11	E	5 P.M. 49	A	21s.43	SAG	2

Ya-honk! he says, and sounds it down to me like an invitation;
The pert may suppose it meaningless, but I listen closer,
I find its purpose and place up there toward the November sky.
— *Walt Whitman*

Farmer's Calendar

In the old days householders in my neighborhood would cut evergreen boughs in the late fall and pile them around the foundations of their houses to protect their cellars and floors from the winter wind. The pine, spruce, and hemlock branches blocked the wind until the snow began to fall. Then, when the snow arrived, they held it, affording more protection. "House banking," the pine boughs stacked against the foundation were called.

One or two houses around here still use evergreen branches for banking, but most of us have turned to plastic sheeting. Each year around this time my house, like hundreds of others, gets its feet wrapped like those of a Chinese princess. Some people cover the outer walls of their houses with heavy plastic film clear to the top of the first-floor windows. More often you just run a band of plastic around the foundation from the ground to a couple of feet up the wall and make it fast.

I take a fat roll of plastic and anchor it at a corner of the house with a rock. Then I unroll it along the wall and around the next corner. I staple the top edge of the sheet to the clapboards near the bottom of the wall and nail battens made of sections of wood lath over the staples to secure the plastic to the house. Then I weight the lower edge of the sheet on the ground with boards and rocks. I work quickly. By the time I've gone around the house with my roll of plastic there are something like 110 feet of sheet hanging out. One year a big north wind came over the field before I had my banking sheet battened down. One end of the sheet was fast, and I held the other. The sheet filled like a spinnaker and pulled me into the air. I was carried by the wind — you can believe this or not — clear to Palm Beach, where I found that few people banked their houses against the winter wind at all and those who did used hundred-dollar bills.

D.M.	D.W.	Dates, Feasts, Fasts, Aspects, Tide Heights	Weather ↓
1	W.	**All Saints** • Great Lisbon earthquake, 1755 • Tides {8.9 {10.0 • *Danks*
2	Th.	**All Souls** • ☾ runs low • Marie Antoinette born, 1755 • {8.7 {9.8 • *for*
3	Fr.	♂♂☾ • ♂♭☾ • ♂♀☿ • Tides {8.5 {9.6 • *nothing.*
4	Sa.	10' floodwater, Montpelier, Vt., 1927 • Tides {8.3 {9.5 • *Mellow*
5	A	**25th ☉. af. ℙ.** • Gunpowder Plot, 1605 • *glow;*
6	M.	**St. Leonard** • ☾at ☊ • 98 m.p.h. winds, Block Island, R.I., 1953 *Hello,*
7	Tu.	♂♳☉ • ♂♀☿ • First cartoon of Republican elephant, 1874 • *snow!*
8	W.	♀ Gr. Elong. East (47°) • Hitler jailed after Beer Hall Putsch, Munich, 1923 • *Ground*
9	Th.	☾ on Eq. • "Freshwater Fury" storm sank 8 ore-carriers, Great Lakes, 1913 • *hardens,*
10	Fr.	☿ sup. ♂ • Saybrook, first English town in Conn., founded, 1635 • {10.8 {10.3 *cover*
11	Sa.	**Veterans Day • St. Martin** • Indian Summer begins. • *your*
12	A	**26th ☉. af. ℙ.** • ☾at peri. • ♂♭♅ • *gardens.*
13	M.	Full Beaver ○ • Karen Silkwood died in auto crash, 1974 • Tides {12.3 {10.7 • *Just*
14	Tu.	Kilauea erupted, Hawaii Is., 1959 • Year's highest A.M. tide: 12.4' • *flurries,*
15	W.	☾ runs high • ♂♀♅ • ♂♀♄ • Tides {10.5 {12.1 • *but*
16	Th.	♂♃☾ • Oklahoma statehood, 1907 • Tides {10.2 {11.7 • *get*
17	Fr.	**St. Hugh of Lincoln** • Tornado hit Washington, D.C., 1927 • *out*
18	Sa.	*Nothing makes a man or woman look so saintly as seasickness.* • Tides {9.4 {10.4 • *your*
19	A	**27th ☉. af. ℙ.** • ☾at ☊ • *furries!*
20	M.	**St. Edmund** • Indian Summer ends. • Tides {8.9 {9.3 *Awful*
21	Tu.	Prune grapevines now. • Cigar lighter patented, 1871 • Tides {8.9 {9.0 *nice*
22	W.	**St. Cecilia** • ☾ on Eq. • First flakes of 56" snow, Randolph, N.H., 1943 • *for*
23	Th.	**Thanksgiving Day • St. Clement** • Tides {9.3 {8.8 • *the*
24	Fr.	☾ at apo. • Scott Joplin born, 1868 • Tides {9.5 {8.8 • *wild*
25	Sa.	**St. Catherine** • 28" snowfall, Pittsburgh, Penn., 1950 • {9.7 {8.8 *rice.*
26	A	**28th ☉. af. ℙ.** • ♂♂☾ • Tides {9.9 {8.8 • *Only a*
27	M.	*If there be ice in November that will bear a duck, There'll be nothing thereafter but sleet and muck.* • *Viking*
28	Tu.	New ● • "Hopalong Cassidy" made NBC-TV debut, 1948 • {10.1 {8.8 *would*
29	W.	*The first 40 years of life give us the text; the next 30 supply the commentary.* • *go out*
30	Th.	**St. Andrew** • ☾ runs low • ♂♂☾ • ♂♀☾ *hiking.*

*Fish, to taste right, must swim three times —
in water, in butter, and in wine.*

DECEMBER, THE TWELFTH MONTH

The Eastern Hemisphere sees Mars hide a star in the dawn sky on the 5th. With a telescope, you might pick out the Andromeda Nebula, our closest neighbor galaxy. On the 14th, Venus reaches greatest brilliancy, and even Jupiter is not so bright, rising around sunset. Saturn is a dim few degrees south of Mercury on the 16th. Viewing of the Geminid meteors is hampered by a nearly full Moon on December 13-14. At mid evening, Cygnus's Northern Cross stands upright and is bathed with the Milky Way in the northwest. The winter solstice arrives on the 21st at 4:22 P.M. EST. On the 23rd, Mercury reaches greatest elongation and might be seen low in the west after sunset. The new Moon on the 27th runs low. Jupiter is in opposition, Venus is stationary, and there is a conjunction of Uranus with the Sun. Note the many-colored darting rays of Sirius when it is low.

ASTRONOMICAL CALCULATIONS

☽	First Quarter	5th day	20th hour	26th min.
○	Full Moon	12th day	11th hour	31st min.
☾	Last Quarter	19th day	18th hour	55th min.
●	New Moon	27th day	22nd hour	21st min.

FOR POINTS OUTSIDE BOSTON SEE KEY LETTER CORRECTIONS — PAGES 80-84

Day of Year	Day of Month	Day of Week	☉ Rises h. m.	Key	☉ Sets h. m.	Key	Length of Days h. m.	Sun Fast m.	Full Sea Boston A.M.	Full Sea Boston P.M.	☽ Rises h. m.	Key	☽ Sets h. m.	Key	Declination of sun ° '	☽ Place	☽ Age
335	1	Fr.	6 54	E	4 13	A	9 19	27	$12\frac{3}{4}$	$12\frac{3}{4}$	9 A.M. 55	E	6 P.M. 54	B	21s.52	SAG	3
336	2	Sa.	6 55	E	4 13	A	9 18	27	$1\frac{1}{2}$	$1\frac{1}{2}$	10 31	E	8 03	B	22 01	CAP	4
337	3	**A**	6 56	E	4 12	A	9 16	26	$2\frac{1}{4}$	$2\frac{1}{4}$	11 02	E	9 13	C	22 09	CAP	5
338	4	M.	6 57	E	4 12	A	9 15	26	3	$3\frac{1}{4}$	11 28	D	10 24	C	22 17	CAP	6
339	5	Tu.	6 58	E	4 12	A	9 14	25	4	4	11 A.M. 51	D	11 P.M. 35	D	22 25	AQU	7
340	6	W.	6 59	E	4 12	A	9 13	25	$4\frac{3}{4}$	5	12 P.M. 14	C	— —	–	22 32	PSC	8
341	7	Th.	7 00	E	4 12	A	9 12	25	$5\frac{3}{4}$	6	12 37	C	12 A.M. 47	D	22 39	PSC	9
342	8	Fr.	7 01	E	4 12	A	9 11	24	$6\frac{1}{2}$	7	1 03	B	2 03	E	22 46	PSC	10
343	9	Sa.	7 01	E	4 12	A	9 11	24	$7\frac{1}{2}$	8	1 33	B	3 21	E	22 52	PSC	11
344	10	**A**	7 02	E	4 12	A	9 10	23	$8\frac{1}{4}$	9	2 10	B	4 42	E	22 57	ARI	12
345	11	M.	7 03	E	4 12	A	9 09	23	$9\frac{1}{4}$	10	2 58	A	6 02	E	23 02	TAU	13
346	12	Tu.	7 04	E	4 12	A	9 08	22	$10\frac{1}{4}$	11	3 57	A	7 16	E	23 06	TAU	14
347	13	W.	7 05	E	4 12	A	9 07	22	11	$11\frac{3}{4}$	5 06	A	8 19	E	23 10	AUR	15
348	14	Th.	7 06	E	4 12	A	9 06	21	—	12	6 21	B	9 09	E	23 14	GEM	16
349	15	Fr.	7 06	E	4 12	A	9 06	21	$12\frac{1}{2}$	$12\frac{3}{4}$	7 34	B	9 48	E	23 17	CAN	17
350	16	Sa.	7 07	E	4 13	A	9 06	20	$1\frac{1}{2}$	$1\frac{1}{2}$	8 45	C	10 17	E	23 20	CAN	18
351	17	**A**	7 08	E	4 13	A	9 05	20	$2\frac{1}{4}$	$2\frac{1}{2}$	9 53	C	10 42	D	23 22	LEO	19
352	18	M.	7 08	E	4 13	A	9 05	19	$3\frac{1}{4}$	$3\frac{1}{2}$	10 57	D	11 04	D	23 24	LEO	20
353	19	Tu.	7 09	E	4 14	A	9 05	19	4	$4\frac{1}{4}$	11 P.M. 59	D	11 23	C	23 25	LEO	21
354	20	W.	7 09	E	4 14	A	9 05	18	5	$5\frac{1}{4}$	— —	–	11 A.M. 42	C	23 26	VIR	22
355	21	Th.	7 10	E	4 15	A	9 05	18	$5\frac{3}{4}$	$6\frac{1}{4}$	1 A.M. 01	E	12 P.M. 02	B	23 26	VIR	23
356	22	Fr.	7 10	E	4 15	A	9 05	17	$6\frac{3}{4}$	$7\frac{1}{4}$	2 02	E	12 24	B	23 26	VIR	24
357	23	Sa.	7 11	E	4 16	A	9 05	17	$7\frac{1}{2}$	8	3 05	E	12 49	B	23 26	VIR	25
358	24	**A**	7 11	E	4 16	A	9 05	16	$8\frac{1}{4}$	9	4 08	E	1 20	A	23 24	LIB	26
359	25	M.	7 12	E	4 17	A	9 05	16	9	$9\frac{3}{4}$	5 12	E	1 59	A	23 23	SCO	27
360	26	Tu.	7 12	E	4 18	A	9 06	15	$9\frac{3}{4}$	$10\frac{1}{2}$	6 11	E	2 45	A	23 20	SCO	28
361	27	W.	7 12	E	4 18	A	9 06	15	$10\frac{1}{2}$	11	7 06	E	3 41	A	23 18	SAG	0
362	28	Th.	7 13	E	4 19	A	9 06	14	11	$11\frac{3}{4}$	7 53	E	4 44	B	23 15	SAG	1
363	29	Fr.	7 13	E	4 20	A	9 07	14	$11\frac{3}{4}$	—	8 32	E	5 53	B	23 12	SAG	2
364	30	Sa.	7 13	E	4 20	A	9 07	13	$12\frac{1}{2}$	$12\frac{1}{2}$	9 04	E	7 04	B	23 08	CAP	3
365	31	**A**	7 13	E	4 21	A	9 08	13	1	$1\frac{1}{4}$	9 A.M. 32	D	8 P.M. 16	C	23s.04	CAP	4

Unwarmed by any sunset light
The gray day darkened into night,
A night made hoary with the swarm
And whirl-dance of the blinding storm . . .
— John Greenleaf Whittier

D.M.	D.W.	Dates, Feasts, Fasts, Aspects, Tide Heights	Weather ↓
1	Fr.	☌♄☾ • Father Flanagan founded Boys Town, Nebraska, 1917 • {8.7 10.0 •	North
2	Sa.	*Marriage has many pains, but celibacy has no pleasures.* •	buried,
3	A	**1st Sun. in Advent** • ☾ at ☊ • {8.7 9.8	south
4	M.	83 m.p.h. winds, Atlantic City, N.J., 1898 • Tides {8.8 9.7 •	varied.
5	Tu.	*Most women are not so young as they are painted.* •	Bears
6	W.	**St. Nicholas** • ☾ on Eq. • Ira Gershwin born, 1896 • {9.4 9.5 •	nap
7	Th.	Gas refrigerator patented, 1926 • Johnny Bench born, 1947 • Tides {9.9 9.5 •	in
8	Fr.	**Concept. of V.M.** • John Lennon killed, 1980 • {10.4 9.6 •	cold
9	Sa.	14′ snow drifts, Vevay, Ind., 1917 • Kirk Douglas born, 1918 • {11.0 9.7 •	snap.
10	A	**2nd S. in Adv.** • ☌☿⛢ • ☾ at peri. •	This
11	M.	20° F., San Francisco, 1932 • Tides {11.8 10.0 •	is
12	Tu.	Full Cold ○ • Kenya declared independence, 1963 • {12.0 10.0 •	surprising;
13	W.	**St. Lucy** • ☾ runs high • ☌♃☾ • Tides {12.0 10.0 •	the
14	Th.	♀ at Greatest Brilliancy • ☌☿♆ •	mercury's
15	Fr.	*No man is rich enough to buy back his past.* • {9.9 11.4 •	rising!
16	Sa.	☾ at ☋ • ☌☿♄ • Tides {9.7 10.9 •	Get
17	A	**3rd S. in Adv.** • Tides {9.5 10.3 •	hopping
18	M.	*There is more felicity on the far side of baldness than young men can imagine.* •	on
19	Tu.	☾ on Eq. • Climbers reached summit of Vinson Massif, Antarctica, 1966 •	your
20	W.	Ember Day • Calm seas. • Tides {9.0 8.6 •	shopping;
21	Th.	**St. Thomas** • Winter Solstice • Tides {9.0 8.3 •	before
22	Fr.	☾ at apo. • Ember Day • First catamaran launched, 1662 • {9.1 8.2 •	too
23	Sa.	**Chanukah** • ☿ Gr. Elong. East (20°) • Ember Day •	long,
24	A	**4th S. in Adv.** • Tides {9.4 8.2 •	a foot
25	M.	**Christmas Day** • ☌⛢☾ • Tides {9.6 8.3 •	is
26	Tu.	**St. Stephen** • A green Christmas makes a fat churchyard. •	dropping!
27	W.	**St. John** • ☾ runs low • ☌⛢☉ • ♃☍ • ♀ stat. • New ●	
28	Th.	**Holy Innocents** • Iowa joined Union, 1846 • {10.2 8.8 •	Auld
29	Fr.	☌☿☾ • Beware the Pogonip. • 14″ snow, Albuquerque, New Mexico, 1958 •	lang
30	Sa.	☌♀☾ • ☿ stat. • *End the old year square with every man.* •	syne, '89!
31	A	**1st S. af. Christmas** • **St. Sylvester** • ☾ at ☊ •	

Farmer's Calendar

As a democratic people, Americans are supposed to be mostly indifferent to manners and likewise to all other considerations of what used to be called "good breeding." If that's true, they miss a lot of fun, not because manners are really important, but because to ignore them is to lack a whole system for describing the world and making distinctions between things — and that not only in matters of etiquette, but even in the field of weather.

Consider snowstorms. Clearly, our vocabulary for describing them is pretty poor. There are nor'easters and Canadians, dusters and ten-inchers. If we introduce the idea of *snowstorm etiquette*, we immediately acquire far richer, more informative categories.

As with the etiquette of behavior — that is, real manners — so good breeding in winter storms is almost less a matter of what is said and done than it is a matter of timing, setting, inflection, style. A well-bred storm occurs at night — a week night, please, not a Friday or a Saturday night. A well-bred snowstorm knows what it is: a *snow* storm. Therefore it eschews ice, sleet, and rain. A well-mannered storm does not knock out the electric power, any more than a gentleman gets drunk and hurls the hors d'oeuvres against the drawing-room wall. A well-mannered storm knows what is enough; it does not make the loutish error of supposing that if six inches of snow is good, eighteen is three times better. Above all, a well-bred storm, like a well-bred gentleman or lady, knows when to take its leave. It does not linger awkwardly an instant over the time it is wanted. It slips fastidiously away in plenty of time for shoveling, plowing, and road clearing to take place. In weather as in human relations, manners are a way of making life easy, sensible, and especially, predictable. Boreas, take heed.

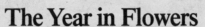

The Year in Flowers

According to a once-popular old poem, it begins with snowdrops on February 2 and ends with love-in-a-mist on November 25. by Andrew E. Rothovius

□ ABOUT 250 YEARS AGO ENGLISH PEriodicals from time to time printed an anonymous poem variously titled "A Calendar of English Flowers," "A Garland of the Seasons," and other similar names. The poem can sometimes be found pasted into diaries and account books of the period. The poem can hardly be older than 1600 or later than the 1640s, these limits being set by datable references within its text and its use of Catholic feast days, whose observance was forbidden under Cromwell's Puritan Commonwealth. For today's flower lovers, the poem still retains its fascination as a floral almanac, and some find it a rewarding project to plan a section of their garden around it.

Although a few of the flowers named do not flourish outside of the moist English climate (at least during our severe northern winters), they are well suited for milder regions of the United States and may even survive and bloom with the aid of shelters in colder areas.

The flower year, according to the poem, commences on **February 2,** the Feast of the Purification of Mary that is observed with the lighting of candles (hence Candlemas Day), but simply Groundhog Day in our prosaic Yankee usage. On that day in old England,

The Snowdrop in purest white array
First rears her head on Candlemas Day;
While the Crocus hastens to the shrine
Of Primrose love on St. Valentine.

Snowdrop bulbs are usually sold under the Latin name of Galanthus or sometimes as "Fair Maids of February." Crocus needs no introduction, and even in New England during a mild winter they may be coaxed into bloom by Valentine's Day **(February 14).** The traditional primrose is early blooming, with clustered flowers of bright colors. All three flowers are traditionally said to be short-lived and symbolic of the transitoriness of earthly things. "Primrose love" is that which is merely flirtatious and impermanent.

Then comes the Daffodil, beside
Our Lady's Smock at Lady-tide.

Daffodils are known to all; but few today are acquainted with the little white flowers of the meadow cress (cardamine) that usually blossomed in the English marshes at the time of the angel's annunciation to Mary, **March 25,** or Lady Day. Hanging in clusters from slender stems, they reminded people of women's smocks drying on the wash line, and the next step was to associate them with that garment of Our Lady.

About St. George, when blue is worn
The blue Harebells the fields adorn;
Against the day of Holy Cross,
The Crowfoot gilds the flowery grass.

St. George's Day, **April 23,** the festival of England's dragon-slaying patron saint, has long been observed with the wearing of blue attire, so it was natural to relate it to the scilla or wild hyacinth with its bell-like blue flowers, usually abundant at that time, and commonly known as harebell.

The festival of the Invention (finding) of the Cross by St. Helena falls on **May 3,** and by that time, both here and in England the buttercup, known as crowfoot, gilds lawns and meadows.

When St. Barnaby bright smiles night and day,
Poor Ragged Robin blossoms in the hay;
The Scarlet Lychnis, the garden's pride,
Flames at St. John the Baptist's tide.

Before England (and its New World colonies) adopted the Gregorian reform of the calendar in 1752, the summer solstice — the year's longest day — coincided with the feast of St. Barnabas on **June 11.** At this time the brightly flowered lychnises become the centers of floral attraction, along with Ragged Robin (a common hayfield flower), continuing through the Feast of St. John the Baptist on **June 24.**

From Visitation to St. Swithin's showers,
The Lily white reigns Queen of Flowers;
And Poppies a sanguine mantle spread
For the blood of the dragon St. Margaret shed.

The visit of the pregnant Virgin Mary to her cousin Elizabeth was made an official annual feast for **July 2** in 1590; two weeks from that date to the feast of St. Swithin **(July 15)** is usually the blossoming peak of the white Madonna lily. Scarlet poppies make a showy display around the **July 20** feast day of St. Margaret, a dragon slayer in one version of her legend.

Then under the wanton Rose again
That blushes for penitent Magdalen
Till Lammas Day, called August's Wheel,
When the long corn stinks of camomile.

Roses may still be found blooming in late July, when they are linked with the feast on **July 22** of St. Mary Magdalene, the penitent sinner for love. **August 1,** Lammas (Loaf-Mass) Day, when the first loaves from the new wheat were offered in church, also finds aromatic camomile (Anthemis in its showier modern forms) flowering amid the uncut wheat ("corn" in England).

When Mary left us here below
The Virgin's Bower is full in blow;
And yet anon, the full Sunflower blew
And became a star for St. Bartholomew.

Clematis is now a large-petaled, early blooming vine, but its wild form is still quite similar to what the English garden of 1600 knew as "Virgin's Bower," which blossomed ("blew") around the time of Mary's Assumption into Heaven on **August 15,** followed quickly by the still familiar sunflower that usually peaks around the **August 24** feast of St. Bartholomew.

The Passion Flower long has blowed
To betoken us signs of the Holy Rood

Discovered by early Catholic missionaries in South America in the 16th century and soon popular in Europe, the showy Passion Flower was seen as a symbol for the Crucifixion. By the time of the **September 14** festival of the Holy Cross (or Rood in Old English), its peak of bloom had passed.

The Michaelmas Daisy, among dead weeds,
Blooms for St. Michael's valorous deeds
And seems the last of flowers that stood
Till the feast of St. Simon and St. Jude;
Save Mushrooms, and the Fungus race
That grow till All-Hallow Tide takes place.

Michaelmas Daisy, today familiar as one of several late-blooming asters, was originally a small-flowered wild white aster that bloomed about the date of Michaelmas (**September 29**) and continued to the **October 28** feast of Simon and Jude. Mushrooms and fungi are typical growths of wet Octobers everywhere, at least to the feast of All Saints (All Hallows) on **November 1.**

Soon the evergreen Laurel alone is green
When Catherine crowns all learned men,
The Ivy and Holly Berries are seen
And Yule Log and Wassail come
  around again.

The Christmas greens and berries of both Old and New England are known to everyone; but few now would be able to guess the floral reference to St. Catherine's feast on **November 25,** when schools and colleges in England once honored their most learned scholars by crowning them with a plaited coronet made from the dried pods of love-in-a-mist (often seen in old-fashioned gardens today).

And so the flower almanac of the year's round comes to its end — and to its new beginning, for Candlemas Day (**February 2**) is also the day for getting rid of Christmas greens. □ □

WIND/BAROMETER TABLE

Barometer (Reduced to Sea Level)	Wind Direction	Character of Weather Indicated
30.00 to 30.20, and steady	westerly	Fair, with slight changes in temperature, for one to two days.
30.00 to 30.20, and rising rapidly	westerly	Fair, followed within two days by warmer and rain.
30.00 to 30.20, and falling rapidly	south to east	Warmer, and rain within 24 hours.
30.20, or above, and falling rapidly	south to east	Warmer, and rain within 36 hours.
30.20, or above, and falling rapidly	west to north	Cold and clear, quickly followed by warmer and rain.
30.20, or above, and steady	variable	No early change.
30.00, or below, and falling slowly	south to east	Rain within 18 hours that will continue a day or two.
30.00, or below, and falling rapidly	southeast to northeast	Rain, with high wind, followed within two days by clearing, colder.
30.00, or below, and rising	south to west	Clearing and colder within 12 hours.
29.80, or below, and falling rapidly	southeast to northeast	Severe storm of wind and rain imminent. In winter, snow or cold wave within 24 hours.
29.80, or below, and falling rapidly	east to north	Severe northeast gales and heavy rain or snow, followed in winter by cold wave.
29.80, or below, and rising rapidly	going to west	Clearing and colder.

Note: A barometer should be adjusted to show equivalent sea-level pressure for the altitude at which it is to be used. A change of 100 feet in elevation will cause a decrease of 1/10th inch in the reading.

TIME CORRECTION TABLES

The times of sunrise, sunset, moonrise, moonset, and the rising and setting of the planets are given for Boston only on pages 48-74 and 36-37. Use the Key Letter shown there and this table to find the number of minutes that should be added to or subtracted from Boston time to give the correct time of your city. The answer will not be as precise as that for Boston, but will be within approxi- mately 5 minutes. If your city is not listed, find the city closest to you in both latitude and longitude and use those figures. Canadi- an cities appear at the end of the list. For a more complete explanation see pages 28-30.

Time Zone Code: -1 — Atlantic Std.; 0 — Eastern Std.; 1 — Central Std.; 2 — Moun- tain Std., 3 — Pacific Std.; 4 — Alaska Std.; 5 — Hawaii-Aleutian Std.

City	North Latitude ° '		West Longitude ° '		Time Zone Code	Key Letters				
						A min.	B min.	C min.	D min.	E min.
Aberdeen, SD	45	28	98	29	1	+37	+44	+49	+54	+59
Akron, OH	41	5	81	31	0	+46	+43	+41	+39	+37
Albany, NY	42	39	73	45	0	+ 9	+10	+10	+11	+11
Albert Lea, MN	43	39	93	22	1	+24	+26	+28	+31	+33
Albuquerque, NM	35	5	106	39	2	+45	+32	+22	+11	+ 2
Alexandria, LA	31	18	92	27	1	+58	+40	+26	+ 9	− 3
Allentown-Bethlehem, PA	40	3	75	28	0	+25	+20	+17	+13	+10
Amarillo, TX	35	12	101	50	1	+85	+73	+63	+52	+43
Anchorage, AK	61	10	149	59	4	−46	+27	+71	+122	+171
Ardmore, OK	34	10	97	8	1	+69	+55	+44	+32	+22
Asheville, NC	35	36	82	33	0	+67	+55	+46	+35	+27
Atlanta, GA	33	45	84	24	0	+79	+65	+53	+40	+30
Atlantic City, NJ	39	22	74	26	0	+23	+17	+13	+ 8	+ 4
Augusta, GA	33	28	81	58	0	+70	+55	+44	+30	+19
Augusta, ME	44	19	69	46	0	−12	− 8	− 5	− 1	0
Austin, TX	30	16	97	45	1	+82	+62	+47	+29	+15
Bakersfield, CA	35	23	119	1	3	+33	+21	+12	+ 1	− 7
Baltimore, MD	39	17	76	37	0	+32	+26	+22	+17	+13
Bangor, ME	44	48	68	46	0	−18	−13	− 9	− 5	− 1
Barstow, CA	34	54	117	1	3	+27	+14	+ 4	− 7	−16
Baton Rouge, LA	30	27	91	11	1	+55	+36	+21	+ 3	−10
Beaumont, TX	30	5	94	6	1	+67	+48	+32	+14	0
Bellingham, WA	48	45	122	29	3	0	+13	+24	+37	+47
Bemidji, MN	47	28	94	53	1	+14	+26	+34	+44	+52
Berlin, NH	44	28	71	11	0	− 7	− 3	0	+ 3	+ 7
Billings, MT	45	47	108	30	2	+16	+23	+29	+35	+40
Biloxi, MS	30	24	88	53	1	+46	+27	+11	− 5	−19
Binghamton, NY	42	6	75	55	0	+20	+19	+19	+18	+18
Birmingham, AL	33	31	86	49	1	+30	+15	+ 3	−10	−20
Bismarck, ND	46	48	100	47	1	+41	+50	+58	+66	+73
Boise, ID	43	37	116	12	2	+55	+58	+60	+62	+64
Brattleboro, VT	42	51	72	34	0	+ 4	+ 5	+ 5	+ 6	+ 7
Bridgeport, CT	41	11	73	11	0	+12	+10	+ 8	+ 6	+ 4
Brockton, MA	42	5	71	1	0	0	0	0	0	− 1
Buffalo, NY	42	53	78	52	0	+29	+30	+30	+31	+32
Burlington, VT	44	29	73	13	0	0	+ 4	+ 8	+12	+15
Butte, MT	46	1	112	32	2	+31	+39	+45	+52	+57
Cairo, IL	37	0	89	11	1	+29	+20	+12	+ 4	− 2
Camden, NJ	39	57	75	7	0	+24	+19	+16	+12	+ 9
Canton, OH	40	48	81	23	0	+46	+43	+41	+38	+36
Cape May, NJ	38	56	74	56	0	+26	+20	+15	+ 9	+ 5
Carson City-Reno, NV	39	10	119	46	3	+25	+19	+14	+ 9	+ 5
Casper, WY	42	51	106	19	2	+19	+19	+20	+21	+22
Chadron, NE	42	50	103	0	2	+ 5	+ 6	+ 7	+ 8	+ 9
Charleston, SC	32	47	79	56	0	+64	+48	+36	+21	+10
Charleston, WV	38	21	81	38	0	+55	+48	+42	+35	+30
Charlotte, NC	35	14	80	51	0	+61	+49	+39	+28	+19
Charlottesville, VA	38	2	78	30	0	+43	+35	+29	+22	+17
Chattanooga, TN	35	3	85	19	0	+79	+67	+57	+45	+36
Cheboygan, MI	45	39	84	29	0	+40	+47	+53	+59	+64
Cheyenne, WY	41	8	104	49	2	+19	+16	+14	+12	+11

City	North Latitude °	'	West Longitude °	'	Time Zone Code	Key Letters A min.	B min.	C min.	D min.	E min.
Chicago-Oak Park, IL	41	52	87	38	1	+ 7	+ 6	+ 6	+ 5	+ 4
Cincinnati-Hamilton, OH	39	6	84	31	0	+64	+58	+53	+48	+44
Cleveland-Lakewood, OH	41	30	81	42	0	+45	+43	+42	+40	+39
Columbia, SC	34	0	81	2	0	+65	+51	+40	+27	+17
Columbus, OH	39	57	83	1	0	+55	+51	+47	+43	+40
Cordova, AK	60	33	145	45	4	−55	+13	+55	+103	+149
Corpus Christi, TX	27	48	97	24	1	+86	+64	+46	+25	+ 9
Craig, CO	40	31	107	33	2	+32	+28	+25	+22	+20
Dallas-Fort Worth, TX	32	47	96	48	1	+71	+55	+43	+28	+17
Danville, IL	40	8	87	37	1	+13	+ 9	+ 6	+ 2	0
Danville, VA	36	36	79	23	0	+51	+41	+33	+24	+17
Davenport, IA	41	32	90	35	1	+20	+19	+17	+16	+15
Dayton, OH	39	45	84	10	0	+61	+56	+52	+48	+44
Decatur, AL	34	36	86	59	1	+27	+14	+ 4	− 7	−17
Decatur, IL	39	51	88	57	1	+19	+15	+11	+ 7	+ 4
Denver-Boulder, CO	39	44	104	59	2	+24	+19	+15	+11	+ 7
Des Moines, IA	41	35	93	37	1	+32	+31	+30	+28	+27
Detroit-Dearborn, MI	42	20	83	3	0	+47	+47	+47	+47	+47
Dubuque, IA	42	30	90	41	1	+17	+18	+18	+18	+18
Duluth, MN	46	47	92	6	1	+ 6	+16	+23	+31	+38
Durham, NC	36	0	78	55	0	+51	+40	+31	+21	+13
Eastport, ME	44	54	67	0	0	−26	−20	−16	−11	− 8
Eau Claire, WI	44	49	91	30	1	+12	+17	+21	+25	+29
El Paso, TX	31	45	106	29	2	+53	+35	+22	+ 6	− 6
Elko, NV	40	50	115	46	3	+ 3	0	− 1	− 3	− 5
Ellsworth, ME	44	33	68	25	0	−18	−14	−10	− 6	− 3
Erie, PA	42	7	80	5	0	+36	+36	+35	+35	+35
Eugene, OR	44	3	123	6	3	+21	+24	+27	+30	+33
Fairbanks, AK	64	48	147	51	4	−127	+ 2	+61	+131	+205
Fall River- New Bedford, MA	41	42	71	9	0	+ 2	+ 1	0	0	− 1
Fargo, ND	46	53	96	47	1	+24	+34	+42	+50	+57
Flagstaff, AZ	35	12	111	39	2	+64	+52	+42	+31	+22
Flint, MI	43	1	83	41	0	+47	+49	+50	+51	+52
Fort Randall, AK	55	10	162	47	4	+62	+99	+124	+153	+179
Fort Scott, KS	37	50	94	42	1	+49	+41	+34	+27	+21
Fort Smith, AR	35	23	94	25	1	+55	+43	+33	+22	+14
Fort Wayne, IN	41	4	85	9	0	+60	+58	+56	+54	+52
Fort Yukon, AK	66	34	145	16	4	+30	−18	+50	+131	+227
Fresno, CA	36	44	119	47	3	+32	+22	+15	+ 6	0
Gallup, NM	35	32	108	45	2	+52	+40	+31	+20	+11
Galveston, TX	29	18	94	48	1	+72	+52	+35	+16	+ 1
Gary, IN	41	36	87	20	1	+ 7	+ 6	+ 4	+ 3	+ 2
Glasgow, MT	48	12	106	38	2	− 1	+11	+21	+32	+42
Grand Forks, ND	47	55	97	3	1	+21	+33	+43	+53	+62
Grand Island, NE	40	55	98	21	1	+53	+51	+49	+46	+44
Grand Junction, CO	39	4	108	33	2	+40	+34	+29	+24	+20
Great Falls, MT	47	30	111	17	2	+20	+31	+39	+49	+58
Green Bay, WI	44	31	88	0	1	0	+ 3	+ 7	+11	+14
Greensboro, NC	36	4	79	47	0	+54	+43	+35	+25	+17
Hagerstown, MD	39	39	77	43	0	+35	+30	+26	+22	+18
Harrisburg, PA	40	16	76	53	0	+30	+26	+23	+19	+16
Hartford-New Britain, CT	41	46	72	41	0	+ 8	+ 7	+ 6	+ 5	+ 4
Helena, MT	46	36	112	2	2	+27	+36	+43	+51	+57
Hilo, HI	19	44	155	5	5	+94	+62	+37	+ 7	−15
Honolulu, HI	21	18	157	52	5	+102	+72	+48	+19	− 1
Houston, TX	29	45	95	22	1	+73	+53	+37	+19	+ 5
Indianapolis, IN	39	46	86	10	0	+69	+64	+60	+56	+52
Ironwood, MI	46	27	90	9	1	0	+ 9	+15	+23	+29
Jackson, MI	42	15	84	24	0	+53	+53	+53	+52	+52
Jackson, MS	32	18	90	11	1	+46	+30	+17	+ 1	−10
Jacksonville, FL	30	20	81	40	0	+77	+58	+43	+25	+11
Jefferson City, MO	38	34	92	10	1	+36	+29	+24	+18	+13
Joplin, MO	37	6	94	30	1	+50	+41	+33	+25	+18
Juneau, AK	58	18	134	25	4	−76	−23	+10	+49	+86
Kalamazoo, MI	42	17	85	35	0	+58	+57	+57	+57	+57
Kanab, UT	37	3	112	32	2	+62	+53	+46	+37	+30

City	North Latitude °	'	West Longitude °	'	Time Zone Code	Key Letters A min.	B min.	C min.	D min.	E min.
Kansas City, MO	39	1	94	20	1	+44	+37	+33	+27	+23
Keene, NH	42	56	72	17	0	+ 2	+ 3	+ 4	+ 5	+ 6
Ketchikan, AK	55	21	131	39	4	−62	−25	0	+29	+56
Knoxville, TN	35	58	83	55	0	+71	+60	+51	+41	+33
Kodiak, AK	57	47	152	24	4	+ 0	+49	+82	+120	+154
LaCrosse, WI	43	48	91	15	1	+15	+18	+20	+22	+25
Lake Charles, LA	30	14	93	13	1	+64	+44	+29	+11	− 2
Lanai City, HI	20	50	156	55	5	+99	+69	+44	+15	− 6
Lancaster, PA	40	2	76	18	0	+28	+24	+20	+17	+13
Lansing, MI	42	44	84	33	0	+52	+53	+53	+54	+54
Las Cruces, NM	32	19	106	47	2	+53	+36	+23	+ 8	− 3
Las Vegas, NV	36	10	115	9	3	+16	+ 4	− 3	−13	−20
Lawrence-Lowell, MA	42	42	71	10	0	0	0	0	0	+ 1
Lewiston, ID	46	25	117	1	3	−12	− 3	+ 2	+10	+17
Lexington-Frankfort, KY ..	38	3	84	30	0	+67	+59	+53	+46	+41
Liberal, KS	37	3	100	55	1	+76	+66	+59	+51	+44
Lihue, HI	21	59	159	23	5	+107	+77	+54	+26	+ 5
Lincoln, NE	40	49	96	41	1	+47	+44	+42	+39	+37
Little Rock, AR	34	45	92	17	1	+48	+35	+25	+13	+ 4
Los Angeles incl. Pasadena and Santa Monica, CA ..	34	3	118	14	3	+34	+20	+ 9	− 3	−13
Louisville, KY	38	15	85	46	0	+72	+64	+58	+52	+46
Macon, GA	32	50	83	38	0	+79	+63	+50	+36	+24
Madison, WI	43	4	89	23	1	+10	+11	+12	+14	+15
Manchester-Concord, NH .	42	59	71	28	0	0	0	+ 1	+ 2	+ 3
McGrath, AK	62	58	155	36	4	−52	+42	+93	+152	+213
Memphis, TN	35	9	90	3	1	+38	+26	+16	+ 5	− 3
Meridian, MS	32	22	88	42	1	+40	+24	+11	− 4	−15
Miami, FL	25	47	80	12	0	+88	+57	+37	+14	− 3
Miles City, MT	46	25	105	51	2	+ 3	+11	+18	+26	+32
Milwaukee, WI	43	2	87	54	1	+ 4	+ 6	+ 7	+ 8	+ 9
Minneapolis-St. Paul, MN .	44	59	93	16	1	+18	+24	+28	+33	+37
Minot, ND	48	14	101	18	1	+36	+50	+59	+71	+81
Moab, UT	38	35	109	33	2	+46	+39	+33	+27	+22
Mobile, AL	30	42	88	3	1	+42	+23	+ 8	− 8	−22
Monroe, LA	32	30	92	7	1	+53	+37	+24	+ 9	− 1
Montgomery, AL	32	23	86	19	1	+31	+14	+ 1	−13	−25
Muncie, IN	40	12	85	23	0	+64	+60	+57	+53	+50
Murdo, SD	43	53	100	43	1	+52	+55	+58	+60	+63
Nashville, TN	36	10	86	47	1	+22	+11	+ 3	− 6	−14
New Haven, CT	41	18	72	56	0	+11	+ 8	+ 7	+ 5	+ 4
New London, CT	41	22	72	6	0	+ 7	+ 5	+ 4	+ 2	+ 1
New Orleans, LA	29	57	90	4	1	+52	+32	+16	− 1	−15
New York, NY	40	45	74	0	0	+17	+14	+11	+ 9	+ 6
Newark-Irvington- East Orange, NJ	40	44	74	10	0	+17	+14	+12	+ 9	+ 7
Nome, AK	64	30	165	25	4	−48	+74	+132	+199	+271
Norfolk, VA	36	51	76	17	0	+38	+28	+21	+12	+ 5
North Platte, NE	41	8	100	46	1	+62	+60	+58	+56	+54
Norwalk-Stamford, CT ...	41	7	73	22	0	+13	+10	+ 9	+ 7	+ 5
Oakley, KS	39	8	100	51	1	+69	+63	+59	+53	+49
Ogden, UT	41	13	111	58	2	+47	+45	+43	+41	+40
Ogdensburg, NY	44	42	75	30	0	+ 8	+13	+17	+21	+25
Oklahoma City, OK	35	28	97	31	1	+67	+55	+46	+35	+26
Omaha, NE	41	16	95	56	1	+43	+40	+39	+37	+36
Orlando, FL	28	32	81	22	0	+80	+59	+42	+22	+ 6
Ortonville, MN	45	19	96	27	1	+30	+36	+40	+46	+51
Oshkosh, WI	44	1	88	33	1	+ 3	+ 6	+ 9	+12	+15
Parkersburg, WV	39	16	81	34	0	+52	+46	+42	+36	+32
Paterson, NJ	40	55	74	10	0	+17	+14	+12	+ 9	+ 7
Pendleton, OR	45	40	118	47	3	− 1	+ 4	+10	+16	+21
Pensacola, FL	30	25	87	13	1	+39	+20	+ 5	−12	−26
Peoria, IL	40	42	89	36	1	+19	+16	+14	+11	+ 9
Philadelphia-Chester, PA ..	39	57	75	9	0	+24	+19	+16	+12	+ 9
Phoenix, AZ	33	27	112	4	2	+71	+56	+44	+30	+20
Pierre, SD	44	22	100	21	1	+49	+53	+56	+60	+63
Pittsburgh-McKeesport, PA	40	26	80	0	0	+42	+38	+35	+32	+29

City	North Latitude °	'	West Longitude °	'	Time Zone Code	Key Letters A min.	B min.	C min.	D min.	E min.
Pittsfield, MA	42	27	73	15	0	+ 8	+ 8	+ 8	+ 8	+ 8
Pocatello, ID	42	52	112	27	2	+43	+44	+45	+46	+46
Poplar Bluff, MO	36	46	90	24	1	+35	+25	+17	+ 8	+ 1
Portland, ME	43	40	70	15	0	− 8	− 5	− 3	− 1	0
Portland, OR	45	31	122	41	3	+14	+20	+25	+31	+36
Portsmouth, NH	43	5	70	45	0	− 4	− 2	− 1	0	0
Presque Isle, ME	46	41	68	1	0	−29	−19	−12	− 4	+ 2
Providence, RI	41	50	71	25	0	+ 3	+ 2	+ 1	0	0
Pueblo, CO	38	16	104	37	2	+27	+20	+14	+ 7	+ 2
Raleigh, NC	35	47	78	38	0	+51	+39	+30	+20	+12
Rapid City, SD	44	5	103	14	2	+ 2	+ 5	+ 8	+11	+13
Reading, PA	40	20	75	56	0	+26	+22	+19	+16	+13
Redding, CA	40	35	122	24	3	+31	+27	+25	+22	+19
Richmond, VA	37	32	77	26	0	+41	+32	+25	+17	+11
Roanoke, VA	37	16	79	57	0	+51	+42	+35	+27	+21
Roswell, NM	33	24	104	32	2	+41	+26	+14	0	−10
Rutland, VT	43	37	72	58	0	+ 2	+ 5	+ 7	+ 9	+11
Sacramento, CA	38	35	121	30	3	+34	+27	+21	+15	+10
Salem, OR	44	57	123	1	3	+17	+23	+27	+31	+35
Salina, KS	38	50	97	37	1	+57	+51	+46	+40	+35
Salisbury, MD	38	22	75	36	0	+31	+23	+18	+11	+ 6
Salt Lake City, UT	40	45	111	53	2	+48	+45	+43	+40	+38
San Antonio, TX	29	25	98	30	1	+87	+66	+50	+31	+16
San Diego, CA	32	43	117	9	3	+33	+17	+ 4	− 9	−21
San Francisco incl. Oakland and San Jose, CA	37	47	122	25	3	+40	+31	+25	+18	+12
Santa Fe, NM	35	41	105	56	2	+40	+28	+19	+ 9	0
Savannah, GA	32	5	81	6	0	+70	+54	+40	+25	+13
Scranton-Wilkes Barre, PA.	41	25	75	40	0	+21	+19	+18	+16	+15
Seattle-Tacoma-Olympia, WA	47	37	122	20	3	+ 3	+15	+24	+34	+42
Sheridan, WY	44	48	106	58	2	+14	+19	+23	+27	+31
Shreveport, LA	32	31	93	45	1	+60	+44	+31	+16	+ 4
Sioux Falls, SD	43	33	96	44	1	+38	+40	+42	+44	+46
South Bend, IN	41	41	86	15	0	+62	+61	+60	+59	+58
Spartanburg, SC	34	56	81	57	0	+66	+53	+43	+32	+23
Spokane, WA	47	40	117	24	3	−16	− 4	+ 4	+14	+23
Springfield, IL	39	48	89	39	1	+22	+18	+14	+10	+ 6
Springfield-Holyoke, MA	42	6	72	36	0	+ 6	+ 6	+ 6	+ 5	+ 5
Springfield, MO	37	13	93	18	1	+45	+36	+29	+20	+14
St. Johnsbury, VT	44	25	72	1	0	− 4	0	+ 3	+ 7	+10
St. Joseph, MO	39	46	94	50	1	+43	+38	+35	+30	+27
St. Louis, MO	38	37	90	12	1	+28	+21	+16	+10	+ 5
St. Petersburg, FL	27	46	82	39	0	+87	+65	+47	+26	+10
Syracuse, NY	43	3	76	9	0	+17	+19	+20	+21	+22
Tallahassee, FL	30	27	84	17	0	+87	+68	+53	+35	+22
Tampa, FL	27	57	82	27	0	+86	+64	+46	+25	+ 9
Terre Haute, IN	39	28	87	24	0	+74	+69	+65	+60	+56
Texarkana, AR	33	26	94	3	1	+59	+44	+32	+18	8
Toledo, OH	41	39	83	33	0	+52	+50	+49	+48	+47
Topeka, KS	39	3	95	40	1	+49	+43	+38	+32	+28
Traverse City, MI	44	46	85	38	0	+49	+54	+57	+62	+65
Trenton, NJ	40	13	74	46	0	+21	+17	+14	+11	+ 8
Trinidad, CO	37	10	104	31	2	+30	+21	+13	+ 5	0
Tucson, AZ	32	13	110	58	2	+70	+53	+40	+24	+12
Tulsa, OK	36	9	95	60	1	+59	+48	+40	+30	+22
Tupelo, MS	34	16	88	34	1	+35	+21	+10	− 2	−11
Vernal, UT	40	27	109	32	2	+40	+36	+33	+30	+28
Walla Walla, WA	46	4	118	20	3	− 5	+ 2	+ 8	+15	+21
Washington, DC	38	54	77	1	0	+35	+28	+23	+18	+13
Waterbury-Meriden, CT	41	33	73	3	0	+10	+ 9	+ 7	+ 6	+ 5
Waterloo, IA	42	30	92	20	1	+24	+24	+24	+25	+25
Wausau, WI	44	58	89	38	1	+ 4	+ 9	+13	+18	+22
West Palm Beach, FL	26	43	80	3	0	+79	+55	+36	+14	− 2
Wichita, KS	37	42	97	20	1	+60	+51	+45	+37	+31
Williston, ND	48	9	103	37	1	+46	+59	+69	+80	+90
Wilmington, DE	39	45	75	33	0	+26	+21	+18	+13	+10

City	North Latitude ° '		West Longitude ° '		Time Zone Code	Key Letters				
						A min.	B min.	C min.	D min.	E min.
Wilmington, NC	34	14	77	55	0	+52	+38	+27	+15	+ 5
Winchester, VA	39	11	78	10	0	+38	+33	+28	+23	+19
Worcester, MA	42	16	71	48	0	+ 3	+ 2	+ 2	+ 2	+ 2
York, PA	39	58	76	43	0	+30	+26	+22	+18	+15
Youngstown, OH	41	6	80	39	0	+42	+40	+38	+36	+34
Yuma, AZ	32	43	114	37	2	+83	+67	+54	+40	+28
CANADA										
Calgary, AB	51	5	114	5	2	+13	+35	+50	+68	+84
Edmonton, AB	53	34	113	25	2	− 3	+26	+47	+72	+93
Halifax, NS	44	38	63	35	−1	+21	+26	+29	+33	+37
Montreal, QC	45	28	73	39	0	− 1	+ 4	+ 9	+15	+20
Ottawa, ON	45	25	75	43	0	+ 6	+13	+18	+23	+28
St. John, NB	45	16	66	3	−1	+28	+34	+39	+44	+49
Saskatoon, SK	52	10	106	40	1	+37	+63	+80	+101	+119
Sydney, NS	46	10	60	10	−1	+ 1	+ 9	+15	+23	+28
Thunder Bay, ON	48	27	89	12	0	+47	+61	+71	+83	+93
Toronto, ON	43	39	79	23	0	+28	+30	+32	+35	+37
Vancouver, BC	49	13	123	6	3	0	+15	+26	+40	+52
Winnipeg, MB	49	53	97	10	1	+12	+30	+43	+58	+71

KILLING FROSTS AND GROWING SEASONS

Courtesy of National Climatic Center

Dates given are averages; local weather and topography may cause considerable variation.

City	Growing Season (Days)	Last Frost Spring	First Frost Fall	City	Growing Season (Days)	Last Frost Spring	First Frost Fall
Montgomery, AL	279	Feb. 27	Dec. 3	St. Louis, MO	220	Apr. 2	Nov. 8
Little Rock, AR	244	Mar. 16	Nov. 15	Helena, MT	134	May 12	Sept. 23
Phoenix, AZ	318	Jan. 27	Dec. 11	Omaha, NE	189	Apr. 14	Oct. 20
Tucson, AZ	262	Mar. 6	Nov. 23	Reno, NV	141	May 14	Oct. 2
Eureka, CA	335	Jan. 24	Dec. 25	Concord, NH	142	May 11	Sept. 30
Los Angeles, CA	*	*	*	Trenton, NJ	211	Apr. 8	Nov. 5
Sacramento, CA	321	Jan. 24	Dec. 11	Albuquerque, NM	196	Apr. 16	Oct. 29
San Diego, CA	*	*	*	Albany, NY	169	Apr. 27	Oct. 13
San Francisco, CA	*	*	*	Raleigh, NC	237	Mar. 24	Nov. 16
Denver CO	165	May 2	Oct. 14	Bismarck, ND	136	May 11	Sept. 24
Hartford, CT	180	Apr. 22	Oct. 19	Cincinnati, OH	203	Apr. 5	Oct. 25
Washington, DC	201	Apr. 10	Oct. 28	Toledo, OH	184	Apr. 24	Oct. 25
Miami, FL	*	*	*	Oklahoma City, OK	224	Mar. 28	Nov. 7
Macon, GA	252	Mar. 12	Nov. 19	Medford, OR	178	Apr. 25	Oct. 20
Pocatello, ID	145	May 8	Sept. 30	Portland, OR	279	Feb. 25	Dec. 1
Chicago, IL	192	Apr. 19	Oct. 28	Harrisburg, PA	201	Apr. 10	Oct. 28
Evansville, IN	217	Apr. 2	Nov. 4	Scranton, PA	173	Apr. 24	Oct. 14
Fort Wayne, IN	179	Apr. 24	Oct. 20	Columbia, SC	252	Mar. 14	Nov. 21
Des Moines, IA	182	Apr. 20	Oct. 19	Huron, SD	149	May 4	Sept. 30
Wichita, KS	210	Apr. 5	Nov. 1	Chattanooga, TN	229	Mar. 26	Nov. 10
Shreveport, LA	271	Mar. 1	Nov. 27	Del Rio, TX	300	Feb. 12	Dec. 9
New Orleans, LA	302	Feb. 13	Dec. 12	Midland, TX	217	Apr. 3	Nov. 6
Portland, ME	169	Apr. 29	Oct. 15	Salt Lake City, UT	203	Apr. 12	Nov. 1
Boston, MA	192	Apr. 16	Oct. 25	Burlington, VT	148	May 8	Oct. 3
Alpena, MI	156	May 6	Oct. 9	Richmond, VA	220	Apr. 2	Nov. 8
Detroit, MI	181	Apr. 25	Oct. 23	Spokane, WA	175	Apr. 20	Oct. 12
Marquette, MI	156	May 14	Oct. 17	Parkersburg, WV	188	Apr. 16	Oct. 21
Duluth, MN	125	May 22	Sept. 24	Green Bay, WI	160	May 6	Oct. 13
Minneapolis, MN	166	Apr. 30	Oct. 13	Madison, WI	176	Apr. 26	Oct. 19
Jackson, MS	248	Mar. 10	Nov. 13	Lander, WY	128	May 15	Sept. 20
Columbia, MO	198	Apr. 9	Oct. 24	*Frosts do not occur every year.			

TIDE CORRECTIONS

Many factors affect the time and height of the tides: the coastal configuration, the time of the Moon's southing (crossing the meridian) at the place, and the phase of the Moon. This table of tidal corrections is a sufficiently accurate guide to the times and heights of the high water at the places shown. (Low tides occur approximately 6 hours before and after high tides.) No figures are shown for most places on the Gulf of Mexico, since the method used in compiling this table does not apply there. For such places and elsewhere where precise accuracy is required, consult the Tide Tables published annually by the Distribution Div. C44, National Ocean Survey, Dept. of Commerce, Riverdale, MD 20840.

The figures for Full Sea on the left-hand Calendar pages 48-74 are the times of high tide at Commonwealth Pier in Boston Harbor. The heights of these tides are given on the right-hand Calendar pages 49-75. The heights are reckoned from Mean Low Water, and each day listed has a set of figures — upper for the morning, lower for the evening. To obtain the time and height of high water at any of the following places, apply the time difference to the daily times of high water at Boston (pages 48-74), and the height difference to the heights at Boston (pages 49-75).

	TIME DIFFERENCE: HR. MIN.	HEIGHT FEET
MAINE		
Bar Harbor	−0 34	+0.9
Belfast	−0 20	+0.4
Boothbay Harbor	−0 18	−0.8
Chebeague Island	−0 16	−0.6
Eastport	−0 28	+8.4
Kennebunkport	+0 04	−1.0
Machias	−0 28	+2.8
Monhegan Island	−0 25	−0.8
Old Orchard	0 00	−0.8
Portland	−0 12	−0.6
Rockland	−0 28	+0.1
Stonington	−0 30	+0.1
York	−0 09	−1.0
NEW HAMPSHIRE		
Hampton	+0 02	−1.3
Portsmouth	+0 11	−1.5
Rye Beach	−0 09	−0.9
MASSACHUSETTS		
Annisquam	−0 02	−1.1
Beverly Farms	0 00	−0.5
Boston	0 00	0.0
Cape Cod Canal		
East Entrance	−0 01	−0.8
West Entrance	−2 16	−5.9
Chatham Outer Coast	+0 30	−2.8
Inside	+1 54	*0.4

	TIME DIFFERENCE: HR. MIN.	HEIGHT FEET
Cohasset	+0 02	−0.07
Cotuit Highlands	+1 15	*0.3
Dennisport	+1 01	*0.4
Duxbury (Gurnet Pt.)	+0 02	−0.3
Fall River	−3 03	−5.0
Gloucester	−0 03	−0.8
Hingham	+0 07	0.0
Hull	+0 03	−0.2
Hyannis Port	+1 01	*0.3
Magnolia (Manchester)	−0 02	−0.7
Marblehead	−0 02	−0.4
Marion	−3 22	−5.4
Monument Beach	−3 08	−5.4
Nahant	−0 01	−0.5
Nantasket	+0 04	−0.1
Nantucket	−0 56	*0.3
Nauset Beach	+0 30	*0.6
New Bedford	−3 24	−5.7
Newburyport	+0 19	−1.8
Oak Bluffs	+0 30	*0.2
Onset (R.R. Bridge)	−2 16	−5.9
Plymouth	+0 05	0.0
Provincetown	+0 14	−0.4
Revere Beach	−0 01	−0.3
Rockport	−0 08	−1.0
Salem	0 00	−0.5
Scituate	−0 05	−0.7
Wareham	−3 09	−5.3
Wellfleet	+0 12	+0.5
West Falmouth	−3 10	−5.4
Westport Harbor	−3 22	−6.4
Woods Hole Little Harbor	−2 50	*0.2
Oceanographic Inst.	−3 07	*0.2
RHODE ISLAND		
Bristol	−3 24	−5.3
Sakonnet	−3 44	−5.6
Narragansett Pier	−3 42	−6.2
Newport	−3 34	−5.9
Pt. Judith	−3 41	−6.3
Providence	−3 20	−4.8
Watch Hill	−2 50	−6.8
CONNECTICUT		
Bridgeport	+0 01	−2.6
Madison	−0 22	−2.3
New Haven	−0 11	−3.2
New London	−1 54	−6.7
Norwalk	+0 01	−2.2
Old Lyme (Highway Bridge)	−0 30	−6.2
Stamford	+0 01	−2.2
Stonington	−2 27	−6.6
NEW YORK		
Coney Island	−3 33	−4.9
Fire Island Lt.	−2 43	*0.1
Long Beach	−3 11	−5.7
Montauk Harbor	−2 19	−7.4
New York City (Battery)	−2 43	−5.0
Oyster Bay	+0 04	−1.8
Port Chester	−0 09	−2.2
Port Washington	−0 01	−2.1
Sag Harbor	−0 55	−6.8
Southampton	−4 20	*0.2
(Shinnecock Inlet)		
Willets Point	0 00	−2.3

	TIME DIFFERENCE: HR. MIN.	HEIGHT FEET
NEW JERSEY		
Asbury Park	−4 04	−5.3
Atlantic City	−3 56	−5.5
Bay Head (Sea Girt)	−4 04	−5.3
Beach Haven	−1 43	*0.24
Cape May	−3 28	−5.3
Ocean City	−3 06	−5.9
Sandy Hook	−3 30	−5.0
Seaside Park	−4 03	−5.4
PENNSYLVANIA		
Philadelphia	+2 40	−3.5
DELAWARE		
Cape Henlopen	−2 48	−5.3
Rehoboth Beach	−3 37	−5.7
Wilmington	+1 56	−3.8
MARYLAND		
Annapolis	+6 23	−8.5
Baltimore	+7 59	−8.3
Cambridge	+5 05	−7.8
Havre de Grace	+11 21	−7.7
Point No Point	+2 28	−8.1
Prince Frederick	+4 25	−8.5
(Plum Point)		
VIRGINIA		
Cape Charles	−2 20	−7.0
Hampton Roads	−2 02	−6.9
Norfolk	−2 06	−6.6
Virginia Beach	−4 00	−6.0
Yorktown	−2 13	−7.0
NORTH CAROLINA		
Cape Fear	−3 55	−5.0
Cape Lookout	−4 28	−5.7
Currituck	−4 10	−5.8
Hatteras		
Ocean	−4 26	−6.0
Inlet	−4 03	−7.4
Kitty Hawk	−4 14	−6.2
SOUTH CAROLINA		
Charleston	−3 22	−4.3
Georgetown	−1 48	*0.36
Hilton Head	−3 22	−2.9
Myrtle Beach	−3 49	−4.4
St. Helena		
Harbor Entrance	−3 15	−3.4
GEORGIA		
Jekyll Island	−3 46	−2.9
Saint Simon's Island	−2 50	−2.9
Savannah Beach		
River Entrance	−3 14	−5.5
Tybee Light	−3 22	−2.7
FLORIDA		
Apalachicola	−7 53	*0.18
Cape Kennedy	−3 59	−6.0
Clearwater	−9 01	−6.4
Daytona Beach	−3 28	−5.3
Everglades City	+16 12	−7.3
Fort Lauderdale	−2 50	−7.2
Fort Myers	−7 45	*0.12
Fort Pierce Inlet	−3 32	−6.9
Jacksonville		
Railroad Bridge	−6 55	*0.10
Key West	+11 24	−9.1
Miami Harbor		
Entrance	−3 18	−7.0
St. Augustine	−2 55	−4.9
St. Petersburg	−9 53	−7.6
Sarasota	−11 31	*0.22
Suwannee River		
Entrance	−9 01	−6.4

	TIME DIFFERENCE: HR. MIN.	HEIGHT FEET
CALIFORNIA		
Carmel	−0 22	*0.5
Catalina Island	−1 23	*0.5
Crescent City	−2 05	−4.1
Eureka	+1 35	−3.4
Laguna Beach	−1 38	*0.5
Long Beach	−1 30	*0.5
Los Angeles	−1 33	−4.7
Mendocino	+0 03	−4.4
Monterey	−0 31	−4.9
San Diego	−1 41	−4.3
San Francisco	+0 45	−4.4
Santa Barbara	−1 10	*0.5
Santa Cruz	−0 34	−4.9
Santa Rosa Is.	−0 03	−4.5
OREGON		
Astoria	+2 21	−1.5
Empire-North Bend	+1 48	−3.4
Gold Beach	+1 45	−3.4
(Rogue R. Entrance)		
Tillamook	+2 28	*0.6
WASHINGTON		
Aberdeen	+2 09	−0.1
Bellingham	−6 18	−1.4
Cape Flaherty	+1 26	*0.8
Columbia River		
Entrance (Ilwaco)	+1 35	−2.2
Everett	−6 30	+1.1
Long Beach	+1 07	*0.8
Pacific Beach	+1 10	*0.9
Port Townsend	−7 04	−1.6
Seattle	−6 21	+1.3
South Bend	+2 08	−0.2
Tacoma	−6 14	+1.8
ALASKA		
Anchorage	−4 58	+17.5
Juneau	+3 08	+6.1
Kodiak	+1 53	−1.7
CANADA		
Alberton, P.E.I.	−5 45**	−7.5
Charlottetown, P.E.I.	−0 45**	−3.5
Halifax, N.S.	−3 23	−4.5
North Sydney, N.S.	−3 15	−6.5
St. John, N.B.	+0 30	−8.0
St. John's, Nfld.	−4 00	−6.5
Vancouver, B.C.	−5 25	+4.2
Yarmouth, N.S.	−0 40	+3.0

* Where the difference in the "HEIGHT/FEET" column is so marked, height at Boston should be multiplied by this ratio.

** Varies widely; accurate only within 1½ hours. Consult local tide tables for precise times and heights.

Example: The conversion of the times and heights of the tides at Boston to those of Yorktown, Virginia, is given below:

Sample tide calculation June 1, 1989:

High tide Boston (p. 62)	8:30 A.M. EST
Correction for Yorktown	−2:13 hrs.
High tide Yorktown	6:17 A.M. EST
Tide height Boston (p. 63)	9.9 ft.
Correction for Yorktown	− 7.0 ft.
Tide height Yorktown	+2.9 ft.

Turn ugly brush piles into valuable, FREE Wood Chips, Mulch, Compost!

Why put up with unsightly brush piles that ruin the good looks of your place? Turn *all* your organic "throwaways" into useful wood chip mulch and compost material...and *beautify* your home, instead!

Have the kind of place you've always dreamed of — more easily than you ever thought possible — with the quick and efficient SUPER TOMAHAWK Chipper/Shredder! Send for FREE INFORMATION!

Now 3 Models!
One's right for your property!

For smaller properties
4HP TOMAHAWK

Mid-size workhorse
5HP SUPER TOMAHAWK

Top-of-the-Line
8HP SUPER TOMAHAWK

Beautifully Landscape your home with the TROY-BILT® TOMAHAWK! Your free woodchips become landscaping chips, mulch or compost, for easier care, less watering and better looks.

© 1989 Garden Way Inc.

For FREE DETAILS CALL
1-800-453-5800 Dept. 926B
Anytime, or MAIL THIS COUPON!

The Consumer's Guide to 1989

Based on an analysis of statistics, sales trends, and human behavior, a professional forecaster offers a glimpse of what the year ahead might hold. by Kim Long

□ IN THE BIBLE IT SAYS, "A PROPHET IS NOT WITHOUT HONor, save in his own country and in his own house" (Matthew 13:57). In other words, those who talk about what is to come may find it hard to impress their neighbors. The challenge of accurate forecasting — being right as often as possible — means that sometimes what you have to say sounds either too obvious or too absurd. For 1989 an increase in taxes may sound obvious and fake caviar may sound absurd, but both are part of the picture for the coming year.

The following predictions are based on facts and figures. Statistics, sales records, interviews, and analysis are all used and have yielded an 80-percent success rate in the past six years. Nevertheless, forecasting often can resemble more of an art than a science, because when it comes right down to it, a lot of people out there don't act like sheep.

Consumer Trends

- Can't drink a whole can of pop at once? The beverage industry will soon have the solution: resealable cans. The first sodas to get this new packaging will be available nationally soon after test marketing in 1988. The new aluminum cans will be used for selected carbonated beverages — colas and diet colas at first — in 16-, 24-, and 32-ounce containers. Cost will be similar to beverages now packaged in glass and plastic containers. The resealable cans will eventually be used for everything from juice and beer to powdered and granulated mixes.
- If you are tired of plain old milk, flavored milk is on the way. New flavors will include banana, boysenberry, cherry, peach, and strawberry.
- Fake foods have prospered in recent years as the food industry has cranked out numerous substitutes for popular foods. Next to appear down the pike: fake caviar, made from vegetable products and fish flavors.

- Convenience has become the password at grocery stores in the 1980s. Consumers are getting hooked on prepared foods, kitchen shortcuts, and anything that will fit in a microwave oven. Fast-food restaurants are looking to snag a piece of this market — Wendy's, for one, will soon be selling its own brand of ground beef in selected stores in 1989.
- Low-calorie is the hottest buzzword in food packaging, and more and more products are being developed or altered to attract fat-conscious consumers. The next food category to get this treatment will be snack foods.

VITAL STATISTICS

	1979	1989 (est.)
Population:	225.1 mil.	248.9 mil.
Births:	3.5 mil.	4.1 mil.
Deaths:	1.9 mil.	2.2 mil.
Adoptions:	135,000	165,000
Marriages:	2.3 mil.	2.5 mil.
Divorces:	1.2 mil.	1.0 mil.

Look for low-calorie tortilla chips to lead the way.

• Scratch-and-sniff ads have become an accepted gimmick for fragrance makers. Next ploy in odor-emphasis will be scented newspaper ink. Plans are underway to print ads in some papers with appropriate smells, including strawberry and coffee.

• Hair-care products for an aging population will experience a boom in the next few years as the baby boomers are entering middle age and gaining the gray hairs to prove it.

• Piggyback ads, called "co-parenting" in the food industry, are the coming thing. These promotional ploys use multiple messages on packages to let customers know what's inside. Duncan Hines cookies, for instance, also advertise Hershey's milk chocolate, and Betty Crocker mixes share box space with Dole pineapple. Brand name clout will be the goal of packagers as they push these packaging combinations to extremes.

• Mail-in rebates are on the way out. At the latest count, there are more than 50 billion coupons a year, offering rebates on a wide variety of products. Surveys show that less than ten percent of shoppers actually use them. Companies offering these promotions face rising costs in managing the rebate system without gaining much in sales. Large companies such as Black & Decker and large retailers such as K Mart will lead the switch away from rebates.

• Looking for a head start on the collectibles of the future? There are many factors that aren't always obvious when you are trying to pick undervalued items that will be hot in tomorrow's auctions and antique stores. Some places to start in 1989: folk art (from paintings to stoneware), Depression-era furniture, 1960s dolls and toys, promotional giveaways from fast-food restaurants, psychedelic relics (from posters to record albums), Art Deco items (from jewelry to household appliances), and plastic model kits from the 1950s and 1960s (unassembled, in original boxes).

• Sex is out. Well, sort of. It's being replaced by romance, at least according to indications from the advertising, television, and movie industries. It isn't that people's habits are changing because of the AIDS crisis so much as the aging of the baby boomers. In 1989 baby boomers will be hitting their forties in record numbers, and most of them are married or too old for the singles' bar scene. Hollywood and Madison Avenue are answering this change with a new emphasis on traditional romantic images, flirting, and subtlety.

• A growing trend: cities banning billboards. Among the already converted metropolises: Jacksonville, Florida; Tucson, Arizona; Beaufort, South Carolina; and Anchorage, Alaska. Ballot drives to control or remove more outdoor advertising signs will spring up across the nation in the next few years.

• Compact-disc players are rapidly taking over from record players in the music industry. Within a few years the last LP may be pressed, the victim of consumer enthusiasm for the new digital systems. The next generation of high-tech music machines, however, may give CDs a run for their money. Digital audio tape (DAT for short) uses the same digital system to record as in CDs, creating almost perfect reproductions of original sounds. The difference is in the playback: DAT uses small, matchbox-size tape cassettes and cigarette-pack-size players, allowing greater portability. The new DAT cassettes will also be cheaper than CDs to produce, making them an enticing alternative to consumers. One drawback is the price of DAT players: $800 to $1,500 for the first year or two.

- Home videos in 3-D? New 3-D video camcorders will allow folks to make their own.
- New high-tech interactive games will give players more fun next year. For example, an interactive mystery game has more than 40,000 possible combinations of plot, characters, and situations. Other interactive TV shows will allow viewers to pick answers, take chances, even choose camera angles. Participants will need special equipment to participate.
- New computerized mirrors will allow some shoppers to try on clothes, makeup, and hairdos — electronically. These high-tech devices capture your image, then allow you to manipulate the picture. Other uses for interactive mirrors include plastic surgery and criminal investigation.
- Bar codes — those little vertical lines on most packaged goods — are an important tool for grocery stores. They already speed up the checkout time and provide customers with itemized receipts. Soon they will allow customers to become better shoppers. Handheld bar-code scanners will be offered in some stores, allowing shoppers to keep track of total purchases, compare brand prices, find discounted items, and even check on the calorie counts for different products. In the kitchen the latest microwave ovens will allow busy cooks to "scan" recipes, automatically setting oven times and temperatures.

Automotive Trends

Changes are on the way for our favorite vehicles, but not all of them will be welcomed by everyone. Sure to create controversy are the new federal guidelines for passenger restraints, requiring airbags or passive harness protection on all cars by 1992. In 1989 from 10 to 20 percent of all new cars will feature these safety devices; all domestically made Chrysler models will have airbags by 1990. One new high-tech feature that will not be mandatory is an electronic warning system that can be installed in rear bumpers, warning of obstacles in the way when backing up.

Other automotive changes include:
- Small, fuel-efficient cars will be getting even more gas stingy. Weight reduction and engine improvements will add extra mileage to economy models, with improvements in mileage up to ten percent. Within a few years, new two-cycle engines — advanced versions of engines used in motorcycles and lawn mowers — will arrive, promising even greater mileage. Some drivers, however, may be more excited about the exotic muscle cars that are the opposite trend. BMW, Cadillac, Mercedes, and Subaru, led by the success of Jaguar, are all developing 12-cylinder engines.
- Car washes are modernizing. Trends include more upscale services and installation of new "touchless" wash systems that rely on computer-guided water pressure — no brushes allowed — to clean auto surfaces with a minimum of damage to the paint. Car owners will be increasingly interested in car care because the average period of ownership is growing longer.
- Satellite technology is providing new navigational features for some cars and trucks. With these computerized systems, drivers can pinpoint their location, find their way through complex highway systems (such as that of Los Angeles), avoid construction delays and traffic snarls, and be warned about changes in speed limits. Some

large trucking companies are already using the systems. Other uses may bring more satisfaction to the average consumer: pizza delivery vehicles will find it easier to deliver products hot by having the right route at their fingertips.

- Full-service gas stations are coming back. Along with traditional services such as filling tanks, washing windshields, and checking under the hood, new stations will offer convenience items such as groceries and snacks.

Where there are cars, there are always drivers grumbling about parking meters. High-tech meters are on the way to some cities, featuring slots that read special credit cards. Drivers purchase blocks of time that are electronically encoded on the cards; each use automatically deducts payment from the card according to the time used. Electronic meters with quartz-timing mechanisms are also being developed, avoiding the problem of inaccurate mechanical clocks. Another advance in parking control is a hand-held computer to allow parking-control officers to check on motorists' records instantly and deal with parking scofflaws quickly. And this also involves a trend: the infamous "Denver boot."

No one but parking authorities likes this invention, which allows parking officers to immobilize a car by locking a cumbersome clamp to one wheel. Use of the boot is spreading fast. More than half a dozen cities, including Chicago, Boston, Philadelphia, Los Angeles, and Washington, D.C., now have this device in their arsenals of weapons against parking violators.

Travel Trends

- Computer design and advanced materials have combined to produce a new generation of super-efficient, quiet, propeller-driven airplanes. The new planes are fuel stingy — they can save up to 40 percent of the fuel of compa-

rably sized jetliners. These advanced aircraft get their power from propfan engine designs, capable of quietly pushing planes through the sky at almost 500 miles an hour at altitudes of more than 30,000 feet.

- Frequent-flier programs will be under attack. The problem: too many takers. Many popular air routes are becoming saturated with fliers cashing in their frequent-flier bonuses, cutting and even eliminating profits for airline companies. Triple-mileage programs may eventually drive one or more airlines into bankruptcy. The solution: airlines will reduce awards, add restrictions for earning bonus miles, and remove bonuses on some heavily traveled flights. In addition, the IRS won't be able to resist much longer: taxation on "free" flights is soon to come. Some companies, stung by continued misuse of business bookings to earn employees extra awards, will also begin stricter controls over travel reservations.

- A time-travel event will occur in 1989: the 20th anniversary of the Woodstock Festival, a climactic event of the hippie era. This giant rock festival will be remembered by many on August 15. Two decades later, most of the 400,000 participants have left the drop-out movement of the 1960s far behind. Nostalgia for these "good old days," however, will create a booming Woodstock revival, with posters, books, TV specials, and major articles in leading publications. A return of the antics and attitudes commonplace in 1969 will not accompany this nostalgia. After all, Woodstock veterans have their hands full with teenage kids, careers, and maintaining the status quo.

- For most vacationers, 1989 will be marked by higher gas prices, larger crowds at the major national parks, and more trips close to home. Those looking for foreign adventures will find the best bargains in Mexico and the Caribbean. One of the biggest overseas events will be a celebration in Paris on July 14, marking the 200th anniversary of the fall of the Bastille. Many motorists may also wish to have their own celebrations here in the U.S. on November 26, honoring the 200th anniversary of the first road map published in this country.

Wallet Shock

- Planning on sending junior to college? College costs will increase again for the 1989-1990 school year. Average cost (tuition plus room and board) for a year of schooling at public institutions will be about $6,500. Average cost of private institutions: about $13,300.
- Taxes are due for an increase in 1989. In the wake of the 1988 presidential elections, state and federal authorities will be facing up to the problems of budget shortfalls by raising tax rates on income and adding to the existing taxes on some goods, from gasoline to cigarettes. At the same time, to speed up the paperwork, the IRS is moving into the future with an experimental high-tech plan to accept tax returns directly from home computers. Another new IRS option

will be tax payments with credit cards.
- Another $1 coin? Despite the disastrous experience with the Susan B. Anthony dollar, the U.S. Treasury is likely to bow to pressure from Congress and the vending machine industry and approve the production of a new copper coin that would debut by 1992. The vending machine industry isn't waiting around for this to happen: look for the first credit card machines within the next few years, along with many more units that will take currency in $1, $5, and $10 denominations. Higher-priced products from vending machines — made possible with the ability of the machines to take larger payments — will include clothes, batteries, film, and cosmetics.

City Living — Big vs. Small

More major cities are developing "urban villages" where distinct neighborhood centers are being revitalized. Instead of moving to the suburbs, many people are fixing up older buildings; they include professionals, white-collar workers, young couples, and others dissatisfied with suburban living. As the neighborhoods improve, new businesses move in and city governments lend a hand by fixing up streets, sidewalks, and parks.

For those not interested in urban lifestyles, rural neighborhoods are also a growing trend. Also referred to as satellite communities, these small towns and villages are usually beyond the geographical fringes of suburbs and have small-town charm, safety, and character, all attractive features for those who find cities too big and suburbs too bland. Small towns — stung with declining revenue-sharing from the federal government and a rapid exodus by younger generations seeking other sources of jobs and excitement — are eager to support this new trend. And with the U.S. workplace changing character, more jobs such as data processing, information handling, and electronic services can be performed away from most major metropolitan centers.

Suburbs, on the other hand, are not suffering from this social shunning. There is a growing trend for those who prefer this 20th-century life-style to find all of their needs within suburban boundaries. Among the characteristics of this trend are: more wage earners finding employment in suburban locations, more suburb-to-suburb commuting, and more entertainment and shopping facilities being developed in suburbs to keep customers near home.

Job Trends

Trends in employment are often linked to the baby-boom generation. The latest to come from these 23- to 45-year-olds is a growing urge to start their own businesses. Many baby boomers are now earning top dollars in their fields, but as middle age approaches, the potential to leave their jobs and work for themselves grows.

Franchising fever is one result — a rapidly expanding notion, with franchises springing up in many new fields from law to business management. Franchise classes, consultants, seminars, self-help audio and video tapes, and books will be popping up to take advantage of this market. Other baby boomers — especially those with upscale incomes — will be looking for early retirements, taking advantage of pensions, perks, and bonuses to find other more enjoyable ways to fill their time.

At the other end of the employment picture, more blue-collar jobs will be falling victim to mechanization and automation. Among developments in robot technology are machines that can harvest hard-to-pick fruits and vegetables — from apples to tomatoes — and take over many traditional jobs in the lumber industry. Remote-control timbering machines can fell, strip, and carry trees under the supervision of a single employee. While many of these manual-labor jobs are being replaced by machines, other hands-on jobs will go unfilled. Craftsmen such as masons and finish carpenters are in short supply in some areas. Because these skills require intensive training and apprenticeship, they cannot be easily filled from the ranks of the unemployed or by dissatisfied career workers.

One of the most important trends in employment and career training will be the value of education. There is already a direct link between the amount of education and future earnings: "The more you learn, the more you earn." In the future, this will become even more important, as new specialized jobs are created, more workers compete for higher-paying positions, and job requirements demand a wider range of skills and ability.

• Not enough work to go around in 1989: house construction, mining, railroad work, electronic equipment assembly, automotive assembly, post office jobs, meter reading, stocking, stenography, typing, data entry, and shoe repair.

For 1989, these are the economic and employment prospects around the country:

• Better-than-average growth: California (especially Los Angeles, Orange County, San Diego), Washington, Oregon, Minneapolis, Des Moines, Phoenix, Houston, Dallas, New Orleans, Alabama, Kentucky, Tennessee (especially Nashville), Georgia (especially Atlanta), Florida, Virginia, Pennsylvania, Washington, D.C., New York City, Boston, and Hartford.

• Worse-than-average growth: Rocky Mountain region (except for Denver), most of the north-central region (especially Detroit, Milwaukee), Texas (except major cities), Louisiana (except New Orleans), West Virginia, and most of rural New England.

Trends in Activities

The trends in 1989 will spotlight established activities such as bowling (with gutterless bowling growing in popularity), croquet, pool and billiards, model building, cross-country skiing, and water skiing. Newer activities that are taking off include snowboarding, off-road bicycling, and interval aerobics (alternating from hard to soft versions). Diehard runners and joggers are moving away from marathons and will get more kicks from shorter races. For baseball fans awaiting the debut of this sport as an official Olympic sport in 1992, watch out for the Soviet Union, Australia, Israel, and China. All of these countries are planning to organize Little League teams. Golfers, avoid overcrowded links in California and Florida.

Meanwhile, a surprise visitor at many schools will be a return to physical education. P.E. boosters, health professionals, and parents are finally getting the message that there are too many overweight, out-of-shape kids. The loser in 1989 for kids and adults: television. Average viewing time in front of the TV set will decline slightly.

Health Trends

- A new, holographic contact lens. This lens system will provide focusing for near and distant objects without requiring eye movement.
- Legal euthanasia. California is likely to become the first state to allow legalized "mercy killing" in 1989. Even if voters pass this referendum, the ruling may be challenged at the Supreme Court.

- More wrinkle treatments. Research now underway indicates that products derived from common fruits may be effective in reducing or removing many facial wrinkles. Meanwhile, sales of Retin-A — a wrinkle-fighting product introduced in 1987 — will continue to boom, and the Food and Drug Administration will increase its efforts to stop false advertising about wrinkle control with over-the-counter cosmetic products.
- Nosedrops and lollipops that contain relaxants are being tested for use on children before surgery.
- New drugs being tested or awaiting approval from the FDA include ones that block production of cholesterol, slow or stop complications from diabetes, control appetite, stop neurological damage that is caused by head or spinal-cord injuries, reduce loss of memory that accompanies Alzheimer's disease, fight infections with new antibiotics that don't cause upset stomachs or diarrhea, fight cardiovascular diseases, heal ulcers, reduce the effects of asthma, and boost the human body's own effective pain killers.
- Mail-order drugs. More and more people are filling their prescriptions through the mail; more than 55 million scripts will be filled this way by the end of 1988. By 1990 10 percent of all prescriptions will likely fall into this category.
- Anti-poison-ivy compound. The U.S. Forest Service has developed an effective spray that keeps poison ivy from reacting with human skin.
- Less tobacco smoke than ever. Growing public and government pressure will put the damper on more smokers. Cigarette haters may wish to celebrate on January 11 to mark the 25th anniversary of the original Surgeon General's report against smoking in 1964.
- And finally, all advances in medicine also come with bad news: the cost for hospital stays, doctors' care, and drugs will be rising faster than the cost of living in 1989; eight- to ten-percent increases can be expected.

FARM FACTS

	1965	1975	1980	1989
total acres	1.14 bil.	1.06 bil.	1.04 bil.	1.0 bil.
# of farms	3.4 mil.	2.5 mil.	2.4 mil.	2.0 mil.
cattle	109 mil.	132 mil.	111 mil.	102 mil.
dairy cows	14.9 mil.	11.1 mil.	10.8 mil.	10 mil.
sheep & lambs	25.1 mil.	14.5 mil.	12.7 mil.	10.0 mil.
hogs	56.1 mil.	54.7 mil.	67.3 mil.	49 mil.
chickens	394 mil.	380 mil.	392 mil.	380 mil.

Agricultural Trends

Farming will begin to bounce back in 1989, recovering a little from its problems of recent years. Land prices will increase, but not in all areas. Meanwhile, agricultural products will get a boost from bioengineering and scientific advances in the next few years. Among the advances are:

• Garden vegetables that tolerate extremes of temperature — including frost — and resist insects without needing applications of chemicals.
• Eggs that have lower cholesterol.
• The first test-tube chickens, which will lead the way in developing birds that mature faster, lay more eggs, and have more resistance to disease.
• Leaner beef from crossbreeding and new feeding methods. Consumers will respond by eating more beef. Hot cattle breeds will be Piedmontese and Belgian Blue crossbreeds.
• "Skinny pigs" — the same size as regular hogs but with 70 percent less fat — will be commercially available in the next year or two. The new lean porkers are being created by manipulating a growth-hormone molecule that is naturally present in these animals. Also underway is work on a similar hormone for cattle.
• Baby watermelons, about the size of cantaloupes.
• A new insecticide that begins working when exposed to sunlight and is non-toxic.
• Artificial cooking oils will hit the market within the next few years. Farmers may be worried about these products

lowering the demand for soybeans, a major source of oils, but science gives as it takes away. At least one of the new no-cholesterol oils will be made from soybeans. Each pound of the new oil will take about 1.3 pounds of soybeans to manufacture.
• Meanwhile, some traditional but little-known vegetables and grains will gain favor with consumers. Some of these include arrowroot, daikon, cipolines, fava beans, mung beans, amaranth, quinoa, sesame, and rapeseed.

A Final Filthy Trend

For those folks who think the world is going downhill fast and all these scientific advances and new technology are just so much garbage, prepare for one last surprise in 1989. With much of the country running out of room for its garbage, charges for landfill, dumping, and refuse pickup will all increase in the next year. As a final insult, don't be surprised if the ultimate indignity for modern consumers doesn't surface soon: garbage rationing. □ □

THE AUTHOR: *Kim Long has been researching and writing about consumer trends for the past six years. He is a syndicated newspaper columnist with a weekly column ("The American Forecaster") about trends and is the author of* THE AMERICAN FORECASTER *(an annual book about the future published by Running Press, Philadelphia).*

Huchthausen

The Truth About Beauty

While researching the burning question of precisely (down to tiny fractions of an inch) what constitutes the ideal woman's face, a psychologist at the University of Louisville learned it is also safer to be beautiful.

by Geoffrey Elan

'Tis not a lip, or eye, we beauty call,
But the joint force and full result of all.
— Alexander Pope

□ SORRY, MR. POPE. THE LATEST RE-search on attractiveness shows it *is* a lip, or eye, or some other feature of a woman's face that we call beauty. We even know exactly how wide those lips and how high those eyes ought to be.

Dr. Michael Cunningham, a psychologist at the University of Louisville, showed 150 male college students

pictures of 50 women's faces and asked his subjects to rate the attractiveness of those faces on a six-point scale. The students didn't know that 27 of the 50 women rated were Miss Universe contestants. The others were randomly selected college seniors.

To no one's surprise, the beauty contestants scored much higher than the college seniors. The women rated most attractive had certain features in common: large, widely spaced eyes, small noses and chins, prominent cheekbones, narrow cheeks, arched eyebrows, wide smiles, and dilated pupils.

That happened to be just what Cunningham had expected. He had a theory that what men would find beautiful in a woman's face would be a combination of two things. One would be what he calls "neonate features" — large, widely spaced eyes, and small noses and chins — that we associate with children, thus triggering subconscious feelings of warmth and protectiveness. The other would be features that suggest sexual maturity and responsiveness: prominent cheekbones, narrow cheeks, arched eyebrows, wide smiles, and dilated pupils.

"The sum total of the features signifies someone who is slightly young and helpless, though sexually mature and friendly," Cunningham concluded in *The Journal of Personality and Social Psychology.* "And men find that combination compelling."

Cunningham and his assistants got out their micrometers and measured the faces of the highest-rated women to come up with an idealized model of a beautiful woman's face. The ideal mouth, they found, should be exactly half the width of the face at mouth level. The eyes should be one-fourteenth the height of the face and three-tenths of the width of the face at eye level. The pupils should be one-fourteenth the distance between the cheekbones. The distance from the center of the eye to the bottom of the eyebrow should be one-tenth the height of the face. The chin should be one-fifth the length of the face, and the total area of the nose (length from bridge to tip times the distance between the outer edges of the nostrils) should be no more than five percent of the total area of the face.

Cunningham admits that this is not an absolute standard of female beauty, but one that college men of this time and place agree upon. Every culture has had its own image of the beautiful woman. "Blacker is her hair than the darkness of night, blacker than the ber-

ries of the blackberry bush," says an Egyptian scroll. Greek and Roman statuary favored tall women with straight noses, low foreheads, and powerful shoulders, like those of the *Venus de Milo.* "The reign of the blonde in modern literature is but a continuation of her reign in Greece and Rome," wrote the aptly named classical scholar M. B. Ogle.

Medieval love poems celebrated blonde women with large, light blue eyes and "brent (smooth) brows," according to historian Walter Curry, who adds that "I have failed entirely to find any mention of beautiful ears." He should have consulted the 16th-century Italian Firenzuola, author of *The Beauty of Women,* who wrote: "For perfect beauty the ears should be middle-sized, with the shell finely turned and of a livelier tint than the flat part; and the roll which borders all round must be transparent and of a brilliant hue like the seed of a pomegranate."

A Spanish poet insisted that a woman should have 27 beauties:

— three white: skin, teeth, and hands
— three black: eyes, lashes, and brows
— three red: lips, cheeks, and nails
— three long: body, hair, and hands
— three short: teeth, ears, and legs
— three large: breasts, forehead, and the space between her brows
— three slender: waist, hands, and feet
— three plump: arms, hips, and thighs
— three thin: fingers, hair, and lips

Lola Montez, the scandalous Irish-Spanish mistress of the King of Bavaria, was said to meet 26 of those standards. In 1858 she wrote a book called *The Arts of Beauty,* filled with sensible advice for women about exercise and care of their skin and hair. She denounced the appalling practice of some women who drank from arsenic springs to give their skins a transparent whiteness and said of such common measures as eating chalk: "I have no doubt that this is a good way to get a pale complexion, for it destroys the health."

Ill health was fashionable in America in the years before the Civil War. The ideal American woman was a frail creature with a receding chin. Girls were taught to say the words "peas, prunes, and prisms" before entering a room or posing for a photograph, in order to achieve a perfect "rosebud" mouth. Women starved themselves or suffered severe internal injuries inflicted by corsets to achieve an 18-inch waist. Harriet Beecher Stowe wrote in outrage: "We in America have got so far out of the way of a womanhood that has any vigor of outline or opulence of physical proportions that, when we see a woman made as a woman ought to be, she strikes us as a monster."

By the 1880s, though, plumpness was in. The Statue of Liberty, dedicated in 1886, portrays a large-waisted, broad-shouldered woman. It is interesting that Peter Paul Rubens was a Dutch painter whose richly endowed women were popular when Holland was becoming a world power. When the United States started throwing its weight around on the world stage, actress Lillian Russell's Rubenesque proportions were considered ideal. Some scholars wonder if a nation's drive for expansion can be measured in the bustlines of its most popular women.

Whatever the reason, the pendulum swung back toward thinness and didn't stop until it reached the rail-like flappers of the Roaring Twenties. Then came the backswing to voluptuousness that peaked with Marilyn Monroe in the 1950s. And so it continues, even to this day.

But no matter how fashion may change, research by Cunningham and many others shows that women perceived to be beautiful benefit from those perceptions in a host of ways. Not only are they sought after for dating and marriage, but they tend to get better grades in school, do better in job interviews, get higher pay, and are more likely to be acquitted by juries. The studies are virtually unanimous: it's better to be beautiful.

It's safer, too. In another experiment, Dr. Cunningham showed pictures of 16

On the world stage, actress Lillian Russell's Rubenesque proportions were considered ideal.

women's faces to 82 male college students and asked them for which of the women would they be most likely to:
— help load furniture on a truck
— donate a pint of blood
— donate a kidney
— loan $500 for car repairs
— buy a $100 birthday present
— cosign a $10,000 loan
— swim half a mile to rescue
— enter a burning building
— leap on a terrorist's hand grenade.

The men studied, Cunningham reports, would be most willing to lend money to a woman with a small nose. They'd be more inclined to donate a kidney to a woman with a small nose and greater-than-average eye height. And women with small noses, greater eye height, and greater eye width, would be most safe from a terrorist grenade attack. "Such results," Cunningham concluded, "suggest that the possession of attractive facial features may be of survival value for adults."

So get out those rulers and calculators. If your total nose area is, say, *six* percent of the area of your face, plastic surgery may be worth the price. You can always get a loan from a college man — *afterwards*. □ □

Everything You Never Thought You Could Do with Vinegar

How to clean, polish, unclog, deodorize, and soothe nearly anything in the world, using just white vinegar and elbow grease.

By Earl W. Proulx

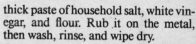

APPLIANCES AND HOUSEHOLD FIXTURES:

Dishwasher: To help keep the drainline clean and sweet smelling, add ½ cup white vinegar to the rinse cycle.

Steam iron: To clean, fill the tank full of white vinegar and let it stay overnight, then rinse out thoroughly with warm water. (Be sure to keep the cord dry.)

Humidifier: To clean the filter, remove it and soak it in a pan of white vinegar until all sediment is off, then wash in detergent and water.

Garbage disposal: If the rubber shield smells after much use, remove it and soak it in a pan of white vinegar.

Oven: Dampen a cleaning rag in vinegar and water and wipe out the interior. This will prevent grease buildup.

Showerhead: To unclog, soak in diluted white vinegar overnight, or put some vinegar in a plastic bag, tie it around the showerhead, and leave on overnight.

Chrome fixtures: Clean off soap and stains with a mixture of 1 teaspoon salt dissolved in 2 tablespoons white vinegar.

Stainless steel: White hard-water stains can be removed by rubbing with white vinegar.

Toilet bowl: Clean and deodorize by pouring undiluted white vinegar into it. Let stand for 5 minutes, then flush. Spray stubborn stains with vinegar, then scrub vigorously.

Brass, copper, and bronze: Make a thick paste of household salt, white vinegar, and flour. Rub it on the metal, then wash, rinse, and wipe dry.

Faucets: Remove hard white calcium deposits by soaking toilet tissue with white vinegar and placing it around the stains. Leave tissue in place for an hour or two.

Bathtub film: Wipe with white vinegar and then baking soda, and rinse clean with water.

Countertops: Plastic laminate counters and tabletops can be cleaned by rubbing with a soft cloth soaked in white vinegar. This also makes them shine.

Drip coffee makers: To clean, fill the reservoir with white vinegar and run it through a brewing cycle.

Washing machine: Fill the machine with water and add a quart of white vinegar. Run the machine through a complete cycle. This will help clean out the hoses and deodorize the tub as well.

FLOORS, WALLS, AND FURNISHINGS:

No-wax vinyl flooring: To clean and shine, add ½ cup white vinegar to ½ gallon warm water.

Carpets: To bring out the color in rugs and carpets, brush them with a mixture of 1 cup white vinegar and 1 gallon water. Animal urine odors can usually be vanquished by using a half-and-half mixture of white vinegar and water. Sponge it into the carpet and then blot it up with thick towels. If the stain is near the wall, also wash the wall with the mixture about 18 inches up, as the culprit may have been a male cat.

Wood paneling: To clean, mix 1 ounce olive oil with 2 ounces white vinegar and 1 quart warm water. Dampen a soft cloth with this and wipe the paneling; then wipe with a dry soft cloth.

Furniture: Clean discolored or dirty wood with a mixture of equal amounts of turpentine, white vinegar, and mineral oil. Shake well before and during use. Apply with a soft cloth and rub vigorously. To take apart a piece of furniture, warm some white vinegar and brush on and around the joints to be separated. Let set a few minutes; repeat if necessary.

Plastic shower curtains: Wash them in the machine with a bath towel. Add 1 cup white vinegar to rinse cycle. Briefly tumble dry.

Painted and varnished surfaces: Use a solution of 1 cup ammonia, ½ cup white vinegar, and ¼ cup baking soda in a gallon of warm water. It does not have to be rinsed or dried and does not dull the finish.

Carpet and upholstery shampoo: Mix ¼ cup mild detergent powder with a quart of water and a tablespoon of white vinegar. Whip into a stiff foam, using an egg beater. Apply foam only to the fabric with a soft brush, sponge, or terry cloth, rubbing gently and using even pressure to prevent streaking. Scrape away soiled foam with a dull knife. Wipe off residue with a damp cloth or sponge.

STAINS, SPILLS, AND YUCKY DEPOSITS:

Stain remover: Make a solution of 1 teaspoon liquid detergent, 1 teaspoon white vinegar, and 1 pint lukewarm water. To remove *non*oily stains, apply with a soft brush or towel, rub gently, and rinse with a towel dampened with clean water. Blot dry and repeat until stain is gone. Dry quickly using a fan or hair dryer.

Coffee on carpet: Blot up excess coffee, then rub the stain with a solution of white vinegar, detergent, and water.

Ball-point ink: Saturate with hair spray, allow to dry, then brush lightly with a solution of half vinegar, half water.

Aluminum pans: Remove dark stains by boiling water containing 1 tablespoon white vinegar for each quart of water.

Aluminum screens: For corrosion, apply white vinegar, let stand a few minutes, then scrub off.

Salt and water stains: White vinegar takes these stains off leather boots and shoes. Wipe over the stained area only, then polish.

White rings on furniture: Rings from wet glasses may be rubbed with a mixture of equal parts olive oil and white vinegar. Rub with the grain of the wood only, then apply a coat of polish.

Chalky deposits: Place dinnerware and glasses in dishwasher. Place cup filled with white vinegar on bottom rack. Run machine for 5 minutes. Stop machine and empty cup (now full of wa-

ter) and refill with vinegar. Complete cycle. Follow with another complete cycle using dishwasher detergent.

Windows, mirrors, glasses: Add 2 tablespoons white vinegar to 8 ounces water and put in a spray bottle. Spray lightly and wipe with old crumpled newspapers. Keep away from the edges of mirrors as moisture will spoil the silver on the back.

Hair dye stains on clothing: Wash in detergent with white vinegar added, then bleach with hydrogen peroxide and relaunder.

Greasy residue: Filmy dirt and grease on tops of stove and refrigerator come clean with a wiping of full-strength white vinegar.

Clogged drains: Pour ½ cup baking soda down the drain, then ½ cup vinegar. Close the drain and let work for a while, then open the drain and let hot water pour through for 3 or 4 minutes.

Leather goods: Clean with a mixture of 1 cup boiled linseed oil and 1 cup white vinegar.

HANDY TRICKS OF THE TRADE:

Air freshener: Set out a shallow dish of white vinegar.

Smoke odors on clothes: Fill bathtub with hot water and add 1 cup white vinegar. Hang clothes above the steaming water.

Pest fighter: A teaspoon of vinegar for each quart of drinking water helps keep your pet free of fleas and ticks. (This ratio of vinegar to water is for a 40-pound animal.)

Baby's clothes and diapers: Add 1 cup vinegar to each load during the rinse cycle. Vinegar naturally breaks down uric acid and soapy residue, leaving clothes soft and fresh.

Washing silks: Add ½ cup Woolite and 2 tablespoons white vinegar to 2 quarts very cold water. Dunk silks up and down in the mixture but do not soak. Roll in a heavy towel and iron while still damp. If you are uncertain about washability, test item by dipping the tail of a blouse or other inconspicuous part in the solution.

Making plastic antistatic: Add a tablespoon of white vinegar to each gallon of rinse water when washing plastic curtains. Vinegar cuts down on the attraction of dust. Plastic upholstery also can be wiped clean with a damp cloth wrung out from a water and vinegar solution.

Hair care: After washing, rinse hair well with 1 cup water containing 1 tablespoon white vinegar. This removes soapy film.

Relieves itching: White vinegar is a time-honored remedy for wasp stings, bruises, chapped hands, sunburn, and hives. It relieves the itching of mosquito and other insect bites. Apply full-strength unless area is raw. □ □

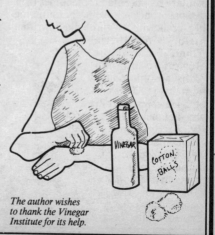

The author wishes to thank the Vinegar Institute for its help.

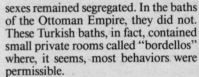

A Look Back: Plumbing and Sanitation in the Good(?) Old Days

It wasn't so long ago that bathing was considered dangerous.
And do you dare imagine why most bathrooms or privies were supplied with a pile of mussel shells?

by Kenneth Mirvis

☐ ST. FRANCIS OF ASSISI, ONE OF HIStory's true lovers of life, taught that dirtiness was a sign of holiness. St. Jerome was ashamed of his followers because they were too clean. St. Catherine of Siena publicly gave up washing for good, and St. Agnes reputedly died without ever having washed. They could have kept themselves clean; they just didn't want to.

Knowledge of sanitation, in fact, has been with us for centuries. More than 4,000 years ago, residents of the island of Crete built a palace that included a fresh water supply, a complete sewage system, and even wooden-seated flushing toilets. Nevertheless, almost 3,800 years passed before the toilet came into widespread use.

Despite painfully slow advances in sanitary practices (and sometimes their disappearance altogether), plumbing has been with us throughout written history. In imperial Rome, for example, elegant communal baths accommodated as many as 3,000 people. However, bathing was not necessarily for getting clean. The baths were social gathering places, suitable for conversation, relaxation, and who knows what else. In Rome the sexes remained segregated. In the baths of the Ottoman Empire, they did not. These Turkish baths, in fact, contained small private rooms called "bordellos" where, it seems, most behaviors were permissible.

While there may not be a connection, such "friendly" bathing habits immediately preceded the Middle Ages, Europe's darkest years. Plagues swept across the continent, wiping out 25 million people — a quarter of the population. Sanitation simply did not exist. Among the few great achievements of the Middle Ages were the remarkable castles built throughout Europe. They were small fortresses, cities under a single roof. Some, not so small, contained as many as 1,500 rooms. Their defense, as we all learned in grade-school history class, relied in part on the moats that surrounded them. But alas, that explanation is not entirely true. In fact, the moats did provide effective protection from invading enemies, but not by design. The castles contained no bathrooms. They did, however, have privies built into the outside walls that were dumped directly into the moats. The moats were nothing more than stagnant cess-

pools that must have been incomprehensibly disgusting. Only a fool would have crossed through one.

Medieval moats highlight the difficulties accompanying waste disposal. In 17th-century England, the problem reached staggering proportions. In 1609 London built a water system that brought clean water from a distance of 40 miles. With plenty of available water, the use of the water closet flourished. Then came the Industrial Revolution. Millions of people moved from rural areas to the city for work. In 1778 Joseph Brahma (and not, as legend would have it, John Crapper) received a patent for the float-and-valve flushing system still in use today. While water closets became more common, they were connected to cesspools by unventilated pipes. Not only did these WCs stink to high heaven, but they were also serious sources of bacteria and infection. In the true spirit of treating the symptom instead of the disease, the Stink Trap was patented in 1782. It successfully eliminated the smell but did nothing to stop the spread of disease.

Society simply did not know how to deal with the problems created by industrialization. In 1847 the British Parliament created a sewer commission and required that every house have some sort of sanitation: an ash pit, a privy, or a water closet. In 1848 they passed the National Public Health Act, a model plumbing code that much of the world has followed. But changes were slow in coming. Between 1849

and 1854, 20,000 Londoners died of cholera. The Thames — the source of most of London's drinking water — was also its sewer! The city had a population of three million and no waste treatment. All of the city's human and industrial waste flowed into the Thames River.

In 1859 Parliament actually had to be suspended for a short time because of the unbearable stench. In 1861 Prince Albert died from typhoid. In 1871 the Prince of Wales almost died from the same disease. Moved by his illness, his recovery, and the related sanitary conditions, he reportedly said that were he not a prince, he'd like to be a plumber.

From that point on, sanitation became a public concern, but it was hard to change old habits and fears. For example, a 19th-century administrator at Oxford College, a Dr. Routh, saw no reason to install showers or baths in the dormitories because "undergraduates were only in residence for eight weeks at a stretch."

Later that century, Mrs. Isabella Beeton — a "helpful hints" journalist of the day — wrote, "Baths are invaluable aids in promoting and preserving health, if properly used in suitable cases; but may become dangerous agents, causing even fatal results, if employed by the wrong individuals, at improper times, or with excessive frequency. Baths should never be taken

LOO!

immediately after a meal, nor when the body is very much exhausted by fatigue or excitement of any kind, nor during nor just before menstruation; and they should be sparingly and guardedly used by pregnant women."

Perhaps such fearfulness about things related to hygiene or bodily functions provides an explanation for a particularly interesting plumbing-related phenomenon: for 4,000 years the place where a person goes to do his or her "business" has never had a straightforward name. The bath or bathroom, after all, is not just for taking a bath, and the "necessary room" is a little oblique. The Israelis went to the "house of honor"; the Egyptians, to the "house of the morning"; Romans, to the "necessarium"; and Tudors went to the "privy," or the "house of privacy" (or they went to the "Jakes" — Jack's place, because everyone had to go — now known as the "John"). Even sailors, a hardy lot with a reputation for direct language, go to the "head."

Another favorite is the "loo." The word entered the vocabulary in one of several ways. Whenever a Frenchman tossed a load from his window, he first hollered, *"Guardez l'eau"* — watch out for the water. It was shortened to *l'eau* and soon became loo. Or, another story goes, it derived from an abbreviation of a common name for the necessary room, *la*

chambre sent, the smelly room. Apparently in order to avoid being quite so crude, the people changed the "s" to a "c" — *la chambre cent,* and the common name for the bathroom became Room 100. Soon the numeral 100 became loo, and it stuck.

Of course, before leaving the necessarium, the user must have a brief encounter with toilet paper — or some culturally appropriate equivalent. Toilet paper as we know it dates back to 1880 when it was introduced by the British Perforated Paper Company. Before that time, the cleaner of choice in the West was a scraper, usually a mussel shell. In the world's eastern countries, people ate only with their right hand; the left hand had another function (and to this day it is considered extremely gauche, so to speak, to eat with one's left hand in the Far East). The Romans used a stick with a sponge on one end — ergo the expression "the wrong end of the stick." In desert regions, sand was the cleaner of choice. In my home state of Georgia, there was the trusty corncob, and of course, the legendary Sears-Roebuck catalog. One mathematically inclined privy manager once estimated that if a Sears catalog were placed in a family's three-holer in January, they'd be to the harness section by June, if they didn't have too many visitors.

But cleansing by means of paper was not limited to the pages of the Sears-Roebuck catalog — any paper worked just fine. As one diligent correspondent replied to a friend after receiving a letter, "I am seated in the necessary house. I have your letter before me. Soon it will be behind me." □ □

President Garfield's Two Months of Agony

Through the years, all Americans have vicariously experienced, through exhaustive media coverage, horrendous national tragedies. But this was perhaps the longest.

Courtesy of John Robinson

☐ SHORTLY BEFORE HIS ASSASSINATION, Abraham Lincoln dreamed that he saw a casket in the White House, guarded by soldiers. When he asked one of them who was dead, the soldier said, "The president."

Sixteen years later, on June 30, 1881, President James A. Garfield was winding up the last Cabinet meeting before his vacation trip to New England. For some reason, he asked Secretary of War Robert Todd Lincoln to tell the story of his father's dream. Two days later, at 9:30 in the morning of July 2, Garfield was shot in a Washington railroad station. For the next 80 days the nation seemed to hold its collective breath as the president struggled to live.

The desperate effort to save the president enlisted the best that 19th-century medicine and science could offer. It caused a political and constitutional crisis such as the nation had never experienced and led in time to reforms that changed the face of American government. It was also the first national drama to be experienced vicariously, as it happened, by all 50 million American citizens. As the *New York Tribune* pointed out, "By the everyday miracle of the telegraph and the printing press, the whole mass of the people have been admitted to his bedside."

Although the assassination occurred during the slowest time of the year for the Washington press corps — in midsummer, when Congress and anyone else with any sense fled the hot, humid, malarial swamp that was the nation's capital — some 275,000 words were transmitted by correspondents via Western Union on that Saturday in July. That broke the previous all-time high of 190,000 words, set only four months earlier on the day Garfield was inaugurated.

Garfield had been a surprise choice as the nominee of the Republican Party in 1880. The convention had become deadlocked between the so-called "Stalwarts," who wanted to renominate Ulysses S. Grant, and the reform-minded "Half-Breeds," who favored James G. Blaine. Garfield was a compromise, with "Stalwart" Chester Arthur as his running mate.

But once elected, Garfield angered the "Stalwarts" by refusing to name their men to his Cabinet. A bizarre character named Charles Guiteau, who had been making a pest of himself seeking a diplomatic post, decided that God had chosen him to set things aright. He bought a pistol — spending an extra dollar on a bone handle that he thought would look good in a museum

— and practiced his marksmanship on the banks of the Potomac within earshot of the White House. Then he began stalking Garfield. On two occasions he was close enough to kill; once he decided against it because the president was with his wife, Lucretia. The other time, Guiteau felt too hot to bother.

He was cooler on the morning of July 2 — cool enough to drop the pistol after he fired the shots and surrender to a stunned policeman, saying, "I did it and want to be arrested. I am a Stalwart, and Arthur is president. Take me to the police station."

"In every city, in every town, in every village of the United States, groups formed about the telegraph and newspaper offices," wrote William Balch in his biography of Garfield hastily published later that year. "Before noon there was scarcely a man, woman, or child who did not know that the Chief Magistrate had been shot and probably killed." A great crowd of people waited outside the White House, where two companies of infantry under the personal command of General William Tecumseh Sherman stood guard.

Garfield was alive but grievously wounded. The assassin had fired two shots from close range; one merely grazed the president's shoulder, but the other smashed into his lower back, a few inches to the right of his spine. The first doctor to reach him tried to reassure Garfield that the wound was not serious, but the president was a Civil War veteran and more realistic: "I am a dead man," he said calmly.

At first, the doctors who examined Garfield thought the bullet had entered the liver and that he could not last the night. The president was taken to the White House, and his wife, who had been recovering from malaria in the New Jersey coastal resort of Elberon, was sent for. The Cabinet sent an urgent message to Vice President Arthur, who was in New York, telling him to be ready to take the oath of office.

But the president, a powerfully built six-footer who had been turning handsprings with his teenage sons the morning of the shooting, rallied. Out of a swarm of doctors, Garfield chose a boyhood friend, Dr. Willard Bliss, to supervise his treatment. Dr. Bliss, in turn, chose three physicians to assist him, ordering one of them, Army surgeon J. J. Woodward, not to reveal any unfavorable medical news to the president or the press.

Thus, as the summer wore on, millions in America and overseas clung hopefully to bulletins such as that of August 23: "The president continues to take by mouth and retain an increased quantity of liquid food. At the morning dressing the wound looked well, and the pus was of a healthy character. . . . "

"At the morning dressing the wound looked well, and the pus was of a healthy character."

Woodward's personal log for that same day had a starker tone: "In spite of our efforts to nourish the president, he is emaciating so rapidly that it is distressing to look at him. His weight has gone from 210 down to about 130 pounds. . . ."

The quality of the president's pus became a subject of intense public interest. "I should think the people would be tired of having me dished up to them in this way," said the wounded president of the daily bulletins.

Unsolicited medical advice came from all over the country. One man proposed that the president's body be "inverted for some hours in order that the bullet might gravitate downwards." Another outlined a plan to run a rubber tube into the wound until it made contact with the bullet, which could then be sucked out by an air pump. An Irish maid in the White House surreptitiously sprinkled holy water in the invalid's oatmeal.

Garfield's doctors were obsessed with locating the bullet, and one or another of them seemed to be poking an unsterile finger or probe into the open wound every day.

On July 26 Alexander Graham Bell and an assistant showed up at the White House with a new invention, a precursor of the metal detector, that he hoped would locate the bullet. A large group of spectators, including the conscious president and his wife, watched in fascination as Bell moved the contraption around Garfield's body, listening through earphones for a telltale click. He got no results that day but came back on August 1 for another try and announced that he had found it, in the president's groin. That was where Bliss and the others believed it to be all along. But the risk of exploratory surgery was too great.

All his doctors could do was try to keep him comfortable — a difficult task in the tropical heat. A team of Navy engineers devised the world's first workable air-conditioning unit that reduced the indoor temperature from 90 to 75 degrees. The president was dosed with quinine to prevent malaria.

While the doctors dithered, politicians wondered who was in charge of the country. The Constitution, which provided for the assumption of duties by the vice president during presidential disability, gave no guidelines on how such a decision should be made. Chester Arthur, after one courtesy call on the White House, tactfully remained in New York.

In all the 80 days Garfield survived, he performed only one official act — the signing of an extradition order on August 10. Fortunately for the nation, July, August, and the first part of September passed without any external threat or internal disorder.

On September 6 the dying president was moved from Washington to a seaside cottage in Elberon, where the climate was thought to be cooler and less dangerous. A baggage car was specially modified for the trip. The bed was delicately balanced so that the motion of the train would not jar the invalid, and a trial run was made, with Dr. Bliss taking the place of his patient, to try it out at various speeds.

The most spectacular preparations involved laying 3,200 extra feet of track

to take the president to the door of the house in which he would stay. Three hundred railroad workers and volunteers worked all night long to lay the track by lantern light, while the Elberon Hotel provided coffee and sandwiches.

When the train reached Elberon, Garfield's car was uncoupled and pushed by hand along the spur leading

Thousands lined railroad tracks to see the president's body borne home for burial.

to the 20-room cottage owned by a Mr. Francklyn. The president was tired but happy to be able to see the ocean and grumbled that he should have come three weeks earlier. "I am myself again," he said, to the excitement of all.

The president began to experience chest pains and to hallucinate. On September 18 he suddenly asked one of his aides, "Do you think my name will have a place in human history?"

The aide replied, "Yes, a grand one, but a grander one in human hearts. You must not talk that way. You have great work yet to perform."

"No, my work is done," Garfield whispered.

The president died on the night of September 19. Curiously, his body was embalmed before an autopsy took place, which added fuel to a fiery medical controversy over his treatment and cause of death that has hardly died out to this day. The official verdict of the autopsy was that Garfield died of a hemorrhage of his splenic artery, presumably nicked by the bullet, which was found nowhere near the place his doctors had predicted. Critics questioned why the artery should have waited 80 days to begin bleeding. The word "bacteria" does not appear in the report, although the evidence is strong that it was a raging infection that killed the president.

Charles Guiteau went to the gallows insisting that it was not he, but the doctors who killed James Garfield, and there were medical men who agreed with him. "It is indeed humiliating to the historian to record such a mass of irretrievable blunders," wrote one outraged physician to a medical journal. In the lay press, Bliss was taken to task for concealing the president's true condition — one newspaper went so far as to charge that he did it to make a profit on the stock market. He did not help his cause by engaging in an unseemly squabble with Congress over the size of his fee.

Many doctors, however, objected to the second-guessing. One recommended sarcastically that someone "gather into one volume — or a dozen volumes — all the plans of treatment which would, beyond question, have saved the life of our late president."

For the second time in a generation, thousands of Americans lined railroad tracks to see a president's body borne home for burial. Though he had only been in office four months, Garfield's death caused an outpouring of grief that exceeded that following Lincoln's murder. "There is no longer any South, North, East, or West," wrote Balch. "Guiteau's bullet will accomplish much to better our political life, to make purer our political purposes."

And in fact, it did. Chester A. Arthur, to the surprise of all, especially his friends in the New York political machine, pushed through a willing Congress a civil service reform bill that largely ended the frantic office-seeking that corrupted earlier administrations.

Perhaps that is the answer to Garfield's deathbed question about his place in history. His long suffering and dying, the agonizing spectacle that brought the nation to his bedside, united it in sorrow and put an end to the spoils system that had divided it in triumph. Garfield may have had some glimmer of that fact during his last days, for at one point he called for pen and paper and seemed to write his own epitaph: *Strangulatus Pro Republica.* Tortured for the Republic. □ □

The Only Foolproof Way to Hypnotize a Lobster

Anyone who plans to campaign for any elected office in the state of Maine would be well advised to master this technique.

by Edmund S. Muskie

☐ BACK WHEN I WAS CAMPAIGNING for governor of Maine, I would occasionally be called upon to demonstrate a technique taught to me by a fisherman from Owls Head, Maine: I would hypnotize a lobster.

A simple procedure, really. But be warned. There are a few things you must memorize before you mesmerize.

1. CHOOSING A LOBSTER: I never met a lobster I didn't like. A couple of prerequisites are:

— a firm grip
— good eye contact

To add to the drama of the demonstration, make sure your lobster is vigorous. Quite vigorous (see number two).

2. GETTING TO KNOW YOUR LOBSTER: Grasp him or her in your left hand, making sure you place your fingers just on the carapace (where the body and tail meet). Now see if your hand-held *Homarus americanus* is a flapper — you know, if the tail flaps quite a bit. If it does, then you've got a good one. Presumably you're trying this in front of a crowd, so wait until everyone is duly impressed before you move on to number three.

3. PUTTING YOUR LOBSTER IN A TRANCE: Now, when I was a senator, I listened to occasional speeches here and there that I thought were enough to put any self-respecting lobster to sleep. But here is a simpler way. Holding the lobster in your left hand, start stroking (with your right) the lobster's tail in a downward motion, curling it as you go. Do this until the lobster is inert.

4. MAKING YOUR LOBSTER DO SOMETHING LOBSTERS NORMALLY WOULDN'T DO: Moving carefully, you may now stand your lobster on his head, using the claws for support. In other words, you make a tripod. He'll stand like that until you wake him up.

5. WAKING UP YOUR LOBSTER: Grasp the lobster by the carapace — either hand, it doesn't matter — and shake. To arouse a particularly stubborn lobster, shake and whisper, "Drawn butter, drawn butter." ☐ ☐

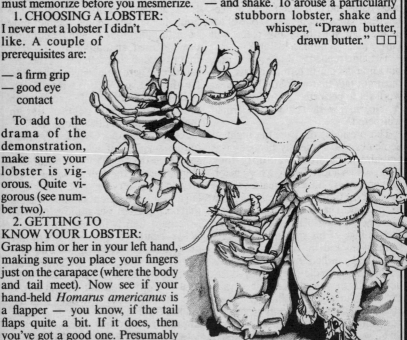

Home Sweet Ohio

Just when you thought you knew absolutely everything, we offer up this entertaining compendium of matters of fact about the Buckeye State.

Home of the Greenback: It was Lincoln's Secretary of the Treasury Salmon P. Chase (former Governor of Ohio) who ordered that federal currency be printed in green ink. He also gave us "In God We Trust" when he put the four words on a two-cent coin in 1864.

Ohioans of Banknote:

Ulysses S. Grant . . . . $50 bill
William McKinley . . . . $500 bill
Salmon P. Chase . . . . . . $10,000 bill

Home of Zane Grey, Zanesville dentist who sold his office equipment to finance his first novel, *Betty Zane,* the story of a pioneer ancestor who singlehandedly saved an Ohio River fort. Grey's subsequent books — among them *Riders of the Purple Sage* — went on to sell more than 130 million copies.

Home of the phrase "Rock 'n' Roll": In 1951 Cleveland disc jockey Alan Freed of WJW was the first to broadcast this Black idiom.

Home of the last surviving soldier of the American Revolution, John Gray, who died in Hiramsburg on March 29, 1868, at age 104. Gray had worked for George Washington at Mount Vernon and was present at Yorktown when Cornwallis surrendered. His epitaph: *John Gray, the Last of Washington's Companions. The Hoary Head Is a Crown of Glory.*

Home of the last passenger pigeon, Martha, who died at 1 P.M. on September 1, 1914, at the Cincinnati Zoo.

Home of the first air-conditioned department store, F. R. Lazarus Company, Columbus, 1934.

Home of the disposable diaper, Pampers, from Procter & Gamble of Cincinnati, 1962.

Home of the world's largest cuckoo clock, 24'x24', at the Alpine-Alpa Cheese House in Wilmont.

Home of the world's largest convention of twins (1,181 sets), at Twinsburg, August 1985.

Home of the world's largest lawn mower, the 60-foot-wide Big Green Machine, owned by Jay Edgar Frick of Monroe; it mows one acre per minute.

Home of the longest chicken flight on record, 302 feet 6 inches, by Lola B., at the Bob Evans Farm Chicken Flying Meet in Rio Grande in 1979.

Home of a 13½-pound radish grown by W. H. McKloskey of Perry Township, 1909. Also home to a 10-foot-long potato sprout found in his cellar by Frank Fitzpatrick of Sidney in 1910. Then there was the world's longest gourd, an 82-inch wonder produced in 1977 by Mark and Randy Ohlin of Poland (who fed it with horse manure and tucked it in at night with a blue blanket).

Ohio, home of seven presidents, all Republicans.

U·S·G·

R·B·H·

J·A·G·

Wm·M·

B·H·

Wm·H·T·

W·G·H·

Home of the world's most overdue book, a treatise on febrile diseases checked out of the University of Cincinnati Medical Library in 1823 and returned by the borrower's great-grandson in 1968. (Fine of $2,646 was waived.)

Home of the only diner owned by a historical society — Joe's, an Akron landmark deeded to the Summit County Historical Society.

Home of the only roller coaster that turns riders upside down six times during the ride, the Vortex at Kings Island.

Home of the only single-repeating-digit zip code, 44444, Newton Falls.

Home of many inventions that help keep chaos at bay: the automatic traffic signal (Garrett A. Morgan, Cleveland, 1923); the cash register (James S. Ritty, Dayton, 1879); the floating soap (Ivory, by Procter & Gamble, Cincinnati, 1879); the motorized spaghetti fork (William Miscavich and Paul Shutt, Canton, 1969); the vacuum cleaner (Murray Spangler, Canton, 1907).

Home of the towns of Fizzleville (Brown County), Knockemstiff (Ross County), Pee Pee (Pike County), and Dull (Van Wert County; named for James Monroe Dull, who owned the land). Not to mention 40 places named Washington and 38 named Madison.

Home of seven presidents in seven decades between the Civil War and Roaring Twenties — Grant, Hayes, Garfield, Harrison, McKinley, Taft, and Harding. Only one of them took us to war. Harrison was the last president (to date) to have a beard; Taft, the last to sport a moustache. Both Garfield and Harding weighed 10 pounds at birth. Taft, at 332 pounds adult weight, was the largest U.S. president. Grant suffered from fierce migraine headaches; Harding, from heartburn. All of them were Republicans.

Home of the Johnny Marzetti, a beef-cheese-tomato-macaroni casserole created by Mary Marzetti of Columbus around the turn of the century and named for her husband. It has become a cafeteria classic.

Home of Life Savers, originally available only in peppermint flavor ("for that Stormy Breath"), brought to us by Clarence Crane of Cleveland in 1912.

Home of many old jokes about Cleveland, including:

"What's the difference between Cleveland and the *Titanic*?"

"The *Titanic* had better restaurants."

And this one-liner:

"Cleveland is Detroit without the glitter."

Home of Laura Mae Whitlock McMartin Corrigan, a milkmaid who became a renowned international socialite of the 1920s. Husband Jimmy Corrigan provided her with a lavender Rolls Royce and liveried footman, appropriate trappings for the woman known as the "Flagpole Kelly of Social Climbers."

Home of Adib Karam and James Matz of Akron, who left that city in 1925 with one dollar, traveled by wit and grit to the Sahara, Bombay, and Peking, and returned home with five cents, a loaf of bread, and the makings of a book, *A Vagabond Journey Around the World — On Nothing.*

Home of the first aluminum saucepan, made in Cleveland in 1890 by Henry Avery and used faithfully by Mrs. Avery for 43 years.

Home of Crisco, the first hydrogenated oil, invented by Procter & Gamble in 1911.

Home of Little Miss Sure Shot (Annie Oakley), King of the Cowboys (Roy Rogers), Liberator of Bulgaria (J. A. MacGahan), Old Iron Pants (General Curtiss LeMay), Drummer Boy of Shiloh (Johnny Clem), and The Red Napoleon (Tecumseh); home of Porkopo-

lis (Cincinnati), Pierogi Capital of America (Cleveland), High School Reunion Capital of the U.S. (Dayton), and Earthquake Capital of Ohio (Anna). Home of The King (Clark Gable).

Home of Columbus's Mary Catherine Campbell, who in 1922 became the first Miss America. She took the title again in 1923 to become the only two-time winner ever. Her boyish figure with its 30-inch bosom set the style for Roaring Twenties flappers.

Home of Berea Grit, also known as Berea sandstone, a cache of light sedimentary rock that made Berea the grindstone capital of the world in the 1800s and provided Ohio with some of its firmest foundations.

Home of Rock of Ages, the biggest rock ever found in Ohio, a 430-million-year-old limestone mass that covers most of an acre. It was left by glaciers near the north fork of Olive Branch not far from Oregonia.

Home of Orville and Wilbur Wright of Dayton, and of a dubious editor at the local newspaper who, when told of the brothers' first successful flight at Kittyhawk, reportedly responded, "Fifty-seven seconds? If it had been fifty-seven minutes it *might* have been a news story." Instead he ran an item saying the brothers would be home for Christmas, thereby becoming editor of the greatest story never told. □ □

Excerpted with permission from *Ohio Matters of Fact,* published by Orange Frazer Press, Inc., P.O. Box 610, Wilmington, OH 45177. Editor Damaine Vonada welcomes additions to her collection of Ohioana; readers may write to P.O. Box 31101, Dayton, OH 45431.

The Day George Washington Became President (200 Years Ago)

It was reportedly cloudy. The president-elect made his audience wait for an hour and ten minutes. He wore a brown suit. He was so nervous he trembled, and he didn't give the speech he had originally written.   by Christopher Roberts

☐ AT SUNRISE ON APRIL 30, 1789, George Washington awoke to the familiar sound of gunfire. Thirteen cannons at the south end of Manhattan roared a salute; then all the church bells of New York began to ring. Today he would be inaugurated as the first president of the United States.

He was alone. Martha had stayed at Mount Vernon, and Washington probably wished he had, too. The night before he left, he wrote to friends: "I approach the chair of government with feelings not unlike those of a culprit who is going to his place of execution."

There had been so many guards of honor, triumphal arches, and other civic festivities on his way north that he was exhausted. He had written to New York's Governor Clinton asking that he

be allowed to enter the city without ceremony, but when he reached the Jersey shore to cross over to Manhattan, he was placed in a fancy barge manned by 13 sea captains and rowed to the Battery through a flotilla of cheering spectators.

Washington was supposed to have been inaugurated on the fourth of March, as specified in the Constitution. The delay was due to muddy roads that postponed the arrival of the new Congress and then a lengthy debate over how the new president should be addressed. Fire companies and cricket clubs had presidents, said vice president-elect John Adams. The dignity of the nation required something grander: "His Highness the President of the United States and Protector of the Rights of the Same" was Adams's suggestion. Congress decided to stick with "Mr. President," but certain members began referring to the plump vice president as "His Rotundity."

Washington, who probably would have balked at being called "your Highness," rose shortly after sunrise, powdered his hair, and put on his sword and a suit of brown woolen broadcloth with silver buttons. His suit was a gift from the just-opened Hartford Manufacturing Company in Connecticut, the first U.S. wool-fabric maker. Wearing it was a political statement that the new nation had no need to buy its clothes from England. It was also a coup for Congressman Jeremiah Wadsworth of Connecticut, who was behind the idea of the gift. He knew that fashionable New Yorkers would pay close attention to what the president wore to his inauguration and promised he could sell another 100 yards afterwards. Indeed, brown broadcloth from Hartford became all the rage.

A little after noon a delegation from Congress arrived at the house where Washington was staying to escort him to the Federal Hall, where the ceremony would take place. They climbed into a carriage drawn by four horses and started making their way slowly through the huge crowds. The short trip, through what is now Pearl Street and then to Broad, was so delayed by the throng that it took more than an hour.

No one knows for sure what the weather was like. Sixty-five years after the fact, the aged Washington Irving recalled that it was cloudy early in the day but that the sun came out around nine. Mary Hunt Palmer, who was 14 at the time, had a different recollection. She reported in 1858 that it had rained so furiously that Washington himself had carried an umbrella on his way to the Federal Building. Contemporary accounts are silent on the weather, which suggests that nothing so remarkable as a heavy rain occurred.

If it had, it surely would have been recorded by Senator William Maclay of Pennsylvania, whose eyewitness account of the inauguration is the most entertaining, if somewhat biased, guide to what truly happened. Maclay was a republican with a small "r," one of those who, like Jefferson, disdained pomp and detested "His Rotundity."

According to Maclay, the Senate met at 11:30 that morning, and while waiting for the President-elect to arrive, got embroiled in a furious debate, initiated by Adams, over whether the Senators should stand or sit during Washington's inaugural speech.

Before the issue could be settled, the clerk of the House of Representatives came to the door with a message from the Speaker. This touched off a new debate over how such a message should be received — should the clerk be allowed into the Senate Chambers? Who should escort him? Adams was in a dither.

The crisis intensified when word came that the Speaker himself and all the Representatives were now cooling their heels at the door. "Confusion ensued," Maclay commented. Finally the Speaker and the House were permitted to enter, where, Maclay recorded, "we sat an hour and ten minutes before the president arrived."

Finally the great man appeared. Adams welcomed him, saying: "Sir, the Senate and the House of Representatives are ready to attend you to take the oath required by the Constitution." Then, wrote Maclay, Adams "seemed to have forgot what he was to say, for he made a dead pause and stood for some time . . . in a vacant mood."

Adams eventually bowed and led Washington and other dignitaries to a balcony overlooking Wall and Broad streets. The streets, windows, and rooftops were packed, and when the people saw their hero on the balcony, they howled with delight. The general was

---

"He trembled, and several times could scarce make out to read."

---

apparently overcome with emotion; he bowed three or four times, placed his hand over his heart, then sank into a chair for a few moments. Then he stood and placed his hand on the Bible. The tumult ceased.

Robert Livingston, the Chancellor of New York, asked: "Do you solemnly swear that you will faithfully execute the office of president of the United States and will, to the best of your ability, preserve, protect, and defend the Constitution of the United States?"

Washington swore the oath, then kissed the Bible. Livingston turned to the crowd and cried, "Long live George Washington, president of the United States!" The masses repeated the accolade and gave the new president three mighty cheers. The flag was hoisted to the cupola of the Federal Building, cannons boomed, and the church bells clanged again. Washington bowed to the crowd a few more times, then went back into the Senate chambers to deliver his inaugural speech. The legislators, still in the dark about protocol, rose when he did, but he bowed and everyone sat down again.

It was not a very good speech, nor was it well delivered. Maclay noted that "this great man was agitated and em-barrassed more than ever he was by the leveled cannon or pointed musket. He trembled, and several times could scarce make out to read." Washington nervously transferred his speech from one hand to the other, placing the free hand in his trouser pocket, and at one point made a flourish with his right hand, "which left rather an ungainly impression." Maclay blamed the president's poor showing on the "dancing-masters" who insisted on unrepublican formality. But he admitted that "the composition may be termed heavy, dull, stupid."

Maclay might have liked better the inaugural speech that Washington didn't give. It was 62 pages long, and only fragments of it remain, but what's there is colorful and compelling. In it, Washington seems obsessed with the dangers of unchecked ambition: ". . . no Wall of words . . . no mound of parchment can be so formed as to stand against the sweeping torrent of boundless ambition," he warns the legislators, and repeats, "they should guard against ambition as their greatest enemy."

No one knows why he chose not to make that speech. Washington was a man of strong passions — Gilbert Stuart, after painting his portrait, said, "Had he been born in the forests, he would have been the fiercest man among the savages" — but he kept them under stern control. Looking at the unbridled language of his first draft, he may have decided that it revealed too much and that it was safer to stick to the bland text he mumbled in New York. Even in war, Washington was better at avoiding disaster than achieving brilliant victories.

After the speech, everyone walked uptown to St. Paul's Chapel for divine services. That evening there were fireworks and illuminations, and a round of parties featuring "transparent paintings." One historian, harking back to Revolutionary War defeats on the same ground, declared that "at last, after many years, Washington had captured New York." □ □

Straight Facts About Warts (and Some Surefire Cures)

The amazing thing about wart remedies is that they all work . . . if you believe in them.

by Tim Clark

"Say — what is dead cats good for, Huck?"
"Good for? Cure warts with!"
　　　　　— The Adventures of Tom Sawyer

☐ DEAD CATS, MASHED ANTS, DANDElion juice, chicken feet, dirt from a fresh grave — they're all good for curing warts. You can talk them off, hypnotize them away, wish them on a gray horse's backside, or lick them every morning until they disappear. There are probably more folk remedies for warts than for any other complaint, and the amazing thing is that they all work — *if* you believe in them.

"The strangest thing about warts is that they tend to go away," says Dr. Lewis Thomas of the Memorial Sloan-Kettering Cancer Center in New York. "And they can be made to go away by something that can only be called thinking or something like thinking."

In his essay "On Warts," which originally appeared in *The New England Journal of Medicine*, Dr. Thomas describes an experiment in which 14 patients with stubborn cases of warts on both sides of their bodies were hypnotized. While under trance, each was told that the warts on one particular side of his or her body would go away. Within a few weeks, eight of the patients had lost all the warts on the suggested sides of their bodies. A ninth, who got his left and right mixed up, lost all the warts on the side of his body *opposite* to the one suggested.

Though we are still ignorant of what makes warts go away, we know that they are caused by human papilloma virus. The virus has been photographed and studied in detail. It is a tiny thing with a head and a tail. The head is so small you could fit 127 million of them side by side in one inch. There are at least 15 different papilloma viruses, and they cause different kinds of warts.

You can get warts from another person who has them, or they can spread from one part of your body to another. But the virus seems to grow at different speeds depending on the individual. Scientists have inoculated volunteers with papilloma virus to see how long it takes before warts appear. For some people it took a few weeks, for others more than a year. They disappear with the same disdain for consistency, but disappear they surely

will. Half of all warts clear up within one year, two-thirds within two years. Many folk sayings associate warts with evil ("a wart on the chin is a devil within"), but in some places they are considered lucky or a sign of wealth. To dream of warts means you have a secret lover, but a wart on the neck means you will be hanged. In Kentucky, people think you can cure a toothache by cutting a wart off a horse's leg and rubbing it on the sore gums. Some people are proud of their warts: the English dictator Oliver Cromwell told a painter that if his portrait didn't include his warts, he wouldn't pay a farthing for it.

- Give your warts names, and think good things about them.
- Sell the wart to someone and don't spend the money.
- Point your finger at it and say "Tige" three times.
- Rub it on St. Abdon's Day (July 30).
- Rub it with the sole of your shoe.
- Rub it with an onion.
- Wish your warts onto a gray horse's backside.
- Cross two pins over a wart then hide them.
- Wrap a pea in a rag and throw it down a well.

BIZARRE AND COMPLICATED
- Put as many stones as you have warts in a bag and toss it over your right shoulder onto a road; whoever picks up the bag will get the warts.
- Find a bone, turn it over, then throw it away; walk off without looking back.
- Have a child who has never seen its father breathe on it.
- Cut an apple in half, rub each half over the wart, tie the halves together, and throw them away.
- Rub it with coffee grounds, put the grounds in a bag, and bury it.
- Rub it with seven kernels of corn, then feed the corn to your neighbor's chickens.
- Look at the new moon and rub the wart three times, saying "You grow and you go" each time.
- Write a wish on a piece of paper, go to a crossroads, then tear it up and scatter it to the wind.

50 Ways Our Grandparents Used to Make Warts Go Away

SIMPLE AND EASY
- Buy five cents worth of candy and eat it all.
- Rub with dandelion juice.
- Rub seven times with a gold ring.
- Wash your hands in water used to boil potatoes.
- Count them each night for nine nights.
- Give a pin to a girl who is not related to you.

Though their Latin name, *Verruca vulgaris*, suggests that warts are commonplace, it is we who should feel humble in their presence — or rather in their absence — because *something* makes a wart go away, and that something is a lot smarter than we are. "If my unconscious can figure out how to manipulate the mechanisms needed for getting around that virus and for deploying all the various cells in the correct order for tissue rejection, then all I have to say is that my unconscious is a lot further along than I am," says Lewis Thomas. "I wish I had a wart right now, just to see if I am that talented." □□

— When you see the new moon, pick up any object on which your foot rests, and rub it on the wart; then walk backwards ten steps and throw it over your right shoulder.
— Without telling anyone, pick up a stone at midnight, spit on it, then put it on a rafter in the attic; after eight weeks, turn it over.

FAINTLY REPELLENT
— Prick the wart with a pin, put the blood on a cloth, and drop it in the path of a stranger; if he picks it up, he gets the wart.
— Tie a dog's hair very tightly around the wart.
— Rub it with a fish.

— Make the wart bleed, smear blood on a bean leaf, hide it under a stone, and walk away backwards.
— Wait until someone dies, then go to the graveyard at midnight and call to the devil; he will take your warts away.
— Kiss the wart, then kiss someone else.
— Rub it with a pebble, then toss the pebble into an open grave.
— Rub it with a chicken foot.
— Rush up and seize the person with the wart, then spit on it.
— Lick the wart when you awaken, before eating or drinking.

EXTREMELY DISGUSTING
— Rub it with cow's urine.
— Rub it with chicken intestines.
— Rub it with a snail.
— Rub it with a rooster's head.
— Cover it with cow manure.
— Mash ants on it.
— Rub it with dirt from a new grave.

DOWNRIGHT CRIMINAL
— Wish your warts on someone whose name you know, but whom you've never met.
— Rub stolen meat on it, then bury the meat.
— Steal a dishcloth and hide it.
— Steal a piece of chalk, rub it on the wart, then throw it away.
— Kill a black cat, take it to a graveyard at midnight, rub it on the wart.
— Wash the wart in the blood of a black cat killed in the light of the moon.
— Rub it with the hand of a corpse.
— Rub it with dead man's spit.

An Hour of Flood, a Night of Flame

On the afternoon of May 31, 1889, the dam burst and 20 million tons of water raged down the Little Conemaugh Valley toward Johnstown, Pennsylvania. . . .　　　　by Norm D. Blume

☐ THE REVEREND H. L. CHAPMAN, minister of the Methodist Church in Johnstown, Pennsylvania, had just sat down to begin work on his next sermon. The text was: "But man dieth, and wasteth away: yea, man giveth up the ghost, and where is he?" The doorbell rang. He answered it and found his wife's cousin, Mrs. A. D. Brinker, standing on the front porch, agitated and soaking wet from the rain that had been falling all night.

The wretched woman was terrified that the South Fork dam would burst on account of the high water and that the town would be deluged. "Johnstown is going to be destroyed today!" she wailed.

The minister, however, remained calm. "Well, Sister Brinker, you have been fearing this for years, and it has never yet happened," Chapman said. "I don't think there is much danger."

It was May 31, 1889, and Mrs. Brinker's prophecy, repeated so many times that her neighbors laughed about it, was about to be fulfilled. Before the day was over, the dam would indeed burst, and most of Johnstown and several neighboring communities would be smashed, swamped, or burned. More than 2,200 persons would die in

The force of the flood waters left such surreal scenes as the Schultz house with a tree through the second story.

America's worst flood — a disaster at first seen as a visitation from God, but later revealed to have been man-made and avoidable.

The dam was 37 years old in 1889 and held 450 acres of water suspended 450 feet above the streets of Johnstown, 14 miles of narrow river valley away. Originally planned as a reservoir that would supply water to the Pennsylvania Canal, the completion of a railroad line through the Allegheny Mountains made it obsolete before it was finished. It was purchased in 1879 by the South Fork Fishing and Hunting Club, whose members included some of the wealthiest and most powerful men in the country: Andrew Carnegie, future Treasury Secretary Andrew Mellon, and future Secretary of State Philander Knox. In Pittsburgh, where most of the members lived, it was known as the "Bosses Club."

The old dam had burst once before, in 1862, but the water was low and little damage occurred. When the rich men of Pittsburgh took over, they ordered the dam repaired so that they could stock the reservoir with fish and ply its waters with sailboats. The materials dumped against the clay foundation of the dam included rock, mud, brush, hay, and horse manure. A fish screen was placed across the spillway to ensure that none of the expensive black bass with which the lake had been stocked could slip downstream to be caught by nonmembers. There was no discharge pipe, so there was no way that the water level could be lowered in an emergency.

Such an emergency seemed most unlikely. The two rivers that met at Johnstown — the Little Conemaugh and the Stony Creek — ran high every spring, often inundating parts of the town. There had been floods in 1885, 1887, and 1888. Though everyone talked about the possibility of the dam letting go, it never had. In time it became a local joke, the bogey of nervous ladies like Mrs. Brinker.

But an ecological catastrophe was in the making. The population of Johns-

town tripled to 30,000 after the Civil War, when it became a steel-making center. The steep hillsides were stripped of timber, causing severe erosion. April had been snowy, and a storm on the night of May 30 dumped seven inches of rain on the barren slopes around the reservoir. The fish screen in the spillway was clogged with debris, reducing its flow to a trickle. The water began to rise, to lap over the top of the dam. Men worked frantically to stop it, but at ten minutes after three on the afternoon of the 31st the dam gave way. Twenty million tons of water went rampaging down the Little Conemaugh valley.

Legend says that a horseman named Daniel Peyton raced ahead of the angry waters, Paul Revere-like, spreading the alarm. He never existed. But Johnstown had been warned. Three messages had been sent from the dam, by telegraph and by foot, saying the flood was imminent. They were paid no more heed than Mrs. Brinker.

The wave smashed the little valley villages first: South Fork, Mineral Point, East Conemaugh, Woodvale. Their only warning came from a Pennsylvania Railroad engineer named John Hess who heard a noise like a hurricane and saw "a commotion in the timber." He drove his engine toward East Conemaugh with the whistle shrieking and gave many people there the chance to scramble uphill. Hess wanted to go all the way into Johnstown, but the track wasn't clear. He jumped out of his cab to safety.

The people of Johnstown heard a rumble, a roar, a sound like "a lot of horses grinding oats." The few survivors who actually saw the 35-foot wall of water approaching said it looked like a hill covered with rubbish — rooftops, trees, pieces of houses — preceded by a black mist, "a mist of death."

Buildings went down like dominoes. Every tree in the city park was ripped out by the roots and flung, along with houses, freight cars, horses, cows, and people, against the mountainside on the other end of town. After the gigantic wave crashed against the hill, the backwash sped up the untouched valley of the Stony Creek, dealing death and destruction. The center of the city was erased in ten minutes.

The wave had spent much of its force in hitting the hillside, so the stone bridge downstream from the place where the Little Conemaugh and the Stony Creek joined survived. As debris piled up around its arches, a new dam

Twenty million tons of water went rampaging down the Little Conemaugh valley. As darkness fell, the whole twisted heap caught fire "with all the fury of hell."

was formed, along with a lake 30 feet deep in places. The bridge saved hundreds of people who had ridden their houses or rooftops with the flood; they climbed, many of them naked and bleeding, over the wreckage to the roadway and fled to higher ground. But many were trapped inside the mound of rubbish, and they suffered the most hideous fate of all. As darkness fell, the whole twisted heap caught fire. It burned "with all the fury of hell," wrote one witness, throughout the night. Perhaps as many as 80 people were cremated alive.

The stories of those who survived verged on the miraculous. Six-year-old Gertrude Quinn was swept away on a mattress. There she bobbed along like a cork until a man named Maxwell McAchren jumped off a floating rooftop and joined her. He managed to throw her from the little raft to rescuers in the window of a building that was left standing. McAchren was pulled out of the water farther downstream.

James Walters, a lawyer, was carried on a piece of debris from his home all the way to the Alma Hall, a sturdy brick building downtown. When he hit the building, he flew off his raft into a window and found himself in his own office. Eighty-year-old Ann Buck spent the night in a tree. Rose Clark had a leg pinned under the wreckage at the bridge, and as the fire approached, rescuers nearly decided to cut her leg off. Luckily, she was pulled out, whole, before the flames reached her.

In the days immediately following the disaster, it was feared that as many as 10,000 might have perished. The actual count came to 2,209, though bodies continued to be discovered as late as 1906. Fifty undertakers were needed to bury the victims. The property damage was estimated at $17 million.

The Johnstown Flood was the story of the decade. It occupied every inch of the front page of *The New York Times* for five days running. More than $3.7 million in cash was sent to help the city rebuild, along with tons of food and clothing and other supplies for the victims. Clara Barton showed up with her new American Red Cross and stayed for five months, working every day.

Some of the millionaire members of the South Fork Fishing and Hunting Club gave generously to relief efforts. Some gave nothing at all. Neither the club nor any of its members paid a dime in damages. But a man named Isaac Reed, remembering the fish screens that blocked the spillway of the South Fork dam, wrote a poem that summarized the feelings of the nation:

An hour of flood, a night of flame,
A week of woe without a name,
A week when sleep with hope had fled,
While misery hunted for its dead,
A week of corpses by the mile,
A long, long week without a smile,
A week whose tale no tongue can tell,
A week without a parallel!
All the horrors that hell could wish,
Such was the price that was paid — for fish!

Note: For a complete account of the tragic flood, the editors recommend David McCullough's *The Johnstown Flood,* first published in 1968 and now available in paperback from Simon and Schuster.

Profits from the Trash Bin

Here's a fascinating sampler of different ways folks have found to make a good living selling things most people would throw away.

by Art Sordillo

☐ OVER 20 YEARS AGO, REYNolds Aluminum decided to recycle cans. Of course Reynolds had to rely on can collectors — folks who decided to pick up and sell what most people would just kick. The idea caught on: over the years, the aluminum industry has collected 268 billion cans. Can collectors have collected $4 billion. And somewhere in America there is a man or woman with a big bank account living in a big house, just because he or she collected cans in a very big way.

Mark Twain complained that he was seldom able to see an opportunity until it had ceased to be one. But that's precisely the logic that the junk dealer, or anyone on the lookout for an unlikely profit, uses to an almost unfair advantage. It's a simple rule — "Why throw it away when you can sell it?"

RAGS

Dennis McGurk and Ed Callahan have cornered the market on rags. Ed will tell you, "Hey, we carry a full line." Their company, Industrial Wiper Supply, in Chelsea, Massachusetts, has done pretty well. A good year might net them over $3 million. Old diapers are the best. Ed looks at an old diaper as if it were the Golden Fleece. "Strictly our top-of-the-line item — nothing beats them. Although sometimes we pick up some good things from hotels — their old towels and stuff." And from old towels, old diapers, and old pants you get rags, which in turn are washed, baled, and sold for industrial-size mop-ups. However, their business has created some by-products nobody can market: "We have a lot of old zippers and buttons." Ed has four people working in sales going from factory to factory, wherever a customer might have something that needs to be wiped up. His partner Dennis does some sales as well. Ed laughs and says, "Yeah, Dennis keeps all his samples in the trunk of his Mercedes."

GREASE

In the *Wall St. Journal* you will always be able to find a cash-price commodity quote on grease (choice, white). Rendering fat and grease is a billion-dollar-a-year industry in the United States (grease is used in livestock feed) — but before you can render it, you have to collect it. Tom Driscoll is the route manager for Baker Commodities in Vernon, California. Tom makes sure his drivers get out and get the grease. "We use a vacuum tank truck. It has a hose to suck it up." Tom sends his drivers out to fast food establishments, taco stands, butcher shops — anywhere the oil boils and the suet sits. Mr. Driscoll wouldn't get really specific and talk numbers. But each truck (he has several) collects 24,000 pounds of grease every other day, and according to Tom, "We've been in business quite awhile."

OLD CARS

Call him Captain Crunch. Larry Danielle keeps a beast named "Big Mac" in his junkyard, and it's not a dog. It's his automobile crusher. "It's a nice machine," he says. Mr. Danielle has 18 acres of old cars that make up "Danielle Used Auto, Truck & Foreign Parts" in Davie, Florida. First an old car comes in and is stripped completely for parts. Next it's crushed and then loaded onto a truck and brought to a steel shredder. "I guess it takes about a minute for it to go through the shredder," Larry says. (Last year, the U.S. exported over 60 million tons of shredded steel.) Larry won't mention money, but he looks pretty comfortable. "Buy American," he'll tell you. His favorite cars for Big Mac are anything foreign: "The foreign cars scrunch easy and don't strain the crusher so much."

FEATHERS

"Down is down right now," says Dorothy Hobbs with some disappointment. Dorothy and her husband Don know where to buy and sell feathers. They own Hobbs Feather Company in West Liberty, Iowa. At first Dorothy was hesitant to talk much about the company: "We have to be careful with our competitors." But in a business that's not just for the birds, the stakes are high. "We sell over 100,000 pounds of feathers a year: turkey, goose, duck, and fancy ones, too." The feathers are washed, dried, and fluffed right on the premises. Mostly, they're sold to fly-tyers and bedding companies. "We also dye feathers — we have 63 different colors." Dorothy is always looking to buy bird feathers and bird skins, so give her a call if you have any. Maybe you'll catch her on a good day, when the market for down is up.

CHICKEN FEET

An average chicken foot weighs an ounce. Rockingham Poultry Marketing Cooperative in Broadway, Virginia, has a lot of chicken feet. "We sell about 50 metric tons a month overseas, mostly to China," says Henry Holler, vice president of sales. He continues, "They eat them spiced, as hors d'oeuvres." Mr. Holler gets serious when he discusses how the trade evolved. "In the chicken-foot business, it's important to sell a good product. Now most of your high-speed pluckers break the feet, so we came up with a better way — to see to it nobody buys a broken leg." Holler has succeeded where others have failed. He has cracked the overseas market. Henry doesn't like throwing around dollar signs but allows, "Let's just say that the new machinery we developed will pay for itself."

SUNKEN SHIPS

Sidney J. Simon is in the sunken-ship business. Sidney moves around pretty well for a fellow who's 71 — that's probably why he couldn't be pinned down. But Mrs. Simon, at home in Miami, Florida, was able to fill in the cracks here and there. Estabelle estimates that

Sidney owns about a dozen or so wrecks off the coast of Nova Scotia. "They're all registered with Lloyd's of London — you can check if you like." Most of the ships were acquired by Sidney's father from insurance companies. Sidney bought the ships from his Dad back in the 1940s. He has been interested in finding a buyer ever since. If you can find Sidney, you may find your pot of gold: salvage is big business. "Sidney's up in Canada, so I can't contact him right now," said Estabelle, "but he's worth a story." No doubt.

According to Mrs. Simon, "If you bought one of those ships, you could probably buy a house like Michael Jackson's." Some of the underwater highlights are a World War I destroyer, a hospital ship, and a couple of cargo ships with sizable bronze propellers (worth $50,000 each). So make Sidney an offer. But where is Sidney? Sometimes Estabelle isn't quite sure. "That Sidney," says Estabelle, "he's so independent . . . a typical Scorpio."

PIG TAILS

There's at least one part of the pig that doesn't go in a hot dog, and William Redd sells it: the tail. At Gwaltney Meat Packing in Smithfield, Virginia, Redd is vice president of sales and seems to have reinvented the squeal.

"Well, on average, I'd guess there's about three pig tails to the pound; 'course that depends on the size of the pig." Right. Pig tails go for about 45¢ a pound overseas. Mr. Redd sells most of his tails to South America, where they are pickled. We took Mr. Redd's word for this. The next question was how many tails are sold. "Hard to say, but we process about 1,000 pigs an hour."

OLD TIRES

In North Haven, Connecticut, Bruce Eber collects tires. He stores them on his 42-acre site, which right now has 12 million tires on it. "I have the capacity to store 40 million," he says. Bruce hasn't found a market for old tires, but as owner of Tire Salvage Inc., he's working on it. "You have to remember," warns Bruce, "that I don't buy them. People pay me to take them away." And how much is that? Mr. Eber charges two dollars to pick up a car tire. Two dollars a tire, 12 million tires. Pretty easy to figure. And the tires keep rolling in, 100,000 every month.

AN UNLIKELY TAX DEDUCTION

So maybe you go into an unlikely business and make a lot of money. As we all know, donating to a nonprofit agency is one way of cutting back on taxable income. Get in touch with Jeanne Sallman in Phoenix, Arizona; Jeanne will be happy to accept your donation — just so long as it's a collection of brand-new, never been worn, odd shoes. Sallman is director of the National Odd Shoe Exchange. "People who need one shoe, usually for some medical reason, contact me (1-602-246-8725). Sometimes they join our network. It's $7.50 to join and $7.50 a year dues." Each member submits a record of his shoe size, and Jeanne keeps it on file. "We get donations from shoe stores, department stores — anyplace that would have a supply of new, single shoes." Jeanne also can obtain a pair of shoes for you even if your feet are two different sizes. "After all," says Jeanne, "I know how hard it is to find what you need; my left foot is size six, and my right is size four." □ □

Forgotten Holidays

Unfortunately the reason for celebrating certain dates in certain places has been lost in the mists of time. Here are a few that should always be remembered.
by Don Bousquet

January 9
The banks close and the kids are out of school in Yorba Linda, California. It's "Nixon's Birthday."

February 13
"Anti-Arbor Day"
Minnesota

March 16
"St. Vinnie's Day"
Patron saint of
auto mechanics.

April 5
"All Quahogs Day"
The entire population
of Rhode Island dons
quahog suits to honor
the state's favorite
creature, the hard-
shelled clam.

May 2
"Purple Martin Day"
At the world center for
the study of the purple martin.

June 18
"Brother-in-Law Day"
Be nice to your brother-in-law.

November 3
"Sanitation Truck Grand Prix and Cookout Day"
Kankakee, Illinois

November 23
"Franklin Pierce
Day of Atonement"
New Hampshire
The entire state practices self-
flagellation on this date for being
the birthplace of the 14th
president.

GENERAL WEATHER FORECAST
1988-1989

(For details see regional forecasts beginning on page 134.)

NOVEMBER THROUGH MARCH will be warmer than normal over most of the country, with the central Great Plains through the Ohio River Valley to the south Atlantic seaboard having well-above-normal temperatures. Only New England, southern Florida, and the desert Southwest are anticipated to have slightly below-normal values. Precipitation is anticipated to be well above normal in coastal New England, the Mississippi River Valley, east Texas, and the Pacific Northwest. Slightly above-normal amounts are expected in portions of the middle and south Atlantic states and southern Florida, the Ohio River Valley, and the western Great Lakes. The rest of the country may see below-normal precipitation, with the Southwest, the western Great Plains, the eastern Great Lakes to western New England, and northern Florida in particular having well-below-normal amounts. Snowfall will be above normal in southern and coastal New England down through the middle Atlantic states and across to the eastern Great Lakes and the Ohio River Valley to the Mississippi. The Great Plains, Great Lakes, southern Great Basin, and much of California are anticipated to have below-normal amounts, while the rest of the West should have above normal, particularly in the northern Rockies and Cascades.

APRIL THROUGH OCTOBER: Spring will be warmer than usual over the whole country except for the Northeast from the Great Lakes through New England and in a few isolated areas such as southern Florida and the central Pacific coast. The Rocky Mountain region on east through the central and northern Great Plains and the upper Ohio River Valley, in particular, may have well-above-normal temperatures. The Eastern Seaboard is expected to have above-normal precipitation, except that central and southern Florida will be drier than normal, with well-above-normal amounts in the Ohio River Valley, the Gulf states, and southern California. Most of the rest of the country will have below-normal amounts, with the Northwest and southwestern sections of the Great Plains and Great Lakes being particularly dry.

Summer will be slightly cooler than normal over most of the eastern half of the country and slightly warmer than normal from the western Great Plains to the Pacific coast. The greater part of the country will have below-normal precipitation, particularly so in the southern Great Lakes, Ohio and lower Mississippi river valleys, the southwestern Great Plains, and the extreme Northwest. Above-normal rainfall is expected in New England, the mid-Atlantic states, southern Florida, the northern Great Plains, and the desert Southwest.

Fall will be quite variable, with warm and dry spells alternating with cool and wet ones. The northern half of the country east of the Rockies will be slightly warmer than normal, but the rest slightly cooler or very close to normal. The country will be wetter than normal except for New England, the middle Atlantic states, Florida, and the region from the southern Great Lakes to eastern Texas.

U.S. WEATHER REGIONS

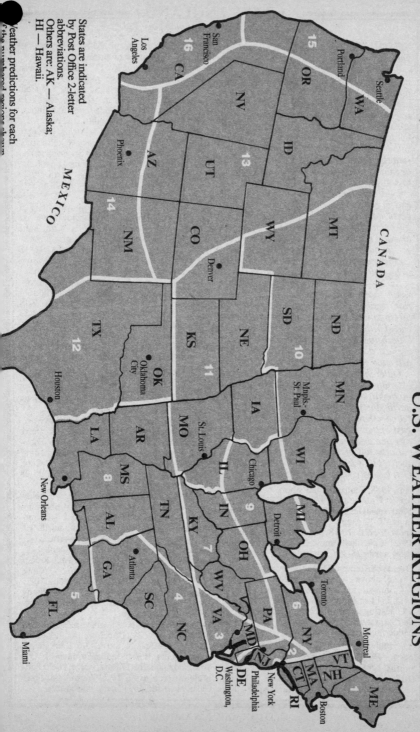

States are indicated by Post Office 2-letter abbreviations. Others are: AK — Alaska; HI — Hawaii.

Weather predictions for each of the numbered regions shown

For regional boundaries, see map page 133.

SUMMARY: *The winter is expected to be variable, with southern and coastal sections averaging cooler than normal with above-normal precipitation and snowfall, while the northern interior will be milder with below-normal precipitation and snowfall. Following a mild first half of November and a seasonable and wet latter half, but with abundant snow in the mountains, a considerably colder and snowier than normal December is anticipated. Watch for a northeaster at the beginning of the month, heavy rain changing to snow in the south before midmonth, and snowstorms just before Christmas and the end of the year. Following a snowstorm in early January and a thaw the second week, the balance of the month and most of February and the first few days of March should see frequent snowstorms and below-normal temperatures. But most of March is expected to be sunnier and warmer than normal.*

Spring is expected to be slightly cooler and wetter than normal, except for northern interior sections that will have below-normal precipitation. After a minor heat wave at the end of March, temperatures should remain a little below normal except for warm spells the last days of April and May, with a wet May and early June to follow a dry April.

Other than a heat wave at the end of June extending into the first week of July, few major departures from normal are anticipated, particularly in the north. More frequent thundershowers and cool spells during August in the south will be balanced by a sunnier and drier than normal September.

Early fall should see warm and sunny spells, but watch for a major storm early in October, with snow in the mountains.

Nov. 1988: Temp. 46° (0.5° above ave.); Precip. 4.5″ (0.5″ above ave.). 1-3 Clear, cold nights. 4-6 Mild, sprinkles. 7-9 Rain & sleet, snow mountains. 10-12 Sunny & warm. 13-15 Rain then snow & cold. 16-18 Rain south, snow north. 19-21 Cold, light snow. 22-27 Storm, heavy snow north. 28-30 Clear, cold.

Dec. 1988: Temp. 27.5° (6° below ave.); Precip. 7″ (2.5″ above ave. south; 1″ below northwest). 1-4 Snowstorm, northeaster south. 5-9 Very cold, light snow. 10-12 Severe snowstorm. 13-15 Clearing, mild. 16-22 Very cold, snow. 23-24 Snowstorm. 25-28 Extreme cold. 29-31 Milder; snow, heavy southeast.

Jan. 1989: Temp. 29° (0.5° below ave.; 2° above north); Precip. 5″ (1″ above ave.; 0.5″ below north). 1-5 Snowstorm. 6-8 Cold wave, sunny. 9-12 January thaw, sprinkles. 13-18 Mild, intermittent sleet & snow. 19-22 Severe cold, flur-

ries. 23-25 Snowstorm. 26-28 Clear, seasonable. 29-31 Heavy snowstorm, clearing.

Feb. 1989: Temp 27.5° (3° below ave.; ave. north); Precip. 2.5″ (1″ below ave.). 1-2 Clear & cold. 3-6 Snowstorm, light north. 7-9 Cold wave. 10-12 Snowstorm, seasonable. 13-16 Partly cloudy. 17-19 Mild; rain, snow mountains. 20-22 Sunny; seasonable, cold nights. 23-25 Snowstorm, cold. 26-28 Clearing, milder.

Mar. 1989: Temp. 44° (6° above ave.); Precip. 3″ (1″ below ave.; ave. north). 1-4 Snowstorm. 5-7 Sleet & snow. 8-10 Clear & warm. 11-13 Rain. 14-16 Snow. 17-19 Sunny, very warm. 20-23 Clear; mild days, cold nights. 24-26 Clear, very warm. 27-31 Colder; then rain.

Apr. 1989: Temp. 49° (0.5° above ave.; 1.5° above north); Precip. 2.5″ (1″ below ave.). 1-2 Clear & hot. 3-5 Cold wave. 6-10 Rain, some heavy; snow mountains. 11-12 Sunny, normal. 13-15 Cold; rain, snow mountains. 16-18 Clearing, mild. 19-24 Sun & light rain; seasonable. 25-27 Clear; warm north. 28-30 Rain.

May 1989: Temp. 58° (1° below ave.); Precip. 4.5″ (1″ above ave.). 1-2 Heavy rain, cold. 3-5 Sprinkles, seasonable. 6-8 Cold, sunny. 9-13 Storm, cold. 14-18 Rain, then clearing. 19-23 Rain, cold. 24-26 Showers. 27-29 Clear & hot. 30-31 Rain, cold.

June 1989: Temp. 66° (2° below ave.); Precip. 3.5″ (0.5″ above ave.; 1″ below north). 1-2 Cold; showers, heavy south. 3-4 Clear, hot; rain north. 5-7 Rain, heavy south; cold. 8-10 Cold, showers. 11-17 Intermittent rain, warm. 18-20 Clearing, cold. 21-26 Warm; some sun, showers. 27-30 Clear & hot; showers north.

July 1989: Temp. 72.5° (1° below ave.; ave. north). Precip. 1.5″ (1″ below ave.; 0.5″ above north). 1-4 Hot, scattered showers. 5-6 Thunderstorms. 7-12 Sunny, seasonable. 13-17 Cloudy; showers then clearing. 18-19 Cool; scattered showers. 20-24 Clearing, hot. 25-28 Thundershowers, cool. 29-31 Sunny.

Aug. 1989: Temp. 69° (3° below ave.; 1.5° below north); Precip. 8″ (5″ above ave.; 1″ above inland). 1-3 Sunny, hot. 4-7 Rain, cool. 8-10 Sunny, warm. 11-12 Rain south, sunny north. 13-18 Showers, cool. 19-20 Sunny, warm. 21-24 Rain. 25-26 Sunny. 27-31 Showers, cool.

Sept. 1989: Temp. 65° (0.5° above ave.); Precip. 1.5″ (2″ below ave.; 1″ below north). 1-3 Showers. 4-6 Warm. 7-9 Partly cloudy, cool. 10-12 Clear & warm. 13-15 Showers. 16-18 Cloudy, cool. 19-25 Clear, warm. 26-29 Rain, seasonable. 30 Clear & warm.

Oct. 1989: Temp. 56° (1° above ave.; 2° above north); Precip. 2″ (1″ below ave.; 2″ above north). 1-2 Clear & warm. 3-6 Rain, heavy snow mountains. 7-11 Indian Summer-like. 12-14 Cloudy, cool. 15-17 Rain, warm. 18-20 Partly cloudy, seasonable. 21-23 Warm; rain. 24-29 Clear, pleasant. 30-31 Scattered showers.

Be Your Own Boss and Make

$18.00 to $30.00 AN HOUR!

Find out how by sending now for your Free Lifetime Security Fact Kit!

Your FREE Lifetime Security Fact Kit tells you how to make $18.00 to $30.00 an hour in your own Foley-Belsaw Full-Service Saw and Tool Sharpening Business. Your FREE Fact Kit explains how you can:

— be your own BOSS!
— work full time or part time, right at home.
— do work you enjoy and take pride in.
— operate a CASH business where 90¢ of every dollar you take in is clear cash profit.

And it is so easy to learn. Foley-Belsaw gives you all the facts and instructions. No previous experience or special training necessary. All you need is the desire and ambition to be your own boss. Foley-Belsaw tells you everything you need to know to be successful. There's plenty of business where you live to keep you busy. It doesn't matter whether you live in a big city, small town or a small farm community.

Earn While You Learn

You'll quickly be able to develop the skills necessary to earn a steady income. You'll be able to sharpen all types of saws, garden and shop tools for home, farm and industry. Profits from your Foley-Belsaw Full-Service Sharpening Business can provide...

... CASH for future security or supplemental income
... CASH for travel, vacations, fishing trips
... CASH for things you've always wanted!

And you'll be able to set your own hours and not have to worry about layoffs and strikes. There are no franchise fees. Best of all — age or physical condition is no barrier — any age person can succeed.

You can be like Steve Taylor of Brookville, Ohio, who told us:
"... the first year I grossed $21,000.00."

Or James B. Jones, of Albuquerque, NM who reported:
"This past summer my sales and service amounted to almost $6,000.00 a month."

But you've got to get the FACTS before you can get started. So WRITE NOW for your FREE Lifetime Security Fact Kit. It's yours to keep with NO OBLIGATION!

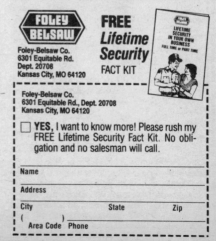

FOLEY BELSAW

Foley-Belsaw Co.
6301 Equitable Rd.
Dept. 20708
Kansas City, MO 64120

FREE Lifetime Security FACT KIT

Foley-Belsaw Co.
6301 Equitable Rd., Dept. 20708
Kansas City, MO 64120

☐ **YES,** I want to know more! Please rush my FREE Lifetime Security Fact Kit. No obligation and no salesman will call.

Name _____

Address _____

City _____ State _____ Zip _____

( ) _____
Area Code Phone

2. GREATER NEW YORK—NEW JERSEY

For regional boundaries, see map page 133.

SUMMARY: *The winter is expected to be milder than normal, with below-normal precipitation, although the snowfall should be above normal early in the season. Following a mild November until Thanksgiving time, the balance of the year will be much colder and snowier than normal. A January thaw before midmonth will balance out colder than normal weather near month's end, while February may see several snowy cold snaps balanced by frequent mild spells. The season is expected to close with a warm and comparatively dry March.*

Spring should start out warmer and drier than normal because of brief warm spells through April, with frequent but light shower activity; however, the season is anticipated to be cooler and wetter overall as a result of heavy rainfall during the latter part of May and early June, with accompanying cooler than normal temperatures.

The summer is expected to be slightly cooler than normal, with average precipitation in southern sections, but below normal in northern ones. Aside from brief hot spells early and late in July, temperatures should remain at or below normal until the middle of September, when they are expected to be well above normal. Heavy thundershowers should bring above-normal rainfall during July; less activity during the rest of the season is anticipated in the north.

Early fall is anticipated to be generally warm and pleasant, with the main shower activity expected at the end of September and middle of October.

Nov. 1988: Temp. 49° (2° above ave.); Precip. 2.5″ (1″ below ave.). 1-3 Clear & mild. 4-6 Seasonable. 7-9 Cold wave; light rain, snow north. 10-13 Sunny, warm. 14-18 Rain, snow mountains. 19-21 Clearing & cold. 22-26 Intermittent heavy rain & sleet, snow north. 27-30 Partly cloudy, cold snap.

Dec. 1988: Temp. 30° (6° below ave.); Precip. 5″ (1.5″ above ave.). 1-4 Rain changing to snow, cold. 5-6 Sunny & cold. 7-8 Flurries. 9-11 Snowstorm. 12-13 Sunny & mild. 14-18 Cold wave, intermittent snow. 19-22 Partly sunny, very cold. 23-24 Snowstorm. 25-28 Clear, very cold. 29-31 Snow turning to rain.

Jan. 1989: Temp. 33.5° (1.5° above ave.); Precip. 3″ (Ave.). 1-5 Seasonable, then snowstorm. 6-8 Sunny, cold snap. 9-10 Clear, turning mild. 11-16 Some rain, mild. 17-19 Clearing, seasonable. 20-23 Cloudy, cold. 24-27 Snow then clearing, cold. 28-29 Snowstorm north, light south. 30-31 Seasonable.

Feb. 1989: Temp. 33° (Ave.; 1° above south); Precip. 2.5″ (0.5″ below ave.). 1-2 Sunny, quite cold. 3-4 Rain & sleet, mild. 5-9 Sunny, very cold. 10-14 Intermittent snow, sleet south; seasonable. 15-16 Clearing. 17-19 Rain, mild. 20-22 Clear & mild. 23-24 Snowstorm. 25-26 Clearing, cold. 27-28 Snow.

Mar. 1989: Temp. 47° (6° above ave.); Precip. 3″ (1″ below ave.). 1-4 Snow & sleet. 5-7 Cloudy, sprinkles. 8-10 Clear & warm. 11-13 Rain, quite mild. 14-16 Cold snap. 17-18 Clear, warm. 19-23 Cloudy, intermittent rain; colder. 24-27 Clear, warm. 28-31 Heavy rain, mild.

Apr. 1989: Temp. 53° (1° above ave.); Precip. 2″ (2″ below ave.). 1-2 Clear, very warm. 3-5 Rain then clearing, seasonable. 6-8 Rain, cold. 9-11 Sprinkles, cold; mild south. 12-13 Rain. 14-17 Partly cloudy, cold. 18-20 Sprinkles. 21-24 Clear, mild; then showers. 25-28 Sunny & warm. 29-30 Rain, cooling.

May 1989: Temp. 61° (1° below ave.); Precip. 6″ (2.5″ above ave.). 1-4 Intermittent rain, cold. 5-7 Sunny, warm. 8-12 Cold snap, intermittent rain. 13-14 Clear, seasonable. 15-23 Variable, some heavy rain; seasonably warm. 24-26 Partly cloudy, showers. 27-29 Clear, warm. 30-31 Storm, heavy rain.

June 1989: Temp. 69° (2° below ave.); Precip. 4″ (1″ above ave.; 1″ below south). 1-2 Cold & rainy. 3-4 Clear, warm. 5-10 Storm, heavy rain north, then sprinkles; cool. 11-15 Sunny & warm. 16-18 Rain, heavy south. 19-21 Sunny, cool, then warming. 22-25 Unseasonably cool, rain. 26-30 Clear, brief heat wave.

July 1989: Temp. 75° (1° below ave.); Precip. 4.5″ (1″ above ave.). 1-3 Showers, heavy south. 4-6 Thunderstorms, seasonable. 7-10 Partly cloudy, showers. 11-12 Sunny, hot. 13-16 Sprinkles, cooler. 17-20 Sunny & warm, then sprinkles. 21-24 Clear, hot. 25-28 Heavy thunderstorms, milder. 29-31 Partly cloudy.

Aug. 1989: Temp. 71° (4° below ave.); Precip. 3″ (1″ below ave.). 1-4 Clear, seasonable. 5-9 Showers, cool; then clearing & warm. 10-12 Thundershowers, cooler. 13-15 Sunny & warm; few showers. 16-20 Cool, intermittent showers. 21-25 Rain, then clearing. 26-27 Rain, milder. 28-30 Sunny & mild. 31 Showers.

Sept. 1989: Temp. 68° (Ave.); Precip. 2.5″ (1″ below ave.; ave. south). 1-3 Rain, cooler. 4-6 Clear, seasonably warm. 7-10 Partly cloudy & mild; sprinkles. 11-14 Sunny, very warm; few showers. 15-18 Cloudy & cool. 19-24 Clear, unseasonably warm. 25-29 Showers, very heavy south. 30 Clear & warm.

Oct. 1989: Temp. 60° (2° above ave.); Precip. 2″ (1″ below ave.). 1-2 Sunny & warm. 3-5 Heavy rain, cold snap. 6-13 Indian Summer-like. 14-17 Rain, cool. 18-21 Clear & pleasant. 22-24 Cool, showers. 25-29 Clear & warm. 30-31 Rain, scattered north; warm.

3. MIDDLE ATLANTIC COAST

For regional boundaries, see map page 133.

SUMMARY: *Late fall and winter will be quite variable, but end up slightly milder and drier than normal overall, except for central and western sections that should have above-normal precipitation. The total snowfall is expected to be above normal due to excessive snow in early winter compensating for below-normal snow later in the season. After Thanksgiving, unseasonably cold and snowy weather should prevail much of the time through December and the latter part of January, with some relief due to a January thaw at midmonth. Thereafter, frequent warm spells will become more and more dominant through February and March.*

Spring is expected to be slightly milder than normal with well-above-normal precipitation. The end of March through April should be warmer and slightly drier than normal, despite a cold and wet spell at mid-April, while frequent cold and wet periods will make May a very wet month. June will have quite variable temperatures that will average out cooler than normal, with less than normal rainfall being anticipated.

The summer will be cooler and a little wetter than normal, largely because of heavy thundershower activity in early and late July and early August. Only brief hot spells are expected in July, while temperatures should remain at and below normal for most of the rest of the season.

The early fall will be mostly warm and pleasant, despite rains at the end of September and the middle and end of October.

Nov. 1988: Temp. 51° (2° above ave.); Precip. 2.5″ (0.5″ below ave.). 1-5 Unseasonably warm, increasing clouds. 6-9 Rain, cold snap; snow west. 10-13 Sunny & warm. 14-16 Cold & rainy. 17-19 Heavy rain. 20-21 Sunny & mild. 22-26 Intermittent heavy rain, seasonable. 27-30 Partly cloudy, unseasonably cold.

Dec. 1988: Temp. 33° (6° below ave.); Precip. 5″ (2″ above ave.). 1-3 Rain & sleet, cold; snow west. 4-6 Partial clearing, milder. 7-10 Snowstorm, cold. 11-13 Sunny & mild. 14-16 Turning very cold, snow. 17-19 Flurries, frigid. 20-21 Clear, continued cold. 22-24 Snowstorm. 25-28 Clear & very cold. 29-31 Snowstorm, changing to rain.

Jan. 1989: Temp. 37° (1° above ave.); Precip. 2.5″ (Ave.). 1-4 Storm, heavy east, snow west. 5-7 Cold, sunny. 8-10 Clear & warm. 11-13 Rain, mild. 14-18 Sunny; showers east. 19-21 Cold snap; rain, snow west. 22-23 Sunny, milder. 24-26 Snowstorm, cold wave. 27-28 Clear, frigid. 29-31 Warming, then rain.

Feb. 1989: Temp. 40° (2° above ave.); Precip. 3″ (0.5″ above ave.). 1-2 Clear, seasonable. 3-5 Storm, snow west. 6-8 Cold snap, partly cloudy. 9-12 Light rain & snow, milder. 13-15 Storm, heavy snow west. 16-19 Sunny & mild, then showers. 20-22 Clear, pleasant. 23-25 Snowstorm, cold. 26-28 Clear & mild, showers east.

Mar. 1989: Temp. 53° (7° above ave.); Precip. 1.5″ (2″ below ave.). 1-3 Sunny & warm, scattered showers. 4-6 Cloudy, sprinkles. 7-10 Clear, very warm. 11-13 Rain, heavy west, cooler. 14-15 Cloudy, cold. 16-18 Clear, warm. 19-23 Storm, cold wave. 24-26 Sunny, very warm. 27-28 Cloudy, cool. 29-31 Showers, warm.

Apr. 1989: Temp. 59° (2° above ave.); Precip. 2.5″ (0.5″ below ave.). 1 Clear & warm. 2-4 Storm, cooler. 5-8 Sunny, warm; showers north. 9-11 Sunny & pleasant. 12-14 Rainy & cold. 15-16 Warm, showers. 17-21 Sprinkles; cool. 22-24 Clear, very warm. 25-27 Cloudy then clear & warm. 28-30 Rainstorm, cold.

May 1989: Temp. 65.5° (0.5° below ave.); Precip. 6″ (3″ above ave.). 1-2 Clear & cold. 3-5 Rain, scattered east; warm. 6-9 Cold wave, rainstorm. 10-15 Mostly sunny, warm; few showers. 16-19 Rain, heavy east; cool. 20-22 Rain, locally heavy, warm. 23-25 Showers, some sun. 26-29 Clear, warm & pleasant. 30-31 Very heavy rain, seasonably warm.

June 1989: Temp. 72.5° (2° below ave.); Precip. 2″ (1″ below ave.). 1-2 Rain, heavy east; cool. 3-5 Clear & hot. 6-8 Storm, cool. 9-15 Clear, turning hot. 16-19 Rain, heavy east & north; cooling. 20-22 Clearing, hot. 23-25 Storm, heavy west; very cool. 26-30 Clear & warm.

July 1989: Temp. 78° (1° below ave.); Precip. 5″ (1″ above ave.). 1-6 Thundershowers, seasonably warm. 7-9 Cloudy, sprinkles; milder. 10-14 Showers, heavy central & west; warm. 15-20 Seasonable, scattered showers; then rain west. 21-24 Clear & hot. 25-27 Heavy thundershowers. 28-31 Showers then clearing.

Aug. 1989: Temp. 74.5° (3° below ave.); Precip. 4″ (0.5″ below ave.). 1-3 Clear, seasonable. 4-6 Showers, heavy east; cooler. 7-9 Sunny, warm. 10-12 Thundershowers. 13-15 Clear, warm. 16-19 Showers east; milder. 20-22 Thundershowers, hot. 23-27 Scattered showers, heavy east; seasonable. 28-31 Few showers, milder.

Sept. 1989: Temp. 70° (1.5° below ave.); Precip. 3.5″ (Ave.). 1-4 Showers, heavy west; mild. 5-9 Clear & pleasant. 10-13 Partly cloudy, showers east; turning hot. 14-16 Rain, milder. 17-23 Clear & pleasant. 24-28 Intermittent rain, locally heavy; warm. 29-30 Clear, warm.

Oct. 1989: Temp. 60° (0.5° above ave.); Precip. 2.5″ (0.5″ below ave.). 1-2 Clear, warm. 3-5 Rain, heavy east; cold. 6-12 Indian Summer-like. 13-17 Rainstorm, cool. 18-21 Clear, pleasantly warm. 22-25 Rain, very cool. 26-29 Sunny & pleasant. 30-31 Heavy rain, milder.

For regional boundaries, see map page 133.

SUMMARY: *Late fall and winter are expected to be warmer than normal, with above-normal precipitation in southern sections, but slightly below normal elsewhere. Western sections may anticipate well-above-normal snowfall. Although several cold snaps are expected during November, the month as a whole should be warmer and drier than normal, in marked contrast to December, which will be quite cold, wet, and much snowier than usual. January temperatures may be quite variable, while precipitation is expected to be above normal, but thereafter the balance of the season is anticipated to be progressively warmer and drier.*

Spring will be cool and wet except for some east-central sections that may be warmer and drier than normal. April is expected to have frequent warm and dry spells, more than offsetting a cool and wet period at the middle of the month and again the last few days, while May should see frequent spells of cooler and wetter than normal weather, which will extend on into June.

Summer is expected to continue cooler and wetter than normal, with temperatures varying between normal and subnormal, and showers distributed fairly uniformly over the period. Occasional thundershowers may be anticipated.

Fall temperatures will be slightly below normal, with heavy showers in late September and at the middle and end of October.

Nov. 1988: Temp. 53° (2° above ave.); Precip. 2″ (1″ below ave.). 1-6 Sunny, unseasonably warm. 7-9 Cold wave; rain, heavy east. 10-13 Sunny, very warm. 14-16 Cloudy, showers. 17-19 Cold snap; showers, heavy northeast & west. 20-21 Clearing, warmer. 22-26 Cloudy, heavy rain west. 27-30 Cold wave, clearing.

Dec. 1988: Temp. 37° (6° below ave.); Precip. 5.5″ (2″ above ave.). 1-2 Rain, seasonable; dry south. 3-7 Clear & cold. 8-10 Cold wave; storm, heavy snow north & west. 11-13 Sunny, milder. 14-16 Very cold; some snow. 17-19 Snowstorm. 20-23 Clearing, then more snow. 24-27 Sunny, seasonable. 28-31 Snowstorm.

Jan. 1989: Temp. 45° (2.5° above ave.); Precip. 4.5″ (1″ above ave.). 1-4 Rainstorm, snow west; seasonable. 5-7 Cold snap. 8-9 Sunny & warm. 10-12 Rain, very heavy west; warm. 13-16 Cloudy, showers west. 17-18 Cloudy, cold. 19-21 Storm; snow west. 22-23 Seasonable. 24-26 Showers, heavy south; cold. 25-31 Clearing.

Feb. 1989: Temp. 47.5° (2.5° above ave.); Precip. 4″ (Ave.; 1″ below south). 1-2 Sunny, seasonable. 3-5 Rain; mild. 6-7 Clear & warm. 8-10 Rain north, sunny south. 11-12 Sunny, mild. 13-15 Rain, heavy west; cooler. 16-17 Clear & warm. 18-21 Sun & showers. 22-24 Rain, heavy south; cooling. 25-26 Clear, warm. 27-28 Showers, cool.

Mar. 1989: Temp. 56.5° (6° above ave.); Precip. 3″ (2″ below ave.). 1-2 Warm & sunny. 3-5 Showers, seasonably cool. 6-10 Clear, quite warm. 11-13 Rain, colder. 14-17 Clear & cold. 18-21 Warm, rain, heavy west. 22-24 Cold snap; showers, moderate rain north. 25-29 Clear & warm. 30-31 Showers, heavy south.

Apr. 1989: Temp. 63° (3° above ave.); Precip. 3″ (0.5″ below ave.). 1-3 Rain, very heavy west; seasonable. 4-10 Sunny, very warm. 11-13 Rain north, sunny south; warm. 14-16 Cold wave, rain. 17-19 Sunny & pleasant. 20-21 Cold wave, rainstorm. 22-24 Clear, warm. 25-27 Partly cloudy. 28-30 Heavy rain, cooler.

May 1989: Temp. 68° (0.5° below ave.); Precip. 5.5″ (2″ above ave.). 1-2 Clearing, very cold. 3-5 Rain north, sunny south. 6-8 Cold snap, heavy rain. 9-10 Clear & warm. 11-12 Showers, cool. 13-15 Clear, seasonable. 16-19 Heavy rain. 20-26 Showers west, heavy rain east; cool. 27-29 Partly cloudy. 30-31 Heavy rain north.

June 1989: Temp. 76° (1° above ave.; 1° below south); Precip. 2″ (1″ below ave.; ave. south). 1-4 Sunny; showers north. 5-8 Rain, heavy south; cool. 9-13 Clearing, hot. 14-16 Very warm. 17-20 Rain, heavy east. 21-23 Clear, unseasonably hot. 24-26 Rain, heavy east. 27-30 Sunny, seasonably warm; showers west.

July 1989: Temp. 78.5° (Ave.; 1° below south); Precip. 4″ (Ave.). 1-5 Showers, heavy south. 6-8 Rain, heavy north; cool. 9-11 Rain northeast from tropical storm. 12-17 Seasonable, few showers. 18-20 Rain south, scattered north; cooler. 21-24 Clear & hot. 25-27 Rain, heavy east. 28-31 Sunny then showers.

Aug. 1989: Temp. 76° (2° below ave.); Precip. 4.5″ (1″ above ave.). 1-2 Partly cloudy, cooler. 3-5 Rain, heavy east. 6-7 Seasonable. 8-10 Showers, heavy south. 11-13 Sunny & hot; rain north. 14-16 Showers, milder. 17-21 Clear, hot. 22-25 Rain, scattered west. 26-29 Showers, heavy east. 30-31 Cloudy, cool.

Sept. 1989: Temp. 73° (3° below ave.); Precip. 3″ (Ave.; 2″ above south). 1-3 Showers, cooler. 4-6 Sunny & pleasant. 7-9 Showers west; cooler. 10-12 Rain, clearing west. 13-14 Clear & warm. 15-17 Rain, cooler. 18-21 Showers, heavy south; cool. 22-28 Rain, heavy east then west. 29-30 Sunny, warm.

Oct. 1989: Temp. 61° (Ave.; 2° below south); Precip. 4″ (2″ above ave.). 1-4 Showers, cooling. 5-10 Clear & pleasant. 11-13 Rain, heavy south; cool. 14-15 Sunny, warm. 16-17 Rain, light southeast, cool. 18-20 Clear, cool. 21-23 Sunny, warm. 24-26 Sprinkles; cool. 27-28 Clear, warm. 29-31 Heavy rain.

5. FLORIDA

SUMMARY: *Late fall and winter are expected to be warmer and drier than normal in the north and cooler and wetter than normal in the south. Warmer than normal temperatures will outweigh brief cold spells until a cold wave sweeps into northern sections just after Thanksgiving, after which frequent cold snaps will predominate through most of a wet December. Prolonged warm periods during January will more than offset the few brief cold spells, while precipitation should be above normal in the north. Temperatures during February and March should fluctuate between normal and above normal, with the precipitation being below normal.*

Spring is anticipated to be warmer and wetter than normal in the north and slightly cooler and drier in the south. Precipitation should be fairly uniformly distributed from the latter part of April through May and June, but with above-normal intensity in the north.

Summer temperatures are anticipated to remain fairly close to normal, while frequent showers are expected throughout the season, but with greater than normal intensity in the south during July and in central sections during August and September.

Fall should see temperatures alternating from above to below normal, with below-normal precipitation after mid-October.

Nov. 1988: Temp. 66° (1° below ave.; 2° above north); Precip. 3″ (0.5″ above ave.). 1-6 Cloudy, heavy rain south; warm. 7-9 Rain, cold snap. 10-11 Warming, clear. 12-15 Showers, warm. 16-18 Rain, seasonable. 19-23 Sunny & pleasant. 24-26 Sprinkles, showers north; warm. 27-29 Cold wave, scattered north; hard frost. 30 Clear & warm.

Dec. 1988: Temp. 59° (3° below ave.); Precip. 1.5″ (0.5″ below ave.; 2″ above north). 1-2 Warm, sunny, sprinkles. 3-7 Clear & cold, then warming. 8-10 Cold & rainy. 11-14 Clear & pleasant. 15-17 Partly cloudy, cooler. 18-19 Rain, heavy north. 20-21 Cold snap, frost. 22-24 Cool, showers. 25-27 Sunny, warm. 28-31 Showers, heavy north.

Jan. 1989: Temp. 62° (1.5° above ave.; 4° above north); Precip. 3″ (1″ above ave.; ave. north & south). 1-4 Heavy showers, warm. 5-7 Cold snap. 8-16 Partly cloudy, showers north; very warm. 17-20 Seasonable; showers, rain north. 21-24 Clear & warm. 25-28 Rain, heavy north; cold. 29-31 Clear, warming.

Feb. 1989: Temp. 63.5° (2° above ave.); Precip. 1″ (2″ below ave.). 1-4 Sunny & warm, sprinkles south. 5-7 Cloudy, cool. 8-17 Alternating sunny & warm, showers & mild central and north; sprinkles south. 18-19 Rain, warm. 20-22 Cloudy, seasonable. 23-24 Rain, scattered south; mild. 25-28 Clearing.

Mar. 1989: Temp. 68° (1° above ave.; 4° above north); Precip. 2″ (1″ below ave.). 1-2 Clear, seasonable. 3-5 Heavy rain, cool. 6-10 Sunny; warm north. 11-13 Partly cloudy, showers north. 14-17 Sunny & mild. 18-21 Rain, heavy north; very warm. 22-24 Showers, cool. 25-30 Partly cloudy, very warm. 31 Rain.

Apr. 1989: Temp. 73° (1° above ave.; 1° below south); Precip. 2″ (0.5″ below ave.; 1.5″ above north). 1-2 Heavy rain. 3-5 Cloudy & mild, sprinkles. 6-16 Clear & very warm. 17-19 Partly cloudy, mild. 20-22 Showers, heavy north; cool. 23-27 Variable clouds, seasonable. 28-30 Rain north, light south.

May 1989: Temp. 78° (1° above ave.; 1° below south); Precip. 4.5″ (0.5″ above ave.; 1″ below south). 1-5 Sunny, warm; sprinkles south. 6-8 Heavy rain, seasonable. 9-12 Showers, heavy north. 13-16 Sunny, seasonably warm. 17-21 Heavy rain. 22-25 Showers, locally heavy. 26-31 Few showers, sun; seasonable.

June 1989: Temp. 80° (1° below ave.; ave. north); Precip. 6″ (1″ below ave.; 0.5″ above south). 1-5 Sunny & hot; heavy showers south. 6-8 Rain, locally heavy; milder. 9-11 Clear, seasonable; showers south. 12-16 Sprinkles, rain south. 17-20 Rain, seasonably hot. 21-24 Clear, hot. 25-27 Rain, scattered south; milder. 28-30 Partly cloudy, showers south.

July 1989: Temp. 82.5° (Ave.; 1° below south); Precip. 9″ (2″ above ave.; 4″ above south). 1-6 Heavy thundershowers, warm. 7-13 Sunny & hot; showers, locally heavy. 14-21 Showers, heavy north, scattered south; seasonable. 22-24 Showers, heavy central. 25-27 Scattered showers, slightly mild. 28-31 Showers, heavy thundershowers south.

Aug. 1989: Temp. 82.5° (Ave.; 1° below south); Precip. 9″ (3″ above ave.; 1.5″ below north and south). 1-4 Heavy showers, mild. 5-7 Seasonable; showers, heavy central. 8-11 Heavy showers north, light south. 12-18 Scattered showers. 19-25 Thunderstorms, scattered south. 26-31 More showers, hot.

Sept. 1989: Temp. 80° (1° below ave.); Precip. 7″ (1.5″ above ave.; 1″ below north & south). 1-3 Heavy thundershowers. 4-7 Sunny, showers; milder north. 8-12 Thundershowers, warm. 13-16 Showers, heavy central & north. 17-23 Thundershowers, heavy central; cooling. 24-30 Scattered showers, hot.

Oct. 1989: Temp. 75° (Ave.; 0.5° above north); Precip. 3″ (Ave.; 1″ below south). 1-4 Showers, scattered north. 5-9 Sunny & pleasant. 10-12 Showers, heavy central & north; mild. 13-17 Clear & hot, showers north. 18-21 Sunny, milder; sprinkles south. 22-28 Sunny, warm. 29-31 Scattered showers.

6. UPSTATE N.Y.—TORONTO AND MONTREAL

For regional boundaries, see map page 133.

SUMMARY: *Late fall and winter are expected to be milder than normal, with below-normal precipitation. Snowfall is anticipated to be above normal in central and southern sections, but below normal in the north. Look for warmer and drier than normal weather until Thanksgiving, but then much colder weather on through most of December, with frequent and heavy snowstorms. A January thaw will make it a milder than normal month with below-normal snowfall, while cold snaps and mild spells will about balance each other in February. Following snowstorms at the end of February and in early March, generally mild weather is in the offing.*

Spring is anticipated to be cooler and drier than average, with cool spells being longer than warm spells. Precipitation will occur frequently through the season, although in light amounts during April, while May should be quite wet and June slightly less so.

Summer temperatures will be only slightly below normal, with brief heat waves occurring only during the early part of the season. Eastern sections should receive slightly greater than normal rainfall due to thundershower activity in July, while western sections receive slightly less than normal.

Fall will be generally sunny, warm, and pleasant, but watch for an early snowstorm in early October.

Nov. 1988: Temp. 40° (1° above ave.); Precip. 3″ (Ave.; 1″ below west). 1-5 Sunny & mild, then freezing rain north. 6-8 Cold snap, rain & snow. 9-13 Clearing, unseasonably warm. 14-15 Cold snap, snow. 16-20 Mild, rain; then cold, snow. 21-24 Seasonable, rain & snow. 25-27 Snowstorm. 28-30 Cold, snow.

Dec. 1988: Temp. 21° (5° below ave.); Precip. 3″ (Ave.; 2″ above west). 1-4 Snowstorm, heavy west; cold. 5-8 Clearing, intermittent snow. 9-11 Milder, moderate snow. 12-14 Sunny, milder than normal. 15-17 Very cold, flurries. 18-20 Blizzard. 21-28 Intermittent sun & snow, unseasonably cold. 29-31 Snowstorm, milder.

Jan. 1989: Temp. 26° (3° above ave.); Precip. 1.5″ (1″ below ave.). 1-4 Snowstorm, heavy east; slightly mild. 5-7 Cold snap, flurries. 8-10 Partly cloudy, quite mild. 11-15 Rain & snow, intermittent north; mild. 16-19 Cold wave, moderate snow. 20-24 Unseasonably cold, light snow. 25-26 Snowstorm. 27-31 Light snow.

Feb. 1989: Temp. 23.5° (Ave.; 1.5° above west); Precip. 2″ (0.5″ below ave.). 1-2 Sunny. 3-6 Snow, normal temperature. 7-9 Clearing, very cold. 10-11 Snow, moderate north; milder. 12-16 Partly cloudy, flurries. 17-19 Light rain & snow; quite mild. 20-23 Cold, intermittent snow. 24-25 Snowstorm, cold wave. 26-28 Partly clear, seasonable.

Mar. 1989: Temp. 40° (6° above ave.); Precip. 2.5″ (0.5″ below ave.). 1-4 Snowstorm, very cold. 5-9 Seasonable, clear then snow. 10-13 Mild; rain, heavy north. 14-16 Cold snap, light snow. 17-18 Clear & warm. 19-20 Showers. 21-25 Mostly sunny & warm. 26-28 Seasonable, rain & snow. 29-31 Rain, very mild.

Apr. 1989: Temp. 47.5° (1° above ave.); Precip. 1.5″ (1.5″ below ave.). 1-2 Clear, very warm. 3-5 Severe cold wave. 6-8 Rain, mild. 9-14 Cold, intermittent rain & snow. 15-18 Sunny, turning warm. 19-24 Partly cloudy, cold; some rain & snow. 25-27 Clear, very warm. 28-30 Rain changing to snow & cold.

May 1989: Temp. 55° (2° below ave.); Precip. 4″ (1″ above ave.). 1-3 Cold wave, snow. 4-6 Sunny & mild. 7-16 Rainy & cold, snow mountains. 17-19 Partly cloudy, rain east; seasonable. 20-23 Cloudy, cold & rainy. 24-26 Seasonably mild, heavy rain. 27-29 Sunny, very warm. 30-31 Cold, heavy rain central & south.

June 1989: Temp. 63° (2.5° below ave.); Precip. 3.5″ (0.5″ above ave.; 0.5″ below west). 1 Cold, heavy rain central. 2-4 Clear, warm. 5-6 Heavy rain, cold. 7-10 Light rain, cool. 11-14 Rain then partly cloudy. 15-17 Thundershowers, seasonable. 18-21 Clear & pleasant. 22-25 Thundershowers, cool. 26-30 Clearing, heat wave.

July 1989: Temp. 72° (0.5° above ave.); Precip. 4″ (1″ above ave.; 0.5″ below west) 1-4 Showers central & south; very warm. 5-6 Heavy thundershowers. 7-10 Sunny, seasonably warm. 11-13 Showers, warm. 14-16 Cloudy; showers, locally heavy. 17-23 Clear & warm, few showers. 24-28 Heavy thundershowers, cool. 29-31 Sunny & pleasant.

Aug. 1989: Temp. 67° (2° below ave.); Precip. 2″ (1″ below ave.; ave. west). 1-3 Clear & warm. 4-6 Rain, locally heavy; cool. 7-13 Sunny, scattered showers; warm. 14-16 Rain, heavy north; mild. 17-19 Partly cloudy, mild. 20-22 Thundershowers, warm. 23-25 Light rain. 26-28 Mild. 29-31 Showers.

Sept. 1989: Temp. 62° (1° above ave.); Precip. 3.5″ (0.5″ above ave.). 1-3 Rain, cooler. 4-7 Sunny & cool, showers central & west. 8-10 Clear & warm. 11-15 Rainstorm. 16-18 Clearing & cold. 19-24 Clear, unseasonably warm. 25-27 Rain, heavy east; mild. 28-30 Heavy showers then clearing; seasonable.

Oct. 1989: Temp. 52.5° (2° above ave.); Precip. 3″ (Ave.). 1-3 Clear, very warm. 4-6 Severe cold wave; heavy snow north, rain south. 7-11 Indian Summer-like. 12-13 Cloudy, cold. 14-15 Showers, warm. 16-17 Heavy rain, cool. 18-20 Sunny, mild. 21-23 Rain, heavy north; cold. 24-29 Clear & mild. 30-31 Rainstorm, warm.

GET IN ON THE PROFITS OF SMALL ENGINE SERVICE AND REPAIR

START YOUR OWN MONEY MAKING BUSINESS & BEAT INFLATION!

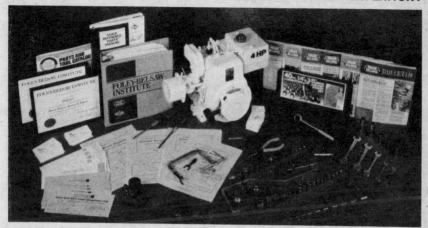

**You get all this Professional equipment with your course,
PLUS 4 H.P. Engine... ALL YOURS TO KEEP... All at NO EXTRA COST.**

Work part time, full time right at home. In just a short time, you can be ready to join one of the fastest growing industries in America... an industry where qualified men are making from **$25.00 to $30.00 per hour.** Because the small engine industry has grown so quickly, an acute shortage of qualified Small Engine Professionals exists throughout the country. When you see how many small engines are in use today, it's easy to understand why qualified men command such high prices — as much as $49.95 for a simple tune-up that takes less than an hour.

65-million small engines are in service today!

That's right — there are over sixty-five million 2-cycle and 4-cycle small engines in service across the U.S.A.! With fully accredited and approved Foley-Belsaw training, you can soon have the skill and knowledge to make top money servicing these engines. Homeowners and businessmen will seek you out and pay you well to service and repair their lawn mowers, tillers, edgers, power rakes, garden tractors, chain saws, mini-bikes, go-carts, snowmobiles... the list is almost endless.

No experience necessary.

We guide you every step of the way, including tested and proven instructions on how to get business, what to charge, how to get free advertising, where to get supplies wholesale... all the 'tricks of the trade'... all the inside facts you need to assure success right from the start.

Send today for FREE facts!

You risk nothing by accepting this offer to find out how Foley-Belsaw training can give you the skills you need to increase your income in a high-profit, recession-proof business of your own.
Just fill in and mail coupon below (or send postcard) to receive full information and details by return mail. DO IT TODAY!

FOLEY-BELSAW INSTITUTE
6301 Equitable Rd., Dept. 51502
Kansas City, MO 64120

NO OBLIGATION... NO SALESMAN WILL CALL

RUSH COUPON TODAY FOR THIS FACT-FILLED FREE BOOKLET!

Tells how you quickly train to be your own boss in a profitable Spare time or Full time business of your own PLUS complete details on our 30 DAY NO RISK Trial Offer!

SUMMARY: *Late fall and winter are expected to have above-normal temperatures, with above-normal precipitation in the west, but below normal in the east. The total snowfall is anticipated to be above average over the region. Large temperature swings are in the offing for November, together with frequent and fairly heavy precipitation, while a very cold and snowy latter half of December may follow a close-to-normal first half. Except for brief cold snaps, the balance of the season should see well above-normal temperatures and below-normal snowfall except for a comparatively snowy February.*

Despite much drier than normal weather through April, with drought developing in some eastern sections, spring is expected to be much wetter than normal overall due to frequent and heavy rains in May and June. Temperatures will start out well above normal through early April, but then have alternating cool and warm spells until the latter part of June.

Summer is anticipated to be drier then normal with less frequent shower activity, with temperatures near normal in the west, but above normal in the east. July will have a number of brief hot spells, but then cooler periods are expected through early September. Early fall will be variable, but with spells of warm weather predominating, while heavy shower activity, particularly in the east, will bring above-normal rainfall.

Nov. 1988: Temp. 47.5° (3° above ave.); Precip. 3.5″ (1″ above ave.). 1-5 Sunny & warm, showers east. 6-8 Heavy rain, snow east; turning very cold. 9-12 Clear then cloudier, very warm. 13-15 Rain & snow, cold. 16-18 Rain, mild. 19-20 Cloudy & cold. 21-24 Intermittent rain, mild. 25-28 Snow, cold snap. 29-30 Sunny, cold.

Dec. 1988: Temp. 30° (5° below ave.); Precip. 2.5″ (1″ below ave.). 1-4 Heavy rain changing to snow; cold. 5-8 Seasonable, flurries. 9-11 Snow, cold. 12-13 Clear & mild. 14-15 Cold wave, flurries. 16-18 Snowstorm. 19-21 Clear, severe cold. 22-24 Snowstorm, cold. 25-27 Clearing, cold. 28-31 Heavy snowstorm, then milder.

Jan. 1989: Temp. 34° (4° above ave.); Precip. 1.5″ (1.5″ below ave.). 1-2 Flurries, seasonable. 3-5 Light snow, milder. 6-8 Cold snap. 9-10 Cloudy, very mild. 11-16 Intermittent rain, mild. 17-20 Partly cloudy, seasonably cold, flurries. 21-23 Sunny & mild. 24-26 Snowstorm, cold wave. 27-28 Sunny, milder. 29-31 Light snow.

Feb. 1989: Temp. 38° (4.5° above ave.); Precip. 3.5″ (1″ above ave.; ave. east). 1-2 Sunny. 3-7 Showers & sun; mild. 8-11 Snow changing to

heavy rain. 12-13 Clear & mild. 14-16 Cold, light snow. 17-19 Warm, heavy rain. 20-22 Cloudy, seasonable. 23-25 Snowstorm. 26-27 Sunny, mild. 28 Light snow, cold.

Mar. 1989: Temp. 51° (8° above ave.); Precip. 4.5″ (0.5″ above ave.; 0.5″ below east). 1-3 Rain changing to snow. 4-5 Clearing, mild. 6-10 Very warm, showers. 11-13 Rainstorm, turning cold. 14-15 Light snow, cold. 16-17 Clear & warm. 18-23 Intermittent rain, mild. 24-26 Sunny, warm. 27-31 Rainy, mild.

Apr. 1989: Temp. 58° (3° above ave.); Precip. 2″ (1.5″ below ave.). 1-2 Sunny, very warm. 3-4 Cold, rainy. 5-8 Clear, very warm; showers east. 9-12 Cloudy, rainy & cold. 13-16 Unseasonably cold, light rain. 17-18 Clear, mild. 19-20 Rain, cold. 21-24 Sunny, warming. 25-27 Very warm, clear then showers. 28-30 Rain, mild.

May 1989: Temp. 63° (1° below ave.; 1° above east); Precip. 6″ (2″ above ave.; 0.5″ above east). 1-2 Cold snap. 3-8 Cold & rainy. 9-10 Sunny & warm; rain east. 11-15 Cool, intermittent rain. 16-17 Clearing, mild. 18-22 Heavy rain, cool. 23-25 Partial clearing then rain. 26-27 Clear & warm. 28-31 Rainstorm, cooler.

June 1989: Temp. 73° (0.5° above ave.); Precip. 5.5″ (1.5″ above ave.). 1 Rain ending, cold. 2-4 Clear & warm. 5-9 Heavy rain then slackening, cold. 10-15 Sunny, very warm; showers east. 16-18 Heavy rain, seasonably warm. 19-20 Partly cloudy. 21-25 Very heavy rain, quite warm. 26-30 Sunny, unseasonably warm.

July 1989: Temp. 77.5° (1.5° above ave.); Precip. 3.5″ (0.5″ below ave.). 1-3 Scattered showers, hot. 4-6 Rain, scattered east; milder. 7-9 Sunny, seasonable. 10-13 Heat wave, showers. 14-16 Sunny & showers, seasonable. 17-20 Sunny, warm; thundershowers east. 21-23 Clear & hot. 24-26 Thundershowers, cooler. 27-28 Hot. 29-31 Showers, milder.

Aug. 1989: Temp. 74° (1° below ave.); Precip. 2.5″ (1″ below ave.). 1-3 Showers, sunny east. 4-7 Sunny & warm; rain east. 8-9 Sunny, hot. 10-11 Heavy rain. 12-13 Clear, very warm. 14-18 Mild, scattered showers. 19-22 Heavy rain, warm. 23-25 Clear & pleasant. 26-31 Sunny, mild; few scattered showers.

Sept. 1989: Temp. 69° (0.5° above ave.; 1.5° above east); Precip. 2″ (1″ below ave.). 1-3 Cool, showers. 4-6 Sunny, pleasant; showers west. 7-12 Clear, unseasonably warm. 13-15 Showers, heavy east; mild. 16-25 Sunny & pleasantly warm; then showers east. 26-28 Heavy thundershowers. 29-30 Clear & warm.

Oct. 1989: Temp. 58° (2° above ave.); Precip. 2.5″ (Ave., 1″ above east). 1-2 Clear, very warm. 3-5 Cold snap; sprinkles, moderate rain east. 6-11 Indian Summer-like. 12-14 Seasonable, showers. 15-17 Rain, heavy east; cold. 18-20 Sunny & mild. 21-23 Heavy rain, cool. 24-27 Clear & pleasant. 28-31 Rain, then clearing.

8. DEEP SOUTH

For regional boundaries, see map page 133.

SUMMARY: *Late fall and winter are expected to be milder than normal overall, with well-above-normal precipitation. Warm, dry spells should be interrupted by cold and wet ones, with heavy precipitation in the north through November and early December, before the advent of very cold, wet and snowy weather during the latter part of December and beginning January. Fluctuating, but generally milder than normal, temperatures will prevail during the balance of the season, but heavy rains at mid-January and mid-February should cause some flooding.*

Spring is anticipated to start out with a very warm and dry early April, but become progressively wetter, with little overall temperature change through May and June, ending up slightly warmer than normal overall and much wetter than normal in the south, but drier than normal in the north.

Summer is expected to have temperatures fairly close to normal except for cool and wet spells that are anticipated in early and late July, bringing heavy rains to southern sections, and frequent but light precipitation through August and late September. Brief hot, dry periods may be expected after mid-July and mid-August and early September.

Early fall is anticipated to have periods of sunny, pleasantly warm and dry weather, interspersed with brief spells of cold and wet weather, with below normal precipitation in southern sections.

Nov. 1988: Temp. 57° (2° above ave.); Precip. 3″ (1″ below ave.; 2″ above north). 1-5 Clear, pleasantly warm. 6-7 Showers, heavy north-central; cold snap. 8-12 Sunny & warm. 13-18 Rain, heavy central & northwest; cold. 19-21 Clear, mild. 22-26 Rain, heavy central, snow north; very cold. 27-30 Clear & mild.

Dec. 1988: Temp. 45° (4° below ave.); Precip. 4.5″ (1″ below ave.). 1-2 Rain; seasonably cold. 3-6 Clearing, cold. 7-9 Heavy rain, changing to snow; very cold. 10-12 Sunny & mild. 13-16 Cold snap, snow east. 17-18 Heavy rain, snow north. 19-21 Cloudy, very cold. 22-23 Snowstorm. 24-26 Sunny, seasonable. 27-31 Heavy rain, light west; clearing south.

Jan. 1989: Temp. 47° (1° above ave.); Precip. 7″ (2″ above ave.). 1-6 Showers, snow east; cold. 7-13 Unseasonably warm; very heavy rain, light south. 14-16 Turning cold; rain, heavy central & north. 17-18 Cloudy & quite cold. 19-21 Cold wave; snow, heavy rain south. 22-23 Clear, very cold. 24-25 Heavy rain, seasonable. 26-31 Clearing, milder.

Feb. 1989: Temp. 51° (2° above ave.); Precip. 7″ (2.5″ above ave.; ave. north). 1-2 Cold snap. 3-5 Rain, milder. 6-7 Clear & mild. 8-11 Heavy rain, then clearing. 12-14 Rain, changing to snow north; cold. 15-16 Sunny & mild. 17-18 Rain. 19-21 Clear, mild. 22-23 Rain. 24-26 Clearing & cold. 27-28 Showers, warm.

Mar. 1989: Temp. 60° (4° above ave.); Precip. 7″ (1″ above ave.; ave. north). 1-2 Clear & warm. 3-4 Rain, heavy east; cold. 5-9 Sunny, warm. 10-12 Heavy rain, cooler. 13-16 Partly cloudy, cold. 17-20 Intermittent rain, warm. 21-24 Cloudy, cold. 25-29 Sunny & warm; showers north. 30-31 Rain, seasonable.

Apr. 1989: Temp. 68° (3° above ave.); Precip. 2″ (1″ below ave.). 1-2 Heavy rain ending. 3-9 Mostly sunny, unseasonably warm. 10-13 Scattered showers, cooler. 14-15 Heavy rain. 16-18 Cold snap, clear. 19-21 Rain, very heavy northwest; cold. 22-26 Clear, very warm. 27-30 Heavy rain, light central; mild.

May 1989: Temp. 72° (0.5° below ave.); Precip. 7″ (2″ above ave.; ave. north). 1-2 Clear & cool. 3-7 Rain, heavy west; warm. 8-10 Clear & cool. 11-13 Partly cloudy, light showers. 14-15 Heavy rain, seasonable. 16-18 Showers, cool. 19-24 Heavy rain, warm. 25-27 Clear & pleasant. 28-31 Very heavy rain then clearing; mild.

June 1989: Temp. 78° (1° below ave.); Precip. 5″ (2″ above ave.; 0.5″ above north). 1-3 Sunny, seasonably warm. 4-6 Heavy rain, cool. 7-10 Clearing, very cool. 11-13 Partly cloudy, showers; hot. 14-19 Sunny & hot; heavy rain northeast. 20-22 Clear & hot. 23-25 Thundershowers. 26-28 Clear. 29-30 Heavy showers.

July 1989: Temp. 81° (0.5° below ave.); Precip. 6″ (2″ above ave.; 1″ below north). 1-4 Thundershowers, hot. 5-8 Cloudy, rain south & east; milder. 9-13 Heavy rain. 14-15 Clear & hot. 16-22 Scattered showers, sunny & hot. 23-26 Showers, heavy south & east. 27-31 Clear north, showers south & east.

Aug. 1989: Temp. 80.5° (1° below ave.); Precip. 1.5″ (2″ below ave.). 1-3 Rain, very heavy northwest; mild. 4-6 Sunny, rain south. 7-10 Moderately heavy rain, hot. 11-13 Sunny, very hot. 14-15 Thunderstorms, milder. 16-21 Clear, hot. 22-24 Rain, heavy north; seasonable. 25-28 Clear, warm. 29-31 Showers, milder.

Sept. 1989: Temp. 75.5° (1° below ave.); Precip. 1.5″ (2″ below ave.). 1-4 Scattered showers, mild. 5-8 Showers, heavy north; warm. 9-12 Clear & hot. 13-15 Showers, heavy east; milder. 16-18 Clear, pleasantly warm. 19-21 Showers, cool. 22-24 Sunny, seasonable. 25-27 Heavy rain, milder. 28-30 Clear & warm.

Oct. 1989: Temp. 65° (Ave.); Precip. 1.5″ (1″ below ave.; ave. north). 1-4 Showers, heavy north; cooling. 5-12 Clear, pleasantly warm. 13-16 Rain, heavy northeast; turning cold. 17-19 Clear, seasonably warm. 20-24 Scattered showers, rain northwest. 25-27 Clear & warm, showers north. 28-31 Heavy rain then clearing.

9. CHICAGO & SOUTHERN GREAT LAKES

For regional boundaries, see map page 133.

SUMMARY: *Late fall and winter will have well-above-normal temperatures over most of the region except for the northwest which will be only slightly above normal. Precipitation is expected to be below normal in the east, but slightly above in the west, with above-normal snowfall in southern sections and below in northern ones. A snowstorm at Thanksgiving will usher in colder than normal weather, with the latter half of December being particularly frigid. December is anticipated to be much snowier than usual, but thereafter below-normal snowfall is expected until the latter half of February. Following a January thaw, temperatures should be above normal, with only brief cold snaps.*

Spring will be slightly cooler than normal, despite a warm start, due to frequent cool spells. April and early May will be quite dry, but then above-normal rainfall is in the offing, with June being quite wet, particularly in eastern sections.

The summer is expected to be considerably drier than normal, with fewer thundershowers than usual. Frequent hot spells should make July a warmer than normal month, but then cooler than normal periods are expected the balance of the summer.

Early fall may expect frequent periods of unseasonable warmth, interspersed with brief cold snaps, resulting in above-normal temperatures. Normal amounts of precipitation are anticipated.

Nov. 1988: Temp. 41.5° (1° above ave.); Precip. 2.5" (0.5" above ave.; 1" below east). 1-4 Sunny then sprinkles, mild. 5-7 Rain changing to snow, cold snap. 8-10 Warming, sunny. 11-13 Rainstorm, mild. 14-15 Cold snap. 16-17 Rain, mild. 18-20 Partly cloudy, cold. 21-24 Scattered showers, mild. 25-27 Snowstorm, cold. 28-30 Cloudy, unseasonably cold.

Dec. 1988: Temp. 24° (5° below ave.); Precip. 2" (0.5" below ave.). 1-3 Snowstorm. 4-9 Cloudy, intermittent light snow. 10-12 Sunny & mild. 13-16 Cold wave, flurries. 17-18 Snowstorm. 19-21 Severe cold, clear. 22-24 Snow, unseasonably cold. 25-27 Partial clearing, snow north. 28-31 Snowstorm.

Jan. 1989: Temp. 27° (3° above ave.); Precip. 2.5" (0.5" above ave.; ave. east). 1 Sunny, milder. 2-4 Snow. 5-7 Cold snap, flurries. 8-10 Rain, mild. 11-12 Cold, sleet. 13-16 Snowstorm. 17-22 Mild; light snow north. 23-25 Cold wave, snow. 26-29 Clearing then snow, milder. 30-31 Very cold, snow north.

Feb. 1989: Temp. 30° (1.5° above ave.); Precip. 1" (0.5" below ave.). 1-2 Partly cloudy, milder. 3-5 Sleet & snow. 6-7 Sunny, cold. 8-10 Mild, rain changing to snow. 11-14 Sunny, mild then cold. 15-18 Snowstorm. 19-21 Clear, very cold. 22-24 Snow, seasonable. 25-28 Light snow.

Mar. 1989: Temp. 48° (7° above ave.); Precip. 3" (Ave.). 1-3 Cold, snow. 4-7 Warming then light rain. 8-10 Rain, heavy north; mild. 11-14 Turning colder, then snow, heavy west. 15-16 Sunny, mild. 17-22 Rain, locally heavy; mild. 23-25 Clear, very mild. 26-28 Rain, seasonably cold. 29-31 Clearing & warm.

Apr. 1989: Temp. 52° (2° above ave.); Precip. 2" (2" below ave.). 1-4 Clear & warm, then cold snap. 5-6 Showers, very mild. 7-9 Cloudy, cold; snow north. 10-12 Rain, snow north. 13-16 Cloudy, raw. 17-19 Rain, turning warm. 20-23 Mild, sprinkles. 24-27 Showers, warm spell. 28-30 Turning cold, sprinkles.

May 1989: Temp. 58° (2.5° below ave.); Precip. 3" (Ave.). 1-2 Cold snap, sprinkles. 3-6 Warm spell, sunny then rain west. 7-9 Rain, cool. 10-12 Cloudy, cold; rain west. 13-17 Rain, then cloudy, cold. 18-24 Warm, then cool; intermittent rain. 25-26 Sunny, warm. 27-29 Rainstorm. 30-31 Cloudy, cool.

June 1989: Temp. 68.5° (2° below ave.); Precip. 4.5" (0.5" above ave.; 1.5" above east). 1-3 Clear & warm. 4-6 Rain, heavy east; cold. 7-10 Sunny, warming; showers east. 11-13 Cloudy, mild; showers north. 14-16 Thundershowers. 17-20 Clearing, mild. 21-24 Heavy thundershowers. 25-30 Sunny, turning hot; few showers.

July 1989: Temp. 75.5° (0.5° above ave.; 1.5° above east); Precip. 3.5" (0.5" below ave.; 1.5" below east). 1-2 Sunny & hot. 3-5 Thundershowers, heavy west. 6-11 Partly cloudy, mild then hot. 12-14 Heavy thundershowers west, sprinkles east. 15-17 Sunny & warm, showers east. 18-21 Scattered showers. 22-24 Hot; thundershowers east. 25-29 Scattered showers. 30-31 Mild.

Aug. 1989: Temp. 72° (1.5° below ave.); Precip. 2.5" (1" below ave.). 1-2 Sunny, very warm. 3-6 Seasonable, showers. 7-11 Scattered showers. 12-14 Thundershowers, heavy west; warm. 15-17 Partly cloudy, mild. 18-22 Thundershowers, very warm. 23-25 Milder, showers east. 26-28 Cool. 29-31 Clear, warm.

Sept. 1989: Temp. 65° (1° below ave.; 0.5° above east); Precip. 2" (1" below ave.). 1-2 Rain, cold snap. 3-4 Sunny, warm. 5-8 Showers, cool; then clearing. 9-11 Showers, heavy northwest; warm. 12-14 Rain, locally heavy. 15-17 Cloudy, very cool. 18-23 Clear, warm. 24-27 Rain, heavy west. 28-30 Sunny, mild.

Oct. 1989: Temp. 57° (2.5° above ave.); Precip. 2.5" (Ave.). 1-2 Clear, warm. 3-5 Showers, cold snap. 6-11 Clear, pleasant. 12-13 Cloudy, cool. 14-16 Rain, cold. 17-19 Sunny & warm. 20-22 Rain, cold. 23-27 Sunny, warming. 28-29 Rain, cool. 30-31 Sunny & warm.

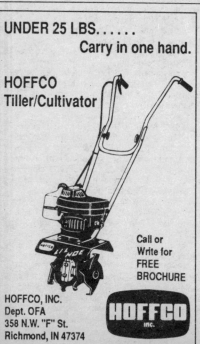

10. NORTHERN GREAT PLAINS—GREAT LAKES

For regional boundaries, see map page 133.

SUMMARY: *Late fall and winter are expected to be milder than normal, with slightly above-normal precipitation over most of the region with the exception of the southwest, which may be well below normal. Snowfall will be below normal except for an excess in the Black Hills. November and December will be colder and snowier than usual, with the latter half of December being particularly frigid, while January may have more mild spells to outweigh the cold ones, as well as above-normal snowfall. March will be warmer and drier than normal.*

Spring should be warmer than normal in the west, but slightly cooler than normal in the east, with above-normal precipitation except for a slight deficiency in the southwest. April through May should be quite warm and dry, but then cool and wet weather is expected for the rest of the season except for occasional clear and warm periods.

Summer is expected to be cooler and wetter than normal, except for the southeast that may be warmer and drier than usual. Other than a heat wave in the west in early August, temperatures will generally be near or slightly below normal until greater excursions above and below normal are encountered in September. The latter half of July through most of August will be fairly dry, but September should be quite wet.

Large variations above and below normal are anticipated in the early fall. Precipitation and snowfall will both be above normal.

Nov. 1988: Temp. 31.5° (2° below ave.); Precip. 1″ (0.5″ below ave.). 1-2 Clear & mild. 3-5 Rain & sleet. 6-8 Snow, heavy southeast; cold. 9-10 Clear, mild. 11-13 Snowstorm, cold wave. 14-15 Seasonable. 16-18 Cold snap, snow. 19-21 Clearing, milder. 22-23 Cloudy, cold. 24-26 Snowstorm, cold. 27-30 Seasonable, flurries.

Dec. 1988: Temp. 14° (5° below ave.); Precip. 1.5″ (0.5″ above ave.). 1-2 Sunny west, snow east. 3-4 Cloudy, cold. 5-7 Snow, moderate south. 8-10 Clear & mild. 11-13 Cold wave; snow, heavy north. 14-16 Sunny & seasonable. 17-18 Snowstorm. 19-21 Severe cold. 22-26 Snowstorm, light west. 27-29 Snow, very cold. 30-31 Cloudy, milder.

Jan. 1989: Temp. 15° (3.5° above ave.); Precip. 1″ (Ave.). 1-4 Light snow, seasonably cold. 5-7 Sunny & mild. 8-10 Snow, heavy southeast. 11-15 Partly cloudy, mild. 16-18 Flurries, seasonable. 19-22 Clear & mild. 23-26 Cold snap; snow, flurries west. 27-29 Light snow, milder. 30-31 Clear, very cold.

Feb. 1989: Temp. 18° (0.5° above ave.); Precip. 1″ (Ave.). 1-2 Mild; partly cloudy, snow north.

3-5 Light snow, cold wave. 6-8 Very cold. 9-11 Snowstorm, mild. 12-14 Sunny, seasonable. 15-18 Flurries, turning cold. 19-21 Clear & mild. 22-24 Snow, flurries west. 25-28 Cloudy, light snow north; slightly mild.

Mar. 1989: Temp. 36° (7° above ave.); Precip. 1.5″ (0.5″ below ave.). 1-3 Cold snap; snowstorm, light west. 4-8 Sunny, very mild. 9-14 Snowstorm, flurries west; seasonable. 15-18 Sunny, warm. 19-21 Freezing rain, heavy central. 22-24 Clear & warm. 25-27 Rain, heavy southwest; mild. 28-31 Clear, very warm; showers east.

Apr. 1989: Temp. 51° (5° above ave.); Precip. 1″ (1″ below ave.). 1-4 Very warm, rain north. 5-6 Cloudy & cool. 7-9 Seasonable; rain & snow, heavy central. 10-12 Sunny south, rain north. 13-15 Partly cloudy, rain west. 16-23 Sunny, very warm; showers north. 24-26 Rain, light west. 27-30 Partly cloudy & warm.

May 1989: Temp. 56° (2° above ave.); Precip. 3″ (Ave.). 1-3 Sunny, sprinkles; warm. 4-6 Heavy rain west, sunny east. 7-9 Rain, very cool. 10-12 Partly cloudy, warmer. 13-16 Cold wave, light rain & snow. 17-20 Scattered showers, mild. 21-28 Intermittent heavy rain, cool. 29-31 Clearing, very warm.

June 1989: Temp. 67.5° (0.5° below ave.); Precip. 6″ (2″ above ave.). 1-2 Sunny, very warm; rain west. 3-5 Cold wave, heavy rain. 6-8 Clear, warming. 9-11 Showers, hot. 12-13 Seasonable. 14-16 Rain, heavy southeast, cooler. 17-20 Sunny & hot. 21-24 Heavy rain, cool. 25-27 Clear and hot. 28-30 Showers, warm.

July 1989: Temp. 73.5° (0.5° above ave.); Precip. 3″ (0.5″ below ave.). 1-4 Rain, heavy east; seasonably warm. 5-9 Partly cloudy, showers west. 10-13 Thundershowers, hot. 14-16 Sunny & warm. 17-21 Seasonable, showers west. 22-24 Showers, heavy central. 25-28 Cooler, scattered showers. 29-31 Clear & warm.

Aug. 1989: Temp. 70° (0.5° below ave.); Precip. 1.5″ (2° below ave.; 1″ above west). 1-6 Showers; clear & hot west. 7-9 Clear & warm; showers central, mild. 10-11 Seasonable. 12-14 Heavy rain, sunny west; mild. 15-17 Partly cloudy, showers west. 18-20 Showers, hot. 21-24 Heavy rain east. 25-31 Seasonable; showers west.

Sept. 1989: Temp. 60° (1° below ave.); Precip. 4.5″ (2″ above ave.). 1-2 Cold & rainy. 3-8 Clear & warm; cold nights. 9-13 Heavy rain, cold. 14-17 Showers, warm. 18-21 Unseasonably warm. 22-24 Rain, mild. 25-26 Sunny & warm. 27-30 Cold & rainy, then clear.

Oct. 1989: Temp. 49° (0.5° below ave.; 3° below west); Precip. 3″ (1″ above ave.). 1-3 Rain, cool. 4-6 Indian Summer-like. 7-8 Showers south; cool. 9-12 Heavy rain, snow north. 13-16 Snowstorm. 17-19 Sunny, mild; snow west. 20-21 Cold, snow east. 22-27 Clear & mild. 28-31 Cold, snow south.

11. CENTRAL GREAT PLAINS

For regional boundaries, see map page 133.

SUMMARY: *Late fall and winter are expected to have extremely variable temperatures but end up much milder than normal over all. Precipitation will be unevenly distributed, with northwest and central sections being drier than normal, southern sections slightly so, but with the northeast having well-above-normal amounts. Despite a very snowy December, the seasonal snowfall is anticipated to be well below normal in the north and southwest, slightly below in south-central sections but slightly above in the southeast. Most of December will be unusually cold, but thereafter few excursions of below-normal temperatures and numerous mild spells are anticipated.*

Spring is expected early and should be well above normal in temperature with below-normal precipitation in the north and west, but above in the southeast. May and parts of June may be cool and wet, but otherwise warm and drier weather should prevail.

The summer is anticipated to be warmer and drier than normal in the west, but cooler and wetter than normal in the east. Drought is expected in some south-central and western sections, while rains in the east may cause local flooding. Hot and mild spells should alternate, with a cool period at the end of August.

The fall will not depart significantly from normal, with sunny and warm periods alternating with cold, wet ones.

Nov. 1988: Temp. 40.5° (2° above ave.); Precip. 1″ (0.5″ below ave.). 1-3 Sunny & warm. 4-7 Cold snap, rain. 8-11 Clear, very warm. 12-14 Cold wave; rain, heavy east, snow north. 15-18 Warmer; rain east, showers west. 19-23 Sunny & mild. 24-26 Cold wave; snowstorm, light west. 27-30 Sunny, cold.

Dec. 1988: Temp. 19.5° (6° below ave.); Precip. 2″ (1″ above ave.; 0.5″ below south). 1-4 Sunny & mild west; cloudy, rain southeast. 5-7 Cold wave; snowstorm north. 8-12 Clear & mild. 13-15 Cold wave. 16-18 Snow, very cold. 19-23 Severe cold, snow. 24-26 Partly sunny, warming. 27-29 Snowstorm. 30-31 Cloudy, cold.

Jan. 1989: Temp. 25° (4° above ave.); Precip. 2″ (1″ above ave.; 0.5″ below northwest). 1-2 Sunny, mild. 3-5 Cold snap; snow, sunny west. 6-10 Mild; sunny; then heavy rain central & south. 11-16 Seasonable, snow & rain, heavy southeast. 17-22 Sunny, quite mild. 23-25 Cold wave; snowstorm. 26-28 Light snow, rain southeast. 29-31 Sunny & mild; snow west.

Feb. 1989: Temp. 29.5° (5° above ave.); Precip. 0.5″ (0.5″ below ave.; 1″ above southeast). 1-4 Snow, showers south; cold. 5-7 Cloudy, cold. 8-

10 Mild; snow & rain, heavy southeast. 11-16 Seasonable; flurries, sprinkles south. 17-19 Storm, very heavy southeast. 20-23 Sunny then rain. 24-28 Sunny & mild; showers east.

Mar. 1989: Temp. 44° (9° above ave.); Precip. 3″ (1″ above ave.; 0.5″ below south). 1-3 Cold, snow east. 4-7 Sunny, warm; rain southeast. 8-12 Rain, snow north; cold. 13-18 Clearing & warming, then rain east. 19-21 Rain, cool. 22-24 Cloudy, mild, then rain east. 25-27 Rain, warm. 28-31 Sunny & warm, then showers.

Apr. 1989: Temp. 56.5° (6° above ave.); Precip. 1.5″ (1.5″ below ave.). 1-3 Very warm, scattered showers. 4-8 Partly cloudy, showers west. 9-11 Light rain, milder. 12-15 Cold wave; rain, snow north. 16-19 Sunny & warm, then rain. 20-24 Clear, very warm. 25-27 Rain, heavy east; milder. 28-30 Clear & pleasant.

May 1989: Temp. 59° (3° below ave.); Precip. 3″ (1″ below ave.; 3″ above southeast). 1-4 Warm; showers, heavy south. 5-7 Cold wave; heavy rain. 8-9 Clear, warm. 10-15 Scattered showers, then rain; cool. 16-18 Sunny & pleasant. 19-24 Rain, cooler. 25-26 Seasonable. 27-31 Rain, locally heavy, then clearing & warm.

June 1989: Temp. 71.5° (Ave.; 0.5° above west); Precip. 4.5″ (1″ above ave.; 1″ below south). 1-3 Clear & warm; thundershowers west. 4-6 Cold wave, rain. 7-14 Sunny & hot. 15-18 Cloudy, showers west. 19-23 Rain; turning cool. 24-27 Clear, very warm. 28-30 Rain, heavy east.

July 1989: Temp. 76° (Ave.; 1° above south); Precip. 2″ (1″ below ave.). 1-2 Sunny & hot, showers west. 3-5 Thundershowers, seasonable. 6-8 Sunny, hot. 9-12 Showers, light east. 13-15 Thundershowers, light west. 16-18 Sunny, hot. 19-21 Rain north, hot. 22-25 Thundershowers. 26-28 Sunny, mild. 29-31 Showers.

Aug. 1989: Temp. 72° (2° below ave.; 1° above west); Precip. 5″ (1″ above ave.; 1″ below northwest). 1-4 Showers, sunny west; hot. 5-10 Showers, heavy east; milder. 11-15 Partly cloudy, light showers; warm. 16-18 Sunny & warm; heavy showers southeast. 19-22 Heavy showers, hot. 23-25 Sunny, hot. 26-31 Intermittent showers, locally heavy; mild.

Sept. 1989: Temp. 64.5° (0.5° below ave.); Precip. 2.5″ (0.5″ below ave.; 2″ below south). 1-4 Partly sunny & pleasant; showers west. 5-7 Sunny, mild; heavy showers south. 8-9 Clear, very hot. 10-15 Heavy rain, warm; then clearing. 16-22 Showers west; pleasant. 23-27 Rain, heavy east; warm. 28-30 Clear and warm.

Oct. 1989: Temp. 55° (1° above ave.; ave. west); Precip. 3.5″ (1.5″ above ave.; ave. south). 1-2 Heavy rain, light south; cool. 3-6 Clear, warm. 7-11 Heavy rain central & west, sunny & warm east. 12-15 Sunny, warm then heavy rain. 16-19 Clear & mild, showers west. 20-22 Heavy rain, light west; cold wave. 23-27 Sunny, mild. 28-29 Rain east, sunny west. 30-31 Clear & warm.

12. TEXAS—OKLAHOMA

For regional boundaries, see map page 133.

SUMMARY: *Late fall and winter may see temperatures well above normal in the east and slightly above in central and western sections, with central and southeastern sections receiving well-above-normal precipitation while below-normal amounts are expected in northern and western sections. Except for a very cold period during the middle of December and another subnormal spell in the latter part of January, temperatures generally will vary between normal and well above normal, with an occasional cold snap. Frequent and heavy precipitation is expected in central & southeastern sections, but northwestern sections may experience drought before getting relief after mid-January.*

Spring is anticipated to be warmer than normal, much wetter than normal in the south and much drier in the north. A very warm and dry period in early spring should give way to more seasonable temperatures and frequent shower activity, with southeastern and south-central sections experiencing very heavy amounts in late May and June.

Summer temperatures should be above normal in the south and west, but slightly below in the north. Precipitation is expected to be much below normal in the northeast, with drought developing, but well above normal in southern and western sections. Except for showers at the very beginning of the season, little rainfall is expected until heavy showers arrive at the end of August.

Early fall is expected to see cool and wet spells, with heavy rain in the south and west, interspersed with sunny and warm ones.

Nov. 1988: Temp. 59° (3° above ave.); Precip. 2.5″ (Ave.; 2″ below north & west). 1-6 Sunny, warm. 7-9 Cold snap, clear. 10-12 Cloudy, warm. 13-16 Rain, heavy central & east, cold. 17-21 Sunny & warm. 22-25 Rain east, clear west. 26-28 Cold. 29-30 Clear & warm.

Dec. 1988: Temp. 44.5° (4° below ave.; 0.5° below south); Precip. 1″ (1″ below ave.; 2″ above southeast). 1-4 Sunny, warm. 5-7 Cold wave; snow northeast, heavy rain south. 8-12 Clear & warm. 13-14 Cold wave, hard frost. 15-20 Rain & snow, then very cold. 21-22 Rain & snow, cold. 23-25 Clear, cold. 26-28 Showers, heavy east. 29-31 Clear, mild.

Jan. 1989: Temp. 46° (1° above ave.); Precip. 3″ (1″ above ave.). 1-6 Sunny & mild. 7-10 Rain, heavy east, light west; warm. 11-13 Cold wave; rain, snow north, light west. 14-19 Alternating sun and rain, locally heavy, snow north; very cold. 20-22 Clear & mild. 23-26 Showers, cold. 27-31 Clear, very warm.

Feb. 1989: Temp. 51.5° (2° above ave.); Precip. 4″ (2″ above ave.; 0.5″ below west). 1-3 Cold; rain, snow north. 4-6 Sunny, mild. 7-9 Showers, heavy east; sunny west. 10-14 Sunny, rain east; cold. 15-23 Sun & rain; cold. 24-25 Seasonable. 26-28 Clear & warm.

Mar. 1989: Temp. 60° (3° above ave.); Precip. 2.5″ (0.5″ above ave.). 1-3 Cloudy, mild; showers south. 4-7 Clear & warm. 8-10 Rain, heavy east. 11-15 Clear & warm. 16-19 Rain, heavy east. 20-24 Cloudy, cool; rain northeast. 25-27 Sunny & pleasant. 28-31 Rain east, light west.

Apr. 1989: Temp. 70.5° (4° above ave.); Precip. 2.5″ (2″ below ave.). 1-5 Clear, heat wave. 6-12 Partly cloudy, very warm. 13-15 Scattered showers, seasonable. 16-18 Clear & pleasant. 19-20 Rain, heavy east, scattered west. 21-24 Clear & warm. 25-28 Rain, heavy central; warm. 29-30 Clear, warmer.

May 1989: Temp. 72° (1.5° below ave.; 1.5° above south); Precip. 5″ (0.5″ above ave.). 1-2 Clear, warm. 3-4 Rain. 5-8 Showers, heavy northeast, sunny west. 9-11 Mild; rain central. 12-15 Rain east, sprinkles west. 16-20 Rain; cold then mild. 21-24 Showers. 25-26 Cold. 27-31 Rain, light west; warm.

June 1989: Temp. 81° (1° below ave.); Precip. 6″ (3″ above ave.; 1″ below north & west). 1-5 Rain, very heavy east; seasonable. 6-8 Partly cloudy, cool. 9-11 Sunny & warm. 12-14 Showers, heavy east, few west. 15-17 Lighter showers. 18-21 Sunny & hot. 22-27 Milder, thundershowers. 28-30 Scattered showers, hot.

July 1989: Temp. 86.5° (Ave.); Precip. 1″ (1″ below ave.; 1″ above southeast). 1-4 Seasonably hot; heavy showers north. 5-8 Rain south, heavy southeast; milder. 9-11 Clear & hot; showers east. 12-17 Clear, very hot. 18-20 Partly cloudy, sprinkles east. 21-23 Clear, hot. 24-26 Rain east, light west. 27-31 Clear, hot.

Aug. 1989: Temp. 86.5° (1° above ave.); Precip. 1″ (1″ below ave.). 1-7 Hot, scattered showers. 8-10 Partly cloudy, showers north. 11-14 Very hot, showers. 15-22 Showers, seasonable. 23-25 Showers, heavy north; milder. 26-27 Clear. 28-31 Showers, cooling.

Sept. 1989: Temp. 76° (2° below ave.; ave. south); Precip. 5.5″ (2″ above ave.; 1″ below north). 1-6 Heavy showers, light northeast; mild. 7-9 Sunny, hot. 10-12 Showers, sunny north. 13-15 Clear & hot; showers north. 16-22 Cooler; showers. 23-25 Cloudy, mild; showers north. 26-30 Showers, heavy east; mild.

Oct. 1989: Temp. 67° (1° below ave.; 1° above south); Precip. 2.5″ (1″ below ave.; 1.5″ above south & west). 1-3 Showers, heavy east, light west; cool. 4-7 Clear & pleasant. 8-14 Heavy rain central & west, few showers east, then heavy; seasonable. 15-18 Clear & warm. 19-21 Rain. 22-26 Sunny, seasonable. 27-29 Showers, heavy east. 30-31 Clear & warm.

For regional boundaries, see map page 133.

SUMMARY: *Late fall and winter are expected to be milder than normal, with below-normal precipitation in the south and well above normal in the north. Most sections should receive above-normal snowfall, particularly in the northwest, but the southwest will have below normal. November and December should be quite variable but have several prolonged cold and snowy periods that bring well-above-normal snowfall to central and northern sections. Thereafter temperatures should remain closer to normal, with brief excursions above and below.*

Spring is anticipated to be warmer and drier than normal, except for above-normal precipitation in the south. April through early May should see warm and dry spells before cooler and wetter weather prevails through the latter part of May and early June. More sunny and warm spells should close out the season.

Summer is expected to be warmer than normal in central and southern sections and slightly cooler than normal in the north. Above-normal precipitation is anticipated in northern and southern sections, but below normal across the central portion of the region. Frequent, but brief, hot and dry spells should alternate with milder, showery ones through most of the season.

Fall is expected to start out sunny and pleasant, but cold fronts in the middle and latter parts of October should bring cooler and wetter than normal weather.

Nov. 1988: Temp. 40° (Ave.); Precip. 2″ (1″ above ave.). 1-2 Clear & mild. 3-6 Cold wave; rain central & north, heavy northwest. 7-8 Sunny, mild. 9-12 Cold snap; snow, heavy north. 13-19 Intermittent snow, heavy north, flurries south. 20-23 Sleet & snow, cool. 24-28 Clear & cold. 29-30 Seasonable; rain west.

Dec. 1988: Temp. 31° (1° above ave.; 1° below north); Precip. 1.5″ (Ave.; 0.5″ above north). 1-3 Clear & warm east; rain west & north. 4-7 Cloudy cold; snow north. 8-11 Snow north, light south; mild. 12-16 Very cold, snow. 17-19 Flurries, cold north. 20-22 Snowstorm. 23-25 Sunny; frigid north. 26-31 Snowstorm, mild.

Jan. 1989: Temp. 31° (2° above ave.); Precip. 1″ (0.5″ below ave.). 1-2 Snowstorm north, sunny south. 3-5 Sunny & mild. 6-12 Snow, seasonably cold. 13-19 Sunny, extreme cold; flurries south. 20-25 Cold, sunny; scattered snow south. 26-29 Snowstorm, light east. 30-31 Cloudy & cold, scattered snow north.

Feb. 1989: Temp. 35° (1° above ave.; 2° below north); Precip. 0.5″ (0.5″ below ave.). 1-3 Snow, light north; cold. 4-6 Sunny; light snow west. 7-9 Cloudy, cold; snow east. 10-12 Sunny, season-able; snow north. 13-16 Cold, snow. 17-20 Sunny, normal. 21-25 Cloudy, light snow. 26-28 Clear & mild, snow west.

Mar. 1989: Temp. 43° (2.5° above ave.); Precip. 1.5″ (Ave.; 0.5″ above north). 1-4 Cloudy, cold; then snowstorm. 5-6 Sunny, mild. 7-11 Snow, cold. 12-15 Clear & warm. 16-19 Rain changing to snow, cold. 20-22 Clearing, warmer. 23-25 Rain, snow mountains; seasonable. 26-29 Rain, snow east. 30-31 Clear & warm.

Apr. 1989: Temp. 54° (5° above ave.; 2° above north); Precip. 1.5″ (0.5″ below ave.). 1-2 Cloudy, warm. 3-6 Rain, turning cold. 7-9 Sunny, mild. 10-13 Rain, snow mountains; cold. 14-17 Sunny & warm east; drizzle west. 18-22 Sprinkles, then clear & very warm. 23-25 Rain, cold wave. 26-30 Clear, very warm.

May 1989: Temp. 60° (1° above ave.; 0.5° below north); Precip. 1″ (0.5″ below ave.). 1-3 Rain. 4-6 Cold snap. 7-11 Sunny, very warm, scattered showers. 12-15 Rain, cold. 16-19 Warm, light showers. 20-23 Clear & warm. 24-26 Cloudy, sprinkles. 27-29 Showers, cool; then clearing. 30-31 Heavy rain.

June 1989: Temp. 68° (Ave.; 1° below north); Precip. 2″ (1″ above ave.; ave. north). 1-2 Rain, snow mountains; cold. 3-5 Sunny & pleasant. 6-8 Clear & hot. 9-11 Sunny, rain west; warm. 12-15 Cloudy, sprinkles; hot. 16-20 Cloudy, mild; rain west & north. 21-25 Clearing, warm. 26-30 Cloudy, mild; rain west & north.

July 1989: Temp. 78.5° (1° above ave.; ave. north); Precip. 0.5″ (0.5″ below ave.). 1-3 Sunny & seasonable; rain west & north. 4-7 Partly cloudy, light showers west. 8-11 Seasonably hot, sprinkles. 12-14 Cloudy, rain west. 15-18 Rain, locally heavy; sunny west. 19-21 Seasonable. 22-26 Sunny, very hot; thundershowers south. 27-31 Milder, showers.

Aug. 1989: Temp. 76° (1° above ave.); Precip. 1″ (Ave.). 1-4 Clear & hot; then scattered showers, milder. 5-9 Sunny, hot; showers south. 10-12 Cloudy, cooler; showers east. 13-14 Clear, hot; rain south. 15-18 Rain, scattered west; warm. 19-23 Sunny; turning hot. 24-26 Milder, scattered showers. 27-31 Rain, seasonable.

Sept. 1989: Temp. 65° (0.5° above ave.; 1.5° below north); Precip. 0.5″ (0.5″ below ave.). 1-4 Showers. 5-6 Sunny; warm. 7-12 Rain west, cloudy east; cool. 13-18 Clear, very warm; sprinkles east. 19-21 Rain, cold wave. 22-24 Clear, seasonable; rain south. 25-27 Cloudy, cool. 28-30 Sunny, very warm; rain north.

Oct. 1989: Temp. 50° (3° below ave.); Precip. 2″ (1″ above ave.). 1-3 Cloudy, warm. 4-6 Rain, cold. 7-12 Cold wave, rain & snow. 13-15 Clearing, warming; light rain east. 16-18 Sunny, seasonable. 19-22 Snowstorm, cold wave. 23-26 Seasonable; snow north. 27-29 Cold snap, snow west. 30-31 Cold, snow.

14. SOUTHWEST DESERT

For regional boundaries, see map page 133.

SUMMARY: *Late fall and winter are expected to be drier than normal over the region, with above-normal temperatures in the east, but below normal in the west. Dry periods, with warm daytime temperatures, are anticipated at the end of one month and the beginning of the following month all through the winter, while cold spells with freezing nighttime temperatures are in the offing during the middle period of the month. Most of the winter's precipitation will come during the cold period in mid-January.*

Spring is anticipated to be warmer than normal, due primarily to an early heat wave in the latter part of April and early May and a briefer but hotter one before mid-June. The precipitation in the west may be limited to brief showers in April, bringing drought to some sections, while eastern sections should get above-normal amounts from the shower activity at the end of April and in early May.

Summer should be warmer and drier than normal in the east, but have near- to below-normal temperatures in the west, with above-normal precipitation. The hot weather will be broken after mid-July by heavy shower activity and milder temperatures, with northwestern sections experiencing much greater than normal precipitation.

Following a hot and dry spell at the end of September, the early fall is expected to remain pleasantly warm with normal scattered showers, except possibly in southern sections where heavy showers should bring above-normal precipitation.

Nov. 1988: Temp. 58.5° (2° below ave.; 2° above east); Precip. 0″ (0.5″ below ave.). 1-5 Partly cloudy, warm; clear, very warm east. 6-8 Clear, very warm. 9-11 Cloudy, mild; very warm east. 12-15 Cold; showers east. 16-18 Cool, cold nights. 19-21 Cloudy, milder. 22-26 Clear, cold nights. 27-30 Clear, warm.

Dec. 1988: Temp. 50° (3° below ave.; ave. east); Precip. 0.5″ (0.5″ below ave.). 1-4 Clear, quite warm. 5-7 Cloudy, mild; showers east. 8-14 Sunny; mild days, cold nights. 15-17 Rainy, turning cold. 18-21 Sunny; cold, hard frost. 22-25 Sunny & milder. 26-28 Rain, locally heavy; seasonable. 29-31 Cloudy.

Jan. 1989: Temp. 51° (1° below ave.); Precip. 1.5″ (0.5″ above ave.; 1″ above south). 1-6 Clearing, very warm. 7-10 Rain, locally heavy, cold. 11-15 Partly cloudy, rain; cold. 16-18 Showers, heavy east; quite cold. 19-20 Sunny, seasonable. 21-25 Rain then sprinkles; cool. 26-28 Cold, frost. 29-31 Clear, warm.

Feb. 1989: Temp. 53° (3° below ave.; 1° below east); Precip. 0.2″ (0.5″ below ave.). 1-3 Sunny & warm. 4-6 Partly cloudy; cold nights, frost. 7-9 Showers, cold. 10-12 Sunny, cold nights. 13-17 Intermittent showers, cold. 18-20 Sunny; mild, cold nights. 21-23 Cloudy, showers east. 24-28 Clear, quite warm.

Mar. 1989: Temp. 61° (0.5° above ave.); Precip. 3″ (0.5″ below ave.). 1-7 Sunny, warm. 8-10 Cold & rainy. 11-15 Clearing, very warm. 16-17 Partly cloudy, seasonable. 18-20 Light rain, cold. 21-22 Clear, very warm; cloudy east. 23-25 Cool, sprinkles. 26-31 Sunny, seasonable; rain east.

Apr. 1989: Temp. 71° (3° above ave.); Precip. 0″ (0.3″ below ave.; ave. east). 1-4 Sunny & warm. 5-12 Some clouds, widely scattered showers; seasonable. 13-17 Clearing & hot. 18-24 Partly cloudy, seasonable then hot. 25-27 Clear & hot; showers east. 28-30 Cloudy, showers; hot.

May 1989: Temp. 78° (1° above ave.); Precip. 0″ (0.1″ below ave.). 1-2 Sprinkles, hot. 3-7 Clear & hot; showers east. 8-10 Clear, hot; widely scattered showers east. 11-13 Partly cloudy, showers east. 14-16 Cloudy, milder. 17-24 Partly cloudy, hot; few showers east. 25-27 Cloudy, milder. 28-31 Sunny, hot.

June 1989: Temp. 86.5° (Ave.; 1° above south); Precip. 0″ (0.2″ below ave.). 1-2 Cloudy, mild; showers east. 3-5 Clear, seasonably hot. 6-9 Heat wave; showers east. 10-12 Partly cloudy, hot. 13-18 Clear, showers east. 19-21 Widely scattered showers. 22-25 Clear, hot; rain east. 26-30 Partly cloudy, thundershowers east.

July 1989: Temp. 91° (1° below ave.); Precip. 1.5″ (0.5″ above ave.; 0.5″ below south & east). 1-5 Clear & hot, thundershowers east. 6-9 Cloudy, showers. 10-12 Sunny, seasonable; showers east. 13-17 Showers, milder. 18-20 Clear, very hot. 21-25 Thundershowers, milder. 26-31 Seasonably hot, scattered showers.

Aug. 1989: Temp. 89.5° (0.5° below ave.; 1° above south & east); Precip 2″ (1″ above ave.; ave. east). 1-6 Very hot, intermittent showers. 7-9 Thundershowers, milder. 10-12 Sunny, seasonable; few showers. 13-15 Showers, milder. 16-22 Partly cloudy, scattered showers; hot. 23-25 Thundershowers. 26-31 Showers, hot.

Sept. 1989: Temp. 84° (1° below ave.; 1° above east); Precip. 2″ (1″ above ave; ave. east & south). 1-4 Rain, locally heavy; milder. 5-10 Clear & hot, showers east. 11-14 Sunny, seasonable, few showers. 15-20 Intermittent showers, hot then milder. 21-23 Thundershowers. 24-31 Clearing, turning hot.

Oct. 1989: Temp. 70° (3° below ave.; ave. east); Precip. 0.5″ (Ave.; 1″ above south). 1-5 Showers, heavy south; mild. 6-11 Partly cloudy, scattered showers; warm. 12-14 Showers, locally heavy. 15-18 Clear, warm. 19-23 Cloudy, then clear & warm. 24-29 Sunny, seasonably warm. 30-31 Rain, cooler.

SUMMARY: *Late fall and winter are expected to be slightly milder than normal and to have below-normal precipitation in the north, but above normal in the south. Snowfall over the region should be greater than normal. November may have considerably above-normal precipitation and snowfall on into early December, with temperatures not markedly different from normal, only to be followed by a very cold and dry period until Christmastime. January should be mild, with above-normal snowfall. February is expected to be comparatively dry in southern sections; close to normal conditions are anticipated elsewhere.*

Spring is anticipated to be significantly warmer and drier than usual, with May in particular having more frequent sunny and warm periods than normal. Brief warm, dry spells in April will make it slightly milder and drier than normal; in June they will be balanced by cool and wet periods.

Summer is expected to be a continuation of the warmer and drier than normal weather of spring. Following a cool and wet first half of July, warmer and sunnier than usual weather is anticipated for the rest of July and through August, with a cool and damp early September partially balanced by alternating warm/dry and cool/wet spells for the rest of the month.

Early fall is anticipated to remain slightly below normal in temperature for an extended period, with close to normal precipitation in the north, but considerably above normal in the south.

Nov. 1988: Temp. 46° (0.5° above ave.; ave. north); Precip. 8″ (3″ above ave.; 1″ above north). 1-6 Heavy rain, seasonable. 7-8 Showers. 9-12 Cold wave, snow. 13-23 Heavy rain, snow mountains; cold. 24-27 Clearing, milder. 28-30 Heavy rain, snow mountains.

Dec. 1988: Temp. 41.5° (0.5° above ave.; 0.5° below north); Precip. 6.5″ (Ave.; 1″ below north). 1-4 Heavy rain, snow mountains; mild. 5-6 Light rain. 7-9 Rain, mild. 10-12 Snowstorm. 13-15 Light snow. 16-18 Clear, unseasonably cold. 19-23 Cold; snow. 24-26 Snowstorm. 27-31 Rain, snow mountains; mild.

Jan. 1989: Temp. 43° (4° above ave.); Precip. 5.5″ (0.5° below ave.). 1-11 Heavy rain, snow mountains; mild. 12-14 Light rain & snow, seasonable. 15-18 Clear, cold wave. 19-21 Light freezing rain, turning mild. 22-24 Light rain, mild. 25-29 Heavy rain, heavy snow mountains. 30-31 Flurries, colder.

Feb. 1989: Temp. 43.5° (0.5° above ave.; 0.5° below north); Precip. 2″ (2″ below ave.; ave.

north). 1-2 Rain & snow. 3-6 Heavy rain, snow mountains. 7-8 Cold drizzle. 9-11 Rain, heavy snow north & mountains. 12-18 Intermittent rain & snow. 19-20 Sunny, mild. 21-28 Rain, heavy north, heavy snow mountains.

Mar. 1989: Temp. 47° (1° above ave.); Precip. 4.5″ (1″ above ave.; ave. north). 1-2 Rain, heavy north. 3-10 Intermittently heavy rain, seasonably cold. 11-14 Sprinkles then clear & cool. 15-19 Heavy rain, lighter north, snow mountains; cold. 20-22 Rain, scattered north. 23-25 Sunny, milder. 26-31 Rain, heavy north; cold then turning milder.

Apr. 1989: Temp. 52° (1.5° above ave.; 0.5° above north); Precip. 1.5″ (1″ below ave.). 1-2 Rain, cold. 3-6 Scattered showers, seasonable. 7-11 Partly cloudy, light showers. 12-15 Moderately heavy rain, cold. 16-21 Sunny & mild; few sprinkles. 22-25 Rain, seasonably cold. 26-28 Clear & warm. 29-30 Rain, seasonable.

May 1989: Temp. 60° (3° above ave.); Precip. 1″ (1″ below ave.). 1-4 Cold & rainy. 5-10 Sunny, warm. 11-12 Scattered pleasantly light showers, cold. 13-15 Clear, very warm. 16-18 Sprinkles, cold. 19-24 Clear, unseasonably warm. 25-28 Cloudy, light showers; cooler. 29-31 Rain, heavy south; cold.

June 1989: Temp. 62.5° (Ave.); Precip. 2″ (0.5″ above ave.). 1-2 Rain; cold. 3-5 Sunny & warm; sprinkles north. 6-9 Intermittent rain, cool. 10-13 Showers, heavier north; seasonable. 14-16 Sunny & warm. 17-20 Rain, heavy north; cold wave. 21-24 Clear, very warm. 25-30 Rain, unseasonably cold.

July 1989: Temp. 68.5° (0.5° above ave.); Precip. 1″ (0.5″ above ave.). 1-4 Rain, heavier north; warming. 5-6 Scattered showers, cooler. 7-11 Sunny, pleasantly warm. 12-14 Heavy rain, cool. 15-17 Cloudy, very cool. 18-20 Rainy & cool. 21-25 Sunny & hot. 26-31 Clear, warmer than average; then sprinkles.

Aug. 1989: Temp. 68 ° (1° above ave.; ave. north); Precip. 0″ (1″ below ave.). 1-3 Cool, sprinkles. 4-8 Sunny, seasonably warm. 9-11 Showers, cool. 12-15 Sunny, very warm. 16-19 Few light showers, cooler than normal. 20-27 Clear, warm. 28-31 Sprinkles, mild.

Sept. 1989: Temp. 62.5° (Ave.); Precip. 1″ (0.5″ below ave.). 1-4 Rain, light north; cool. 5-8 Sunny, then light rain; cool. 9-11 Light showers, locally heavy north. 12-17 Sunny & warm; few showers north. 18-21 Moderately heavy rain, quite cool. 22-26 Sunny & warm, then light showers. 27-30 Sunny, pleasant.

Oct. 1989: Temp. 53° (1° below ave.); Precip. 4″ (1″ above ave.; ave. north). 1-3 Clear, pleasantly warm. 4-7 Rain, cool; 8-10 Scattered showers. 11-13 Rain, cooler than average. 14-16 Sunny, seasonable. 17-20 Partly cloudy, cool; light showers north. 21-22 Light rain; sunny north. 23-31 Heavy rain, seasonably cold.

16. CALIFORNIA

For regional boundaries, see map page 133.

SUMMARY: *Late fall and winter are anticipated to be slightly warmer and considerably drier than normal, with below-normal snowfall in the mountains. Warm spells in November, late December, and late January will make these months warmer than normal despite several cool periods. The Central Valley will need to watch for frost in mid-December and mid-January. February may be colder than normal, particularly at night, but warm spells will predominate during March. Frequent and heavy rains and mountain snows in November and December will result in above-normal precipitation for early winter, but the balance of the season is expected to be much below normal.*

Spring is expected to be slightly cooler and drier than normal in northern sections but warmer and wetter than usual in the south. Early and heavy spring rains are anticipated in the Central Valley and the south, causing most of the seasonal precipitation, although the Central Valley should receive more late in May. Warm periods are expected in late April, early May, and late June, while much of May and early June will be quite cool in the north.

Summer will be typically dry, with cooler than normal temperatures in the north due to mild daytime temperatures interspersed with brief hot spells. Daytime temperatures in the south should fluctuate between normal and above-normal values.

Early fall will see hot periods alternating with mild and rainy ones. Precipitation will be below normal in the north, above normal in the south.

Nov. 1988: Temp. 56° (1° above ave.; ave. south); Precip. 4″ (1.5″ above ave.; 1″ below south). 1-4 Heavy rain, light south; cool. 5-9 Clear & warm. 10-12 Light rain, cold. 13-16 Heavy rain north, snow mountains. 17-18 Sunny, mild. 19-23 Rain, heavy north. 24-27 Clear & warm. 28-30 Rain; cloudy south.

Dec. 1988: Temp. 51° (2° above ave.; 0.5° below south); Precip. 6″ (2.5″ above ave.). 1-4 Clear, then rain, cold. 5-7 Sunny, mild. 8-10 Heavy rain, snow mountains, showers south. 11-15 Cold, light showers. 16-18 Seasonable. 19-20 Light rain; sunny south. 21-23 Cold east. 24-31 Rain, snow mountains; cold.

Jan. 1989: Temp. 52° (3.5° above ave.; 1° above inland); Precip. 1.5″ (2.5″ below ave.). 1-2 Rain north, scattered south. 3-5 Clear, warm. 6-11 Intermittent rain, heavy north. 12-21 Clear, warm days, cold nights, frost interior. 22-24 Cloudy, cold; rain north. 25-31 Clear, unseasonably warm; showers north.

Feb. 1989: Temp. 50° (1.5° below ave.); Precip. 2″ (1″ below ave.). 1-2 Rain. 3-5 Clear, frost inland. 6-8 Heavy rain, snow mountains. 9-13 Sunny south, rain north. 14-15 Cold, light rain. 16-18 Sunny, warm, cold nights. 19-20 Rain, light south; cold. 21-22 Sunny. 23-25 Rain, scattered south. 26-28 Sunny, warm.

Mar. 1989: Temp. 54° (1° above ave.); Precip. 1.5″ (1″ below ave.). 1-4 Scattered showers; sunny south. 5-6 Clear & warm. 7-9 Sprinkles. 10-14 Clear, warm. 15-17 Heavy rain, snow mountains. 18-22 Sunny, warm; showers north. 23-25 Rain, heavy south; snow mountains. 26-31 Sunny, warm; showers north.

Apr. 1989: Temp. 55° (Ave.; 2° above inland & south); Precip. 1.5″ (Ave.; 1.5″ above south). 1-5 Heavy rain, cold. 6-9 Sunny, warm; cold nights. 10-12 Showers, cool. 13-16 Clearing, warm. 17-23 Cool, sprinkles coast; sunny & warm inland. 24-28 Clear, unseasonably warm. 29-30 Partly cloudy, showers north.

May 1989: Temp. 56.5° (1° below ave.; 1° above inland); Precip. 0.3″ (Ave.; 0.5″ above inland). 1-8 Sunny, seasonable; warm inland. 9-12 Unseasonably warm. 13-16 Showers & cool coast, seasonable inland. 17-24 Cloudy, cool, sprinkles; sunny inland. 25-28 Light rain, cool. 29-31 Rain, heavy inland, light south.

June 1989: Temp. 60° (1° below ave.; 2° above south); Precip. 0″ (Ave.). 1-8 Cloudy, cool; clear & warm south. 9-11 showers north, clear & warm south. 12-15 Cool. 16-18 Seasonable, light rain north; very warm south. 19-24 Clear; very warm, hot inland. 25-30 Partly cloudy, sprinkles coast.

July 1989: Temp. 61° (1° below ave.; 1.5°above south); Precip. 0″ (Ave.). 1-2 Cool, few showers. 3-8 Sunny & warm, hot inland. 9-12 Seasonable, few showers. 13-16 Clear, very warm, hot inland. 17-20 Mild; clear, very warm south. 21-27 Cloudy, scattered showers. 28-31 Showers, warmer.

Aug. 1989: Temp. 61° (2° below ave.; 2° above inland & south); Precip. 0″ (Ave.). 1-3 Mild. 4-6 Clear & hot. 7-12 Cooler coast, hot inland. 13-15 Clear; showers southeast. 16-18 Sunny & hot. 19-21 Milder. 22-25 Sunny, hot. 26-31 Clear & warm, hot inland.

Sept. 1989: Temp. 62° (2° below ave.; 1° above south); Precip. 0″ (0.2″ below ave.). 1-5 Sunny, mild. 6-8 Scattered light showers; clear & hot south. 9-14 Clear, seasonably warm. 15-18 Sunny & hot. 19-21 Cloudy, sprinkles, rain north; cool. 22-26 Clear & hot. 27-30 Partly cloudy & cool coast; sunny & hot inland.

Oct. 1989: Temp. 61° (Ave.; 1° below inland); Precip. 0″ (1″ below ave.; 0.5″ above south). 1-3 Clear & hot. 4-8 Showers, cool. 9-12 Seasonable; showers north. 13-17 Clear, very warm. 18-21 Rain, cool. 22-24 Sunny & warm. 25-27 Rain north, sunny south. 28-31 Clear, warm.

About the Virga, Child of the Clouds

Considered one of the small wonders of the natural world, it's often mistaken for the funnel cloud of a tornado.   by Kathleen Cain

☐ IN HIS HIT SONG "ROCKY MOUNtain High," John Denver had a line that fascinated me. "I've seen it rainin' fire in the sky," he sang. I'd seen that many times as I watched the Colorado sunset shining through an elusive cloud that drifted out of the bottom of another cloud and almost touched the ground. As I watched, the sky would catch fire and appear to rain all at once. What I was watching is the virga, that mysterious rain that never reaches the ground, although it makes a fine show in the process.

The virga travels under many other names as well, most of them more descriptive than scientific: fingers of rain, phantom rain, rain that never falls, pillars of cloud, dry rain, walking rain, whiskers of rain. A more scientific but less often used appellation is the fallstreak. Sometimes the virga is described as sinister and ominous, at other times as sinuous and elusive. It's the cloud that amateur weather-watchers most frequently mistake for the funnel cloud of a tornado, and it's a frustrating sight for those who watch it evaporate before it reaches a wheat field or garden in need of moisture. It is no less lovely to watch in winter as a trail of snow.

At a glance, the word virga might seem to have come into the English language through the same door as the word virgin. Truth is, it arrived by another route altogether. From the Latin *virga,* virga carries with it the various meanings of the older word — a branch, twig, or stick — descriptive of its appearance as it hangs down from a cloud in the sky. Another meaning can be found in the word *verge,* which means "to descend towards the horizon or to move in a certain direction."

The *U.S. Weather Almanac* declares the virga to be "water or ice particles falling from a cloud, usually in wisps or streaks, and evaporating before reaching the ground." While some sources specify that the virga falls in the form of rain or snow, others simply state that it can occur as evaporating precipitation, which opens up the possibility for the likes of hail, sleet, graupel, hoarfrost, glaze, rime, and fog-drip.

Although Aristotle, in his *Meteorologica,* recorded the kinds of weather that seemed to follow the appearance of certain kinds of clouds, it was not until 1896 and the International Cloud Year that scientists made systematic worldwide observations about clouds. They listed ten basic cloud types, described by their appearance and location:

- Altocumulus, altostratus — form in the middle region of the atmosphere
- Cirrus, cirrostratus, cirrocumulus — appear high in the sky
- Cumulus, cumulonimbus — develop vertically
- Stratus, stratocumulus, nimbostratus — low in the sky

Cirrus clouds look feathery; stratus clouds appear to be layered or stratified; cumulus clouds have a heaped-up look; nimbus are rain clouds.

Where does the virga fit into all this? All clouds are made of water vapor, but not all clouds are capable of producing precipitation. Two processes control the formation of rain clouds and rain. The first is the sequence in which moist warm air cools as it rises; as it cools, the amount of vapor it can hold decreases. At a temperature called the dew point, the air is saturated; when the temperature drops below that point, the vapor condenses into water droplets, forming clouds. The second process requires the presence of condensation nuclei, minute particles of dust, smoke, salt, and other substances on which water drop-

lets form. As they grow larger, they also become heavier. Average raindrops range in size from 0.02 to 0.25 inch (0.51 to 6.35 mm.) in diameter — the smaller number being about the size of a period on this page.

Size is one reason the virga never makes it to the ground — the drops are too small to sustain themselves all the way down. As raindrops fall, they collide with other raindrops. The larger ones fall to the ground; the small ones are moved back up into the cloud by the air around them, and the process begins again. (This is called the Coalescence Theory.) Scientists estimate that a raindrop with a diameter of 0.004 inch (0.100 mm.) or less will not make it to the ground.

Even if the raindrop or snowflake is larger than the minimum required to fall to the ground, the air beneath a precipitation-bearing cloud is often warmer and drier than the cloud, causing the moisture to evaporate on its way through. The drier the air beneath the mother cloud, the more likely the chances for the virga.

Although the virga can develop anywhere in the world where precipitation occurs, it is most likely to occur in a location with a geography like that of Denver, Colorado, where I live. The nearby mountain barrier robs the low-level atmosphere of moisture, making the air drier beneath the clouds. When the moisture leaves the upper atmosphere and descends in the form of the serpentine virga, its chances of evaporating before it reaches the ground are much higher than they would be in, say, Connecticut or Ireland. The virga occurs frequently in Arizona, New Mexico, Texas, Colorado, Utah, and Nevada, although it is not strictly limited to west of the 100th meridian. Still, only those who live on or near the desert know the special torture of watching much-needed moisture dissipate in the dry string of rain that is the virga.

One group for whom this elusive phenomenon holds special interest is airline pilots. Recent studies have connected the virga to wind shear, the deadly downdraft that has been responsible for several major airline accidents. Wind shear often begins where the virga begins, high in the sky. As rain or snow falls from a cloud, it drags air down with it. As the air moves downward, it cools, becomes denser, and moves faster — sometimes from 60 to 150 miles per hour. Such a downdraft can cause a dust storm on the ground or worse. (This phenomenon is called a microburst.) Understanding a weather event as temporary and mysterious as the virga has been a key toward understanding — and avoiding — the dangers these freaks of the weather might create.

If you look up in the sky as rain clouds begin to gather, and you see a tail or curtain or veil flowing from them, or the rain looks as if it is walking above the horizon, look twice before you think about reporting a tornado. It may be only the virga, that child of the clouds, weaving its way through the sky and vanishing into thin air, one of the small wonders of the natural world. □□

The TROY-BILT TUFF-CUT® High Wheel Mower is

7 Ways Better
than ordinary Lawn Mowers!

"Feather-Touch" Controls *engage blade and wheels separately, precisely.*

1. Better Built.
The TUFF-CUT is the ONLY homeowner mower which carries a 6 Year Warranty! The TUFF-CUT could be the LAST mower you'll ever need to buy.

2. Easy to handle.
Weight of motor (in *rear*) offsets weight of deck (in *front*) for perfect balance. Well thought out controls let you maneuver neatly, precisely, with full safety.

3. Safer to Use.
The TUFF-CUT has many convenient safety features, including a "Blade Brake" that immediately stops the blade without stopping the engine. The blade is way out in front for a large "margin of safety".

Best Warranty in the Business!

Big, pneumatic tires *absorb shocks, turn on a dime, roll over obstacles.*

Power-in-reserve *with up to 8HP! Most powerful walk-behind homeowner mower!*

Super-wide cut *— up to 24" at a pass — gets the job done quicker.*

Never again struggle with
poorly made, underpowered mowers that stall, and make mowing a dreaded chore!

©1989 Garden Way, Inc.

4. Conquers hills easily.

Plenty of GUTS — up to 8HP! — and POWERED wheels take the "push" out of uphill mowing.

5. Steps over obstacles.

Big wheels walk right over ruts, rough ground, landscape timbers — nuisances that stop other mowers cold.

6. Mows foot-tall grass.

Shears tall grass, seldom-mown areas quickly and easily. Never again worry about grass "too tall" to handle!

7. Up to 50% faster.

Extra power, wide cut, and easy maneuvering help you finish up far faster than ordinary mowers . . . even riders!

Small lawns:
5HP, 22"
push model

Large lawns:
8HP, 24" self-
propelled model

Mid-size lawns:
5HP, 22" self-
propelled model

← 22" →

← 24" →

← 22" →

For FREE Catalog

Call TOLL-FREE
1-800-453-9900
24 hours . . . OR . . .
MAIL THIS COUPON
TODAY! ➡

Ten Different Ways to Win with Your Pet

As a special service to our readers, the author compiled this select listing of unique animal races around the country.

by Art Sordillo

☐ MAYBE YOUR PET ISN'T "SHOW MATERIAL." Just because your animal has no pedigree, it doesn't mean you should give up all hope of winning the big one. You can always *race* your critter; long shots pay off every once in a while. So don't get discouraged. Look in your backyard, the farmhouse, the creek, or maybe the kitchen cupboard — you might find a winner.

HORSES
The Kentucky Derby
WHERE: Louisville, Kentucky.
WHEN: First Saturday in May.
WHAT YOU WIN: Your winnings will be well over $600,000.
WHAT IT COSTS TO ENTER: $20,200.

WINNING FORM: Most will agree that you should look for good conformation. "That means," according to Tony Terri, Director of Public Relations at Churchill Downs, "your horse is pretty muscular. Bulked out with fine muscles."

LIZARDS
World's Greatest Lizard Race
WHERE: Lovington, New Mexico.
WHEN: Fourth of July.
WHAT YOU WIN: Some gift certificates to local restaurants and you get your picture in the paper.
WHAT IT COSTS TO ENTER: Free; just enter before July 3.

WINNING FORM: Over at the Chamber of Commerce, Nancy Peacock was willing to share a few tips: "Your lizard should look bold. He should have large pupils and beady eyes. Also, smaller lizards tend to run faster. Make sure you feed your lizard before the race; sometimes a lizard will get distracted trying to eat another contestant — we've had that happen."

CHICKENS
International Chicken Flying Meet

WHERE: Rio Grande, Ohio.
WHEN: Third Saturday in May.
WHAT YOU WIN: $100.
WHAT IT COSTS TO ENTER: Free.
WINNING FORM: Over at Bob Evans' chicken farm, Gale Jones, farm secretary, tells us: "Usually a winner weighs between 32 and 48 ounces. And your chicken should be a loner — mostly keeping to itself and not clucking too much. You should have an enthusiastic trainer; someone willing to help the chicken get started. Please note that the chickens start the race by jumping out of a mailbox." (One year an entrant who trained her chicken by throwing it out the window reported, "Sometimes she flies, sometimes she just falls on the car.") And please be mindful of meet rule number six: "No electrical device may be used to induce the entrant."

CRABS
National Hard Crab Derby

WHERE: Crisfield, Maryland.
WHEN: Labor Day weekend.
WHAT YOU WIN: A trophy 30″ tall.
WHAT IT COSTS TO ENTER: $3.
WINNING FORM: Ruth Custis at the Crisfield Chamber of Commerce advises, "Your crab shouldn't be molting, and he should exhibit a fair amount of stamina. Also, try to keep your crab warm — not too warm though, because you might scare him."

BUGS
Great American Bug Race

WHERE: West Palm Beach, Florida.
WHEN: Second week in October.
WHAT YOU WIN: $100.
WHAT IT COSTS TO ENTER: $7.50.
WINNING FORM: Hugh Mathis works in public relations for Palm Beach Atlantic College (where the race is held) and had this to say: "We do have some standards: no sneakers, no steroids, no wings, and definitely no centipedes, please. On the whole, bugs with lighter-colored legs consistently finish faster. Training your bug is not too hard — just jog, every day, once around the room with it. Big bugs don't always do well — it's the energetic bug that finishes first."

HERMIT CRABS
The Hermit Crab Race
WHERE: Ocean City, New Jersey.
WHEN: Second week of August.
WHAT YOU WIN: A nice plaque.
WHAT IT COSTS TO ENTER: Free.
WINNING FORM: Mark Soifer at City Hall organizes the event and tells us, "Your hermit crab should be small and skinny. Look for long legs. Also, work out with your hermit crab — try to get him to run about three feet going straight. And remember, hermit crabs like to be spritzed with tepid water before they race."

CRAWFISH
Cajun Crawfish Derby
WHERE: Port Arthur, Texas.
WHEN: Last weekend in May.
WHAT YOU WIN: A real big trophy.
WHAT IT COSTS TO ENTER: $20.
WINNING FORM: Chef "Oink" Theriot, culinary professor and crawfish commissioner, heads up the races at the Cajun Festival. "Well, let me tell you, a racing crawfish has to be bred. We breed them to race. And you can always tell a purebred because of the claws — they're darker in color. Females race faster." And please, no crawdad doping allowed; officials constantly check the tails for Tabasco sauce.

EARTHWORMS
Great Worm Race
WHERE: Ashland, Kentucky.
WHEN: Fourth of July.
WHAT YOU WIN: A 24″ (tall) trophy.
WHAT IT COSTS TO ENTER: Free.
WINNING FORM: John Gallaher sponsors the event and says the secret is: "Moistness. Your worm should be moist." He also shared some rules. "No worm can be any longer than eight inches — and we will be checking for stimulants. For our protection and your safety, you should know we're not responsible for any worms trampled, lost, or eaten."

CATFISH
Grand Prix Catfish Race
WHERE: Greenville, Mississippi.
WHEN: First weekend in June.
WHAT YOU WIN: Usually a trip somewhere.
WHAT IT COSTS TO ENTER: $25.
WINNING FORM: The race is sponsored by the local newspaper, so managing editor Sally Gresham is in the know. Sally says, "They all look alike to me, but some are sleeker than others. It might be helpful to get in the water and practice sprinting with your catfish." There is another motivation for your catfish; losers will be eviscerated, cooked, and eaten.

TURTLES
Brennan's Pub Turtle Races
WHERE: Marina Del Rey, California.
WHEN: Every Thursday night.
WHAT YOU WIN: A bottle of champagne.
WHAT IT COSTS TO ENTER: Free.
WINNING FORM: Mike Shaw, manager of Brennan's, tried to help out. "Well, make sure your turtle moves quite a bit. He shouldn't be hibernating. That's about it. Oh yeah, I almost forgot. Please, no pointing at the competitors — they'll stop right where they are and pull their heads back in." □ □

"PRESCRIPTION DRUG KILLS DOCTOR"

(By Frank K. Wood)

An Atlanta doctor has died from a freak drug reaction on a trip overseas. An infection he had didn't clear up after taking a drug so he took a different drug, too. The two drugs reacted with each other and caused crystallization in his kidneys. He had kidney failure and died a few days later.

WHAT YOUR DOCTOR DOESN'T TELL YOU ABOUT THE SIDE EFFECTS OF PRESCRIPTION DRUGS

This tragedy points to the fact that most doctors don't tell their patients about the side effects of the drugs they prescribe.

The reaction that killed the doctor and many other prescription drug side effects are clearly described in a new book, *"Prescription Drug Encyclopedia"*.

THE GOOD EFFECTS OF PRESCRIPTION DRUGS

We all take drugs prescribed by our doctor for their good effects, like relieving pain, fighting infection, birth control, aiding sleep, calming down, fighting coughs, colds or allergies, or lowering heartbeat and blood pressure.

MOTRIN   TETRACYCLINE

TAGAMET   INDERAL

VALIUM   TYLENOL/CODEINE

DO YOU HAVE ANY OF THESE BAD SIDE EFFECTS?

Prescription drugs can cause headache, upset stomach, constipation, stuffy nose, short breath, high blood pressure, fear and ringing sounds.

LATEST FACTS ON EACH DRUG

The book describes more than 400 of the most-often-used drugs. Facts are given in easy-to-understand words.

EASY TO READ

The book lists brand names, money-saving generic names, good effects, side effects, and warnings.

It explains drug categories. (For example: a drug may be called an "analgesic" . . . analgesic means "pain reliever").

Order this 30,000 word, easy-to-understand book explaining more than 400 drugs, edited by two pharmacists, right away.

The Ten Commandments for Making $100,000 on 25 Acres

Actually, what it requires most of all is a healthy dose of common sense.   by Booker T. Whatley

□ A FEW YEARS AGO WARD SINCLAIR of *The Washington Post* wrote an article about me that said "A lone guru in Alabama has found a way for small farmers to make $100,000 from 25 acres." To tell you the truth, I had no conception of what a guru was. I told my wife, "We'd better look that word up and see what that writer called me!"

As a result of that, I came up with what I call "The Guru's Ten Commandments." If you want to be a successful small farmer, you'd better get used to abiding by these principles.

THY SMALL FARM SHALT:
I. PROVIDE YEAR-ROUND, DAILY CASH FLOW.

I recommend that these types of farms have a *minimum* of 10 crops, each representing no more than 10 percent of the gross of that farm. So if you completely lose one crop, you're still operating at 90-percent efficiency. And there are not many things in this country operating at 90-percent efficiency.

II. BE A PICK-YOUR-OWN OPERATION.

A pick-your-own operation greatly reduces the cost of labor. But it requires excellent management and detailed planning. Any successful PYO operation has these features:

— one place to enter the farm and one place to leave it. The husband should greet the ladies when they come to the farm, supervise picking, and teach them how to harvest. The wife should be in charge of the checkout station. If you men get over at the exit, some of those charming ladies are going to jive you right out of all your strawberries.

— parking on both sides of the road near the crop being harvested. Don't build a central parking space and transport your clients to the crops. Let them drive right up.

— comfort stations in the fields. Some farms even have telephone jacks out there so that their clients can call home or the office.

— no pets allowed. Folks will bring dogs and some of these dogs have a way of getting in heat. Then you have half the males chasing the females and the other half fighting.

It's not necessary to advertise if you abide by the third commandment, which is . . .

III. HAVE A CLIENTELE MEMBERSHIP CLUB.

A CMC consists of a group of loyal customers who are seeking wholesome, high-quality, contamination-free fruits and vegetables, fish and game birds, honey, nuts, rabbits, care and feed for their horses, and recreation for their families. To belong to a CMC, we recommend that the farmer charge an annual fee of $25, which gives your clients the privilege of coming to your farm and harvesting produce for 60 percent of what your local supermarket is charging. One 25-acre farm will supply the needs of 1,000 households. People say, "Oh, it would be so hard to get 1,000 of these people!" My reply to that is, well, everything is hard! Life's hard! But where you can provide yourself with a guaranteed market, it's worth it.

Don't accept just anyone. The first thing to ask is, "Do you have a freezer?" If the prospective client doesn't have a freezer, you're wasting your time. You're trying to find people to join your CMC who have the same philosophy as the ant. They believe in preparing for winter. They believe in it religiously. *The CMC is the lifeblood of any diversified small farm operation.*

IV. PROVIDE YEAR-ROUND, FULL-TIME EMPLOYMENT.

You just invite disaster to set up one of these farms and think you're going to work at it part-time or just on Saturdays and Sundays. The farmer says he's going to be open from 9 A.M. to sundown every day of the week.

V. BE LOCATED ON A HARD-SURFACED ROAD WITHIN A RADIUS OF 40 MILES OF A POPULATION CENTER OF AT LEAST 50,000, WITH WELL-DRAINED SOIL AND AN EXCELLENT SOURCE OF WATER.

City folks don't mind driving up to 40 miles. But after that, they are taking a trip, and they're not interested. You need well-drained soil and a good source of water because every inch of this farm is under irrigation.

VI. PRODUCE ONLY WHAT THY CLIENTS DEMAND — AND NOTHING ELSE!

Farmers are notorious for producing what *they* like to grow and then trying to sell it to somebody. But if your clientele demands collard greens, you shouldn't waste your time trying to educate them to eat kale. If they demand collard greens and turnips, that's what you grow. Nothing else.

VII. SHUN MIDDLEMEN AND MIDDLEWOMEN LIKE THE PLAGUE, FOR THEY ARE A CURSE UNTO THEE.

When some people talk about direct marketing, they mean farmers doing all the harvesting and hauling it to a farmers' market. But when I use the words direct marketing, I mean a situation where the clients come to the farmer, do the harvesting, and take it home with them in their own containers. The small farmer cuts down on his cost of production and gets 100 percent of the dollar spent on what he grows.

VIII. CONSIST OF COMPATIBLE, COMPLEMENTARY CROPS THAT EARN A MINIMUM OF $3,000 PER ACRE ANNUALLY.

For example, everybody in this country eats strawberries. The few who don't are allergic to them. You don't have to worry about those people. The same holds true for blackberries, raspberries, blueberries, and root crops. All of us eat greens. All of us who can afford to eat quail and pheasant. All of us like fish. All of us like honey. You can grow Chinese chestnuts, nuts, sweet corn, and lamb. You can stock a pond and sell fishing rights. All of us eat peas and beans. But if you're producing peas and beans, get yourself a sheller. The middle-class American housewife doesn't mind coming out with the kids and picking a few bushels of peas, but she doesn't want to spend the next six months shelling the things.

IX. BE WEATHERPROOF AS FAR AS POSSIBLE, WITH BOTH DRIP AND SPRINKLER IRRIGATION.

This protects you against drought, late spring frosts, and early fall frosts.

X. BE COVERED BY A MINIMUM OF $250,000 WORTH ($1 MILLION IS BETTER) OF LIABILITY INSURANCE.

Now, I talk about city folks and how dumb they are, and a lot of it is true. The reason you want a pick-your-own thing is these city folks will pick sticks and stones and stuff the farmer would never dare pick. That's why you always charge by weight, not volume. But there is one thing that city folks know how to do. *They know how to sue you.*

Now my peers and opponents say the Whatley Small Farm Plan is just too complicated for small farmers in this country. My plan *is* complicated. It requires good management. But my granddaddy, who was born in slavery and never went to school, operated a farm ten times more complicated than this. What the old man had going for him was a head full of common sense.

Farmers in this country are hard working. But they have to be hard planners, hard managers, and hard thinkers, too. □ □

Excerpted with permission from *How to Make $100,000 Farming 25 Acres,* published by the Regenerative Agriculture Association (RAA), a division of the nonprofit Rodale Institute. It is available in softcover ($17.95, postpaid) and hardcover ($24.95, postpaid) from the RAA Library, 222 Main St., Emmaus, PA 18049.

GESTATION AND MATING TABLE

	Proper age for first mating	Period of fertility, in years	No. of females for one male	Period of gestation, in days	
				Range	Average
Ewe	90 lbs. or 1 yr.	6		142-154	147 151[8]
Ram	12-14 mos., well matured	7	50-75[2] 35-40[3]		
Mare	3 yrs.	10-12		310-370	336
Stallion	3 yrs.	12-15	40-45[4] Record 252[5]		
Cow	15-18 mos.[1]	10-14		279-290[6] 262-300[7]	283
Bull	1 yr., well matured	10-12	50[4] Thousands[5]		
Sow	5-6 mos. or 250 lbs.	6		110-120	115
Boar	250-300 lbs.	6	50[2] 35-40[3]		
Doe goat	10 mos. or 85-90 lbs.	6		145-155	150
Buck goat	Well matured	5	30		
Bitch	16-18 mos.	8		58-67	63
Male Dog	12-16 mos.	8			
She cat	12 mos.	6		60-68	63
Doe rabbit	6 mos.	5-6		30-32	31
Buck rabbit	6 mos.	5-6	30		

[1]Holstein & Beef: 750 lbs. Jersey: 500 lbs. [2]Handmated. [3]Pasture. [4]Natural. [5]Artificial. [6]Beef; 8-10 days shorter for Angus. [7]Dairy. [8]For fine wool breeds.

BIRD AND POULTRY INCUBATION PERIODS, IN DAYS

Chicken .. 21 Goose .. 30-34 Guinea 26-28
Turkey ... 28 Swan ...... 42 Canary 14-15
Duck ... 26-32 Pheasant .. 22-24 Parakeet 18-20

GESTATION PERIODS, WILD ANIMALS, IN DAYS

Black bear ..... 210 Seal 330
Hippo .... 225-250 Squirrel, gray ... 44
Moose .... 240-250 Whale, sperm ... 480
Otter ...... 270-300 Wolf 60-63
Reindeer ... 210-240

MAXIMUM LIFE SPANS OF ANIMALS IN CAPTIVITY, IN YEARS

Box Turtle
(Eastern) ... 138
Bullfrog 16
Camel 25
Cat (Domestic) . 23
Cheetah 16
Chicken 14
Chimpanzee ... 37
Cow 20
Dog (Domestic) . 22
Dolphin 30
Eagle 55

Elephant 84
Giant Tortoise . 190
Giraffe 28
Goat 17
Gorilla 33
Grizzly Bear .. 31
Horse
(Domestic) .. 50
Kangaroo 16
Lion 30
Moose 20
Owl 68

Oyster
(Freshwater) 80
Pig 10
Polar Bear ... 41
Rabbit 13
Rattlesnake .. 20
Reindeer 15
Sea Lion 28
Sheep 20
Tiger 25
Timber Wolf .. 15
Toad 36
Zebra 25

REPRODUCTIVE CYCLE IN FARM ANIMALS

	Recurs if not bred	Estrual cycle incl. heat period (days)		In heat for		Usual time of ovulation
	Days	Ave.	Range	Ave.	Range	
Mare	21	21	10-37	5-6 days	2-11 days	24-48 hours before end of estrus
Sow	21	21	18-24	2-3 days	1-5 days	30-36 hours after start of estrus
Ewe	16½	16½	14-19	30 hours	24-32 hours	12-24 hours before end of estrus
Goat	21	21	18-24	2-3 days	1-4 days	Near end of estrus
Cow	21	21	18-24	18 hours	10-24 hours	10-12 hours after end of estrus
Bitch	pseudo-pregnancy	24		7 days	5-9 days	1-3 days after first acceptance
Cat	pseudo-pregnancy		15-21	3-4 days if mated	9-10 days in absence of male	24-56 hours after coitus

In Pursuit of the Weed-Free Garden

It is an endless challenge, but a few simple techniques, a good sense of timing, and knowledge of certain materials can make the battle go more easily.
by Roger A. Kline

☐ ONE OF THE GREATEST EFFORTS GARdeners make is to control or eliminate weeds. This activity is the most time-consuming and persistent throughout the gardening season and often the most unpopular.

Weeds are *other* plants, sometimes interesting, always persistent, and they compete with our vegetable crops for nutrients, water, light, and carbon dioxide. Especially if weeds are vigorous, they cause a reduced yield and poor quality of vegetables. Young vegetable crops, particularly small-seeded crops such as carrots, spinach, and onions, can be devastated by any weed growth. Weeds may also harbor harmful insects and diseases. And if left to form seeds, the weeds will plague the gardener for years to come.

The effects of letting weeds grow freely in the vegetable garden are so destructive that we must either plan to control them or plan not to have a garden. But there is good news: there are many ways to reduce the effect of weeds without becoming obsessed or too exhausted by the chore. Let us state a range of methods from which gardeners may select those suitable to their situation.

In general, it is always more effective to eliminate weeds when they are very young and when the vegetable crop is very young. If weeds are to be neglected, such as when gardeners are on vacation, let that be late in the season when the vegetable crops are large and reaching a harvestable stage.

Studies at Cornell University have

shown some interesting results with peas and beans. In these experiments, weeding was done at different times during the development of these crops. It was found that if the crops were kept weed-free for the first three to four weeks, unabated weed growth after that time did not significantly reduce their yields. (However, before you conclude that you'll stop weeding after the first month, let me remind you of the real danger of letting weeds form their seeds and drop them by the thousands per plant onto your garden soil.)

Weed numbers can be reduced by a few simple techniques. Keeping the surrounding vegetation mowed and not letting any of it go to seed will go a long way toward reducing the number of new weeds in your fertile garden soil. Having the garden occupied by either vegetable plants or a cover crop through most of the year will also discourage weeds.

Each year gardeners normally break the soil with either a plow or a rototiller, or deep hoeing. It is a good practice because it homogenizes the soil, mixing in organic matter, granular fertilizer, old plant debris, and compost. It also redistributes weed seeds or other reproductive parts, which can disrupt the weeds' life cycles. After that initial cultivation the garden looks clean and rich. There are no visible weeds and it seems as if they'll never grow. But be assured they will.

Often weeds will merely be delayed. Quack grass, for instance, spreads by underground rhizomes. Tilling or plowing cuts up the rhizomes and actually tends to spread them more pervasively through the garden soil. Special attention to noxious weeds such as quack grass is needed.

Once the vegetable seeds or transplants are set in the garden there should be no further deep tilling of the soil, partly because it will not be any more effective as weed control than shallow tilling and also because it may prune the roots of the growing vegetables. The first line of weed defense is a well-sharpened

hoe that is scraped along the surface of the soil. If the weed plants are young, they will be cut off or come out easily and die quickly when the roots are exposed to air. (Weeds more than a few inches tall should not only be hoed and pulled out, but raked up and removed lest they reroot.) A wheel hoe is another suitable piece of equipment for shallow scraping of the soil through the aisles of the garden. Hand-pulling is much slower, but very effective, and sometimes mandatory close to vegetable crops.

It was found that if the crops were kept weed-free for the first three to four weeks, unabated weed growth after that did not significantly reduce yields.

If these mechanical ways of eliminating weeds are not attractive to you, try mulch. Mulch is perhaps the most popular and most appealing method of weed control. It is especially good for annual weeds because they come up from seed. Even if weed seeds germinate and begin to grow under a mulch, they do not receive daylight and die without it.

Mulch can be applied in the form of straw, grass clippings, newspapers, leaves, black plastic, wooden boards, or many other creative ideas. Because the object is to block light, the mulch must be applied thickly enough to accomplish that: i.e., six inches of straw, one inch of grass clippings, and so on. (If grass clippings are used, be sure that no herbicide was applied during the growing season.) Do not use hay — it may introduce an abundance of new seeds to plague the garden.

Black plastic comes in rolls from 100

to 2,000 feet long and from 3 to 4 feet wide. About 1 millimeter or thicker is needed to exclude light. Rake the bed smooth and lay the roll of plastic on one end. Dig the furrows so that the plastic can be tucked down into the soil. Furrows should be about 3 inches deep and 3 inches in from the edges of the plastic. Water the bed well if it seems dry. This is the only moisture the young vegetable plants will receive before their roots extend to the aisle beyond the plastic. Roll out the plastic three or four feet at a time, burying the edges as you go. Leave a little bit of slack so it can resist any perennial weeds that may begin to grow underneath. Set transplants through the plastic into the furrows, using a round bulb setter to poke holes. Even seeds can be poked through the plastic using a dibble to make the holes. If you don't like the appearance of the black plastic, spread a thin layer of wood shavings or lawn clippings on top of it. In the fall, loosen the edges of the plastic with a hoe and remove it entirely from the garden.

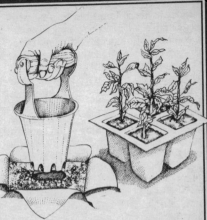

The stale seedbed method works in the opposite way: we try to promote weeds early in the season so they may be hoed or tilled away before vegetable planting is done. Do this by laying a sheet of clear plastic over an area of the garden in late April or early May. This will let in sunlight and warm the soil enough to trigger the germination of most weed seeds. Once the weeds have grown an inch or two, the plastic is removed and the weeds are eliminated with the shallow action of a hoe or wheel hoe; or they may be covered with organic or black plastic mulch as described above. If the soil is left undisturbed, few weeds will be produced for the rest of the season. This part of the garden should be ready by late May.

Crowding the garden soil gives weeds little room to establish and develop. Either plant vegetables close together, or select crops or types that are vigorous and full. For instance, in a weedy part of the garden, the bean plant would offer much more competition than the onion plant. Use "relay planting" (starting warm-weather crops as soon as early spinach or peas are done, for example) to insure that the soil will not be bare for long. At the end of the season, cover crops such as rye grass, winter wheat, or oats can occupy the garden. The garden soil should contain plants of your choosing for twelve months of the year. If you leave the soil vacant, any passerby may root there.

The use of chemicals or herbicides is generally not recommended for the home garden, although they can be effective when establishing a plot of land as a garden. The use of herbicides by untrained applicators can be risky and dangerous to food plants and to animals. Because herbicides are usually very specific, and our gardens contain many different weeds and crops, very few weed-control chemicals are adaptive to the home garden. If you do choose to use herbicides, get all the professional advice that you can beforehand and follow the label instructions exactly. Calibration and rate of application are difficult. Drift due to wind may endanger nearby plants.

All in all there is no magical solution to the perpetual problem of weeds. But we hope that these hints will let the control of weeds become your exercise and your pride and your avenue to a much better home garden. □ □

Searching for the Ideal Northern Grape

*It should combine
Old World quality and
New World hardiness . . .*
by Michael Goc

*A free loose earth is what the vines demand,
Where wind and frost have helped the
    laborer's hand
And sturdy peasants deep have stirred the
    land. . . .*

– Virgil

□ YOU WOULD EXPECT A ROMAN POET
who was also a gentleman farmer to
know how to raise grapes — at least in
balmy Italy. Unlike Virgil, we sturdy
peasants who disguise ourselves as
home vineyardists in the northern
United States and Canada get little help
from the wind and frost. Arctic temperatures threaten our vines every winter, and the sight of deadwood that will
bear no fruit too often blights our
spring. The grape we plant must suit its
location on a frigid continent. Beauty
and taste are important in the north,
but winterhardiness comes first.

Samuel de Champlain learned about
the hazards of planting the wrong grape
for the climate when he brought the
first French vines to Quebec in 1608.
He assumed that they would thrive,
since the banks of the St. Lawrence
were covered with native grapes. Hardy
they were, these native *riparia* grapes,
but unimpressive in terms of size and
taste. The great *vinifera* of France —
sweet, rich-tasting, and pedigreed for
wine — would replace them, Champlain hoped.

But the European grapes failed to
survive even their first winter in the
New World. Bred for the more gentle
weather of their homeland, they froze
in a typical blast of North American
weather. Cold was not the only problem. *Vinifera* imported to parts
warmer than Canada or New England
succumbed to a tiny root parasite
called the phylloxera louse to which native vines were resistant. Even worse,
phylloxera traveled to Europe where it
threatened vines under cultivation
since the Middle Ages. (By the
1900s French vineyardists were

forced to import resistant North American rootstock and graft their treasured vines onto it. Thanks to this forced marriage, the vines of Europe are as much American as European — but don't tell that to the wineshop experts who are convinced that the best vintages must have a pure European pedigree!)

Back in America, colonial vineyardists faced a real dilemma. The European vines they favored would not grow in North America, and hardy North American vines could not produce grapes of European quality. Grape lovers in the Upper Midwest, New England, and Canada have faced the same problem ever since. We've been looking for the grape that combines Old World quality and New World hardiness.

In 1843 Ephraim Bull planted a seed from a grapevine he found growing wild near Concord, Massachusetts. The vine was a member of the native North American *labrusca* line with dark, thick-skinned, big-seeded, strong-tasting fruit. It survived winters in Concord and usually bore fruit before the first killing frost. By 1860 the Concord was twining its way through more American and Canadian arbors than any other grape. It was the first homegrown fruit to gain genuine national popularity. The only jelly that generations of American children tasted was made from Ma's Concord vine, and the heavy purple wine fermented from its grapes was the only intoxicant to stain the lips of their temperance-minded parents.

The Concord was the ideal northern grape in its time, but it is not without drawbacks. It is hardy only to -20°F. (-29° C.). Colder temperatures or windchills, not uncommon north of the Ohio River, will freeze a Concord vine and set back the harvest for at least a year. The Concord also takes a dangerously long time to ripen — as late as mid-October in the Great Lakes and New England. Finally, the Concord tastes "foxy." That's how vinophiles describe the spicy, mouth-puckering sensation caused by even a fully ripe Con-

cord. This is a grape meant to be cooked, not eaten fresh.

No sooner were the Concord's shortcomings noted than vineyardists began to improve on it. Growers and breeders in the New York-Ohio fruit belt and in France, Ontario, and Minnesota have all developed grapes that endure cold, ripen faster, or taste better than the venerable Massachusetts vine.

The New York-Ohio growers, and their Canadian counterparts just north of the Great Lakes, showed the importance of microclimate by developing vines that take advantage of the tempering effects of large bodies of water and a generous snow cover. Delaware, Duchess, Catawba, Niagara, Clinton, Fredonia, Canadice, Elvira, and New York Muscat grapes do well in places where extreme winter temperatures are buffered by water, there is shelter from extreme wind, heavy snows bury the vines, or there is the artificial warmth of an urban area. Move these grapes

By 1860 the Concord was twining its way through more American and Canadian arbors than any other grape.

away from a favored spot, and they are in trouble. For winterhardiness, a good location is worth 10 or 20 degrees of warmth.

Genes help, too. This factor is most evident with the French hybrid grapes like Foch, Baco Noir, Chelois, Aurore, de Chaunac, and Cascade. A century ago, when the French were forced to develop phylloxera-resistant European vines using hardy American rootstock, they unintentionally produced grapes of the finest quality on a vine that could tolerate very low temperatures — lower than what the climate demanded in France's wine-growing provinces. The

French exported their vines to North America, and in the 40 years since their introduction here, the hybrids have displaced the Concord as the most widely grown grape in eastern Canada. With their cachet of French wine-making excellence, the hybrids are favored by home vintners throughout the northern United States.

The development of the hardy French hybrids spawned a Canadian

---

Even hardy grapes should be planted with shelter from the worst cold in mind.

---

breeding program that has produced even more excellent, cold-hardy grapes. Among these are the *V* grapes from the Ontario Research Institute at appropriately named Vineland: Van Buren, Veeblanc, Veeport, Vincent, Vanessa, and Ventura.

Although in many cases the development of new grape varieties has been part of an international industry, viticultural history is still populated by enterprising individuals in the Ephraim Bull tradition. Louis Suelter was a Minnesota farmer who discovered a wild grape flourishing on the banks of the Minnesota River a bit south of Minneapolis. He crossed it with a Concord, called the offspring Beta, and developed the hardiest domestic grape on the continent. It will survive and fruit in an environment — like that of a windswept Dakota fencerow — that would kill any other grape. The only problem with Beta is that it retains the foxy taste of its forebears and is strictly a juice and jelly grape, one to be planted where all others freeze out.

The upper Midwest is not usually thought of as a hothouse where vineyard arts flower, but no one ever told Elmer Swenson. He is a laconic Norwegian-American dairy farmer who

turned to serious grape-breeding after the kids grew up and he sold his cows.

Like Bull and Suelter, Swenson started with a wild vine that was hardy and bore acceptable Concord-like fruit. That was 40 years ago. Today Swenson tends several thousand grapes in a hillside vineyard on the Wisconsin side of the St. Croix River, northeast of St. Paul. He works at developing grapes as refined as a Parisian boulevardier and as hardy as, well, a northern Wisconsin dairy farmer.

Swenson's Edelweiss, Kay Gray, La-Crosse, St. Croix, and Swenson's Red grapes match the French hybrids and their Canadian descendants as today's ultimate cross between quality and winterhardiness. They've inspired an association of grape growers in Minnesota to start a breeding program that crosses winter-hardy vines from the edge of the wild grape's range in Manitoba with proven domestic types. The association hopes to produce the ideal northern grape.

While waiting for the ultimate grape to come along, we northerners can create better growing conditions for the vines we have. One simple and obvious tactic is to avoid planting a vine that is not hardy enough for the local climate. Consult with experienced growers in the area or ask the county agent. The Minnesota Grape Growers Association publishes an excellent guide to grape types and viticulture that is useful in the North (see box for address).

Even hardy grapes should be planted with shelter from the worst cold in mind. A building, solid fence, or evergreen hedge on the weather side of the vines can reduce wind chill and damage. Grapes planted on a hillside with good air drainage or in a warm urban yard are less likely to suffer from freak frosts or extreme cold. Grapes are very often grown on lakeshores or riverbanks because the water moderates the local climate.

Once the vines are planted, don't encourage easily frozen new growth by fertilizing grapes in late summer or fall;

also stop watering after harvest to encourage the onset of dormancy.

Some growers bury their vines. They carefully detach them from the trellis, gently bend the canes to the ground, and cover them with a mulch of straw, shredded cornstalks, or soil. Snow adds further protection. Once buried, even fragile grapes with little resistance to cold can endure frigid weather. However, take care not to crack vines when bending them, for this may open the way to disease and decay. Buried vines are also susceptible to rodent damage.

No one ever said growing grapes in the North was easy, but we have come a long way from Champlain to Bull to Swenson. More grapes of superior quality and hardiness are available than ever before. □□

Choosing a Grape for the Northern Vineyard

Keep three traits in mind when choosing a grape for the North: winterhardiness, early ripening, and whether a grape suits your own needs for jelly, juice, or eating fresh.

Winterhardiness
Beta, Valiant, Concord, President, Ventura, Foch, Kay Gray, St. Croix, Swenson's Red, and *Edelweiss.* Only the half-wild *Beta* can survive regular temperatures below -25° F. (-31.7° C.).

Early Ripening
Van Buren, Himrod, Worden, Price, Aurore, Seneca, Foch, Fredonia, Baco Noir, Elvira. Grapes that ripen early beat autumn frosts, start to harden off earlier, and are better prepared for winter cold.

Best for Wine
Foch, Baco Noir, Aurore, Delaware, LaCrosse, New York Muscat, Ontario Muscat, Niagara, Duchess, Elvira, Vincent, Veeblanc, Ventura. The French hybrids carry the legacy of their homeland's reputation for the finest wines, but many American and Canadian grapes produce excellent vintages.

Best for Jelly
Fredonia, Concord. Any grape, including wild fruits, may be cooked into jelly. The stronger-tasting grapes of American parentage are considered to make the best jelly.

Best for Juice
Beta, Valiant, Concord, Fredonia, Kay Gray, St. Croix.

Seedless Table Grapes
Canadice, Himrod, Suffolk Red, Vanessa. These grapes have been bred to taste best right off the vine without the inconvenience of seeds.

Sources and Nurseries

Growing Grapes in Minnesota is useful throughout the North. Send $5 to Birger Johannessen, Minnesota Grape Growers Association, 1167 Glendon St., Maplewood, MN 55119.

Cold-hardy grapes are available from many nurseries. Here are a few:

Miller Nurseries
West Lake Road
Canandaigua, NY 14424

J. W. Jung Seeds and Nursery
Randolph, WI 53957

Gurney Seed and
Nursery
Yankton, SD 57079

For Canadian
varieties:

Mori Nurseries
Ltd.
RR 2
Niagara on the
Lake
Ontario, L0S 1J0

OUTDOOR PLANTING TABLE, 1989

The best time to plant flowers and vegetables that bear crops above the ground is during the LIGHT of the Moon; that is, between the day the Moon is new to the day it is full. Flowering bulbs and vegetables that bear crops below ground should be planted during the DARK of the Moon; that is, from the day after it is full to the day before it is new again. These Moon days for 1989 are given in the "Moon Favorable" columns below. See pages 48-74 for the exact times and days of the new and full Moons.

The three columns below give planting dates for the Weather Regions listed. (See Map p. 133.) Consult page 84 for dates of killing frosts and length of growing season. Weather regions 5 and the southern half of 16 are practically frost free.

Above Ground Crops Marked(*)	Weather Regions 1, 6, 9, 10, North 13		Weather Regions 2, 3, 7, 11, South 13, 15		Weather Regions 4, 8, 12, 14, 16	
E. means Early / L. means Late	Planting Dates	Moon Favorable	Planting Dates	Moon Favorable	Planting Dates	Moon Favorable
*Barley	5/15-6/21	5/15-20, 6/3-19	3/15-4/7	3/15-22, 4/5-7	2/15-3/7	2/15-20, 3/7
*Beans (E)	5/7-6/21	5/7-20, 6/3-19	4/15-30	4/15-20	3/15-4/7	3/15-22, 4/5-7
(L)	6/15-7/15	6/15-19, 7/3-15	7/1-21	7/3-18	8/7-31	8/7-16, 8/31
Beets (E)	5/1-15	5/1-4	3/15-4/3	3/23-4/3	2/7-28	2/21-28
(L)	7/15-8/15	7/19-31	8/15-31	8/17-30	9/1-30	9/16-28
*Broccoli (E)	5/15-31	5/15-20	3/7-31	3/7-22	2/15-3/15	2/15-20, 3/7-15
(L)	6/15-7/7	6/15-19, 7/3-7	8/1-20	8/1-16	9/7-30	9/7-15, 9/29-30
*Brussels Sprouts	5/15-31	5/15-20	3/7-4/15	3/7-22, 4/5-15	2/11-3/20	2/11-20, 3/7-20
*Cabbage Pl.	5/15-31	5/15-20	3/7-4/15	3/7-22, 4/5-15	2/11-3/20	2/11-20, 3/7-20
Carrots (E)	5/15-31	5/21-31	3/7-31	3/23-31	2/15-3/7	2/21-3/6
(L)	6/15-7/21	6/20-7/2, 7/19-21	7/7-31	7/19-31	8/1-9/7	8/17-30
*Cauliflower Pl. (E)	5/15-31	5/15-20	3/15-4/7	3/15-22, 4/5-7	2/15-3/7	2/15-20, 3/7
(L)	6/15-7/21	6/15-19, 7/3-18	7/1-8/7	7/3-18, 8/1-7	8/7-31	8/7-16, 8/31
*Celery (E)	5/15-6/30	5/15-20, 6/3-19	3/7-31	3/7-22	2/15-28	2/15-20
(L)	7/15-8/15	7/15-18, 8/1-15	8/15-9/7	8/15-16, 8/31-9/7	9/15-30	9/1-15, 9/29-30
*Corn, Sweet (E)	5/10-6/15	5/10-20, 6/3-15	4/1-15	4/5-15	3/15-31	3/15-22
(L)	6/15-30	6/15-19	7/7-21	7/7-18	8/7-31	8/7-16, 8/31
*Cucumber	5/7-6/20	5/7-20, 6/3-19	4/7-5/15	4/7-20, 5/5-15	3/7-4/15	3/7-22, 4/5-15
*Eggplant Pl.	6/1-30	6/3-19	4/7-5/15	4/7-20, 5/5-15	3/7-4/15	3/7-22, 4/5-15
*Endive (E)	5/15-31	5/15-20	4/7-5/15	4/7-20, 5/5-15	2/15-3/20	2/15-20, 3/7-20
(L)	6/7-30	6/7-19	7/15-8/15	7/15-18, 8/1-15	8/15-9/7	8/15-16, 8/31-9/7
*Flowers (All)	5/7-6/21	5/7-20, 6/3-19	4/15-30	4/15-20	3/15-4/7	3/15-22, 4/5-7
*Kale (E)	5/15-31	5/15-20	3/7-4/7	3/7-22, 4/5-7	2/11-3/20	2/11-20, 3/7-20
(L)	7/1-8/7	7/3-18, 8/1-7	8/15-31	8/15-16, 8/31	9/7-30	9/7-15, 9/29-30
Leek Pl.	5/15-31	5/21-31	3/7-4/7	3/23-4/4	2/15-4/15	2/21-3/6, 3/23-4/4
*Lettuce	5/15-6/30	5/15-20, 6/3-19	3/1-31	3/7-22	2/15-3/7	2/15-20, 3/7
*Muskmelon	5/15-6/30	5/15-20, 6/3-19	4/15-5/7	4/15-20, 5/5-7	3/15-4/7	3/15-22, 4/5-7
Onion Pl.	5/15-6/7	5/21-6/2	3/1-31	3/1-6, 3/23-31	2/1-28	2/1-5, 2/21-28
*Parsley	5/15-31	5/15-20	3/1-31	3/7-22	2/20-3/15	2/20, 3/7-15
Parsnips	4/1-30	4/1-4, 4/21-30	3/7-31	3/23-31	1/15-2/4	1/22-2/4
*Peas (E)	4/15-5/7	4/15-20, 5/5-7	3/7-31	3/7-22	1/15-2/7	1/15-21, 2/6-7
(L)	7/15-31	7/15-18	8/7-31	8/7-16, 8/31	9/15-30	9/15, 9/29-30
*Pepper Pl.	5/15-6/30	5/15-20, 6/3-19	4/1-30	4/5-20	3/1-20	3/7-20
Potato	5/1-31	5/1-4, 5/21-31	4/1-30	4/1-4, 4/21-30	2/10-28	2/21-28
*Pumpkin	5/15-31	5/15-20	4/23-5/15	5/5-15	3/7-20	3/7-20
Radish (E)	4/15-30	4/21-30	3/7-31	3/23-31	1/21-3/1	1/22-2/5, 2/21-3/1
(L)	8/15-31	8/17-30	9/7-30	9/16-28	10/1-21	10/15-21
*Spinach (E)	5/15-31	5/15-20	3/15-4/20	3/15-22, 4/5-20	2/7-3/15	2/7-20, 3/7-15
(L)	7/15-9/7	7/15-18, 8/1-16, 8/31-9/7	8/1-9/15	8/1-16, 8/31-9/15	10/1-21	10/1-14
*Squash (L)	5/15-6/15	5/15-20, 6/3-15	4/15-30	4/15-20	3/15-4/15	3/15-22, 4/5-15
*Swiss Chard	5/1-31	5/5-20	3/15-4/15	3/15-22, 4/5-15	2/7-3/15	2/7-20, 3/7-15
*Tomato Pl.	5/15-31	5/15-20	4/7-30	4/7-20	3/7-20	3/7-20
Turnips (E)	4/7-30	4/21-30	3/15-31	3/23-31	1/20-2/15	1/22-2/5
(L)	7/1-8/15	7/1-2, 7/19-31	8/1-20	8/17-20	9/1-10/15	9/16-28, 10/15
*Wheat, Winter	8/11-9/15	8/11-16, 8/31-9/15	9/15-10/20	9/15, 9/29-10/14	10/15-12/7	10/29-11/3, 11/28-12/7
Spring	4/7-30	4/7-20	3/1-20	3/7-20	2/15-28	2/15-20

GARDENING BY THE MOON'S SIGN

The Outdoor Planting Table (opposite) shows how the phases of the Moon can be used as a guide. Gardeners who use the Moon's *astrological* sign listed below (not astronomical place as on pages 48-74) follow these rules: 1) When the Moon is between new and first quarter (see left-hand calendar pages 48-74 for Moon phases), plant or transplant above-ground crops that produce seeds on the outside (i.e. strawberries, corn, leafy and "bolting" vegetables), and cucumbers, when the Moon is in Taurus, Cancer, Scorpio, Capricorn, or Pisces. 2) When the Moon is between first quarter and full, plant or transplant above-ground crops bearing seeds inside the fruit (i.e. tomatoes, squash, peas, beans) when the Moon is in Taurus, Cancer, Scorpio, Capricorn, or Pisces. 3) When the Moon is between full and last quarter, plant below-ground crops when the Moon is in Taurus, Cancer, Scorpio, Capricorn, or Pisces. 4) When the Moon is between last quarter and new, do not plant; use for destroying weeds, brush, pests, and for cultivating and plowing when the Moon is in Aries, Gemini, Leo, Virgo, Libra, Sagittarius, or Aquarius.

Prune to encourage growth when the Moon is in Cancer, Scorpio, or Capricorn; to discourage growth when the Moon is in Aries or Sagittarius. Wean animals when the Moon is in Taurus, Cancer, or Pisces.

MOON'S PLACE IN THE ZODIAC

	Nov 88	Dec 88	Jan 89	Feb 89	Mar 89	Apr 89	May 89	June 89	July 89	Aug 89	Sept 89	Oct 89	Nov 89	Dec 89
1	LEO	VIR	LIB	SAG	SAG	AQU	PSC	TAU	GEM	LEO	VIR	LIB	SAG	CAP
2	LEO	VIR	SCO	SAG	CAP	AQU	ARI	TAU	CAN	LEO	LIB	SCO	SAG	CAP
3	VIR	VIR	SCO	CAP	CAP	PSC	ARI	GEM	CAN	VIR	LIB	SCO	CAP	AQU
4	VIR	LIB	SAG	CAP	AQU	PSC	TAU	GEM	LEO	VIR	SCO	SAG	CAP	AQU
5	VIR	LIB	SAG	AQU	AQU	ARI	TAU	CAN	LEO	VIR	SCO	SAG	AQU	PSC
6	LIB	SCO	CAP	AQU	PSC	ARI	GEM	CAN	LEO	LIB	SCO	SAG	AQU	PSC
7	LIB	SCO	CAP	PSC	PSC	TAU	GEM	LEO	VIR	LIB	SAG	CAP	AQU	ARI
8	SCO	SAG	AQU	PSC	ARI	TAU	CAN	LEO	VIR	SCO	SAG	CAP	PSC	ARI
9	SCO	SAG	AQU	ARI	ARI	GEM	CAN	VIR	LIB	SCO	CAP	AQU	PSC	TAU
10	SCO	SAG	AQU	ARI	TAU	GEM	CAN	VIR	LIB	SCO	CAP	AQU	ARI	TAU
11	SAG	CAP	PSC	TAU	TAU	CAN	LEO	VIR	LIB	SAG	CAP	PSC	ARI	GEM
12	SAG	CAP	PSC	TAU	GEM	CAN	LEO	LIB	SCO	SAG	AQU	PSC	TAU	GEM
13	CAP	AQU	ARI	GEM	GEM	LEO	VIR	LIB	SCO	CAP	AQU	ARI	TAU	CAN
14	CAP	AQU	ARI	GEM	GEM	LEO	VIR	SCO	SAG	CAP	PSC	ARI	GEM	CAN
15	AQU	PSC	TAU	CAN	CAN	LEO	VIR	SCO	SAG	AQU	PSC	TAU	GEM	LEO
16	AQU	PSC	TAU	CAN	CAN	VIR	LIB	SCO	SAG	AQU	ARI	TAU	CAN	LEO
17	PSC	ARI	GEM	CAN	LEO	VIR	LIB	SAG	CAP	PSC	ARI	GEM	CAN	VIR
18	PSC	ARI	GEM	LEO	LEO	LIB	SCO	SAG	CAP	PSC	TAU	GEM	LEO	VIR
19	ARI	TAU	CAN	LEO	VIR	LIB	SCO	CAP	AQU	ARI	TAU	CAN	LEO	VIR
20	ARI	TAU	CAN	VIR	VIR	LIB	SCO	CAP	AQU	ARI	GEM	CAN	VIR	LIB
21	TAU	GEM	CAN	VIR	VIR	SCO	SAG	AQU	PSC	TAU	GEM	LEO	VIR	LIB
22	TAU	GEM	LEO	VIR	LIB	SCO	SAG	AQU	PSC	TAU	CAN	LEO	VIR	SCO
23	TAU	GEM	LEO	LIB	LIB	SAG	CAP	AQU	ARI	TAU	CAN	LEO	LIB	SCO
24	GEM	CAN	VIR	LIB	LIB	SAG	CAP	PSC	ARI	GEM	LEO	VIR	LIB	SCO
25	GEM	CAN	VIR	SCO	SCO	SAG	AQU	PSC	TAU	GEM	LEO	VIR	SCO	SAG
26	CAN	LEO	LIB	SCO	SCO	CAP	AQU	ARI	TAU	TAU	CAN	LEO	LIB	SCO	SAG
27	CAN	LEO	LIB	SCO	SAG	CAP	PSC	ARI	GEM	CAN	VIR	LIB	SCO	CAP
28	LEO	VIR	LIB	SAG	SAG	AQU	PSC	TAU	GEM	LEO	VIR	LIB	SAG	CAP
29	LEO	VIR	SCO	—	CAP	AQU	PSC	TAU	CAN	LEO	LIB	SCO	SAG	CAP
30	LEO	VIR	SCO	—	CAP	PSC	ARI	GEM	CAN	VIR	LIB	SCO	CAP	AQU
31	—	LIB	SAG	—	CAP	—	ARI	—	CAN	VIR	—	SAG	—	AQU

The Secret of Growing Witloof at Home

It's a delicious vegetable in the chicory family —
frost hardy, virtually carefree, not bothered by pests or
insects — and it does best under the cellar stairs.   by Peg Boyles

☐ FROM THE VOLUPTUOUS REDHEADED Italian radicchio to the elegant pale *chicons* of Belgian endive, imported chicories are the rage among the upscale salad crowd these days, fetching upwards of four dollars a pound in some gourmet supermarkets.

I grow my own and feel very smug. I got into chicory long before chicory got chic.

It all started as a chance encounter at a country store one blustery November day some years ago. The elderly gentleman pumping gas into a vintage Ford pickup remarked to no one in particular that it was getting cold. "Guess I

better head home and dig my end ivies before the ground freezes," he said.

"Your end ivies?" I inquired politely.

"Yup. Belgian end ivies."

Ah, yes, I'd seen Belgian endive in the gourmet section of the supermarket — pale, peaked little sprouts, five or six inches long. Tasty little morsels. The man at the gas pump went on to say that he found them easier to grow than a decent cabbage — he left them in the garden all summer, dug up the roots in the fall, put them in boxes of sand, and left them to sprout under the cellar stairs all through the winter.

It didn't take me long to realize that

this veteran gardener was on to something special: a vegetable that was frost hardy, virtually carefree, not bothered by pests or insects, and tolerant of a wide range of adverse growing conditions. Despite the fact that it is a two-stage crop, it seems to thrive on minimal attention. Best of all, he told me, "Two or three boxes of end ivies will give you a good supply of greens from Thanksgiving to April Fool's!"

By the time I'd ordered seed and planted my first crop, I'd learned that Belgian endive isn't even a true endive, but a type of chicory called witloof, which in Flemish means "white leaf," a reference to the fact that the crop is forced in darkness from stored roots. The resulting tightly folded, blanched heads, called *chicons,* provide incomparably tender, fine-grained, crunchy salad and cooking greens, lacking all but the merest hint of the extreme bitterness of the summer foliage.

Native to Europe, wild chicory has been used as a potherb since ancient times. Leaves, roots, and blossoms found their way into the herbalists' pharmacopoeia as treatments for liver, kidney, and bladder ailments, and for treating infections of the skin and eyes.

Europeans started cultivating chicory in the early seventeenth century, having learned that the fleshy bitter root could be dried and ground to provide an excellent adulterant or substitute for expensive imported coffee. The practice of adulterating coffee with chicory became so widespread that in 1832 the British Parliament made it illegal to sell the blend. But the public had by then acquired a taste for chicory-laced coffee and raised an outcry that forced repeal of the law.

Cichorium intybus, the wild European perennial that gave rise to the giant-rooted coffee chicories, was also the progenitor of the forcing chicories like witloof and of the red Italian heading varieties called radicchio. The curly endives and the broad-leaved escaroles sprang from the sibling species *Cichorium endiva,* whose wild ancestors were annual and biennial plants native to the continent of Asia.

For years I grew the standard witloof from seed bought at my local feed store and enjoyed bountiful crops every winter. The past couple of years I've been growing Toner, a new forcing variety developed in France and sold here by Johnny's Selected Seeds in Albion, Maine. Toner is more productive than earlier varieties and tolerant of a broader range of growing and forcing conditions.

I reserve one 3-foot-by-15-foot planting bed for my chicory each spring. Because I'm after strong, husky roots rather than spectacular summer foliage, I dig in a couple of five-gallon pails of mineral-rich wood ashes, avoiding manure or any other nitrogen-rich fertilizers, and loosen the soil deeply.

To lessen the risk of midsummer bolting, I wait until mid-May to sow the seeds. Aside from thinning the seedlings to stand six inches apart and keeping weeds down with a few shallow early cultivations, I pretty much let my chicory bed fend for itself the rest of the growing season. The plants resemble big untidy dandelions. Their broad floppy leaves do a good job of self-mulching to conserve moisture and keep down weeds.

Although commercial growers force roots that are at least two inches in diameter at the crown, healthy roots of virtually any size or shape will produce high-quality blanched sprouts. Sometime soon after the first killing frost of fall I dig up the entire bed of chicory roots with an ordinary garden fork and twist the leaves off each root, leaving an inch or so at the top so as not to injure the crowns from which my crop of *chicons* will emerge.

The older witloof varieties required that the roots be buried in sand or soil during forcing to ensure formation of nice tight heads. This mode of culture also ensured that the growing heads would take on a load of grit that was devilishly difficult to rinse out.

The newer varieties of forcing chicories like Toner produce well-formed heads without being buried. I simply pack the defoliated roots tightly in an upright position in deep, sturdy containers in five or six inches of sawdust, peat moss, or sand. I've raised fine crops in plastic utility pails and wastebaskets, galvanized buckets, wooden crates, waxed cardboard boxes, and ceramic pickle crocks.

It takes about three weeks to get heads of harvestable size in a container behind the cookstove.

I give the roots a couple of weeks' rest in a cool place after harvest, then thoroughly dampen the storage medium surrounding the roots and double-bag the entire container in heavy black plastic garbage bags. This is an inelegant but effective means of excluding light and maintaining high humidity, both essential for producing high-quality witloof.

The warmer the forcing location, the faster the *chicons* will grow. I like to harvest my first crop in time for Thanksgiving dinner and find it takes about three weeks to get heads of harvestable size in a container set behind the kitchen cookstove. Another container or two comes along more slowly in a corner of an unheated upstairs bedroom. I leave others under the cellar stairs, where the temperature hovers just above 50°. This strategy provides me with successive harvests over a four-month growing season.

Throughout the forcing period, it is essential to keep the storage medium moist, but not soggy, and to keep the chicory in total darkness. Even small amounts of filtered light can turn the shoots bitter and tough.

The *chicons* are ready to eat whenever they're big enough to break off, although books suggest five or six inches as optimum length. To harvest,

simply twist or break the head gently from the root. As long as the crown is not damaged during harvest, the root will continue to send forth tiny, loose clusters of blanched leaves long after the main head is harvested. Though less visually impressive than the plump single *chicon,* these loose-leaf clusters possess the same mild flavor and pleasing crunch.

Although witloof *chicons* can be stir-fried or steamed and served sauced or unadorned, cooking does destroy their unique crunchy-silken texture and delicate flavor. Simply halved or quartered lengthwise, arranged in a star shape on a plate, and drizzled with vinaigrette, raw chicory makes a quick, elegant salad. Chopped or sliced, the heads or leaves make a welcome addition to tossed salad. Their semitubular shape and stiffness make the separated raw leaves ideal for stuffing. Any soft filling will do, from herbed cottage or cream cheese to seafood salad, pâté, or hummus. Because raw witloof tends to develop brown spots after exposure to air and water, harvest the heads just before using, and rinse them as little as possible in cold water.

For a spectacular and filling winter salad, alternate whole leaves of witloof with avocado slices around the edge of a salad plate. Add a second layer of thinly sliced rounds of green pepper and navel oranges. Top off the salad with a generous dollop of this dressing: 1 cup cottage cheese, ½ cup low-fat sour cream, 1 clove garlic, and two tablespoons of orange or lemon juice, whirred in a blender until smooth.

Since starting my long-standing relationship with the delicate winter witloof, I have had a brief, impassioned fling with its tempestuous summer sibling, the red-heading chicory called radicchio (pronounced with a hard "chi," as in zucchini). I found it difficult to grow, and developing a taste for the bitter stuff proved even more challenging than growing it. So much for trendy vegetables. If I want chic, I'll stick with witloof. □ □

Magic with Molasses

Today's innovative cooks are finding unusual and tasty ways to use this country's oldest sweetener.   by Jody Saville and Susan Peery

☐ MOLASSES HAS SWEETENED OUR culture for centuries. Every child who studies American history learns about the "triangular trade" — slaves, rum, and molasses — that supported the Colonial economy. Molasses was so important to colonists that the founders of Georgia promised 64 quarts of molasses as a reward to every man, woman, and child who endured a year in the new settlement. Some historians argue that it was not the tax on tea that precipitated the American Revolution, but an earlier tariff on molasses that encouraged civil disobedience. Up until World War I, when the collapse of sugar prices made the refined product affordable for the first time, molasses was the sweetener of choice for most Americans for cooking and table use.

Molasses, like white table sugar, is refined from sugar cane, and both contain from 45 to 50 calories per tablespoon. Although both products hit the bloodstream as sucrose and are the "empty calories" of which nutritionists despair, molasses does have traces of such valuable minerals as calcium, potassium, and phosphorous (there are, of course, many better and less-caloric sources of those nutrients). Light and dark brown sugars are simply white sugar with molasses added for color and moisture, in a ratio of about one part molasses to nine parts sugar. There seems to be some argument about blackstrap molasses, the product of the third "squeezing" of sugar cane: some relegate it to cattle feed and industrial use, while others claim it as an iron-rich health food.

Fortunately, no one needs to justify molasses nutritionally in order to enjoy the taste. It provides distinctive flavor and welcome moistness to many baked goods and cooked foods. We tend to pigeonhole molasses and limit its use to certain foods that seem to begin with "b": baked beans, brown bread, barbecue sauces, bran muffins. But today's cooks are also using molasses in nontraditional ways, such as in stir-fries, dips, salad dressings and marinades, and children's snacks. Perhaps the following tips (courtesy of the Molasses Information Network, P.O. Box 9179, Morristown, NJ 07960) and recipes will encourage you to take up your jar of sticky, sweet molasses and venture beyond baked beans.

MOLASSES TASTE TIPS

* Zip up an omelet or scrambled eggs with ½ teaspoon molasses and a few drops of Tabasco sauce.
* Add a tablespoon of molasses per serving to bean soups, including navy bean, split pea, lentil, and black bean. Add ½ teaspoon per serving to corn chowder or seafood bisques.
* For a low-fat salad dressing, try combining ⅛ cup molasses, ¼ cup balsamic vinegar, and ¾ cup water; shake well.
* Zip up your favorite vinaigrette (1 part wine vinegar to 3 parts oil) by adding 1 tablespoon molasses and 2 tablespoons Dijon mustard.
* Make an innovative spread to use on brown bread and sweet breads (pumpkin, zucchini, and others) by blending 1 tablespoon molasses, the freshly grated rind of 1 orange, and 8 ounces of softened cream cheese.
* Marinate lamb chops in a mixture of 3 tablespoons molasses, 1 teaspoon rosemary, and 3 cloves crushed garlic. Baste frequently while grilling.
* Coat chicken breasts or pieces in a mixture of ½ cup molasses and ½ cup Dijon mustard, and roll in chopped pecans. Chill for an hour or more, then sauté for 10 to 15 minutes per side, until tender.
* Glaze the crust of a chicken or beef pot pie with a mixture of 1 teaspoon molasses, 1 egg yolk, and 1 teaspoon water. Brush over crust before baking.
* Poach halibut, salmon, or other firm-fleshed fish in this broth: 1 quart water, ½ cup white wine, 1 medium onion (sliced), 2 tablespoons molasses, juice of ½ lemon, 5 whole peppercorns, 1 teaspoon salt, and 1 bay leaf. Simmer until fish flakes easily.
* Top baked potatoes with a dollop of the following: mix 2 cups sour cream or plain yogurt, 2 tablespoons molasses, 2 tablespoons each chopped fresh parsley, chives, and dill. Top with crumbled fried bacon.
* For a healthy snack, dip banana slices in molasses and roll in toasted sesame seeds or wheat germ.
* Swirl 1 teaspoon molasses into a cup of plain yogurt and add fresh fruit.
* Make a fine dip to serve with raw vegetables or crackers by combining 1 pound of small-curd cottage cheese with a large grated carrot, small minced onion, ¼ cup Dijon mustard, 2 tablespoons molasses, 3 tablespoons sweet pickle relish, 2 tablespoons minced pimiento, and 1 tablespoon chopped fresh parsley.
* Add 1 teaspoon molasses and ¼ teaspoon curry powder for every six eggs to your favorite deviled-egg mixture.
* Stuff celery sticks with a combination of ½ cup chopped apple, 1 teaspoon lemon juice, 1 tablespoon molasses, and 8 ounces softened cream cheese.
* Drizzle cooked potato pancakes, hash browns, or French fries with a blend of ¼ cup molasses, ¼ cup malt vinegar, and ¼ cup Dijon mustard.
* Dress up cold cooked chicken with a sauce of 1 teaspoon each molasses, grated fresh ginger, and soy sauce; this sauce also goes well with stir-fried vegetables or meats.
* Make baked apples with a filling of 1 teaspoon molasses, 1 tablespoon orange marmalade, and a dash of cinnamon per apple.
* Sauté banana slices in equal amounts of molasses, butter, and lime juice. Sprinkle with cinnamon-sugar and serve warm over vanilla ice cream.

OUR FAVORITE MOLASSES RECIPES

Molasses Curried Fruit

    1 16-ounce can peach halves
    1 16-ounce can pear halves
    1 16-ounce can whole unpeeled apricots
    1 20-ounce can pineapple chunks
    1 cup sultana raisins (seedless)
    ½ cup light molasses
    ⅓ cup melted butter
    2 teaspoons curry powder

Drain fruits. Place in casserole with raisins. Mix molasses, melted butter, and curry powder and pour mixture over fruit. Bake at 325° F. for 1 hour. Cool to room temperature, cover, and refrigerate overnight. Reheat in oven just before serving. Very nice served with ham or sausage. Always a nice addition to a buffet. Can be garnished with a few maraschino cherry halves.

Molasses-Apple Cottage Pudding

2½ tablespoons butter, melted
2 tart apples
6 tablespoons molasses
⅓ cup shortening
⅔ cup sugar
1 egg
1 cup all-purpose flour
1½ teaspoons baking powder
¼ teaspoon salt
½ cup milk
½ teaspoon vanilla

Melt butter and divide equally between six custard cups, swirling butter around to coat sides. Peel, core, chop finely, and divide apples among the custard cups. Add 1 tablespoon molasses to each cup. Cream shortening and sugar, add egg, and beat well. Sift flour, baking powder, and salt together and add alternately with milk to creamed mixture. Add vanilla and mix well. Pour batter over apple mixture, filling cups ¾ full.

Bake at 350° F. for 45 to 50 minutes. To serve, turn each cup upside down on serving dish and top pudding with whipped cream or other sauce of your choice. Best served warm. Makes 6 servings.

Molasses Muffins

2 cups all-purpose flour
⅛ teaspoon baking soda
2 teaspoons baking powder
½ teaspoon salt
½ cup raisins (optional)
1 egg
¼ cup molasses
1 cup milk
3 tablespoons melted margarine

Sift flour, baking soda, baking powder, and salt together. Add raisins if desired. Combine egg, molasses, milk, and margarine and stir into dry ingredients. Mix only enough to blend ingredients; do not beat. Spoon mixture into greased muffin tins, filling about ⅔ full. Bake at 400° F. for 15 to 20 minutes. Makes 10 to 12 large muffins or 18 small muffins.

To vary:

Bran Molasses Muffins: Reduce flour to 1 cup and add ¾ cup unprocessed bran to dry ingredients. Reduce milk to ¾ cup and proceed as above.

Cornmeal Molasses Muffins: Reduce flour to 1 cup and add 1 cup cornmeal. Proceed as above.

Oatmeal Muffins: Reduce flour to 1 cup and add 1 cup rolled oats. Reduce milk to ¾ cup. Proceed as above.

Molasses Brownies

⅔ cup butter or margarine
⅔ cup confectioners' sugar
⅔ cup molasses
1 teaspoon vanilla
1 egg
1¾ cups all-purpose flour
⅛ teaspoon baking soda
1 cup chopped nuts

Cream butter and sugar until fluffy. Stir in molasses and vanilla. Beat in eggs. Sift flour and soda together and add to batter. Mix well and add nuts. Spread batter in two greased 9-inch-square pans. Bake at 350° F. for 25 minutes. Cut into bars. Yield will depend on size of bars.

Jody's Double Gingersnaps

1½ cups butter or margarine
2 cups sugar
2 eggs
½ cup molasses
4 cups flour
2 teaspoons baking soda
2 teaspoons cinnamon
2 teaspoons ground cloves
4 teaspoons ground ginger
    sugar for rolling

Cream butter and sugar. Add eggs and molasses and blend well. Sift dry ingredients together. Add half of dry mixture to creamed mixture and blend with mixer. Add remaining half and blend by hand. Chill dough for several hours. At this point, you may bake whatever portion of the dough you desire, and refrigerate or freeze the remainder. (Dough keeps in the refrigerator, well covered, for at least a week. To freeze, wrap dough well in plastic or foil.) To bake, pull off pieces of dough to make balls the size of a walnut. Roll the balls in sugar and place on ungreased cookie sheets. Bake at 350° F. for about 15 minutes. Balls will flatten out and tops will be crackled. Makes 5 to 6 dozen. (Recipe may be halved or doubled.) □ □

Everything You Always Wanted to Know About Cheesecake

(plus the best cheesecake recipe in the world)

The truth is that a single serving of cheesecake contains the equivalent daily caloric intake of many Third World villages. But oh, it is, as the poet said, "a foretaste of heaven."

by Bob Trebilcock

☐ I GREW UP IN THE MIDWEST in the 1960s, in an era before all Americans were transformed into gourmets. No one-inch-diameter medallions of salmon floated in a perfect pond of saffron cream at our house: we ate real food for real people. Now and then my mother prepared some recipe clipped from the rotogravure section of the Sunday newspaper — usually cream-of-mushroom-soup casseroles and adventuresome concoctions with Jell-O. These attempts to bring a little panache to the table were usually followed the next night with a moist pot roast and tasty apple pie over which otherwise law-abiding citizens might commit the most heinous crime to ensure seconds. You could say that we were food traditionalists who took solace in the conformity of our meals the way businessmen find comfort in the blue suit.

It comes as no surprise, then, that the first cheesecake to find its way to the table met with some skepticism. It was Thanksgiving Day 1969. No one really dug in until halftime of the second football game — after the apple, pumpkin, and mincemeat pies were gone. No doubt there was a little regional snobbery involved here. Cheesecake was prefaced with the words "New York style," and to a Midwesterner, the last good thing to come out of New York City was the Dodgers, and they had the good sense to move west.

But we were wrong about cheesecake. The experience was an epiphany for our taste buds. From then on, holiday dessert for me meant rich, creamy cheesecake. Some thought I was a little fanatical when I insisted my wife-to-be apprentice with my mother, but in cheesecake and marriage, you can't be too careful.

The Dictionary of Calories and Carbohydrates claims that a four-ounce serving of commercial cheesecake contains only 306 calories. Of course, they are dealing with a miserly portion of the kind of airy impostor that resembles the real thing in name only. The truth is, a single serving — what I consider a single serving, at least — contains the equivalent of the daily caloric intake of most Third World villages. I'm certain cheesecake was on the mind of the church when gluttony was designated as one of the seven deadly sins.

The history of cheesecake is almost as rich as its flavor. The ancient Greeks most likely invented the delicacy more than 2,000 years ago: cottage cheese put through a sieve was blended with honey and flour and baked until done. The Greeks accurately described their culinary contribution as "dainty food for mortal man." According to the food writer M. F. K. Fisher, prospective grooms in Argos were presented with cheesecakes prior to the marriage nuptials, presumably as the eating experience most closely resembling the joys of an evening of frolic. Likewise, brides-to-be were given by maiden attendants "cakes delicately shaped like breasts."

The Romans knew a good thing when they saw it: Cato, the Roman soldier and statesman, included a cheesecake recipe with his booty from the conquest of Greece. The recipe survives; in fact, at least one scholar of culinary history (namely me) has wondered whether or not the decline of the Roman Empire might not be traced to a preoccupation with cheesecake.

The Dark Ages, of course, were not nearly as dark as is often thought: cheesecake not only survived, but in pre-Renaissance England it thrived. In 1381 a recipe for cheesecake was published in the *Book of the Table,* leading one English poet to describe the dessert as "a foretaste of heaven with glimpses

Brides-to-be were given by maiden attendants "cakes delicately shaped like breasts."

of higher life and ethereal worlds." By the mid-sixteenth century, "Maids of Honor" were served as the coronation dessert for Elizabeth I. The recipe is said to have sold for 1,000 pounds sterling. In 1662 one Mrs. Leeds included a cheesecake recipe in her book, *The Compleate Cook,* with instructions for determining the proper oven temperature for cheesecake baking: "Let your oven ben hot enough for a Pigeon pye and let a stone stand up till the scorching be passed, then set them in, half an hour will bake them well."

Of course, cheesecake evolution wasn't limited to England. The Italians perfected a ricotta pie with candied fruit, and the Russians developed Pashka, a traditional cottage-cheese dessert served at Easter. Though it's rarely reported, cheesecake played an important role in the French Revolution when Marie Antoinette was mistakenly beheaded after the erroneous report that she said the peasants could eat cake. What she actually said was, "Let them eat cheesecake," a sign not of royal indifference to the masses, but of genuine benevolence.

The first published recipe for the modern dessert we know as cheesecake was probably the one included in Mrs. Glasse's *Art of Cookery Made Plain and Simple,* published in the late 1700s. Early cheesecakes were a rough cousin to the smooth concoction we eat today. The breakthrough came in 1872, when New York dairymen invented cream cheese while attempting to duplicate the flavor of unripened French Neufchâtel. The proprietors of New York's Jewish delicatessens used the new cheese to bake a rich cake with a zwieback or graham-cracker crust.

For a time it looked as if the new dessert might be available only to the rich and famous. Then, on August 27, 1926, *The New York Times* reported that a cartel known as the Brownsville and East New York Cream Cheese Dealers' Association had been broken up. Israel M. Lerner, the state deputy attorney general, predicted a 30-percent reduction in the price of the most crucial of ingredients. Cheesecake lovers across the Big Apple cheered. By the mid-1940s the dessert was popular enough to support a growing number of businesses devoted only to cheesecake. The dessert of choice at Lindy's, the fashionable Broadway haunt of the 1940s and 1950s, was cheesecake. Chef Leo Lidenbaum permitted his recipe to be printed in *Good Housekeeping* and other far-reaching publications, and the moniker "New York style" became as permanently attached to cheesecake as Kansas City to a strip steak.

That was the golden age of cheesecake. In today's era of designer food and pizzas with marinated cactus and duck livers, cheesecake has gone exotic. Lately I've found cheesecake recipes with whole-wheat crusts (whom are they trying to kid?); fillings of blue cheese, Gouda, cottage cheese, ricotta, avocado, buttermilk, cider, tofu, and pumpkin; cheesecakes topped with daiquiris, grapefruit, passion fruit, currants, and cranberries. There is something called Cheesecake Alaska with Pistachio Filling, as well as recipes for low-calorie cheesecake and cheesecake in a flower pot. Under the headline ". . .

Something Completely Different," *The New York Times* once published a recipe for smoked salmon and onion cheesecake. And for the do-it-yourselfer, how about "Your Own Cheese, Your Own Cake." That implies your own cow raised on your own farm. No, thanks — I don't want to get into farming just for dessert.

It's not that I wouldn't try any of these cheesecakes; I'm ecumenical enough to paraphrase Will Rogers's comment on mankind and say I've never met a cheesecake I didn't like. But in a perfect world, I prefer mine served like red wines and German beers: in quantity, plain, and warmed almost to room temperature. With that in mind, I offer my mother's cheesecake recipe. It's simple, rich, and delicious. I think it tastes best when served a day old. My mother prepares it a day earlier than needed, usually so late at night that my father goes to bed rather than wait for it to cool.

Virginia Trebilcock's Cheesecake

Crust:
- 2 cups crushed graham crackers
- ½ cup melted butter
- ¼ cup crushed walnuts

Filling:
- 3 8-ounce packages of cream cheese, at room temperature
- 1½ cups sugar
- 5 eggs
- 3 tablespoons lemon juice

Topping:
- 1 pint sour cream
- ½ cup sugar
- 1 teaspoon vanilla

Preheat oven to 350°. Combine crust ingredients and press evenly across bottom and sides of a 10-inch springform pan. Mix filling ingredients: Combine cream cheese and sugar; add eggs one at a time, beating thoroughly after each one. Beat in the lemon juice. Pour filling over crust, and bake for 45 minutes without opening the oven door.

Remove cheesecake and reduce heat to 300°. Mix topping ingredients and spread topping over cheesecake. Return to oven and bake for 15 minutes longer. Cool on rack for several hours, then refrigerate overnight. Serve plain or topped with fresh fruit.

□ □

WINNING RECIPES IN THE 1988 RECIPE CONTEST
How to Prepare Your Thanksgiving Turkey

FIRST PRIZE:
Pilgrim's Thanksgiving Turkey

- 1½ cups fresh cranberries
- 4 cups cooked wild rice
- ⅓ cup melted butter or margarine
- ⅓ cup golden corn syrup
- 1 small onion, grated
- 1 shallot, minced
- 1 teaspoon salt
- ½ teaspoon marjoram
- ⅛ teaspoon pepper
- ⅛ teaspoon mace
- ⅛ teaspoon basil
- 1 8- to 10-pound turkey
- 8 slices smoked bacon

Grind the cranberries through the coarsest blade of a food chopper into a large saucepan. Add the remaining ingredients except turkey and bacon and cook for 10 minutes, stirring frequently. Cool. Stuff the turkey with the rice mixture and truss the bird. Place the turkey on its side on a rack in a roasting pan. Cover with 4 slices of the bacon and roast at 325° F. for 1 hour. Turn onto the other side and roast for another hour. Turn the bird on its back and place remaining 4 slices of bacon over breast and legs and continue roasting, basting from time to time, for 2 hours or until the thigh meat is fork tender. Serves 8 to 10.

Mrs. Jean Roczniak
Rochester, Minnesota

SECOND PRIZE:
Bagged Roast Turkey with Cornbread, Chestnut, and Sage Stuffing

- 1 large turkey (15-22 pounds)
- 2 plain large brown grocery bags
- 1 cup butter or margarine
- 1 clove garlic, minced

Remove giblets from turkey. Soak turkey in salted water to cover for 1 hour; meanwhile, prepare giblet stock and stuffing (see below). Drain and rinse turkey; pat dry. Rub cavities with minced garlic. Melt butter or margarine and brush inside of bird (or pour into cavities and rotate bird). Bird is ready for stuffing.

Giblet Stock:
- giblets and neck from turkey
- 2 ribs celery, chopped
- 1 clove garlic, minced

- 1 onion, quartered
- 1 parsnip, quartered
- 1 teaspoon each salt, pepper, marjoram, and sage

Combine all and cook in 1 quart water, covered, while turkey is soaking and stuffing is being mixed.

Stuffing:
- 4-6 cups baked cornbread (depending on size of turkey)
- 2 cups wheat bread, in 1″ cubes
- 2 onions, diced
- 2 apples, peeled, cored, and diced
- 2 cups diced celery
- 1 cup diced meat from cooked and peeled chestnuts
- giblets, chopped fine
- ½ cup grated carrot
- 2 tablespoons ground fresh sage
- 2 teaspoons salt
- 1 teaspoon freshly ground black pepper
- 1 cup butter or margarine, melted
- 1 cup giblet stock, strained

Crumble cornbread and toss with bread cubes and remaining ingredients. When stuffing is well mixed, stuff lightly into cavities and sew them shut with needle and cotton thread. Tuck wings in and tie legs together. Place stuffed turkey in one brown bag and slide the second bag over the open end. Place bagged bird in roasting pan and roast at 350° F., allowing 20 minutes per pound. Much of the fat will be absorbed by the paper bag. Check after three-quarters of the time has elapsed and add water if necessary. Cut away paper bags and let turkey brown during last 20-30 minutes of roasting time. Use turkey drippings and remaining giblet stock to make gravy.

June Stewart
Wheeling, Illinois

THIRD PRIZE:
Roast Turkey with Apple-Pecan Stuffing

- 1 10- to 14-pound turkey
- ½ cup soft butter
- salt and pepper

Remove giblets from bird. Massage turkey well with softened butter, then salt and pepper it. Prepare stuffing as directed below.

Stuffing:

- ½ cup butter
- 3 stalks celery, diced
- 2 large onions, diced
- 2 large cooking apples, peeled and diced
- 10-12 cups cubed bread
- 1 cup water
- 2 tablespoons finely chopped fresh parsley
- 1 teaspoon basil
- ⅛ teaspoon nutmeg
- ½ teaspoon paprika
- ½ teaspoon pepper
- 1½ cups chopped pecans
  strips of salt pork or bacon, uncooked

In a large kettle, melt butter and cook celery and onions until tender, stirring occasionally. Add apples and cook 5 minutes longer. Remove from heat; stir in bread cubes, water, seasonings, and pecans. Mix well. Stuff turkey and sew cavities shut with needle and cotton thread. Line bottom of roasting pan with half of the strips of salt pork or bacon, then place turkey breast side up in the pan. Place remaining salt pork or bacon strips over breast. Place in a preheated 450° F. oven and cook for 30 minutes, then reduce heat to 350° F. and continue roasting until the turkey is done (juices run clear and legs move easily). Baste frequently with the liquid in the pan; add additional melted butter if necessary. *Susan Wiker Kinzers, Pennsylvania*

1989 RECIPE CONTEST:
Holiday Cookies and Bars

For 1989, prizes (first prize, $50; second, $25; third, $15) will be awarded for the best original recipes for holiday cookies and bars. All entries become the property of Yankee Publishing Incorporated, which reserves all rights to the materials submitted. Winners will be announced in the 1990 edition of *The Old Farmer's Almanac.* Deadline is April 15, 1989. Address: Recipe Contest, *The Old Farmer's Almanac,* Dublin, NH 03444.

THE OLD FARMER'S ALMANAC COOKBOOK CONTEST

Readers of *The Old Farmer's Almanac* are invited to submit as many as five of their favorite recipes in any category for possible inclusion in the upcoming *Old Farmer's Almanac Cookbook.* All entries become the property of Yankee Publishing Incorporated; readers whose recipes are chosen for inclusion in the book will be compensated. Address: Cookbook Contest, *The Old Farmer's Almanac,* Dublin, NH 03444.

WINNING ESSAYS IN THE 1988 ESSAY CONTEST
"The Secret of a Successful Marriage"

FIRST PRIZE:

Upon noticing the title of this year's essay contest, I approached my husband of 35 years. "What makes our marriage a success?" I asked. "It's not a success," he answered, avoiding my eyes. "Does this mean you're leaving?" I asked. "Just as soon as I get through eating," was his reply. Snatching for his slice of apple pie, my fingers did a sharp pivot in midair to scratch an imaginary itch on my nose as he warbled sweetly, "Honey, this has to be the best pie you've ever made!"

After washing the dishes, I passed him coming in from outdoors with a load of firewood under his arm. "You'd better be on your way," I threatened. "When I get through drying the dishes," he replied.

Later, as I saw him heading for the bedroom in his pajamas, all ready for the night, I said, "Still here?" "Till tomorrow," he countered. "Gotta get you to church tomorrow and pick up the grandchildren for you to babysit tomorrow afternoon." Warming his always-cold feet on mine, he muttered something about my being the only one around with a checkbook.

Well, though he claims our marriage isn't a success, he's still around!

Marie Pemberton
Denver, Colorado

SECOND PRIZE:

What is the secret of a successful marriage? Easy! It's a pot of coffee and 30 minutes of private time each day.

Twelve years ago I married a wonderful woman with two sons. She began bringing two cups of coffee to bed each morning. We even set the alarm a half-hour earlier than really necessary so we would not have to rush through our eye-opener. Our sons soon learned that we were not to be disturbed during our "private time" for anything less than a house fire. The activities of that half hour varied. Sometimes we talked of trivial things, sometimes of money matters or future plans. Sexual activity filled that half hour on occasion. Other times we sat silently in the early morning darkness holding hands while drinking coffee with the other hand. We might talk of happy times or sad. Of our family or work. The subject didn't matter.

The boys are grown and on their own now, but my wife and I still have our "private time" in the morning. Sometimes I make and deliver the coffee, usually she does. We've decided to give the marriage another 12 years to see if it works out. I suspect that in the year 2000 we'll decide to try it for another 24 years, just to give the marriage a chance.

Ed Baldwin
Norfolk, Virginia

THIRD PRIZE:

I have been married for over 40 years to the same woman. Our secret is never to be boring or uninteresting toward one another. We pay attention to each other's needs. We both always have a sense of humor and use it. While I am not an authority on romance, I am often reminded of a Burma Shave classic: "At making love/Pa ain't no whiz,/But he knows how/To keep Ma his."

We never bring up past failures or losses as what is done, is done. For years I've surprised my wife with bouquets from the florist or a dollar item from rummage sales, which she dotes on. Many times I've held back from complaining and am glad of this virtue, as things always turned out fine anyway. I have traveled extensively with this little woman of mine across the country and each time have felt like a groom all over again. Now that I am older, I feel I owe her my love for all the times she put up with me. I'm not a gambler, but I picked a winner 40 years ago. *David Kocsis*
Flint, Michigan

1989 ESSAY CONTEST:
"The Best Advice My Mother Ever Gave Me"

For 1989, prizes (first prize, $50; second, $25; third, $15) will be awarded for the three best 200-word essays on this topic: "The best advice my mother ever gave me." All entries become the property of Yankee Publishing Incorporated, which reserves all rights to the material submitted. Winners will be announced in the 1990 edition of *The Old Farmer's Almanac*. Deadline: April 15, 1989. Essay Contest, *The Old Farmer's Almanac*, Dublin, NH 03444.

RAINY DAY AMUSEMENTS

Answers appear on page 219.

MIDDLE NAME GAME

Do you fancy yourself the type who never forgets a name? How about middle names? Can you recall what the middle initial stands for in the following names?
– Byran Henry

1) B. F. Goodrich
2) John D. Rockefeller
3) George M. Pullman
4) Charles A. Lindbergh
5) Samuel L. Clemens
6) P. T. Barnum
7) Samuel F. B. Morse

8) Adlai E. Stevenson
9) Pablo R. Picasso
10) John J. Pershing
11) Rachel L. Carson
12) Alfred B. Nobel
13) Huey P. Long
14) Robert E. Lee

15) Charles R. Darwin
16) J. C. Penney
17) Robert L. Ripley
18) Ulysses S. Grant
19) William T. Sherman
20) George A. Custer
21) Harry S. Truman

DOUBLE TV TROUBLE

This is a two-part quiz. First match the stars with the television series they starred in; then match their names with their given names.
– Thomas E. Oetzel

1) Robert Blake
2) Amanda Blake
3) Jackie Coogan
4) Barbara Eden
5) Michael Landon
6) Jack Lord
7) Harry Morgan
8) Barbara Stanwyck
9) Connie Stevens
10) Gale Storm

a. Hawaiian Eye
b. I Dream of Jeannie
c. M*A*S*H
d. Baretta
e. My Little Margie
f. Little House on the Prairie
g. Hawaii Five-O
h. The Big Valley
i. Gunsmoke
j. The Addams Family

A. Harry Bratsburg
B. John Leslie
C. Michael Gubitosi
D. Josephine Cottle
E. Ruby Stevens
F. Barbara Huffman
G. Beverly Neil
H. John Joseph Ryan
I. Concetta Ingolia
J. Eugene Maurice Orowitz

NAVAL SHIP FIRSTS

Match the vessel first in U.S. naval history with its identifying phrase.
– John A. Johnston

1) *Nautilus*
2) *Maine*
3) *Skate*
4) *Reuben James*
5) *Enterprise*
6) *Ward*
7) *Langley*
8) *Birmingham*
9) *Patrick Henry*
10) *Red Rover*

a. First aircraft carrier commissioned, March 20, 1922
b. First ship lost in WW II, October 30, 1941
c. First WW II Liberty ship
d. World's first atomic submarine, 1955
e. First hospital ship
f. First battleship (battle cruiser) launched, November 18, 1890
g. First airplane takeoff (cruiser), November 14, 1910
h. First atomic aircraft carrier commissioned, 1961
i. First submarine to surface at North Pole, 1959
j. First to fire on the enemy at Pearl Harbor, December 7, 1941

NEXT IN LINE

Rearrange the cabinet members in correct order of presidential succession.
– Milt Hammer

A) Secretary of Defense
B) Secretary of the Interior
C) Vice President
D) Secretary of Agriculture
E) Speaker of the House
F) Secretary of Health, Education and Welfare

G) Attorney General
H) Secretary of State
I) Secretary of Energy
J) President Pro Tempore of the Senate
K) Secretary of Housing and Urban Development

L) Secretary of the Treasury
M) Secretary of Transportation
N) Secretary of Labor
O) Secretary of Commerce

There's Money Out on Those Frozen Lakes!

Herewith a brief rundown on some of the big-money ice-fishing tournaments for fishermen who really like the cold.
by David Zilavy

☐ NO PRECISE TABS ARE KEPT ON THE ice-fishing tournaments held in the United States and Canada every winter. Most are modest competitions sponsored by local fire stations or Knights of Columbus, with prizes ranging from a couple of lures to the omnipresent Grand Prize — the gas-powered ice auger. But here, together for the first time anywhere, are the top seven prize-winning ice-fishing tournaments in North America.

1. The Great Rotary Fishing Derby, Lake Winnipesaukee, New Hampshire. A round $100,000 in prizes is offered, but you'd best bring a four-leaf clover, a rabbit's foot, and your lucky fishing hat. To win the first prize, a $30,000 Stingray Maxim II speedboat, you have to catch one of 120 tagged fish, then have that tag number drawn from a barrelful of all other tag numbers. Figure the odds on that. Same goes for the Ford Bronco and the $10,000 and $5,000 cash prizes. For a $12 registration fee, your name goes into the pot for $30, $500, and $5,000 cash prize drawings. The ten heaviest perch, pickerel, cusk, bass, and trout fetch awards totaling $8,700. If you'd like to put up a shack in one of the several shantytowns that spring up during the tournament (the first weekend in February), call 603-279-6463.

2. Forest Lakes Ice-fishing Tournament, Forest Lakes, Minnesota. What else would they do in the Land of 10,000 Lakes during winter but ice fish? This is one of the few competitions that actually, absolutely, award all money advertised — $60,000. Angle for trout and bass to win four-wheel-drive trucks, boats, Las Vegas trips, cash, buck knives, and of course, gas-powered ice augers. Tickets will set you back $30, but the fish board, where winning catches are displayed, is vast and generous. Time was when one tagged fish was worth a million dollars. Lloyds of London insured it, but the payments ballooned and now things are done differently at Forest Lakes. Call 612-459-5815.

3. Saratoga Lakes Ice-fishing Derby, Saratoga, Wyoming. The line is $55,000 in prizes. The hitch is that the large prizes come only for catching tagged trout. They release 101 of them. The top total payout ever was $8,000. The biggest trout is worth $500, the second $250, the third $100. If the big one gets away, you can meet the King and Queen Fish, celebrities crowned for some tie to Wyoming. Last year's royalty were England's Prince Charles and Princess Diana, chosen because the sister of the wife of their Master of House lives in Wyoming. The derby is always the weekend between NFL playoffs and the Superbowl. Ten dollars will get you in. Call 307-326-8855.

4. Winter Crazy Days, Detroit Lakes, Minnesota. About $40,000 in prizes are offered on this fourth-Saturday-in-January tournament (it used to be the fifth Saturday, but they ran out of those). There's a good bit of cash to win here; ten increments from $1,500 down to $100 for the top ten catches of bass, crappies, sunfish, northerns, and walleyes. There's also a grab bag of wildlife prints, luggage, grills, VCRs, a truck, and gas-powered ice augers. Tickets are $20. Call 218-847-4427.

5. Annual Eagles Ice-fishing Tournament, Lake Mitigoshi, North Dakota. At four in the morning on the last Saturday in January, officials start drilling holes in the ice; thousands of holes. A horn then blasts at one in the afternoon, and for the next two and a half hours some 4,000 fisherman try for their piece of the $30,000 purse. The largest walleye, perch, or northern nets $1,000; second place is worth $500, on down to $150 for fifth place. Last year just one five-inch walleye was caught; it won the $1,000 prize. If your pop-up doesn't pop, you can check out the dogsled or snowmobile races, the snow sculpture, or the concessions tent. But don't eat too much because your $20 entry fee includes a spaghetti feed. Call 701-662-3912.

6. Lake Simcoe Ice-fishing Derby, Ontario, Canada. The December-through-March contest makes this tourney popular with Americans and Canadians alike — you can work it into your schedule. Lake Simcoe is big.

Fish-hut operators take participants out in Ski-Doos and Arctic Cats (ten miles out!) to party huts, eight-person shanties complete with stoves and bunks. The snowmobile ferries are equipped with extra-large trailers for your own beer and food. Some stay for weeks. Top prizes for trout, perch, walleye, whitefish, herring, and pike are $1,000 each. Periodic raffles hand out fish gear, toques (wool hats), a truck, boats, and the gas-powered auger. Total giveaway: $20,000. It costs $6 (Canadian) to enter. Call 416-476-4301.

7. Fairhaven Rotary's Great Fish Derby, Vermont. During the first weekend in January, all Vermont waters are open for ice fishing. Only 500 usually compete for the $8,000 worth of spoils. Part is given to the three largest northerns, walleyes, bass, trout, and perch. There are also prizes for tagged fish caught from four seeded lakes. The rest of the pot is divvied up by raffles into cash and the gas-powered augers. Call 802-265-3443. □□

BEST FISHING DAYS, 1989
(and other fishing lore from the files of *The Old Farmer's Almanac*)

Probably the best fishing time is when the ocean tides are restless before their turn and in the first hour of ebbing. All fish in all waters — salt or fresh — feed most heavily then.

Best temperatures for fish species vary widely, of course, and are chiefly important if you are going to have your own fish pond. Best temperatures for brook trout are 45° to 65° F. Brown trout and rainbows are more tolerant of higher temperatures. Smallmouth black bass do best in cool water. Horned pout take what they find.

Most of us go fishing when we can get off, not because it is the best time. But there are best times:
- One hour before and one hour after high tide, and one hour before and one hour after low tide. (The times of high tides are given on pages 48-74 and corrected for your locality on pages 86-87. Inland, the times for high tides would correspond with the times the Moon is due south. Low tides are halfway between high tides.)
- "The morning rise" — after sunup for a spell — and "the evening rise" — just before sundown and the hour or so after.

- Still water or a ripple is better than a wind at both times.
- When there is a hatch of flies — caddis or mayflies, commonly. (The fisherman will have to match the hatching flies with *his* fly — or go fishless.)
- When the breeze is from a westerly quarter rather than north or east.
- When the barometer is steady or on the rise. (But, of course, even in a three-day driving northeaster the fish isn't going to give up feeding. His hunger clock keeps right on working, and the smart fisherman will find something he wants.)
- When the Moon is between new and full.

MOON BETWEEN
NEW & FULL

Jan. 7-21	Aug. 1-16
Feb. 6-20	Aug. 31-Sept. 15
Mar. 7-22	Sept. 29-Oct. 14
Apr. 5-20	Oct. 29-Nov. 13
May 5-20	Nov. 28-Dec. 12
June 3-19	Dec. 27-31
July 3-18	

OLD AND NEW MATHEMATICAL PUZZLES

Blanton C. Wiggin, Puzzle Editor

☐ HERE ARE 15 CLASSICAL, ORIGINAL, and timely puzzles for 1989 from our readers. There should be something to interest everyone, and we hope they are challenging. Everyday common sense and a little agility are all you'll need; you won't need calculus, computers, alertness to tricks, or specialized knowledge, though these are sometimes helpful. Some puzzles may require a chart or data from your local library.

We will award one prize of $50 for the best set of solutions to puzzles 12 through 15 received before February 1, 1989. The answers to these four are omitted here.

We use a point system to judge the prize set. A basic, unadorned, correct answer is 20 points. For a thorough analysis, an elegant or novel answer, up to 5 points extra. Numerical errors lose only 2 or 3 points, if it is clear that the method is understood.

Explanations and Prize-Set Answers will be sent after June 15 to anyone sending 50¢ and a self-addressed stamped envelope to "Puzzle Answers," *The Old Farmer's Almanac,* Dublin, NH 03444.

We will also pay $15 for any original puzzles we use in *The Old Farmer's Almanac* for 1990. Closing date for submissions is February 1, 1989. Entries become the property of Yankee Publishing Incorporated and cannot be acknowledged or returned.

We are happy to find that a number of teachers, grades 4 through college, use our puzzles in their classrooms. We've enjoyed talking to some of these college classes. Some of this year's puzzles submitted by students are noted.

The 1988 winner is George Hall, Tucson, Arizona, a frequent entrant, with a masterful entry, scoring 98.5. Hall included clear explanations, background material, and interesting asides. In a year of unusually good answers, runner-up is Tina Virzi, Plattsburgh, New York, with 95.5! She was followed by Arthur Loepp, Kansas City, Missouri, 95.25, and for fourth, a tie between last year's winner, Bob Symons, Waterloo, Ontario, and Bob Matthews, West Hartford, Connecticut, 95.

Congratulations to all!

Have fun with these 1989 puzzles, and send your answers early for puzzles 12-15. Please use a separate sheet for each puzzle or answer. Be sure to put your name and address on each sheet. Good luck!

Answers appear on page 219.

1. Six Stix
Difficulty: 1

a) Arrange 6 toothpicks so that each pick touches every other pick.

b) Rearrange the same 6 to form exactly 4 – only 4 – equilateral triangles.

Ruth Dykstra
Bussey, Iowa

2. Better Barns
Difficulty: 1

Farmer Allen's 2 barns were built 100 years apart.

Their 1989 ages multiplied together equal 1989! When were they built?

Mary E. B. Nightingale
Brookline, New Hampshire

3. Simple Estimates
Difficulty: 1

a) A man calculated the square root of 2 (actually 1.41421 . . .) with an error of about 1 percent by simply dividing two small numbers in his head. How did he do it?

The Old Farmer's Almanac 1966

b) The Greeks calculated π (actually 3.14159 . . .) in the same way. What were their numbers? *Patty Nagy*
Huntington, L.I., New York

4. End States
Difficulty: 2

We're not looking for stability at the end of a nuclear decay chain, just some ordinary geography.

a) Which American state is southernmost, northernmost, westernmost, and which is easternmost?

b) OK? Now how about the lower 48?

c) Fair enough. What about Canadian provinces?

d) You are viewing a lovely sunset. On the other side of the earth, at your antipodes, people are watching the sunrise. What is their latitude and longitude?

Fran Loutrel
Wellesley, Massachusetts

5. Time of the Pharaohs
Difficulty: 2

Using 455 cubic blocks, an Egyptian apprentice constructed a small, square, solid pyramid to earn his diploma. Every block in each level took an equal amount of time to place, but at each higher level, the time per block doubled. He labored 1879 hours to complete the pyramid. How much time did he expend placing the single block at the top? *Jack Tumath*
Plymouth, Michigan

6. Grove of Trees
Difficulty: 3

"I am constrained to plant a grove
to satisfy the maid I love.
This ample grove must be composed
of nineteen trees in nine
straight rows.
And in each row five I must place,
or ne'er expect to see her face.
Ye men of art lend me your aid
to try to please this lovely maid."

How would you arrange the trees?
Cason D. Brinson
circa 1850
Garland W. Brinson
Sneads Ferry, North Carolina

7. Seattle Trip
Difficulty: 3

In this 100th anniversary year of Washington State, Pete Yakima will return to his hometown 3,500 miles from Miami, Florida.

He leaves at sunrise October 25, doesn't touch or wind his electric watch, which keeps perfect time, and drives continuously at a leisurely rate of 270 miles a day, arriving before the anniversary date.

What time will his watch read at moonset in Seattle on the day he arrives there? *Doreen Rowe*
Collinsville, Illinois

8. Double Vision
Difficulty: 3

Little Tommy caught 2 tadpoles and put them in a tank. When they were still, he looked down into the tank and saw View D:

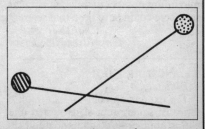

(continued on next page)

Then he looked into the front of the tank, for View F:

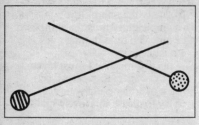

Are the 2 tadpoles touching one another?

T. Bredt Aiken
S. Colton, New York

9. Fruit Salad
Difficulty: 3
A grower has 2 orders for a total of 240 crates of oranges and 260 crates of grapefruit. Customer A wants 300 crates of fruit and customer B, 200. The proportion of grapefruit in the first order is larger than that of oranges in the second. How many fewer crates of oranges go to customer B than grapefruit to A? *Mary Ann Scholten*
Sarasota, Florida

10. A .500 Record
Difficulty: 4
In the old NEFL, 13 teams played each other just once. At season's end, each team had won 6 games and lost 6.
a) How many games were played that year?
b) Defining a "circular set" to be 3 different teams, none of which has beaten both of the others, what is the maximum number of different circular sets there could have been that season?
Charles Townsend
Toms River, New Jersey

11. Nesting Roots
Difficulty: 4
The expression below — an infinite series of square-root signs nested one within another — contains no numbers and yet has an exact numerical value

that can be divined by simple algebra. What is x?

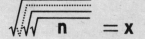

$$\sqrt{\sqrt[4]{\sqrt{\boxed{n}}}} = x$$

Matt Kratter, age 16
Bellevue, Washington

12. Astronomical Clock
Difficulty: 5
The "pointer" stars of the "Big Dipper" are like the hour hand of a clock centered on the North Star. On what nights of the year do they tell the actual time correctly?

Schuyler W. Benson
Belmont, Massachusetts

13. Many Factors
Difficulty: 5
a) Are there 10,000 consecutive non-prime numbers?
b) If a prime is an integer greater than 1 whose only positive integer factors are itself and 1,
1) find a triple of primes (p, q, r) such that p = q + 2 and q = r + 2, and
2) prove that there is only 1 such triple.

Stephen Gettel
San Francisco, California

14. An Eccentric Bias
Difficulty: 5
For a right circular cone of 90 degrees vertex, do the slopes of cutting planes match the eccentricities of the resulting conic sections?

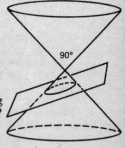

Please explain.

Ed Toll
Jensen Beach, Florida

15. SETI Transnumeration

Difficulty: 5

Suppose the Search for Extraterrestrial Intelligence, "SETI," picked up these 2 unrelated sets of numerical signals in 1989, probably from computers. Each set uses an unusual counting system to show correct calculations. Set A is operationally efficient for machines. Alone, each digit has a familiar value, and position is doubly important.

Set A

98	·832	5603411	821	48971	267
(+) 267	(-) 1045	390619	1934	5854	(+) 1953
145	19807	5992010	18974	6342	?
			56035	1775	
1953	1846	1846	(+) 9862	795	
(+) 122	(-) 26087	(-) 194133	41206	(+) 184915	?
75	195979	027713		000012	2⟌1989267

Successive integers in some segments of the number line:

... 27, 28, 29, 10, 11, 12 ...   ... 17, 18, 19, 0, 1, 2, 3 ...

... 7, 8, 9, 190, 191 ...   ... 199, 180, 181 ...

Set B is both operationally and representationally efficient. Neither will come into common Earth use soon, if ever.

Set B

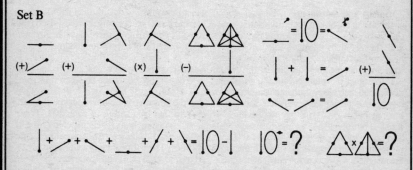

How would you decipher, translate and explain them?

Mineko Matsuno and Pear Currin, students
Lakeside Middle School
Seattle, Washington

Bonus: Make Your Own Puzzle

Difficulty: 5+

(May be substituted in the Prize Set for 12, 13, 14, or 15.)

Construct a cross-number puzzle on a 5x5 grid with the following conditions:

• There are 5 blanks in the grid, no 2 in the same row, column, or diagonal.

• Each digit is used exactly twice, with no leading zeros.

• The smallest composite number, which reads across, is the year of this *Old Farmer's Almanac*.

• Each composite number in the puzzle has a different factor elsewhere in the puzzle.

Bob Lodge
Seattle, Washington

Secrets of the Zodiac
Famous Debowelled Man of the Signs

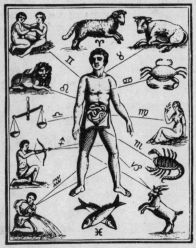

Ancient astrologers associate each of the signs with a part of the body over which they felt the sign held some influence. The first sign of the zodiac — Aries — was attributed to the head, with the rest of the signs moving down the body, ending with Pisces at the feet.

♈ Aries, head. ARI Mar. 21-Apr. 20

♉ Taurus, neck. TAU Apr. 21-May 20

♊ Gemini, arms. GEM May 21-June 20

♋ Cancer, breast. CAN June 21-July 22

♌ Leo, heart. LEO July 23-Aug. 22

♍ Virgo, belly. VIR Aug. 23-Sept. 22

♎ Libra, reins. LIB Sept. 23-Oct. 22

♏ Scorpio, secrets. SCO Oct. 23-Nov. 22

♐ Sagittarius, thighs. SAG Nov. 23-Dec. 21

♑ Capricorn, knees. CAP Dec. 22-Jan. 19

♒ Aquarius, legs. AQU Jan. 20-Feb. 19

♓ Pisces, feet. PSC Feb. 20-Mar. 20

Astrology and Astronomy:

It was the early astrologers who first made the connection between celestial movements and the physical changes that took place here on Earth. Eventually the science of astronomy became the charting of the actual placement of the planets and the constellations, and astrology became the study of how those placements affected aspects of human behavior. Astrology as we know it today is simply a tool we use to time events according to the placement of the two luminaries (the Sun and the Moon) and the eight known planets (Mercury, Venus, Mars, Jupiter, Saturn, Uranus, Neptune, and Pluto) in the 12 signs of the zodiac. Only a qualified astrologer can give a complete interpretation, but Sun signs can aid us in recognizing and understanding some of our abilities and personal timetables.

Astrologers observed that the Sun appeared to move through each of the 12 constellations (or signs) systematically, always starting out in the sign Aries. On the first day of spring (approximately March 21) the Sun crossed over the equator and began moving north, bringing with it warmer weather and the growth of new plants. The Moon, too, had a cycle all its own (approximately every 29½ days), going from a new Moon to a full Moon and back again. On the nights of the full Moon people and animals appeared to be much more active than normal. Many astrologers consider surgery ill-advised during full Moon days (three days before and after) because of excessive bleeding.

Sun Signs and Moon Signs:

What is the difference between Sun signs and Moon signs? Sun signs tell us in what sign the Sun was on our day of birth; they are easy to find by turning to page 204. There are 12 signs; each one rules a specific time of year, certain characteristics, qualities, and abilities. The Moon sign is more complicated to find because it changes every few days. It tells us where the Moon was at the hour of our birth. Astrologically speaking, the Sun represents our goals and the opportunities we will be offered. The Moon represents our instincts and reactions to the world.

Many readers have asked us which signs are best suited for various activities. Astrologers use Moon signs for this determination, and a month-by-month chart showing appropriate times for certain activities is provided below. (To find the astrological place of the Moon in the zodiac, as well as detailed gardening information, see page 181.) Do not confuse this with the astronomical position of the Moon, as listed on the left-hand pages (48-74); because of precession and other factors the astrological and astronomical zodiacs do not agree.

A MONTH-BY-MONTH ASTROLOGICAL TIMETABLE for 1989

Herewith we provide the following yearlong chart, based on the Moon signs, showing the appropriate times each month for certain activities.

by Joanne H. Lemieux

	JAN	FEB	MAR	APR	MAY	JUNE	JULY	AUG	SEPT	OCT	NOV	DEC
Give up smoking	7	6	7	6	5	3	3	1-31	29	29	28	27
Begin diet to lose weight	22-23	28	1 27-28	23-25	21-22 30-31	26-27	23-24	19-20	16-17 24-26	21-23	18-19	15-16
Begin diet to gain weight	15-16	11-12 16-17	10-11 15-16	7-8 11-12	8-10 5	5-6	3	3-5	1	none	12	9-10
Buy clothes	15-16 26-28	11-12 23-24	10-11 22-24	7-8 18-20	4-5 16-17	1-2 12-13	10-11 25-26	6-7 21-23	2-3 18-19	15-16 26-28	12-13 23-24	9-10 20-21
Seek favors	22-23	18-19	17-18	13-15	11-12	7-8	4-6	1-2	24-26	21-22	18-19	15-16
Dental care	7 15-16	11-12	10-11	7-8	5	3-4	7-8	13-14	9-11	7-8	3-4 30	1-2 27-29
End old projects	21	20	22	21	20	19	18	16	15	14	13	12
Hair care	19-20	15-17	15-16	11-12	18-20	14-16	12-13	8-10	14-15	11-12	8-9	5-6
Seek pleasures	22-23	18-19	17-18	13-15	11-12	7-8	4-5	1-2	24-26	21-23	18-19	15-16
Start a new project	7	6	7	6	5	3	3	1 & 31	29	29	28	27
Fishing	11-12 19-21	7-8 15-17	6-7 15-16	3-4 11-12	8-10 27-29	5-6 24-25	2-3 21-22	26-27 17-18	14-15 22-23	11-12 19-20	8-9 16-17	5-6 13-14
Breed	15-16 19-20	11-12 15-17	10-11 15-16	7-8 11-12	5 9-10	5-6	3	none	14	11-12	8-9	9-10
Destroy pests/weeds	1	none	none	5	2-3	26-27	none	28-29	24-26	21-23	23-24	20-21
Graft or pollinate	19-20	15-17	19-21	none	18-20	14-16	12-13	8-10	9-11	7-8	3-4 30	1-2 27-29
Harvest above-ground crops	11-12	7-8	10-11	7-8	8-10	5-6	7-8	3-5 31	1 4-6	2-3 29-30	3-4 30	1-2 27-29
Harvest root crops	19-21	15-17	19-21	16-17	18-20	14-16 19	17-18	13-14	14-15	11-12	8-9 12-13	9-10
Begin logging	4-5 31	1-2 28	1 27-28	5	2-3 23-25	26-27	23-24	19-20 28-29	24-26	21-23	18-19	25-26
Prune or cut hay	2-3	26-27	25-26	none	none	none	29-31	26-27	22-23	19-20	16-17	22-24
Seed grain	26-28	23-24	22-24	18-20	16-17	12-13	9-11	6-7	2-3 29-30	1 26-28	23-24	20-21
Set posts or pour concrete	22-23	5	4-5	1-2 28-29	4 25-26	21-22 28-29	19-20 25-26	21-23 28-29	24-26	21-23	18-19	15-16
Slaughter	21	20-22	22-24	21-23	20-22	19-21	18-20	16-18	15-17	14-16	13-15	12-14
Wean	6	3-4	2-3 29-31	26-27	4-5 23-24	1-2	25-26	21-23	18-19	none	none	27-29
Castrate animals	7	3-4	2-3 29-31	26-27	24	none	none	13	9-11	7-8	3-4 30	1-2 27-29

ARIES March 21-April 20.

Symbol: ♈ The Ram. *Ruling planet:* Mars.
Element: Fire. *Quality:* Assertive. *Ability:* To lead.

Governs: Explorers, pioneers, beginnings, and innovations. *Colors that draw luck:* Shades of red. *Best time of year for:* Personal luck — Mar. 21-Apr. 20; love and recreation — July 23-Aug. 22; travel, meeting new people, and fun — Nov. 23-Dec. 21. *Compatible with:* Fire signs (Leo and Sagittarius) and Air signs (Gemini, Libra, Aquarius). *Places that offer new opportunities:* Puerto Rico, Canada, and Denmark.

TAURUS April 21-May 20.

Symbol: ♉ The Bull. *Ruling planet:* Venus.
Element: Earth. *Quality:* Materialistic. *Ability:* To follow through.

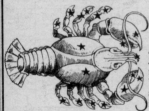

Governs: Builders, farmers, hard work, and possessions. *Colors that draw luck:* Shades of pink. *Best time of year for:* Personal luck — Apr. 21-May 20; love and recreation — Aug. 23-Sept. 22; travel, meeting new people, and fun — Dec. 22-Jan. 19. *Compatible with:* Earth signs (Virgo and Capricorn) and Water signs (Cancer, Scorpio, and Pisces). *Places that offer new opportunities:* Ireland and St. Louis.

GEMINI May 21-June 20.

Symbol: ♊ The Twins. *Ruling planet:* Mercury.
Element: Air. *Quality:* Intellectual. *Ability:* To communicate.

Governs: Writers, siblings, neighborhoods, and ideas. *Colors that draw luck:* Shades of yellow. *Best time of year for:* Personal luck — May 21-June 20; love and recreation — Sept. 23-Oct. 22; travel, meeting new people, and fun — Jan. 20-Feb. 19. *Compatible with:* Air signs (Libra and Aquarius) and Fire signs (Aries, Leo, and Sagittarius). *Places that offer new opportunities:* Belgium, London, and San Francisco.

CANCER June 21-July 22.

Symbol: ♋ The Crab. *Ruling planet:* Moon.
Element: Water. *Quality:* Compassionate. *Ability:* To understand.

Governs: Mothers, elders, endings, and home. *Colors that draw luck:* Shades of sea green. *Best time of year for:* Personal luck — June 21-July 22; love and recreation — Oct. 23-Nov. 22; travel, meeting new people, and fun — Feb. 20-Mar. 20. *Compatible with:* Water signs (Scorpio and Pisces) and Earth signs (Taurus, Virgo, and Capricorn). *Places that offer new opportunities:* Holland, Venice, and New Hampshire.

LEO July 23-August 22.

Symbol: ♌ The Lion. *Ruling planet:* Sun.
Element: Fire. *Quality:* Forceful. *Ability:* To supervise.

Governs: Rulers, leaders, children, and creations. *Colors that draw luck:* Shades of gold and orange. *Best time of year for:* Personal luck — July 23-Aug. 22; love and recreation — Nov. 23-Dec. 21; travel, meeting new people, and fun — Mar. 21-Apr. 20. *Compatible with:* Fire signs (Aries and Sagittarius) and Air signs (Gemini, Libra, and Aquarius). *Places that offer new opportunities:* India, France, Philadelphia, and Chicago.

VIRGO August 23-September 22.

Symbol: ♍ The Virgin. *Ruling planet:* Mercury.
Element: Earth. *Quality:* Curious. *Ability:* To organize.

Governs: Bankers, accountants, health, and place of work. *Colors that draw luck:* Shades of brown. *Best time of year for:* Personal luck — Aug. 23-Sept. 22; love and recreation — Dec. 22-Jan. 19; travel, meeting new people, and fun — Apr. 21-May 20. *Compatible with:* Earth signs (Taurus and Capricorn) and Water signs (Cancer, Scorpio, and Pisces). *Places that offer new opportunities:* Paris, Switzerland, Boston, and Los Angeles.

LIBRA September 23-October 22.

Symbol: ♎ The Scales. *Ruling planet:* Venus.
Element: Air. *Quality:* Idealistic. *Ability:* To relate.

Governs: Diplomats, lawyers, relationships, partners, and politics. *Colors that draw luck:* Shades of blue. *Best time of year for:* Personal luck — Sept. 23-Oct. 22; love and recreation — Jan. 20-Feb. 19; travel, meeting new people, and fun — May 21-June 20. *Compatible with:* Air signs (Gemini and Aquarius) and Fire signs (Aries, Leo, and Sagittarius). *Places that offer new opportunities:* Manhattan, China, Japan, and South Carolina.

SCORPIO October 23-November 22.

Symbol: ♏ The Scorpion. *Ruling planet:* Pluto.
Element: Water. *Quality:* Powerful. *Ability:* To concentrate.

Governs: Detectives, researchers, secrets, and passions. *Colors that draw luck:* Shades of dark red. *Best time of year for:* Personal luck — Oct. 23-Nov. 22; love and recreation — Feb. 20-Mar. 20; travel, meeting new people, and fun — June 21-July 22. *Compatible with:* Water signs (Cancer and Pisces) and Earth signs (Taurus, Virgo, and Capricorn). *Places that offer new opportunities:* Colorado, Norway, Rio de Janeiro, and Washington, D.C.

SAGITTARIUS November 23-December 21.

Symbol: ♐ The Hunter. *Ruling planet:* Jupiter.
Element: Fire. *Quality:* Expansive. *Ability:* To be versatile.

Governs: Hunters, scholars, travel, and religion. *Colors that draw luck:* Shades of purple. *Best time of year for:* Personal luck — Nov. 23-Dec. 21; love and recreation — Mar. 21-Apr. 20; travel, meeting new people, and fun — July 23-Aug. 22. *Compatible with:* Fire signs (Aries and Leo) and Air signs (Gemini, Libra, and Aquarius). *Places that offer new opportunities:* Australia, Spanish Riviera, and the Grand Canyon.

CAPRICORN December 22-January 19.

Symbol: ♑ The Mountain Goat. *Ruling planet:* Saturn.
Element: Earth. *Quality:* Trustworthy. *Ability:* To be disciplined.

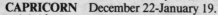

Governs: Authoritarian figures, fathers, time, and status. *Colors that draw luck:* Shades of gray and black. *Best time of year for:* Personal luck — Dec. 22-Jan. 19; love and recreation — Apr. 21-May 20; travel, meeting new people, and fun — Aug. 23-Sept. 22. *Compatible with:* Earth signs (Taurus and Virgo) and Water signs (Cancer, Scorpio, and Pisces). *Places that offer new opportunities:* Alaska, Brussels, Georgia, Rhode Island, and Mexico.

AQUARIUS January 20-February 19.

Symbol: ♒ The Water Bearer. *Ruling planet:* Uranus.
Element: Air. *Quality:* Independent. *Ability:* To be inventive.

Governs: Scientists, astronomers, changes, and television. *Colors that draw luck:* Electric blue and indigo. *Best time of year for:* Personal luck — Jan. 20-Feb. 19; love and recreation — May 21-June 20; travel, meeting new people, and fun — Sept. 23-Oct. 22. *Compatible with:* Air signs (Gemini and Libra) and Fire signs (Aries, Leo, and Sagittarius). *Places that offer new opportunities:* Massachusetts, Arizona, Peru, and New Zealand.

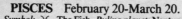

PISCES February 20-March 20.

Symbol: ♓ The Fish. *Ruling planet:* Neptune.
Element: Water. *Quality:* Imaginative. *Ability:* To be psychic.

Governs: Fishermen, poets, dreams, and inspirations. *Colors that draw luck:* Shades of white. *Best time of year for:* Personal luck — Feb. 20-Mar. 20; love and recreation — June 21-July 22; travel, meeting new people, and fun — Oct. 23-Nov. 22. *Compatible with:* Water signs (Cancer and Scorpio) and Earth signs (Taurus, Virgo, and Capricorn). *Places that offer new opportunities:* Maine, Vermont, and Portugal.

CLASSIFIED ADVERTISING

BABY CHICKS, Hubbard White Mountains, Cornish-rock giants, reds, barred rocks, sex-links, leghorns, also turkeys (bronze or white), guineas, pheasants, books, equipment, incubators, hatching eggs. Brochure $1 (refundable). Case Hatchery, 335F Brodbecks, PA 17329. 717-235-2050.

RAISE BANTAMS, CHICKENS, turkeys, ducks, guineas, geese for hobby, food, and profit. Send 50¢ for big picture catalog showing all kinds of fancy poultry. Clinton Hatchery, Box 548-FA, Clinton MO 64735

ALL KINDS of day-old baby chicks. Rare, fancy, exotic, popular, and old-time-favorite breeds. Send 50¢ today for big colorful picture catalog. Show them all. MasterCard and Visa accepted. Nesttest Hatchery, Box 46-95, Windsor, MO 65360. Telephone 816-647-3101

MINIATURE BANTAM CHICKS. Exotic and standard breed chicks. Over 75 breeds. Shipped safely to your postal office. Incubators, books, medications, hatching eggs, equipment. Crow Poultry, Box 106-18, Windsor MO 65360

FREE BEAUTIFUL CATALOG with pictures in color. Country's largest selection. Over 100 varieties. Baby chicks, bantams, ducklings, goslings, turkeys, guineas, pheasants, partridge, and hatching eggs. Also incubators, books, supplies. 72 years supplying large, small, and hobby flocks for eggs, meat, and exhibition. Safe shipment entire U.S. & Canada. Special 4-H, FFA offers. Surprise gift and special bargains for early orders. Write or call. Murray Mc Murray Hatchery, C 101, Webster City IA 50595. Phone: 515-832-3280

WORLD FAMOUS Colonial Chicks. FREE 100 or more heavy breed chicks with regular order to introduce 300-egg pedigree-bred layers. Free catalog in full color. Phone 816-987-3127 or write; Dept. 771, Colonial Poultry Farms, Pleasant Hill MO 64080

PRODUCTION AND BROILER CHICKS. Turkey poults, pheasant & quail, started pullets, hatching eggs, capons, dealer inquiries welcome. Catalog & prices available. Hall Brothers Hatchery, P.O. Box 1026, Norwich CT 06360. 203-269-4447

BABY DUCKS, geese, turkeys, chicks, bantams, guineas, and pheasants. Color catalog — $1 (refundable). Heart of Missouri Hatchery, Box 954FA, Columbia MO 65205

REAL ESTATE

OZARK ACREAGE, HOMESITES, recreational land, mountains, rivers, lakes. 9% interest. Nothing down. Unusual catalog. Woods & Waters, Box 1-FA, Willow Springs MO 65793. (417) 469-3187

480,000,000 ACRES valuable government land. Now available low as $6.80 per acre. Campsites, farms, homesites. Fabulous business opportunities. Latest report $2. Satisfaction guaranteed. American Land Disposal, Box 1409-OFA, Holland MI 49422

FREE NEW REAL ESTATE catalog. Thousands of property descriptions & photos. Farmsteads, country homes, lakefront retreats, much more. Top values from coast to coast. Call or write for your free copy today! United National Real Estate, 4700-BYF, Belleview, Kansas City MO 64112. Ph: Toll free 1-800-999-1020

GOVERNMENT LANDS from $10. Repossessed homes, $1. Drug/tax seizures. Surplus recreational, agricultural, commercial properties. Nationwide directory, $3. Lands, Box 19107-JM, Washington DC 20036

RECIPES

NEW ORLEANS CREOLE-CAJUN recipes. Delicious. Nutritious. Economical. Different! $2 plus 50¢ postage. Box 5930-FA, Metairie LA 70009-5930

GRANDMA SAYS, old-fashioned recipes best. Complete theory and instructions for breads, cakes, or pies, $5.95 each. Marilyn's Kitchen, Box 12270, Charleston SC 29412

HOME COOKIN'. Secret farm recipes passed generation to generation. $1, SASE, Home Cookin', Dept. A, 431 SE Pleasantview Dr., Des Moines IA 50315

BEST PEANUT BRITTLE candy making secret recipe. Order today. How you can make quick, easy, crisp, fresh, tasty peanut candy at home anytime. Plus bonus recipes included. Send $2 and LSASE to: Wilcox, Box 20868A, Philadelphia PA 19141

BEST REMEMBERED GOODIES from Grandmother's pantry. The special few most treasured as a meal. Boy. $3, GLH, Box 169Y, Franklin VT 05457

RELIGION

BECOME AN ORDAINED MINISTER. Free ministerial credentials legalize your right to the title "Reverend." Write: Ministry of Salvation Church, 659-B Third Ave., Chula Vista CA 92010

HELP FROM GOD: 50 powerful healings! Conquer life, end self-doubt. $1. Newlife, Box 684-JZ, Boulder City NV 89005

STAMPS

FREE — 10 Israel and 10 Iraq stamps. To approval applicants. W-B Stamps 7A, Wilkes-Barre PA 18703-0758

FREE — The 1966 U.S. Sipex souvenir sheet, mint, is yours free with your request for approvals. Colonie, Box 12113, Albany NY 12212

WANTED

TOP PRICES PAID for your goose and duck feathers. S&H Green Stamps. Send for price quotations. Northwestern Feather Co., 635 Evergreen SE, Grand Rapids MI 49507

BOTANICALS. We buy wild roots and herbs. For price list contact Wilcox Natural Products, Box 37, Eolia MO 63344

AUTOGRAPHS, LETTERS, PHOTOS of famous people wanted. Herb Gray, P.O. Box 5084, Cochituate MA 01778. 617-877-5254

SLOT MACHINES, any condition, or related parts. Also Wurlitzer jukeboxes and Nickelodeons. Paying cash. 312-985-2742

SQUIRREL TAILS WANTED. Hunters, save your squirrel tails! Top prices, prompt payment. We pay up to 21¢ for good quality fox, gray and red squirrel tails. Parcel Post and UPS charges refunded on shipments over 50. Send tails or write: Mepps, 626 Center Street, Dept. OFA, Antigo WI 54409-2496

WORK CLOTHES

WORK CLOTHES. Save 80%. Shirts, pants, coveralls. Free folder. Write: Galco, 4004 East 71st St., Dept. OF-5, Cleveland OH 44105

ANECDOTES AND PLEASANTRIES

A motley collection of amazing (if sometimes useless) facts, strange stories, and questionable advice kindly sent to us during 1988 by readers of this 197-year-old publication.

WHY DO TEXANS IN DALLAS EAT MORE CANNED SPINACH?
(Discriminating people want to know.)

Dallas consumes more canned spinach than any other city in the United States. (After all, *somebody* has to be first.)

So, now that you're in the mood, here's a list of other well-known foods along with the cities where each enjoys the highest consumption per capita or per household. . . .

WELL, we don't know why. They just *do*. According to industry market research statistics, the city of

THE PRODUCT	WHERE THEY LIKE IT BEST
Twinkies	Chicago *(Where, in 1930, they were invented.)*
Prune Juice	Miami *(The older people there are just regular folk.)*
Campbell's Mushroom Soup	Grand Rapids, Michigan *(They say that 80% goes into casseroles.)*
V-8 Juice	Denver *(Health enthusiasts love Colorado.)*
Ocean Spray Cranberry Juice Cocktail	Boston *(Sure. The company headquarters is in nearby Plymouth.)*
Bubble Gum and Cracker Jacks	Salt Lake City *(There are lots of young people in Mormon families.)*
Kraft's Cheez Whiz	Puerto Rico *(They use it as a bread spread.)*
Fritos	Dallas *(Invented, however, in San Antonio.)*
Wheatena	New England *(Hits the spot on nippy mornings.)*
Breyer's Ice Cream	Philadelphia *(Probably because it was first introduced there in 1866.)*
Baby Food	Miami *(J. Heinz baby food sells best in Pittsburgh.)*
Ketchup	Charlotte, North Carolina *(Again, the Heinz variety prize goes to Pittsburgh.)*
Cheerios	Seattle-Tacoma *(60% more than anywhere.)*
Spam	Hawaii *(A nice island tradition since WWII.)*
Skippy Peanut Butter and Jell-O	Des Moines, Iowa *(Skippy was once made there. But why Jell-O? It was invented in LeRoy, New York.)*
Prego Spaghetti Sauce	Albany, New York *(Most pasta, too.)*
Perrier	Miami *(Probably the company wishes it were New York. Sounds more sophisticated.)*
Wonder Bread	New York City *(No, not rye, whole wheat, or pumpernickel.)*
Popcorn and Reese's Peanut Butter Cups	Portland, Maine *(For the same reason Texans in Dallas like canned spinach.)*

Facts courtesy of Trish Hall and The New York Times

DO YOU VOTE OR WATCH THE SUPER BOWL?

Not everyone does both. And many do neither...

LAST January (1988), an estimated 110 million Americans watched the Redskins whomp the Broncos in the Super Bowl. In the presidential election of November 1984, exactly 92,643,136 Americans went to the polls and voted. Now of the 110 million who watched the Super Bowl, maybe ten million were kids who aren't old enough to vote. So that would leave 7,356,864 Super Bowl watchers who, although eligible to vote, didn't.

There were, at the time of the election four years ago, 174,447,321 Americans of voting age. So exactly 81,804,185 of them didn't bother going to the polls.

Now what we *don't* know is whether most of the 100 million voting-age Americans who watched the Super Bowl last year were mainly comprised of the 92,643,136 who voted in the last election or whether they were mainly comprised of the 81,804,185 who didn't vote in the last election. Either way, it is, of course, obvious that many millions of voting-age Americans neither watched the 1988 Super Bowl *nor* voted in the last elections.

Editor's note: In next year's *Old Farmer's Almanac*, we'll report what *they* usually do with their time.

RECIPE FOR HARDTACK
(You'd have to be desperate.)

MIX one cup of flour with ½ teaspoon of salt, one teaspoon of sugar, and water to moisten. Roll paper-thin and bake for ten minutes in a hot oven. Will keep for 50 years or more, although they say weevils might get in it. (However, some people maintain that weevils are a sort of benefit in that they create little tunnels that soften the crust.)

HOW TO GET YOUR CHILD INTO AN IVY LEAGUE COLLEGE

Here's real scientific information with statistics and stuff...

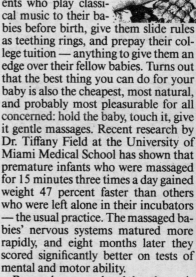

WE read all the time about parents who play classical music to their babies before birth, give them slide rules as teething rings, and prepay their college tuition — anything to give them an edge over their fellow babies. Turns out that the best thing you can do for your baby is also the cheapest, most natural, and probably most pleasurable for all concerned: hold the baby, touch it, give it gentle massages. Recent research by Dr. Tiffany Field at the University of Miami Medical School has shown that premature infants who were massaged for 15 minutes three times a day gained weight 47 percent faster than others who were left alone in their incubators — the usual practice. The massaged babies' nervous systems matured more rapidly, and eight months later they scored significantly better on tests of mental and motor ability.

Researchers speculated that the positive response to touch is part of a survival system in all mammals. A mother mammal's absence (hence, lack of touch) raises levels of beta-endorphin in babies, which in turn slows metabolism, conserves energy, and slows the rate of growth. The mother's touch reverses that process, and normal growth continues. Studies of infant laboratory rats show that a particular pattern of touch by the mother rat — in this case, licking — inhibits the production of beta-endorphin. Researchers also found they could effectively simulate the mother's rough tongue by stroking the baby rats with a wet paintbrush.

For those who want to massage their human infants (a practice that not only leads to fat and happy babies, but virtually assures early admission to an Ivy League school), here are a few guidelines to follow:

1. The best stroke is gentle, firm, and slow. Too light a touch tickles and can overstimulate and even irritate a baby.

2. Massaging the back, neck, and legs will soothe a baby; touching the face, tummy, and feet will excite a baby.

3. Using a few drops of baby oil or pure sesame oil will help keep the baby's skin soft.

4. Use your hands. It's just not polite to use a wet paintbrush on a little baby.

WHAT ST. LOUIS KIDS HAVE TO SAY ABOUT THE WEATHER

The following are true quotes from the classroom of Harold Helfer, an elementary school teacher in St. Louis, Missouri . . .

- When lightning goes through them, clouds start making sounds. So would anybody.
- Rain is saved up in cloud banks.
- Water vapor gets huddled and snuggled together in a cloud. When it is big enough to be called a drop, it does.
- Humidity is the experience of looking for air and finding rain.
- Some oxygen molecules make rain while others help fires to burn. Sometimes it is brother against brother.
- The difference between air and water is that air can be made wetter but water cannot.
- The water cycle is a cycle made out of water that you can pedal along on. I don't believe it has been invented yet.
- A blizzard is when it snows sideways.
- The main value of tornadoes is yet to be discovered.
- You can listen to thunder after light-

ning and tell how close you came to getting hit. If you don't hear it, you got hit, so never mind.

- Listening to meteorologists is one of the chief by-products of bad weather.
- It is so hot in some parts of the world that the inhabitants there have to live somewhere else.
- The wind is like the air, only pushier.
- In order to have different seasons, we had to get the earth tilted over on its axis. But it has been worth it.
- Meteorologists look something like people.

ANOTHER BORING OLD PUZZLE
(Why don't you just skip over this item?)

A 90-year-old Algonquin Indian chief died and left his 17 ponies to his three sons, saying they were to be divided as follows:

½ of them to the oldest,
⅓ of them to the middle son,
⅑ of them to the youngest.

Question: How did the oldest son figure out how to fulfill his father's wishes? (And you can't use *half* ponies either.)

Answer: Well, he went over to the next reservation and borrowed one pony. Which meant he then had eighteen ponies. Then he gave ½ of 18 or 9 to himself. He gave ⅓ of 18 or 6 to the middle son. And ⅑ of 18 or 2 to the youngest son.

Once the distribution of the 17 ponies was made (9+6+2=17), he was able to return the borrowed pony.

Courtesy of Reba Lewis

FLASH! A PASSIONATE KISS BURNS THE CALORIES IN ONE POTATO CHIP

Here are a few mildly interesting potato-chip facts — plus a good recipe . . .

AMERICA has been in the chips since 1853, the year George Crum, hotel chef in Saratoga, New York, created them by accident for railroad tycoon Cornelius Vanderbilt. Cornelius, goes the story, had grumbled about the fried potatoes, complaining they weren't delicate enough for his taste. In a fury, Crum grabbed a cleaver and slashed a batch of spuds as thinly as he could, hurled the slices into a kettle of sizzling lard, fished them out oily and crackling brown, salted them, and served them. The rest, as they say, is history.

Here are a dozen amazing facts about America's favorite munch-a-bunch snack:

1. Annual chip earnings are three billion dollars — as much as the total earnings of all the country's health-food stores.

2. Chain snacking: If all the potato chips Americans eat each year were lined up end to end, the chain would stretch eight million miles — enough to circle the world 336 times.

3. Nearly 50 cents of every snack dollar is spent on potato chips.

4. World's record for potato-chip chomping: 20 two-ounce bags in 24 minutes and 33 seconds.

5. Ten potato chips supply as much fat as two pats of butter, says the Center for Science in the Public Interest.

6. Annual per capita consumption of potato chips is five pounds, except in Pittsburgh where it's eight.

7. There are 250 brands of chips in America, but 52 percent of all chips sold are Frito-Lay.

8. A passionate kiss burns the calories in one potato chip.

9. Potato chips sell eight times as well as pretzels.

10. Potato chips are half as nutritious as an apple, one-third as nutritious as a carrot, and four times more nutritious than a chocolate bar, says the CSPI's Nutrition Scoreboard.

11. A one-ounce bag of chips has the calories and nutrition of a three-ounce baked and buttered spud, says the Potato Promotion Broad.

12. It takes 12 pounds of oil to deep-fry 25 pounds of chips.

Recipe for Old-Fashioned "Saratoga-Style" Potato Chips:

> 2 large baking or white potatoes
> Vegetable oil, for deep frying
> Salt or other seasoning

Peel baking potatoes. Rinse in cold water. Slice crosswise into rounds, thin and uniform, by hand. Or use a vegetable slicer that works by hand or attaches to an electric mixer.

Soak sliced potatoes in several changes of very cold water for two hours, adding ice cubes to the last change of water. Turn potato slices into a towel and dry thoroughly. Fill a deep-fat fryer with 3 inches vegetable oil and heat to 375° F. Using a frying basket or large spatula, fry only a few slices at a time, shaking the basket to prevent sticking. Chips should be golden in 4-5 minutes. Drain chips on paper towels or brown paper bag. Salt just before serving.

• *Tips for home chip makers:* Adding 2 tablespoons of white vinegar to each quart of oil before frying keeps potato slices from absorbing excess fat . . . Cottonseed is the oil used commercially, but peanut oil produces a tastier chip and is healthier.

Compiled by Frances Sheridan Goulart

A PLUMBING NIGHTMARE

For some (maybe everyone), here is the worst thing that could happen to you while you're in the bathroom . . .

FOR almost a week last summer Laurie and Jules Lamothe of Hamilton, Canada, had noticed the toilet in their 12th-floor two-bedroom apartment operating in a rather sluggish fashion. Didn't seem to flush properly. Then, on August 9, 1987, Laurie discovered the reason. When she looked into the toilet bowl, there, toward the bottom but apparently squirming to reach the surface of the water was the

head of what turned out to be a very much alive five-foot-long boa constrictor. When Laurie screamed and sounded the alarm in no uncertain terms, the snake retreated back from the bowl into the sewer system to which it had escaped from a neighboring apartment a week earlier.

During the following several days, members of the Hamilton Society for the Prevention of Cruelty to Animals attempted to capture the elusive boa by putting dead rats and a guinea pig into the Lamothe toilet bowl. To no avail. It all ended on August 12th when a plumber found a blockage in one of the sewer pipes directly below the Lamothe apartment. Turned out the blockage was the boa, which had suffocated to death.

Says Laurie Lamothe of her experience, "From now on, I'll always be playing peekaboo with the toilet seat."

*Courtesy of Nora Underwood
and* Maclean's *Magazine*

Editor's note: So that all almanac readers (and editors) won't also be playing toilet peekaboo from now on, it should be said that SPCA officials stated it was the first time they'd ever encountered a boa constrictor caught in a drainpipe. Ever.

WHY SHOULD YOU KEEP YOUR NOSE TO THE GRINDSTONE?

(This is the only time for the next 50 years that we're ever going to explain this.)

TO grind corn in the old-time grist mills, the corn was fed through a hole in the runner stone, and then, by means of centrifugal force, was carried between two great stones, grinding all the way. However, these two great stones never touched. To accommodate the different grain sizes, the miller was able to adjust the gap between the stones by means of a wheel that was connected by a rod to a lever upon which the central shaft rested. The movement of this adjusting wheel moved one of the great grinding stones, the runner stone, from the other, called the bed stone. *By keeping his nose to the grindstone* (either the runner or the bed stone), the miller could detect the smell of granite, which indicated that the two grinding stones were too close together.

*Courtesy of the Kenyon Corn Meal Co.,
Usquepaugh, Rhode Island*

INSTRUCTIONS FOR THE ASSEMBLY OF JUST ABOUT ANYTHING

GRASP the gizmo in your left hand. With your right hand, insert the doohickey into the little whosie just below the bright red thingamajig and gently — gently! — turn it in a clockwise direction until you hear a click. Attach the long thingamabob to the whatchamacallit. Do not under any circumstances allow the metal whatsit on the end to come in contact with the black plastic thingummy. Failure to follow these instructions will result in damage to the doodad.

By Amos Keetough and Timothy Clark

SOME CHRISTMAS "FIRSTS"

Like, who put up the first Christmas tree in America? Who was the first American to sell Christmas trees? Stuff like that . . .

THE first American Christmas tree can be credited to a Hessian soldier by the name of Henrick Roddmore who was captured at the Battle of Bennington in 1776. He then went to work on the farm of Samuel Denslow in Windsor Locks, Connecticut, where

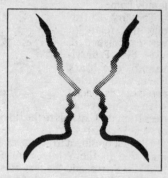

Anecdotes and Pleasantries
continued

for the next 14 years he put up and decorated Christmas trees in the Denslow family home.

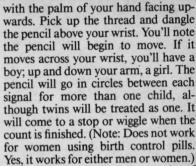

The first Christmas tree retail lot was established in 1851 by a Pennsylvanian, one Mark Carr, who hauled two ox sleds loaded with Christmas trees from the Catskills to the sidewalks of New York City.

The first president to set up a Christmas tree in the White House was Franklin Pierce, and the first president to establish the National Christmas Tree Lighting Ceremony on the White House lawn was Calvin Coolidge.

The first United States Christmas celebration (north of Florida) occurred on St. Croix Island, Maine, in 1604.

The first American to print and sell Christmas cards was one Louis Prang of Roxbury, Massachusetts.

Finally (are you glad this is almost over?), the first department store Santa Claus was James Edgar who, during Christmas seasons beginning in 1890, would wander about his store (the Boston Store) in Brockton, Massachusetts, dressed as Santa Claus, talking to the children of customers.

Courtesy of Richard W. O'Donnell,
Francis X. Sculley, and the dingy files
of The Old Farmer's Almanac.

WANT TO KNOW HOW MANY CHILDREN YOU'LL HAVE?

Well, according to this reader, all you need is a pencil, a needle, and some thread . . .
(You might also throw in a grain of salt, Bunky.)

FIRST, take an ordinary wooden pencil with an eraser and stick a threaded needle into the center of the eraser. Then lay your left arm on a table with the palm of your hand facing upwards. Pick up the thread and dangle the pencil above your wrist. You'll note the pencil will begin to move. If it moves across your wrist, you'll have a boy; up and down your arm, a girl. The pencil will go in circles between each signal for more than one child, although twins will be treated as one. It will come to a stop or wiggle when the count is finished. (Note: Does not work for women using birth control pills. Yes, it works for either men or women.)

For those who doubt the veracity of this method, let me cite my own case. Several years ago I had my tubes tied after I was divorced. At the time, I had two teenage sons, and the pencil would always stop after signaling two boys.

Then I married again and, for fun, tried the method on my new husband, who'd had no previous children. The pencil swung up and down his arm and then across his wrist. A girl and boy still to come! As for me, the pencil signaled two boys, a girl, and then another boy.

Well, I had my tubes untied — and am now the mother of Eric, 18, Ben, 16, Colette, 3½, and Jack, 20 months.
Submitted by Karen C. Okey
Erie, Pennsylvania

JACKSON, MICHIGAN, HOMES ARE MUCH CLEANER THAN RUSSIAN HOMES

But maybe even more surprising is how similar we are . . .

THE following is based on a recent study by the Survey Research Center of the University of Maryland and the Institute for Sociological Research of the Soviet Academy of Sciences. Interviews were conducted with 710 residents of Jackson, Michigan, and 2,181 residents of Pskov, a city midway between Leningrad and Riga. Participants also answered more than 600 written questions and kept diaries for 24 hours.

• 55 percent of the women in Jackson,

Amazing VITASEX ® Formula for MEN & WOMEN

GUARANTEED TO
RENEW VIGOR
IN 20 MINUTES!

POTENT NEW TABLETS

(No Prescription Needed)

REVIVE "YOUR" LOVE LIFE

VITASEX® renews vigor in just 20 minutes and may be the fastest, safest and surest vitamin, mineral tonic and stimulant formula ever released by medical science. Yes, many men and women who have taken these miracle tablets after a tiring working day have found new strength and potency to the point it has made their "love life" come alive again. VITASEX® is the reason many couples are enjoying a happier home life after years of dragging thru each day.

REVITALIZE ENERGY, POTENCY, AND VIGOR

Start today to renew your strength, potency and vigor with the first tablet you take. You don't have to wait days to get results. You get almost immediate new surges of energy because this revolutionary new product is designed to start working instantly. And you won't experience hypertension and jittery energy that accompanies other drugs that you see advertised in certain magazines and newspapers.

AMAZING RESULTS!

VITASEX® is a **scientifically formulated** tonic and stimulant that gives you the EXTRA measure of nutrients and stimulant that you may need to revitalize vigor, energy and stamina. Therefore, you'll also experience the exhilarating, rewarding lift of HEALTHY BODY FUNCTION.

Yes, now instead of being left out of the "good times" you can:

• **Restore healthy body function . . .**
- • **Improve your desire and performance . . .**
- • **Renew your strength, potency and vigor . . .**
- • **And win the desire of your mate regardless of age, or age differences.**

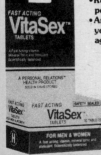

Results with VITA-SEX have **proven** that it gets guaranteed results! Tests show that anyone in good health can renew their strength, stamina and vigor with VITASEX®. **Yes, success in every case.**

RENEW VIGOR IN MINUTES WITH THE FASTEST, SUREST, AND SAFEST TONIC & STIMULANT FORMULA OUR MEDICAL SCIENTISTS HAVE EVER DEVELOPED — ABSOLUTELY GUARANTEED!

In fact, the only way VITASEX® won't work for you is by not using it! It's guaranteed to work for you, even if you've had a problem for years. Even if other formulas have failed you. Even if nothing you've tried in the past had any lasting effect!

That's why we can make this 100% no-risk guarantee. VITASEX® must work for you or your money will be refunded (less postage, of course), and you can keep the first bottle free. ACT NOW!

Michigan, are in the labor force versus 81 percent of the women in Pskov.

- 91 percent of the men in Pskov hold jobs compared to 85 percent of Jackson men.

- Women in Pskov spend 8 hours a week preparing meals. Jackson women spend 6 hours a week.

- Pskov women spend 4 hours a week doing laundry and 4½ hours housecleaning. Jackson women spend 2 hours a week doing laundry and 7 hours in housecleaning.

- Jackson women spend 3 hours a week directly involved with children, like reading to them. Women in Pskov spend 4 hours.

- In both Jackson and Pskov, the women spend about 25 hours a week on household tasks and the men spend 11 hours a week.

- Jackson women have 11 hours more leisure time per week than Pskov women, and Jackson men have 4 more than Pskov men.

- Organizational activities including church attendance: in Jackson, 17 minutes a day; in Pskov, 7 minutes.

- Television viewing: in Jackson, 149 minutes a day; in Pskov, 109 minutes.

- Social pursuits and conversation: in Jackson, 86 minutes; in Pskov, 34 minutes.

- In sports: in Jackson, 15 minutes a day; in Pskov, 9 minutes. (But Pskov residents walk 16 minutes a day to Jackson residents' 4 minutes.)

- Residents in Pskov read for 42 minutes a day, Jackson residents, 27 minutes.

- Jackson residents spend 61 minutes a day eating and 71 minutes caring for personal appearance while Pskov residents spend 48 minutes a day eating and 55 minutes caring for personal appearance.

- Jackson residents sleep 7 hours and 54 minutes a day. People in Pskov sleep 8 hours and 17 minutes.

The Old Farmer's Almanac speaks out!

OUR NOMINATION FOR THE OFFICIAL NATIONAL BUG
(as opposed to insect)

Congress is considering the honeybee. But we have a far more appropriate choice . . .

AS a way to celebrate their centennial in 1989, the Entomological Society of America is suggesting that the United States designate an official national insect this year. We agree. The bald eagle is our bird. The rose is our flower. Time we had a bug.

Well, there seems to be a movement toward that end in Congress. Senator Larry Pressler of South Dakota and Representative Stephen Neal of North Carolina, through separate resolutions in the Senate and the House, are nominating the honeybee.

We disagree.

The honeybee society is very different from our democratic society here in America. Not only is each honeybee born into a strict caste system (drone, worker, and queen) from which there is no chance for advancement, but honeybees exploit their workers, often deliberately starving them. Also, honeybee mothers routinely kill honeybee fathers right after they've made love, "royal" food is available to some privileged honeybees and not to others, and above all, honeybees murder their old queens. Now *that's* un-American.

So instead, we hereby nominate the spider. Even though it's not technically an insect (it's an arachnid), it *could* serve as our official national *bug*. The spider is a talented artist, a skillful architect, and a superb engineer all rolled into one. Besides, spiders eat bugs that are yuckier than they are, and when they reside in your house and you refrain from squashing them, they keep it from raining.

All those in favor of the spider over the honeybee, please write your congressperson. □ □

ANSWERS TO
OLD AND NEW MATHEMATICAL PUZZLES
on pages 198-201

1. a.

b. 3 are above the table.

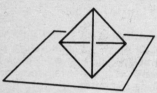

2. 1872 and 1972
3. a. 10/7
   b. 22/7
4. a. South: Hawaii; North, West, and East: Alaska. (Aleutians are partly in high E. longitude.)
   b. South: Florida; North: Minnesota; West: California; East: Maine.
   c. South: Ontario; North: Quebec; West: British Columbia; East: Newfoundland.
   d. Lat.: Same as yours, opposite pole. Long.: 180° minus yours, opposite direction.
5. 64 hours

6.
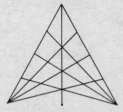

7. No moonset that day, despite all corrections. (His watch will read approximately 7:16 A.M., EDT, Nov. 7, on arrival at 3:16 A.M. in Seattle.)
8. No. An end view:

9. 60, up to 120 crates of oranges to B.
10. a. 78
    b. 91
11. 1
12-15 and Bonus. Prize Set. See instructions on page 198.

ANSWERS TO RAINY DAY AMUSEMENTS
on page 195

MIDDLE NAMES
1) Benjamin Franklin; 2) Davison; 3) Mortimer; 4) Augustus; 5) Langhorne; 6) Phineas Taylor; 7) Finley Breese; 8) Ewing; 9) Ruiz; 10) Joseph; 11) Louise; 12) Bernhard; 13) Pierce; 14) Edward; 15) Robert; 16) James Cash; 17) LeRoy; 18) Simpson; 19) Tecumseh; 20) Armstrong; 21) The S in Harry S. Truman does not stand for anything. He had two grandfathers who both had names beginning with S. To avoid favoritism, his family gave him no middle name.

DOUBLE TV TROUBLE
1) d, C; 2) i, G; 3) j, B; 4) b, F; 5) f, J; 6) g, H; 7) c, A; 8) h, E; 9) a, I; 10) e, D.

NAVAL SHIP FIRSTS
1) d; 2) f; 3) i; 4) b; 5) h; 6) j; 7) a; 8) g; 9) c; 10) e.

NEXT IN LINE
Beginning with the Vice President, the correct order is: C, E, J, H, L, A, G, B, D, O, N, F, K, M, I.

How Long Should Life Be?

Looking at life and death through the patient eyes of evolution,
we see them as the heads and tails of a single coin. . . .
Text and illustrations by Guy Murchie

☐ AS WE GET ALONG IN YEARS, IN-creasingly the thought arises: when will all this end? Or, if we have a choice, how long should life be?

Clearly it is not a simple philosophi-cal question, and it is not one that may ever be satisfyingly answered in this mortal phase of existence. It raises such basic issues as the meaning and pur-pose of life, upon which there is far from general agreement and which the ancients traditionally entrusted to the gods.

To the extent that "how long" is a probe into time, an understanding of time is vital to any judgment of the length or limit of a life. Einstein's The-ory of Relativity says in effect that nei-ther space nor time is fundamental but more truly only an illusion of finitude. Space, therefore, may be viewed as the relation of things to other things, and time as the relation of things to them-selves. The latter concept of course in-volves identity, as between you when you were a child and you as a grown-up, bringing all these periods together in the self that merges your life into a continuum. That is what may be rea-sonably considered a human lifetime on Earth.

Most people seem possessed of an instinct for survival as well as sharing a natural and pervasive wish to postpone their death as long as they comfortably can. And, realizing that even modern science does not yet offer any reason-able means of avoiding death for long,

they latch on to any even slightly plau-sible prospects of immortality they hear about. Thus our civilization has several more or less serious movements working toward immortality, such as cryonics, which freezes bodies immedi-ately after death with the hope that they may be thawed out in some future cen-tury after science has advanced enough to resurrect them into some viable state, if not of real immortality, at least of an indefinite postponement of death.

Certainly mankind has dreamed of vastly elongating its life since time im-memorial as revealed in such traditions as that of the Taoists of ancient China, *Tir na nog* of the ancient Celts, the Hin-du Pool of Youth, and the Hebrew Riv-er of Immortality. Meanwhile, with the progressive accumulation of knowl-edge and acceleration of scientific dis-coveries, the length of an average hu-man life has tripled since the time of Christ and literally doubled just in our present century. Besides, the miracle of genetic engineering is fast moving from fiction to fact. And the scarcely imagin-able transplantation of brains has moved into the realm of research with primitive animals. (This, inevitably, brings up the troublesome question of consciousness. For, if consciousness ac-tually depends on the brain as is widely assumed, then transplanting a brain into another body is the same thing as transplanting a body onto another brain, and who would be *you* after such an operation? Or who would you be?

And might not your brain actually survive and persist through a long succession of bodies of which you could theoretically be conscious for milleniums?)

Few of us seem aware of it, but immortality is in fact already present among us on Earth. I am thinking of the soil amoeba *Dictyostelium discordeum*, known collectively as the slime mold that lives in rotting wood and dead leaves, feeding most of the time in the form of millions of separate, independent, invisible cells that can be considered immortal because they don't have to die. Occasionally, when it has had enough of its bacterial food, this nebulous population swarms and solidifies into a dense, coordinated, visible, mortal mass that oozes about as a small garden slug before suddenly sprouting into a thin-stemmed flower full of spores. In this stage it spews out clouds of fertile powder that drift on the wind to land and start new colonies for miles around; then the stem shifts into reverse and thickens again, pulling the flower back down into the shape of a slug whence it disintegrates once more into its constituent amoebas in order to feed. Thus it flips regularly from mortality to immortality, from visibility to invisibility, and one might almost say, from finitude to infinitude as it alternately propagates and feeds in the real world.

An example of another and different immortal creature is the tiny tentacled pond worm known as a hydra, half an inch long, living in shallow pools, which metabolizes so fast that it replaces almost all its body cells every two weeks, the tissue flowing straight through it like gas in a candle flame at the leisurely speed of a millimeter a day.

In this manner the hydra is so renewed every fortnight that it may never grow old, and barring such a mishap as getting eaten, it could theoretically keep going forever.

Now let us expand our perspective outward into the full sweep of evolution, from where it is obvious that death is far from inevitable, for the kind of death we humans have to deal with (a disintegration of cells) did not even appear in evolution until the latter days of multicelled organisms. The creatures of early evolution — amoebas, bacteria, viruses — indeed were all microscopic. And instead of dying when they reached maturity, they merely divided and kept on dividing while each portion was rejuvenated, leaving no corpse. So true death evolved only in the more advanced colonial and macroscopic stages of life when cells started organizing themselves into complex organisms such as sponges, jellyfish, and worms and learned to diverge into sexes. At the same time, mind you, they kept on evolving as often as not in unsuitable ways that could not be sustained. In other words they needed death to eliminate deformed individuals and misfits and to steer evolution most of the time into more efficient directions. By this means death evolved, and over hundreds of millions of years it became solidly established because, from an evolutionary standpoint, it had survival value. Complex creatures such as our own primate ancestors urgently needed it — and ultimately they could not get along without it. In that sense death has long been an indispensable part of life.

Looking at life and death through the patient eyes of evolution, then, we see

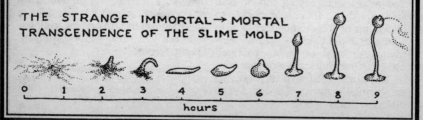

THE STRANGE IMMORTAL → MORTAL
TRANSCENDENCE OF THE SLIME MOLD

0   1   2   3   4   5   6   7   8   9
hours

them as the heads and tails of a single coin, something like the traditional yin-yang polarity of ancient China or the crest and trough of an ocean wave that might be considered the symbolic wave of total being. If we fully accept such life-death polarity, moreover, longevity is diminished thereby in its appeal, and the relatively subtle goal of life's quality may even overshadow the more obvious goal of its quantity. These are inter-relationships that are both natural and reasonable. After all, if one is surely going to die (still our normal expecta-

---

It is obvious that man needs to control the breeding not just of animals but of himself.

---

tion), does it much matter when? Is dying in 1922 predictably more burdensome than dying in 1993? Or is the number of your years in any way more important than your spiritual fulfillment or happiness? Whatever the answer, if you feel confident that you will likely be happier in your soul during your future years on Earth than you have been in past years, then it makes sense to live as long as you can. But if, on the other hand, your ailments, frustrations, and spiritual failures are increasingly weighing you down, wouldn't it almost surely be a blessing if your life should end soon?

Arranging the time of your death, if it should come to that, may not be easy, especially if you are not distressed enough to commit suicide. But you probably do have some choices of action that could alter your expectancy. You might change your job or even your life-style. You could decide to buckle up or forget your seat belt, to accept or avoid risks, to cultivate new friends, to treat or ignore your ailments, to live cautiously or dangerously. You might even take to pondering the spiritual maturity of Socrates, who preferred death to exile.

If you are capable of broadening your perspective enough to contemplate life not as a mere individual but from the viewpoint of all mankind, then many things might come into your ken. Eugenics, for example, could become a serious consideration along with resolving the related world-pollution problem that's beginning to be known as the three Bs (for babies, bombs, and blight). For it is increasingly obvious that there are already too many people on Earth and that man needs to control the breeding not just of animals but of himself. And the bombs are so frighteningly deadly that disarmament treaties probably will disarm them soon. It is also foreseeable that when the oceans and atmosphere get dirty enough the nations of Earth will be forced to cooperate in cleaning them up.

The main thing to realize is that the fate of our world is largely up to us humans. We ourselves are at the cutting edge of evolution in this present unique period when our planet is germinating, when the speed of travel and communication has exploded, when Earth at last has completed the exploration and mapping of herself in this century, opened the atom, cracked the genetic code, leapt into space, and is now moving with some pain and uncertainty toward global freedom and oneness.

Is it not worth living a little longer if we can actually participate in this worldwide movement and help it fulfill its spiritual purpose? If you can say "yes" and really let yourself get absorbed in the universal cause, you will progressively forget yourself and think of all mankind, of all life and more. And you may even burst outside your finite aura of space and time so that it will no longer matter when you die or how long you live. In deepest truth you will then just exist — for all anyone knows, forever.

Guy Murchie is a longtime contributor to The Old Farmer's Almanac. *His book,* The Seven Mysteries of Life, *is available from Houghton Mifflin Co., 2 Park St., Boston, MA 02108.* □□

THE OLD FARMER'S ALMANAC GUIDE TO LUMBER AND NAILS

LUMBER WIDTHS & THICKNESS in Inches

NOMINAL SIZE	ACTUAL SIZE Dry or Seasoned
1 x 3	¾ x 2½
1 x 4	¾ x 3½
1 x 6	¾ x 5½
1 x 8	¾ x 7¼
1 x 10	¾ x 9¼
1 x 12	¾ x 11¼
2 x 3	1½ x 2½
2 x 4	1½ x 3½
2 x 6	1½ x 5½
2 x 8	1½ x 7¼
2 x 10	1½ x 9¼
2 x 12	1½ x 11¼

NAIL SIZES

The nail on the left is a 5d (penny) finish nail; on the right, 20d common. The numerals below the nail sizes indicate the approximate number of common nails per pound.

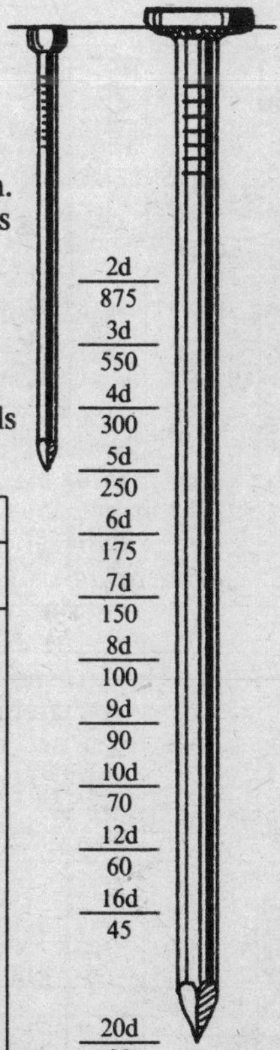

Size	Per pound
2d	875
3d	550
4d	300
5d	250
6d	175
7d	150
8d	100
9d	90
10d	70
12d	60
16d	45
20d	30

LUMBER MEASURE IN BOARD FEET

LENGTH Size in Inches	12 ft.	14 ft.	16 ft.	18 ft.	20 ft.
1 x 4	4	4⅔	5⅓	6	6⅔
1 x 6	6	7	8	9	10
1 x 8	8	9⅓	10⅔	12	13⅓
1 x 10	10	11⅔	13⅓	15	16⅔
1 x 12	12	14	16	18	20
2 x 3	6	7	8	9	10
2 x 4	8	9⅓	10⅔	12	13⅓
2 x 6	12	14	16	18	20
2 x 8	16	18⅔	21⅓	24	26⅔
2 x 10	20	23⅓	26⅔	30	33⅓
2 x 12	24	28	32	36	40
4 x 4	16	18⅔	21⅓	24	26⅔
6 x 6	36	42	48	54	60
8 x 8	64	74⅔	85⅓	96	106⅔
10 x 10	100	116⅔	133⅓	150	166⅔
12 x 12	144	168	192	216	240

1 9 8 8

JANUARY
S	M	T	W	T	F	S
—	—	—	—	—	1	2
3	4	5	6	7	8	9
10	11	12	13	14	15	16
17	18	19	20	21	22	23
24	25	26	27	28	29	30
31	—	—	—	—	—	—

FEBRUARY
S	M	T	W	T	F	S
—	1	2	3	4	5	6
7	8	9	10	11	12	13
14	15	16	17	18	19	20
21	22	23	24	25	26	27
28	29					

MARCH
S	M	T	W	T	F	S
—	—	1	2	3	4	5
6	7	8	9	10	11	12
13	14	15	16	17	18	19
20	21	22	23	24	25	26
27	28	29	30	31	—	—

APRIL
S	M	T	W	T	F	S
—	—	—	—	—	1	2
3	4	5	6	7	8	9
10	11	12	13	14	15	16
17	18	19	20	21	22	23
24	25	26	27	28	29	30

MAY
S	M	T	W	T	F	S
1	2	3	4	5	6	7
8	9	10	11	12	13	14
15	16	17	18	19	20	21
22	23	24	25	26	27	28
29	30	31				

JUNE
S	M	T	W	T	F	S
—	—	1	2	3	4	
5	6	7	8	9	10	11
12	13	14	15	16	17	18
19	20	21	22	23	24	25
26	27	28	29	30	—	—

JULY
S	M	T	W	T	F	S
—	—	—	—	—	1	2
3	4	5	6	7	8	9
10	11	12	13	14	15	16
17	18	19	20	21	22	23
24	25	26	27	28	29	30
31						

AUGUST
S	M	T	W	T	F	S
—	1	2	3	4	5	6
7	8	9	10	11	12	13
14	15	16	17	18	19	20
21	22	23	24	25	26	27
28	29	30	31	—	—	—

SEPTEMBER
S	M	T	W	T	F	S
—	—	—	—	1	2	3
4	5	6	7	8	9	10
11	12	13	14	15	16	17
18	19	20	21	22	23	24
25	26	27	28	29	30	—

OCTOBER
S	M	T	W	T	F	S
—	—	—	—	—	—	1
2	3	4	5	6	7	8
9	10	11	12	13	14	15
16	17	18	19	20	21	22
23	24	25	26	27	28	29
30	31					

NOVEMBER
S	M	T	W	T	F	S
—	—	1	2	3	4	5
6	7	8	9	10	11	12
13	14	15	16	17	18	19
20	21	22	23	24	25	26
27	28	29	30	—	—	—

DECEMBER
S	M	T	W	T	F	S
—	—	—	1	2	3	
4	5	6	7	8	9	10
11	12	13	14	15	16	17
18	19	20	21	22	23	24
25	26	27	28	29	30	31

1 9 8 9

JANUARY
S	M	T	W	T	F	S
1	2	3	4	5	6	7
8	9	10	11	12	13	14
15	16	17	18	19	20	21
22	23	24	25	26	27	28
29	30	31				

FEBRUARY
S	M	T	W	T	F	S
—	—	—	1	2	3	4
5	6	7	8	9	10	11
12	13	14	15	16	17	18
19	20	21	22	23	24	25
26	27	28				

MARCH
S	M	T	W	T	F	S
—	—	1	2	3	4	
5	6	7	8	9	10	11
12	13	14	15	16	17	18
19	20	21	22	23	24	25
26	27	28	29	30	31	—

APRIL
S	M	T	W	T	F	S
—	—	—	—	—	—	1
2	3	4	5	6	7	8
9	10	11	12	13	14	15
16	17	18	19	20	21	22
23	24	25	26	27	28	29
30						

MAY
S	M	T	W	T	F	S
—	1	2	3	4	5	6
7	8	9	10	11	12	13
14	15	16	17	18	19	20
21	22	23	24	25	26	27
28	29	30	31	—	—	—

JUNE
S	M	T	W	T	F	S
—	—	—	1	2	3	
4	5	6	7	8	9	10
11	12	13	14	15	16	17
18	19	20	21	22	23	24
25	26	27	28	29	30	—

JULY
S	M	T	W	T	F	S
—	—	—	—	—	1	
2	3	4	5	6	7	8
9	10	11	12	13	14	15
16	17	18	19	20	21	22
23	24	25	26	27	28	29
30	31					

AUGUST
S	M	T	W	T	F	S
—	—	1	2	3	4	5
6	7	8	9	10	11	12
13	14	15	16	17	18	19
20	21	22	23	24	25	26
27	28	29	30	31	—	—

SEPTEMBER
S	M	T	W	T	F	S
—	—	—	—	—	1	2
3	4	5	6	7	8	9
10	11	12	13	14	15	16
17	18	19	20	21	22	23
24	25	26	27	28	29	30

OCTOBER
S	M	T	W	T	F	S
1	2	3	4	5	6	7
8	9	10	11	12	13	14
15	16	17	18	19	20	21
22	23	24	25	26	27	28
29	30	31				

NOVEMBER
S	M	T	W	T	F	S
—	—	—	1	2	3	4
5	6	7	8	9	10	11
12	13	14	15	16	17	18
19	20	21	22	23	24	25
26	27	28	29	30	—	—

DECEMBER
S	M	T	W	T	F	S
—	—	—	—	1	2	
3	4	5	6	7	8	9
10	11	12	13	14	15	16
17	18	19	20	21	22	23
24	25	26	27	28	29	30
31						

1 9 9 0

JANUARY
S	M	T	W	T	F	S
—	1	2	3	4	5	6
7	8	9	10	11	12	13
14	15	16	17	18	19	20
21	22	23	24	25	26	27
28	29	30	31			

FEBRUARY
S	M	T	W	T	F	S
—	—	—	—	1	2	3
4	5	6	7	8	9	10
11	12	13	14	15	16	17
18	19	20	21	22	23	24
25	26	27	28			

MARCH
S	M	T	W	T	F	S
—	—	—	—	1	2	3
4	5	6	7	8	9	10
11	12	13	14	15	16	17
18	19	20	21	22	23	24
25	26	27	28	29	30	31

APRIL
S	M	T	W	T	F	S
1	2	3	4	5	6	7
8	9	10	11	12	13	14
15	16	17	18	19	20	21
22	23	24	25	26	27	28
29	30					

MAY
S	M	T	W	T	F	S
—	—	1	2	3	4	5
6	7	8	9	10	11	12
13	14	15	16	17	18	19
20	21	22	23	24	25	26
27	28	29	30	31	—	—

JUNE
S	M	T	W	T	F	S
—	—	—	—	1	2	
3	4	5	6	7	8	9
10	11	12	13	14	15	16
17	18	19	20	21	22	23
24	25	26	27	28	29	30

JULY
S	M	T	W	T	F	S
1	2	3	4	5	6	7
8	9	10	11	12	13	14
15	16	17	18	19	20	21
22	23	24	25	26	27	28
29	30	31	—	—	—	—

AUGUST
S	M	T	W	T	F	S
—	—	—	1	2	3	4
5	6	7	8	9	10	11
12	13	14	15	16	17	18
19	20	21	22	23	24	25
26	27	28	29	30	31	—

SEPTEMBER
S	M	T	W	T	F	S
—	—	—	—	—	—	1
2	3	4	5	6	7	8
9	10	11	12	13	14	15
16	17	18	19	20	21	22
23	24	25	26	27	28	29
30						

OCTOBER
S	M	T	W	T	F	S
—	1	2	3	4	5	6
7	8	9	10	11	12	13
14	15	16	17	18	19	20
21	22	23	24	25	26	27
28	29	30	31			

NOVEMBER
S	M	T	W	T	F	S
—	—	—	—	1	2	3
4	5	6	7	8	9	10
11	12	13	14	15	16	17
18	19	20	21	22	23	24
25	26	27	28	29	30	—

DECEMBER
S	M	T	W	T	F	S
—	—	—	—	—	1	
2	3	4	5	6	7	8
9	10	11	12	13	14	15
16	17	18	19	20	21	22
23	24	25	26	27	28	29
30	31					